CW00524136

JAGUAR E-TYPE
Gold Portfolio
<u>1961-1971</u>

Compiled by
R.M.Clarke

ISBN 1 870642 791

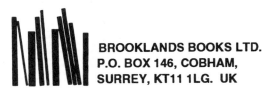

BROOKLANDS BOOKS LTD.
P.O. BOX 146, COBHAM,
SURREY, KT11 1LG. UK

A-JEGP

Printed in Hong Kong

BROOKLANDS BOOKS

BROOKLANDS ROAD TEST SERIES

Abarth Gold Portfolio 1950-1971
AC Ace & Aceca 1953-1983
Alfa Romeo Giulietta Gold Portfolio 1954-1965
Alfa Romeo Giulia Berlinas 1962-1976
Alfa Romeo Giulia Coupés 1963-1976
Alfa Romeo Giulia Coupés Gold P. 1963-1976
Alfa Romeo Spider 1966-1990
Alfa Romeo Spider Gold Portfolio 1966-1991
Alfa Romeo Alfasud 1972-1984
Alfa Romeo Alfetta Gold Portfolio 1972-1987
Alfa Romeo Alfetta GTV6 1980-1986
Allard Gold Portfolio 1937-1959
Alvis Gold Portfolio 1919-1967
AMX & Javelin Muscle Portfolio 1968-1974
Armstrong Siddeley Gold Portfolio 1945-1960
Aston Martin Gold Portfolio 1972-1985
Aston Martin Gold Portfolio 1985-1995
Audi Quattro Gold Portfolio 1980-1991
Austin A30 & A35 1951-1962
Austin Healey 100 & 100/6 Gold P. 1952-1959
Austin Healey 3000 Gold Portfolio 1959-1967
Austin Healey Sprite 1958-1971
Barracuda Muscle Portfolio 1964-1974
BMW Six Cylinder Coupés 1969-1975
BMW 1600 Collection No.1 1966-1981
BMW 2002 Gold Portfolio 1968-1976
BMW 316, 318, 320 (4 cyl.) Gold P. 1975-1990
BMW 320, 323, 325 (6 cyl.) Gold P. 1977-1990
BMW M Series Performance Portfolio 1976-1993
BMW 5 Series Gold Portfolio 1981-1987
Bricklin Gold Portfolio 1974-1975
Bristol Cars Gold Portfolio 1946-1992
Buick Automobiles 1947-1960
Buick Muscle Cars 1965-1970
Cadillac Allanté 1986-1993
Cadillac Automobiles 1949-1959
Cadillac Automobiles 1960-1969
Charger Muscle Portfolio 1966-1974
Chevrolet 1955-1957
Chevrolet Impala & SS 1958-1971
Chevrolet Corvair 1959-1969
Chevy II & Nova SS Muscle Portfolio 1962-1974
Chevy El Camino & SS 1959-1987
Chevelle & SS Muscle Portfolio 1964-1972
Chevrolet Muscle Cars 1966-1971
Chevy Blazer 1969-1981
Chevrolet Corvette Gold Portfolio 1953-1962
Chevrolet Corvette Sting Ray Gold P. 1963-1967
Chevrolet Corvette Gold Portfolio 1968-1977
High Performance Corvettes 1983-1989
Camaro Muscle Portfolio 1967-1973
Chevrolet Camaro Z28 & SS 1966-1973
Chevrolet Camaro & Z28 1973-1981
High Performance Camaros 1982-1988
Chrysler 300 Gold Portfolio 1955-1970
Chrysler Valiant 1960-1962
Citroen Traction Avant Gold Portfolio 1934-1957
Citroen 2CV Gold Portfolio 1948-1989
Citroen DS & ID 1955-1975
Citroen DS & ID Gold Portfolio 1955-1975
Citroen SM 1970-1975
Cobras & Replicas 1962-1983
Shelby Cobra Gold Portfolio 1962-1969
Cobras & Cobra Replicas Gold P. 1962-1989
Cunningham Automobiles 1951-1955
Daimler SP250 Sports & V-8 250 Saloon Gold P. 1959-1969
Datsun Roadsters 1962-1971
Datsun 240Z 1970-1973
Datsun 280Z & ZX 1975-1983
DeLorean Gold Portfolio 1977-1995
Dodge Muscle Cars 1967-1970
Dodge Viper on the Road
ERA Gold Portfolio 1934-1994
Excalibur Collection No.1 1952-1981
Facel Vega 1954-1964
Ferrari Dino 1965-1974
Ferrari Dino 308 1974-1979
Ferrari 328 • 348 • Mondial Gold Portfolio 1986-1994
Fiat 500 Gold Portfolio 1936-1972
Fiat 600 & 850 Gold Portfolio 1955-1972
Fiat Pininfarina 124 & 2000 Spider 1968-1985
Fiat-Bertone X1/9 1973-1988
Fiat Abarth Performance Portfolio 1972-1987
Ford Consul, Zephyr, Zodiac Mk.I & II 1950-1962
Ford Zephyr, Zodiac, Executive, Mk.III & Mk.IV 1962-1971
Ford Cortina 1600E & GT 1967-1970
High Performance Capris Gold Portfolio 1969-1987
Capri Muscle Portfolio 1974-1987
High Performance Fiestas 1979-1991
High Performance Escorts Mk.I 1968-1974
High Performance Escorts Mk.II 1975-1980
High Performance Escorts 1980-1985
High Performance Escorts 1985-1990
High Performance Sierras & Merkurs
Gold Portfolio 1983-1990
Ford Automobiles 1949-1959
Ford Fairlane 1955-1970
Ford Ranchero 1957-1959
Ford Thunderbird 1955-1957
Ford Thunderbird 1958-1963
Ford Thunderbird 1964-1976
Ford GT40 Gold Portfolio 1964-1987
Ford Bronco 1966-1977
Ford Bronco 1978-1988
Holden 1948-1962
Honda CRX 1983-1987
International Scout Gold Portfolio 1961-1980
Isetta 1953-1964
Iso & Bizzarrini Gold Portfolio 1962-1974
Jaguar and SS Gold Portfolio 1931-1951
Jaguar XK120, 140, 150 Gold P. 1948-1960
Jaguar Mk.VII, VIII, IX, X, 420 Gold P. 1950-1970
Jaguar Mk.1 & Mk.2 Gold Portfolio 1959-1969
Jaguar E-Type Gold Portfolio 1961-1971
Jaguar E-Type V-12 1971-1975
Jaguar XJ12, XJ5.3, V12 Gold P. 1972-1990
Jaguar XJ6 Series I & II Gold P. 1968-1979
Jaguar XJ6 Series III 1979-1986
Jaguar XJ6 Gold Portfolio 1986-1994
Jaguar XJS Gold Portfolio 1975-1988
Jaguar XJS Gold Portfolio 1988-1995
Jeep CJ5 & CJ6 1960-1976
Jeep CJ5 & CJ7 1976-1986
Jensen Cars 1946-1967
Jensen Cars 1967-1979
Jensen Interceptor Gold Portfolio 1966-1986
Jensen Healey 1972-1976
Lagonda Gold Portfolio 1919-1964
Lamborghini Countach & Urraco 1974-1980
Lamborghini Countach & Jalpa 1980-1985
Lancia Fulvia Gold Portfolio 1963-1976
Lancia Beta Gold Portfolio 1972-1984
Lancia Delta Gold Portfolio 1979-1994
Lancia Stratos 1972-1985
Land Rover Series I 1948-1958
Land Rover Series II & IIa 1958-1971
Land Rover Series III 1971-1985
Land Rover 90 110 Defender Gold Portfolio 1983-1994
Land Rover Discovery 1989-1994
Lincoln Gold Portfolio 1949-1960
Lincoln Continental 1961-1969
Lincoln Continental 1969-1976
Lotus Sports Racers Gold Portfolio 1953-1965
Lotus Seven Gold Portfolio 1957-1974
Lotus Caterham Seven Gold Portfolio 1974-1995
Lotus Elite 1957-1964
Lotus Elite & Eclat 1974-1982
Lotus Elan Gold Portfolio 1962-1974
Lotus Elan Collection No. 2 1963-1972
Lotus Elan & SE 1989-1992
Lotus Cortina Gold Portfolio 1963-1970
Lotus Europa Gold Portfolio 1966-1975
Lotus Elite & Eclat 1974-1982
Lotus Turbo Esprit 1980-1986
Marcos Cars 1960-1988
Maserati 1965-1970
Maserati 1970-1975
Mazda RX-7 Gold Portfolio1978-1991
Mercedes 190 & 300 SL 1954-1963
Mercedes 230/250/280SL 1963-1971
Mercedes G Wagen 1981-1994
Mercedes Benz SLs & SLCs Gold P. 1971-1989
Mercedes S & 600 1965-1972
Mercedes S Class 1972-1979
Mercedes SLs Performance Portfolio 1989-1994
Mercury Muscle Cars 1966-1971
Messerschmitt Gold Portfolio 1954-1964
MG Gold Portfolio 1929-1939
MG TA & TC Gold Portfolio 1936-1949
MG TD &TF Gold Portfolio 1949-1955
MGA & Twin Cam Gold Portfolio 1955-1962
MG Midget Gold Portfolio 1961-1979
MGB Roadsters 1962-1980
MGB MGC & V8 Gold Portfolio 1962-1980
MGB GT 1965-1980
Mini Gold Portfolio 1959-1969
Mini Gold Portfolio 1969-1980
High Performance Minis Gold Portfolio 1960-1973
Mini Cooper Gold Portfolio 1961-1971
Mini Moke Gold Portfolio 1964-1994
Mopar Muscle Cars 1964-1967
Morgan Three-Wheeler Gold Portfolio 1910-1952
Morgan Plus 4 & Four 4 Gold P. 1936-1967
Morgan Cars 1960-1970
Morgan Cars Gold Portfolio 1968-1989
Morris Minor Collection No. 1 1948-1980
Shelby Mustang Muscle Portfolio 1965-1970
High Performance Mustang IIs 1974-1978
High Performance Mustangs 1982-1988
Nash-Austin Metropolitan Gold P. 1954-1962
Oldsmobile Automobiles 1955-1963
Oldsmobile Muscle Cars 1964-1971
Oldsmobile Toronado 1966-1978
Opel GT Gold Portfolio 1968-1973
Packard Gold Portfolio 1946-1958
Pantera Gold Portfolio 1970-1989
Panther Gold Portfolio 1972-1990
Plymouth Muscle Cars 1966-1971
Pontiac Tempest & GTO 1961-1965
Pontiac Muscle Cars 1966-1972
Pontiac Firebird & Trans-Am 1973-1981
High Performance Firebirds 1982-1988
Pontiac Fiero 1984-1988
Porsche 356 Gold Portfolio 1953-1965
Porsche 911 1965-1969
Porsche 911 1970-1972
Porsche 911 1973-1977
Porsche 911 Carrera 1973-1977
Porsche 911 Turbo 1975-1984
Porsche 911 SC & Turbo Gold Portfolio 1978-1983
Porsche 911 Carrera & Turbo Gold P. 1984-1989
Porsche 914 Gold Portfolio 1969-1976
Porsche 924 Gold Portfolio 1975-1988
Porsche 928 Performance Portfolio 1977-1994
Porsche 944 Gold Portfolio 1981-1991
Range Rover Gold Portfolio 1970-1985
Range Rover Gold Portfolio 1986-1995
Reliant Scimitar 1964-1986
Riley Gold Portfolio 1924-1939
Riley 1.5 & 2.5 Litre Gold Portfolio 1945-1955
Rolls Royce Silver Cloud & Bentley 'S' Series
Gold Portfolio 1955-1965
Rolls Royce Silver Shadow Gold P. 1965-1980
Rolls Royce & Bentley Gold P. 1980-1989
Rover P4 1949-1959
Rover P4 1955-1964
Rover 3 & 3.5 Litre Gold Portfolio 1958-1973
Rover 2000 & 2200 1963-1977
Rover 3500 1968-1977
Rover 3500 & Vitesse 1976-1986
Saab Sonett Collection No.1 1966-1974
Saab Turbo 1976-1983
Studebaker Gold Portfolio 1947-1966
Studebaker Hawks & Larks 1956-1963
Avanti 1962-1990
Sunbeam Tiger & Alpine Gold P. 1959-1967
Toyota MR2 1984-1988
Toyota Land Cruiser 1956-1984
Triumph TR2 & TR3 Gold Portfolio 1952-1961
Triumph TR4, TR5, TR250 1961-1968
Triumph TR6 Gold Portfolio 1969-1976
Triumph TR7 & TR8 Gold Portfolio 1975-1982
Triumph Herald 1959-1971
Triumph Vitesse 1962-1971
Triumph Spitfire Gold Portfolio 1962-1980
Triumph 2000, 2.5, 2500 1963-1977
Triumph GT6 Gold Portfolio 1966-1974
Triumph Stag 1970-1980
TVR Gold Portfolio 1959-1986
TVR Performance Portfolio 1986-1994
VW Beetle Gold Portfolio 1935-1967
VW Beetle Gold Portfolio 1968-1991
VW Beetle Collection No.1 1970-1982
VW Karmann Ghia 1955-1982
VW Bus, Camper, Van 1954-1967
VW Bus, Camper, Van 1968-1979
VW Bus, Camper, Van 1979-1989
VW Scirocco 1974-1981
VW Golf GTI 1976-1986
Volvo PV444 & PV544 1945-1965
Volvo Amazon-120 Gold Portfolio 1956-1970
Volvo 1800 Gold Portfolio 1960-1973
Volvo 140 & 160 Series Gold Portfolio 1966-1975

Forty Years of Selling Volvo

BROOKLANDS ROAD & TRACK SERIES

Road & Track on Alfa Romeo 1949-1963
Road & Track on Alfa Romeo 1964-1970
Road & Track on Alfa Romeo 1971-1976
Road & Track on Alfa Romeo 1977-1989
Road & Track on Aston Martin 1962-1990
R & T on Auburn Cord and Duesenburg 1952-84
Road & Track on Audi & Auto Union 1952-1980
Road & Track on Audi & Auto Union 1980-1986
Road & Track on Austin Healey 1953-1970
Road & Track on BMW Cars 1966-1974
Road & Track on BMW Cars 1975-1978
Road & Track on BMW Cars 1979-1983
R & T on Cobra, Shelby & Ford GT40 1962-1992
Road & Track on Corvette 1953-1967
Road & Track on Corvette 1968-1982
Road & Track on Corvette 1982-1986
Road & Track on Corvette 1986-1990
Road & Track on Datsun Z 1970-1983
Road & Track on Ferrari 1975-1981
Road & Track on Ferrari 1981-1984
Road & Track on Ferrari 1984-1988
Road & Track on Fiat Sports Cars 1968-1987
Road & Track on Jaguar 1950-1960
Road & Track on Jaguar 1961-1968
Road & Track on Jaguar 1968-1974
Road & Track on Jaguar 1974-1982
Road & Track on Jaguar 1983-1989
Road & Track on Lamborghini 1964-1985
Road & Track on Lotus 1972-1981
Road & Track on Maserati 1952-1974
Road & Track on Maserati 1975-1983
R & T on Mazda RX7 & MX5 Miata 1986-1991
Road & Track on Mercedes 1952-1962
Road & Track on Mercedes 1963-1970
Road & Track on Mercedes 1971-1979
Road & Track on Mercedes 1980-1987
Road & Track on MG Sports Cars 1949-1961
Road & Track on MG Sports Cars 1962-1980
Road & Track on Mustang 1964-1977
R & T on Nissan 300-ZX & Turbo 1984-1989
Road & Track on Pontiac 1960-1983
Road & Track on Porsche 1951-1967
Road & Track on Porsche 1968-1971
Road & Track on Porsche 1972-1975
Road & Track on Porsche 1975-1978
Road & Track on Porsche 1979-1982
Road & Track on Porsche 1982-1985
Road & Track on Porsche 1985-1988
R & T on Rolls Royce & Bentley 1950-1965
R & T on Rolls Royce & Bentley 1966-1984
Road & Track on Saab 1972-1992
R & T on Toyota Sports & GT Cars 1966-1984
R & T on Triumph Sports Cars 1953-1967
R & T on Triumph Sports Cars 1967-1974
R & T on Triumph Sports Cars 1974-1982
Road & Track on Volkswagen 1951-1968
Road & Track on Volkswagen 1968-1978
Road & Track on Volkswagen 1978-1985
Road & Track on Volvo 1957-1974
Road & Track on Volvo 1977-1994
R&T - Henry Manney at Large & Abroad
R&T - Peter Egan's "Side Glances"

BROOKLANDS CAR AND DRIVER SERIES

Car and Driver on BMW 1955-1977
Car and Driver on BMW 1977-1985
C and D on Cobra, Shelby & Ford GT40 1963-84
Car and Driver on Corvette 1956-1967
Car and Driver on Corvette 1968-1977
Car and Driver on Corvette 1978-1982
Car and Driver on Corvette 1983-1988
C and D on Datsun Z 1600 & 2000 1966-1984
Car and Driver on Ferrari 1955-1962
Car and Driver on Ferrari 1963-1975
Car and Driver on Ferrari 1976-1983
Car and Driver on Mopar 1956-1967
Car and Driver on Mopar 1968-1975
Car and Driver on Mustang 1964-1972
Car and Driver on Pontiac 1961-1975
Car and Driver on Porsche 1955-1962
Car and Driver on Porsche 1963-1970
Car and Driver on Porsche 1970-1976
Car and Driver on Porsche 1977-1981
Car and Driver on Porsche 1982-1986
Car and Driver on Saab 1956-1985
Car and Driver on Volvo 1955-1986

BROOKLANDS PRACTICAL CLASSICS SERIES

PC on Austin A40 Restoration
PC on Land Rover Restoration
PC on Metalworking in Restoration
PC on Midget/Sprite Restoration
PC on Mini Cooper Restoration
PC on MGB Restoration
PC on Morris Minor Restoration
PC on Sunbeam Rapier Restoration
PC on Triumph Herald/Vitesse
PC on Spitfire Restoration
PC on Beetle Restoration
PC on 1930s Car Restoration

BROOKLANDS HOT ROD 'MUSCLECAR & HI-PO ENGINES' SERIES

Chevy 265 & 283
Chevy 302 & 327
Chevy 348 & 409
Chevy 350 & 400
Chevy 396 & 427
Chevy 454 thru 512
Chrysler Hemi
Chrysler 273, 318, 340 & 360
Chrysler 361, 383, 400, 413, 426, 440
Ford 289, 302, Boss 302 & 351W
Ford 351C & Boss 351
Ford Big Block

BROOKLANDS RESTORATION SERIES

Auto Restoration Tips & Techniques
Basic Bodywork Tips & Techniques
Basic Painting Tips & Techniques
Camaro Restoration Tips & Techniques
Chevrolet High Performance Tips & Techniques
Chevy Engine Swapping Tips & Techniques
Chevy-GMC Pickup Repair
Chrysler Engine Swapping Tips & Techniques
Custom Painting Tips & Techniques
Engine Swapping Tips & Techniques
Ford Pickup Repair
How to Build a Street Rod
Land Rover Restoration Tips & Techniques
MG 'T' Series Restoration Guide
MGA Restoration Guide
Mustang Restoration Tips & Techniques
Performance Tuning - Chevrolets of the '60's
Performance Tuning - Pontiacs of the '60's

BROOKLANDS MILITARY VEHICLES SERIES

Allied Military Vehicles No.1 1942-1945
Allied Military Vehicles No.2 1941-1946
Complete WW2 Military Jeep Manual
Dodge Military Vehicles No.1 1940-1945
Hail To The Jeep
Land Rovers in Military Service
Military & Civilian Amphibians 1940-1990
Off Road Jeeps: Civ. & Mil. 1944-1971
US Military Vehicles 1941-1945
US Army Military Vehicles WW2-TM9-2800
VW Kubelwagen Military Portfolio 1940-1990
WW2 Jeep Military Portfolio 1941-1945

2195

CONTENTS

ACKNOWLEDGEMENTS

Few people would disagree that the Jaguar E-Type - or XK-E as the Americans knew it - was the most charismatic sports car of the 1960s. Yet it was far from typical of the era. Most of its engineering dated from the 1950s, and even its svelte styling was a logical development from Malcolm Sayer's design for the D-Type racers of the previous decade. As the 1970s drew closer and other sports cars were becoming more angular, the E-Type retained its sensuous curves and, as other manufacturers began to flirt with mid-mounted and rear engines, the E-Type retained its conventional front-engine/rear-drive configuration.

Introduced at the 1961 Geneva Show, the car was an immediate sensation. In original form, it came as an open roadster or a sleek fixed-head coupé, in either case with the race-proven six-cylinder 3.8-litre XK engine in triple-carburettor 265bhp tune. From 1964, the 4.2-litre engine was fitted, though this offered little extra in the way of performance and was, in the opinion of many enthusiasts, a rather inferior power unit. Market demand led in 1966 to the introduction of both an automatic transmission option and a "2+2" coupé with stretched wheelbase and rather unhappy styling. But the six-cylinder engine lasted until 1971, when Jaguar's new V12 turned the E-type into a Series III model and completed the transformation from race-bred sports car to grand tourer.

By the standards of the 1980s, the dynamic qualities of those early E-Types are unexceptional. Braking and road-holding are areas in which modern machinery is more competent, but 0-60mph times of under 7 seconds and a top speed of over 140mph are still not to be sniffed at. And the car has retained its essential charisma - so much so that many enthusiasts are prepared to pay enormous amounts of money to restore examples to pristine condition.

A book like this latest volume from Brooklands can only serve to help such enthusiastic endeavours, by conveying impressions of what the cars were like when new. Some of the superlatives perhaps need to be viewed cooly in the context of the car's 1960s heyday, but no enthusiast of the six-cylinder E-Types will want to be without this collection of road tests and other articles from the motoring press of the time. Nor, I suspect, will my fellow motoring writers find they can dispense with it - for where else does such a collection of documentary material on a well-loved classic fall so easily to hand?

This Gold Portfolio could not have been produced without the co-operation of the original publishers and authors. Our thanks go especially to the management of *Autocar, Autosport, Track and Traffic, Cars and Car Conversions, Car and Driver, Cars Illustrated, Classic and Sportscar, Modern Motor, Motor, Motor Racing, Motor Sport, Motor Trend, Popular Imported Cars, Practical Classics, Road & Track, Road Test, Sports Car Graphic, Sports Car World* and the *World Car Catalogue* for allowing us to include their copyright road tests and other stories.

James Taylor

Styling of the coupé is purposeful and beautiful. Centre-lock wire wheels are standard, but white-wall tyres an optional extra

Exciting New 'E'-Type

JAGUAR INTRODUCE 150 M.P.H. COUPÉ AND ROADSTER GRAND TOURING MODELS: 3.8-LITRE ENGINE AND ALL INDEPENDENT SUSPENSION

JAGUAR enthusiasts, particularly Americans, for some time have been asking the company to produce a new two-seater sports car with a flashing performance and plenty of luggage space for long-distance touring. Something based on the competition D-type or its production version, the short-lived XK.SS, would, they thought, provide the desired performance. Of equal importance with high maximum speed and vivid acceleration were the requirements of flexibility for town use and superb road-holding. These demands have now been met by a new 'E' type which makes no pretension of being anything but a two-seater in its two available forms—a G.T. coupé and an open roadster with optionally extra detachable hardtop. Certainly the requirement of adequate luggage space has been met in both forms, though to a lesser extent in the roadster.

In line with established Jaguar policy, prices of the new car are extremely low for the performance and appointments offered; in fact, no other manufacturer of high performance cars approaches them in this respect. Compared with the XK150 S series, the open two-seater is £55 less, and the coupé only £15 more on basic costs.

The new prices are as follows:—

	Basic	Inc. P.T.
Coupé	£1,550	£2,196 19s 2d
Open two seater	£1,480	£2,097 15s 10d

The detachable hardtop is £54; total including P.T., £76 10s. Extras are priced approximately as for the XK150 series.

Basic constructional elements of the car follow very closely those of the D-type, and even more closely in some respects—particularly the independent rear suspension —the experimental competition car entered by Briggs Cunningham for last year's Le Mans 24-hour race. It is thus obvious that a great deal of the experience gained in competition has been applied to this new model. At the same time, much development work has been done to reduce noise in the form of wind roar at high speeds and that transmitted from the road.

Both forms utilize a monocoque body shell and chassis from the bulkhead rearwards; this is constructed of sheet steel with welded joints throughout. Main load-carrying members are the rigid and massive scuttle structure and, just forward of the rear wheels, a deep box section assembly; bracing these points is a very deep boxed sill at each side. Midway along these sills is another top-hat-section cross member. There are also two additional longitudinal floor members running from the bulkhead to the rear cross member structure. At the rear, a considerable degree of stiffness is obtained from the floor of the luggage compartment, which braces the rear cross member of the main hull to the tail section. In the tunnel space so formed, a separate sub-frame carrying the final drive unit and rear suspension assembly is attached separately at four points with rubber mountings to the main hull.

The stiffness of this type of hull construction is such that no additional underfloor reinforcing members are required on the open roadster as compared with the coupé, as is often necessary with some types of integral construction.

The bucket seats are the same for the roadster and coupé. This is the roadster with the detachable hardtop in position showing the hood stowage and side clamps for the hardtop

There are two distinct aspects of the seating and luggage compartment, differing slightly between the coupé and roadster, yet the two cars are basically similar below the window. In each the main floor level, on which the seats are mounted, is below the luggage platform. In their rearmost position, the backs of the bucket seats abut against a short wall formed by the rear cross member and the luggage platform. Thus luggage can be stacked inside the car (in its coupé form) from the seats to the tail. This floor incorporates a hinged flap which can be raised and fixed in retaining catches on each side, an arrangement which prevents heavy luggage moving forward under braking. With this platform raised,

there is then a small space behind the rear seats to accommodate soft baggage and articles needed during a journey.

In the coupé, access to the luggage compartment is through a rear door, side hinged on the left. Its catch is released from an internal pull handle behind the passenger's seat; this initial release opens the door by approximately one inch, just sufficient to get the hand underneath and release the secondary catch. The two hinges incorporate counterbalance springs which lighten the lifting load and hold the door in its over-centre open position but there is also a small retaining stay for use in gusty weather.

On the roadster the rear bulkhead terminates at the same point as the hinged flap of the coupé. This provides a stowage space for small articles behind the seats and the room necessary for the hood stowage. Access to the main luggage compartment is by means of a normal lift-up tail lid released from the passenger compartment. In both cars the spare wheel is mounted horizontally to the right and beneath the floor of the luggage compartment and is provided with a lift-up cover.

To the left side of the spare wheel is the kidney-shaped fuel tank, which has a capacity of 14 gallons. The tank incorporates a Lucas immersed fuel pump with a permanent magnet field electric motor and centrifugal rotor. This unit is a continuous-running type, supplying fuel at a controlled pressure to the carburettors; any flow surplus to the engine requirements is by-passed back to the tank. The advantages of this type of pump is that it reduces vapour lock tendencies by eliminating vacuum on the suction side and maintaining a constant pressure in the feed lines, and is not subject to engine or under-bonnet heat, all of which are contributory causes of vapour lock troubles.

Forward of the bulkhead there is a two-part sub-frame on which the engine is mounted and to which the suspension and steering assemblies are attached. This sub-

The two-seater roadster in its open and one of the two closed forms. Above: The optionally extra glass fibre hardtop which can be fitted with the hood in its stowed position. Below: A roadster in open form. Frameless windows wind down fully into the door recesses. Integrated with the bumpers, a small but efficient air intake is a distinctive styling feature

frame permits easy repair or replacement in the event of an accident, and is constructed of square tubes and box-section members; a separately attached forward section is constructed of circular tubes to which the radiator is mounted, and on which the counterbalanced up-lifting nose section hinges. The rear section of this sub-frame assembly is attached to the bulkhead at six points, each with a four-bolt flange, with a further attachment underneath at each side coincident with the under-floor longitudinal stiffening members of the monocoque hull.

Independent rear suspension is still a rarity on British cars, and Jaguar have not introduced it on the E-type without a great deal of investigation. During development, most of the basic types of independent and de Dion rear suspensions were tried. The de Dion is only a half-way house from the live axle, and although it has the advantage of reducing unsprung weight, the two wheels are still interconnected and reactions from one are transferred to the other. Jaguar engineers considered that the swing

axle type does not permit such good steering control as the basic wishbone pattern finally adopted, because the latter has less change of under- to oversteer characteristics. Basically, the type of suspension used is the same as that of the competition car used at Le Mans last year, but refined in detail to eliminate transmission of road noise.

The Salisbury hypoid final-drive unit and suspension members are attached to a deep and rigid pressed steel sub-frame to form a complete rear end sub-assembly. Suspension members at each side consist of a lower transverse tubular link and a fixed-length double-universal-jointed drive shaft for transverse location; longitudinal location is provided by a radius arm between the lower link and a mounting point on the body structure. The final drive casing is an iron casting with attachment points for mounting to the sub-frame, but the crown wheel and pinion and the taper roller bearings supporting these components are identical with those used in the standard Salisbury beam axle.

Above left: Side windows on the coupé can be opened as shown to assist ventilation. Below left: The driving compartment and facia panel on a left-hand drive open roadster version. The screen of this model has a bracing rod for the central clamp of the hood or hardtop. Below right: The forward-hinged nose permits good access; it can also be removed completely and there are multi-pin plugs for breaking the wiring circuits. This view shows the filter for internal ventilation and the three transparent fluid containers for the clutch and separate brake circuits

Access to the luggage compartment is through the rear hinged door of the coupé. The spare wheel and tools are beneath the removable panel on the right. The luggage retaining board is shown in its raised position

JAGUAR 'E'-TYPE . .

A Powr-Lok limited slip differential is a standard fitting. It incorporates multi-plate clutches adjacent to the differential side gears to provide a torque bias between the drive-shafts when one road wheel has less adhesion than that on the opposite side. By this means wheel spin is controlled, since the internal frame forces have to be overcome before one wheel can slip. These clutches are loaded in two ways: Belleville springs exert sufficient loading to provide traction at one wheel when the opposite one has no resistance; additional loading of the clutches is provided by the separating force of the differential gears through a system of cams.

Inboard Rear Brakes

At the rear, the Dunlop disc brakes are mounted inboard directly to the output shafts of the differential. As this arrangement results in the final drive casing dissipating more heat than normally, the oil seals are made of silicon rubber, which is very resistant to high temperatures.

The wheel carrier is an aluminium casting, inside which are two opposed taper roller hub bearings; this hub comprises two parts. The anti-friction bearings support the hub for the knock-off wheel on their inner diameters; inside this main hub is a splined yoke end for the outboard universal joint, the two being locked together by a castellated nut. Opposed taper roller bearings are used also for the outer pivot of the transverse tubular link; at the inboard pivot joint there are two caged needle roller assemblies at each side for the inner spindle, which is attached by means of a forged carrier to the final drive casing and on each side of the flanges of the sub-frame. There is a normal flange attachment at the drive-shaft inner universal joint; by means of shims between the shaft end and its attachment flange, wheel camber can be adjusted.

Each pressed steel U-section trailing radius arm for the longitudinal location of the suspension is mounted in a conical rubber seating at the body end, and a thick rubber bush at the attachment point to the wheel carrier. These rubber bushings are matched very closely to four—two at each

side—angularly placed V-shaped rubber saddles by means of which the sub-frame and suspension assembly are attached to the cross members of the body hull. Thus the whole unit is insulated on rubber to eliminate road noise and thumps emanating from suspension movements. A great deal of investigation work was necessary to arrive at the positions of these mountings, and the quantity and quality of the rubber used in them, to make sure that any deflections are neutralized and do not result in undesirable wheel movements which could produce rear end steering effects.

There are two suspension units at each side, comprising telescopic dampers and co-axial coil springs. Two small units, as distinct from a larger single assembly, are used for two reasons. They are smaller and therefore can be accommodated without intrusion into the luggage compartment at their top anchorage point. Also, by having one unit placed at either side of the transverse link, there are no offset loads.

A wishbone layout with its inherent low roll centre requires an anti-roll bar to provide roll stiffness. This is mounted transversely in rubber trunnions to the underside of the body hull, and linked to the radius arms at each side by a rubber-bushed drop link.

Front suspension is a direct development from the D-type, consisting of forged wishbones top and bottom, with ball pivots. The lower wishbone at each side is connected to a longitudinal torsion bar anchored at the scuttle assembly. There is an inclined telescopic damper at each side and a transverse anti-roll bar attached to the lower wishbones near the outer ends. Steering is by means of a forward-mounted rack and pinion assembly, gaitered to retain the lubricant, and having a single track rod at either side.

Separate Master Cylinders

The Dunlop self-adjusting disc brakes, 12in. dia., are the same size as those used on the XK150S, but as the E-type is approximately 5 cwt lighter, they have ample capacity for the extra performance. Separate hydraulic circuits with two master cylinders are an important safety feature. Also, the fluid containers for each of these circuits, and that for the clutch, are made of plastic, so that the fluid level is visible externally. In addition, each of the brake containers incorporates a fluid level float wired to a dash warning light.

Separate master cylinders are made possible by a new type of Dunlop mechanical booster. This augments directly the load applied to the brake pedal in definite proportion to the effort applied by the driver, as distinct from the more orthodox method of the servo increasing the hydraulic pressure in the pipe lines at a point between the brake master cylinder and the wheel

The three windscreen wipers in their parked position and the two screen washer jets attached to the scuttle

cylinders. An incidental advantage of this arrangement is a simplification of the hydraulic system, particularly valuable when bleeding the pipe lines.

There are two parts of the brake pedal assembly—the normal pendant pedal and the power lever. One end of the power lever is connected directly to the separate master cylinders through a swinging balance pivot; the other end operates the booster unit, which then applies an added effort to the power lever at this point. The servo unit is mounted on the dash and with the brakes in the "off" position the bellows are fully extended and full of air at normal atmospheric pressure. Initial and very slight movement of the brake pedal operates the master cylinders and, at the same time, a trigger closes an air valve and opens a vacuum valve in the servo unit; this evacuates air from the bellows, which contract and apply a load to the power lever. There is a reserve vacuum tank between the bellows and the engine induction system. The maximum degree of assistance, of course, is proportional to the size of bellows used, induction vacuum being a fairly constant figure. In the event of a breakdown on the servo side, or exhaustion of the vacuum tank, the mechanical linkage to the master cylinders is maintained, but naturally the pedal effort for equal braking would have to be higher.

Proved Power Unit

The power unit is the 3.8-litre version of the famous and well-established XK series and, in fact, is identical with that fitted to the XK150S. In other words, it is a perfectly standard production unit with the directly-operated valves placed in the hemispherical combustion chamber at an included angle of 70 deg., and a 9.0 to 1 compression ratio. The crankcase and cylinder block are a single iron casting with chromium-iron dry type liners. Gross power output is 265 b.h.p. at 5,500 r.p.m., and the maximum b.m.e.p. is 170 p.s.i. at 4,000 r.p.m. There are three 2in. dia. S.U. diaphragm type carburettors, with manual rich mixture control, feeding into straight ports in the aluminium cylinder head. In brief, it is a perfectly tractable and yet very powerful engine; presumably any of the modifications such as the special cylinder head developed for racing purposes will be available for those desiring to enter a car in competitions.

An innovation is the fitting of a thermostatically controlled Lucas electrically-driven coolant fan. This is a two-bladed unit operating in a cowl and comes into use automatically when the water in the header tank reaches a temperature of 80 deg. C., and cutting out when it falls to 73 deg. C. Normal air to the radiator is from a ducted entry at the front of the car, and the efficiency is such that the cooling fan would be in operation only during traffic halts. The advantages of the electrically-driven fan are reduction in noise and a saving in power, while it operates at a high speed when it is needed most, namely at engine idling.

There are two other air ducts from the front of the car, one for a direct supply of cool air to the carburettors and the other to a large filter for the ventilation system. Access to the engine compartment is good, for the complete nose section up to the scuttle hinges upwards on forward pivots. There is a central retainer device released by a hand-operated safety catch after two further locks, adjacent to the scuttle on each side, have been opened with a carriage key. On top of this bonnet section is a central duct, with an exit just forward of the screen.

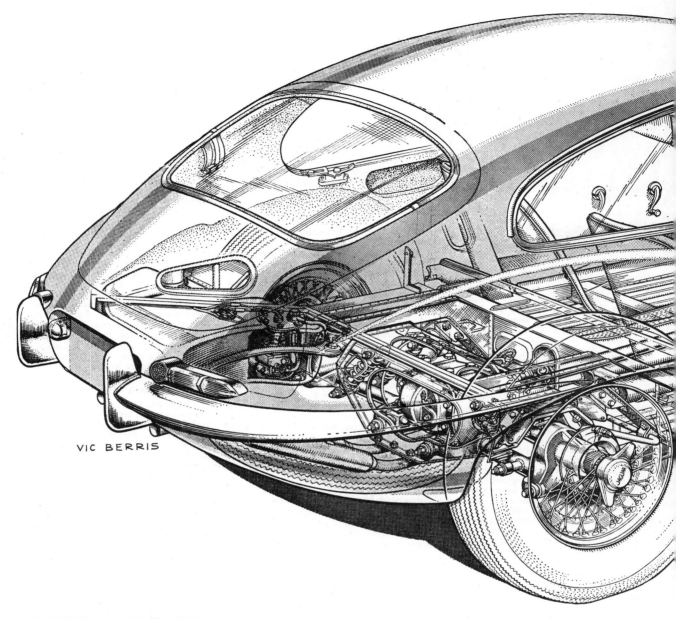

VIC BERRIS

SPECIFICATION

ENGINE

No. of cylinders	...	6 in line
Bore and stroke	...	87 x 106mm (3·43 x 4·17in.)
Displacement	...	3,781 c.c. (230·6 cu. in.)
Valve position and op-eration	...	Opposed valves in hemispherical chambers operated by twin camshafts and inverted tappets
Compression ratio	...	9·0 to 1 (optional 8·0 to 1)
Max. b.h.p. (gross)	...	265 at 5,500 r.p.m.
Max. b.m.e.p.	...	170 p.s.i. at 4,000 r.p.m.
Max. torque	...	260 lb ft at 4,000 r.p.m.
Carburettors	...	Three 2in. dia. horizontal S.U. diaphragm type HD8 with manual rich mixture control
Fuel pump	...	Lucas electric immersed in tank, type 2FP
Tank capacity	...	14 Imp. gallons (63·64 litres)
Sump capacity	...	11 pints (6·25 litres)
Oil filter	...	Full flow
Cooling system	...	Pressurized with pump and thermostat, electrically driven coolant fan, thermostatically operated
Battery	...	12 volt, 57 amp. hr.

TRANSMISSION

Clutch	...	Borg & Beck, 10in. dia. s.d.p. with hydraulic operation
Gearbox	...	Four speeds, synchromesh on 2nd, 3rd and top; central lever control
Overall gear ratios	...	Top 3·31; 3rd 4·25; 2nd 6·16; 1st and reverse 11·18 to 1,
Final drive	...	Salisbury hypoid with limited slip differential. Standard ratio 3·31; optional ratios 2·93, 3·07 and 3·54 to 1

CHASSIS

Brakes	...	Dunlop bridge type disc, outboard front, inboard rear, with servo assistance and separate hydraulic circuits front and rear
Disc dia	...	12in. front and rear
Suspension: front	...	Independent, wishbones with longitudinal torsion bars and telescopic dampers
Suspension: rear	...	Independent, with lower tubular links and fixed length drive shafts for transverse location; longitudinal location by radius arms. 2 coil springs and telescopic dampers each side
Anti-roll bar	...	Front and rear
Wheels	...	Dunlop wire spoke with centre lock hubs
Tyre size	...	6·40—15in. Dunlop RS5 with tubes. Dunlop RS racing tyres optional, 6·00—15in. front, 6·50—15in. rear on special wheels
Steering	...	Rack and pinion
Steering wheel	...	Three-spoke, 16in. dia., adjustable for height and reach
Turns, lock to lock	...	2·75

DIMENSIONS (Manufacturer's figures)

Wheelbase	...	8ft 0in. (243·8cm)
Track	...	4ft 2in. (127cm) front and rear
Overall length	...	14ft 7·3in. (445·3cm)
Overall width	...	5ft 5·2in. (165·6cm)
Overall height	...	4ft 0in. (122cm)
Ground clearance	...	5·5in. (14cm), laden
Turning circle	...	37ft (11·28m)
Dry weight	...	Open two-seater, 2,464lb, 22 cwt (1,118 kg) Coupé, 2,520lb, 22.5 cwt (1,143 kg)

PERFORMANCE DATA

		RS5 tyres	R5 tyres
Top gear m.p.h. per 1,000 r.p.m.	3·31 axle ratio,	23·0	24·6
	2·93 axle ratio,	26·0	27·8
	3·07 axle ratio,	24·8	26·5
	3·54 axle ratio,	21·5	23·0
Torque lb. ft. per cu. in. engine capacity		1·13	
Brake surface area swept by linings		561 sq. in.	
Weight distribution		F, 51 per cent R, 49 per cent	

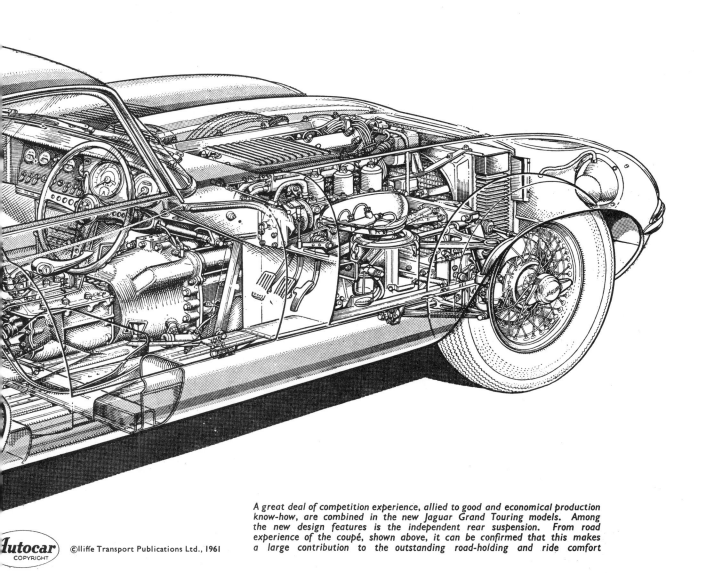

A great deal of competition experience, allied to good and economical production know-how, are combined in the new Jaguar Grand Touring models. Among the new design features is the independent rear suspension. From road experience of the coupé, shown above, it can be confirmed that this makes a large contribution to the outstanding road-holding and ride comfort

Jaguar E-Type

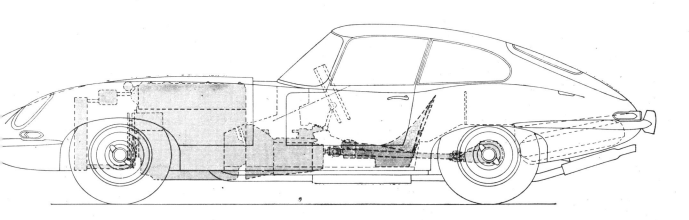

The body form is the result of extensive wind tunnel tests. This outline, reproduced at a 1:25 scale, illustrates the final form developed to solve the conflicting requirements of adequate passenger and luggage space with a body having a low drag factor

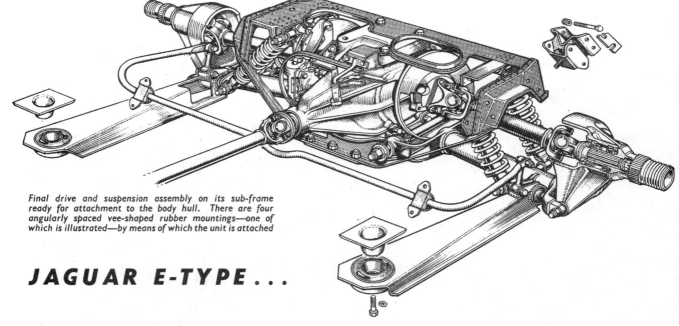

Final drive and suspension assembly on its sub-frame ready for attachment to the body hull. There are four angularly spaced vee-shaped rubber mountings—one of which is illustrated—by means of which the unit is attached

JAGUAR E-TYPE...

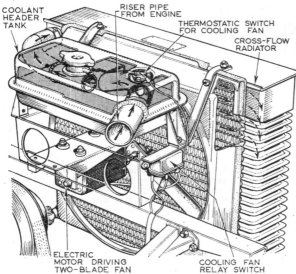

COOLANT HEADER TANK

RISER PIPE FROM ENGINE

THERMOSTATIC SWITCH FOR COOLING FAN

CROSS-FLOW RADIATOR

ELECTRIC MOTOR DRIVING TWO-BLADE FAN

COOLING FAN RELAY SWITCH

Cross flow radiator assembly and its header tank, showing how the water replenishes the coolant system through the break in the pipe run. A thermostat in the header tank operates the electrically driven cooling fan

Air flow from the front of the car is important at high speeds. This diagram shows the three main ducts to radiator, carburettors and internal ventilation filter. The complete nose section hinges upwards at its front pivot points or can be removed completely

the screen, for the release of under-bonnet air pressure.

The gearbox is the standard manually-operated unit fitted in all the company's current models. It has four-speeds, with synchromesh of the constant-load type fitted to the three upper ratios. An overdrive unit is not available, but there are four different final drive ratios available—3·54 to 1, 3·31 to 1, 3·07 to 1 and 2·93 to 1. The standard unit is 3·31 to 1, with which the calculated maximum of 147·6 m.p.h. (on R5 tyres) occurs at the recommended peak engine speed of 6,000 r.p.m. For those who rate acceleration as more important than maximum speed the 3·54 ratio would provide this characteristic. Similarly, should high cruising speeds at relatively low engine r.p.m. be desirable one of the two higher axle ratios would meet such requirements. For normal road use Dunlop RS5 tyres with tubes are fitted. For competition purposes racing tyres—Dunlop R5—and special wheels are available.

A three-spoked wooden rim steering wheel is adjustable for height and reach.

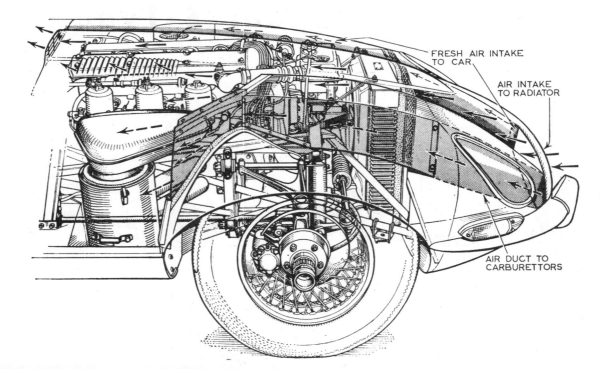

FRESH AIR INTAKE TO CAR

AIR INTAKE TO RADIATOR

AIR DUCT TO CARBURETTORS

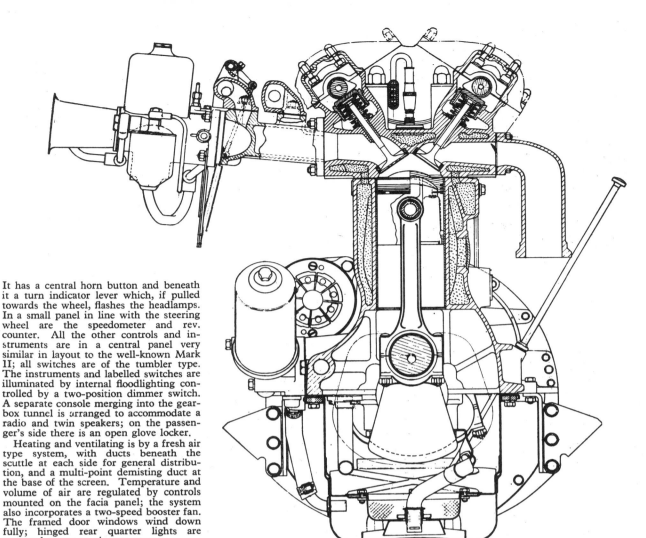

It has a central horn button and beneath it a turn indicator lever which, if pulled towards the wheel, flashes the headlamps. In a small panel in line with the steering wheel are the speedometer and rev. counter. All the other controls and instruments are in a central panel very similar in layout to the well-known Mark II; all switches are of the tumbler type. The instruments and labelled switches are illuminated by internal floodlighting controlled by a two-position dimmer switch. A separate console merging into the gearbox tunnel is arranged to accommodate a radio and twin speakers; on the passenger's side there is an open glove locker.

Heating and ventilating is by a fresh air type system, with ducts beneath the scuttle at each side for general distribution, and a multi-point demisting duct at the base of the screen. Temperature and volume of air are regulated by controls mounted on the facia panel; the system also incorporates a two-speed booster fan. The framed door windows wind down fully; hinged rear quarter lights are arranged to act as air extractors.

With a screen having a relatively high width-to-height ratio the problem of visi-

Evolved from a design which has been under constant development for nearly 14 years and has proved itself in racing, the 3·8-litre engine is the largest in the current Jaguar range. Twin overhead camshafts operate the valves directly through inverted tappets to give long life without frequent attention

VACUUM CONNECTION

VACUUM VALVE

AIR VALVE BUTTON

AIR VALVE

AIR INLET

TWIN MASTER CYLINDERS

Linkage from the brake pedal to the vacuum servo and independent master cylinders. Movement of the bellows tends to carry the air valve button away from the trigger: thus the continuing exhaustion from the bellows occurs only with increased pedal load

bility in wet weather has been overcome by the use of triple wipers linked in unison and operated by a two-speed motor; there are two water jets fed from an electrically driven washer. The twin bucket seats, adjustable for reach, are upholstered in leather over foam rubber cushions. Leather is used throughout for the trim, and the floor covering is of deep pile carpet over thick felt underlay. To eliminate reflections, the top deck of the facia and screen rail are leather covered with foam underlay. The two outer facia panels are finished in matt black paint; the central one and the cover of the console are manufactured in mottled aluminium.

Both the body forms were evolved after extensive wind tunnel testing. Because of its lower drag characteristics, the coupé obviously must be the faster of the two, even when the optionally available glass fibre detachable hardtop is fitted to the roadster. This can be attached without removing the stowed hood.

For the past three weeks we have had a coupé undergoing road test. The most impressive features are the quite outstanding road-holding, suspension and steering and these have been achieved with a very high level of ride comfort and suppression of road noise. From a standing start the quarter mile was covered in 14·7 seconds and 100 m.p.h. reached in 16·2 seconds. This is certainly the fastest car ever tested by this journal; its maximum speed is—see next week!

The Motor Continental Road Test No. 10/61

Make: Jaguar **Type: E-type**

Makers: Jaguar Cars, Ltd., Coventry, England.

Test Data

World copyright reserved; no unauthorized reproduction in whole or in part.

CONDITIONS: *Weather: Dry, warm, wind negligible. (Temperature 63°F. Barometer 30.5 in. Hg.). Surface: Dry tarmacadam. Fuel: Italian "Super" grade pump petrol (98-100 Octane Rating by Research Method).*

INSTRUMENTS

Speedometer at 30 m.p.h.	6% slow
Speedometer at 60 m.p.h.	1% fast
Speedometer at 90 m.p.h.	1% fast
Speedometer at 120 m.p.h.	accurate
Distance recorder	2½% slow

WEIGHT

Kerb weight, (unladen, but with oil, coolant and fuel for approx. 50 miles)	24 cwt.
Front/rear distribution of kerb weight	51/49
Weight laden as tested	28 cwt.

MAXIMUM SPEEDS

Flying Quarter Mile

Mean of opposite runs	149.1 m.p.h.
Best one-way time equals	150.1 m.p.h.

"Maximile" speed. (Timed quarter mile after one mile accelerating from rest.)

Mean of opposite runs	136.4 m.p.h.
Best one-way time equals	136.4 m.p.h.

Speed in gears (at 5,500 r.p.m.)

Max. speed in 3rd gear	107 m.p.h.
Max. speed in 2nd gear	74 m.p.h.
Max. speed in 1st gear	40 m.p.h.

FUEL CONSUMPTION

(Direct top gear)

25 m.p.g. at constant 30 m.p.h. on level.
27 m.p.g. at constant 40 m.p.h. on level.
27½ m.p.g. at constant 50 m.p.h. on level.
27½ m.p.g. at constant 60 m.p.h. on level.
26½ m.p.g. at constant 70 m.p.h. on level.
24 m.p.g. at constant 80 m.p.h. on level.
22½ m.p.g. at constant 90 m.p.h. on level.
21 m.p.g. at constant 100 m.p.h. on level.
17½ m.p.g. at constant 110 m.p.h. on level.
14½ m.p.g. at constant 120 m.p.h. on level.
13½ m.p.g. at constant 130 m.p.h. on level.

Overall Fuel Consumption for 2,859 miles, 144.9 gallons, equals 19.7 m.p.g. (14.35 litres/100 km.).

Touring Fuel Consumption (m.p.g. at steady speed midway between 30 m.p.h. and maximum, less 5% allowance for acceleration) 21.3.

Fuel tank capacity (maker's figure). 14 gallons

STEERING

Turning circle between kerbs:

Left	39 ft.
Right	36½ ft.
Turns of steering wheel from lock to lock	2½

BRAKES from 30 m.p.h.

1.00 g retardation (equivalent to 30 ft. stopping distance) with 115 lb. pedal pressure.
0.96 g retardation (equivalent to 31 ft. stopping distance) with 100 lb. pedal pressure.
0.79 g retardation (equivalent to 38 ft. stopping distance) with 75 lb. pedal pressure.
0.49 g retardation (equivalent to 61 ft. stopping distance) with 50 lb pedal pressure.
0.22 g retardation (equivalent to 136 ft. stopping distance) with 25 lb. pedal pressure.

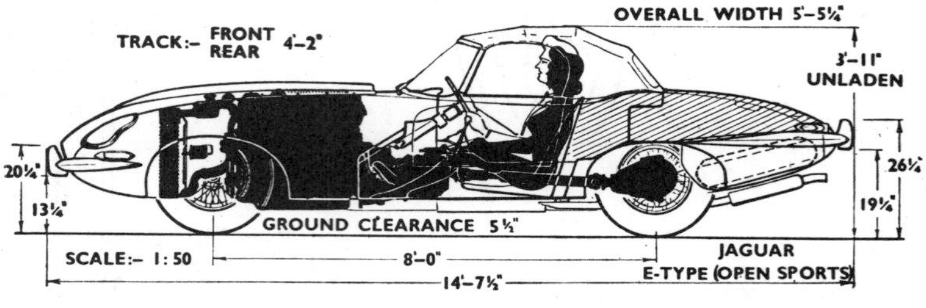

TRACK:– FRONT 4'–2" REAR
OVERALL WIDTH 5'–5¼"
3'–11" UNLADEN
20¼"
13¼"
GROUND CLEARANCE 5½"
26¼"
19¼"
SCALE:– 1:50
8'–0"
14'–7½"
JAGUAR
E-TYPE (OPEN SPORTS)

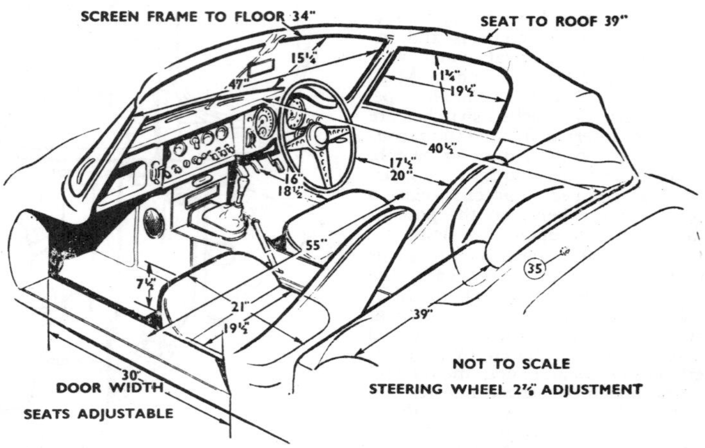

SCREEN FRAME TO FLOOR 34"
SEAT TO ROOF 39"
15¼"
47"
11¼"
19½"
40½"
17½"
20"
16"
18½"
55"
7½"
21"
19½"
39"
35
30"
DOOR WIDTH
SEATS ADJUSTABLE
NOT TO SCALE
STEERING WHEEL 2⅞" ADJUSTMENT

ACCELERATION TIMES from standstill

0-30 m.p.h.	2.6 sec.
0-40 m.p.h.	3.8 sec.
0-50 m.p.h.	5.6 sec.
0-60 m.p.h.	7.1 sec.
0-70 m.p.h.	8.7 sec.
0-80 m.p.h.	11.1 sec.
0-90 m.p.h.	13.4 sec.
0-100 m.p.h.	15.9 sec.
0-110 m.p.h.	19.9 sec.
0-120 m.p.h.	24.2 sec.
0-130 m.p.h.	30.5 sec.
0-140 m.p.h.	39.3 sec.
Standing quarter mile	15.0 sec.

ACCELERATION TIMES on Upper Ratios

	Top gear	3rd gear
10-30 m.p.h.	5.6 sec.	4.2 sec.
20-40 m.p.h.	5.6 sec.	4.3 sec.
30-50 m.p.h.	5.4 sec.	4.0 sec.
40-60 m.p.h.	5.4 sec.	4.0 sec.
50-70 m.p.h.	5.3 sec.	3.9 sec.
60-80 m.p.h.	5.0 sec.	3.7 sec.
70-90 m.p.h.	5.2 sec.	4.2 sec.
80-100 m.p.h.	5.7 sec.	4.8 sec.
90-110 m.p.h.	6.6 sec.	6.5 sec.
100-120 m.p.h.	7.7 sec.	—
110-130 m.p.h.	10.4 sec.	—
120-140 m.p.h.	15.1 sec.	—

HILL CLIMBING at sustained steady speeds

Max. gradient on top gear	1 in 5 (Tapley 440 lb./ton)
Max. gradient on 3rd gear	1 in 3.7 (Tapley 585 lb./ton)
Max. gradient on 2nd gear	1 in 2.4 (Tapley 860 lb./ton)

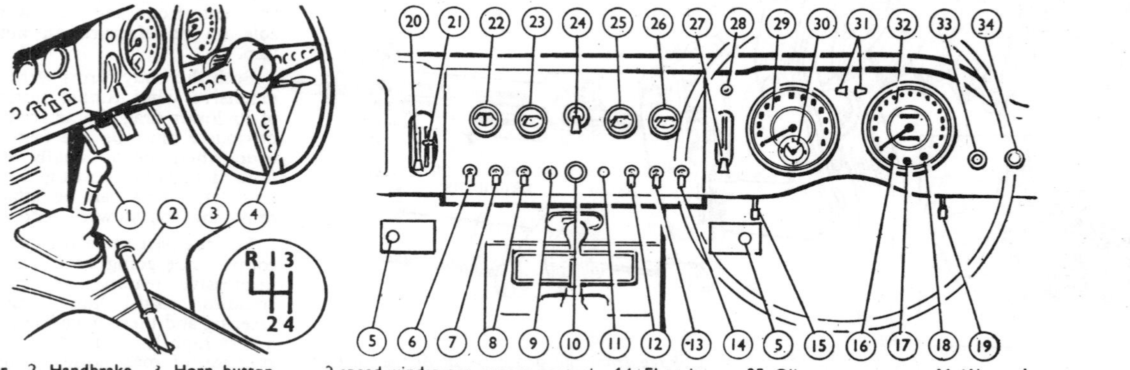

R 1 3
2 4

1, Gear lever. 2, Handbrake. 3, Horn button. 4, Direction indicator and headlamp flasher control. 5, Vent flaps. 6, Interior lights switch. 7, Bright-Dim panel light switch. 8, 2-speed heater fan control. 9. Ignition switch. 10, Cigar lighter 11, Starter 12, Map light switch. 13, 2-speed windscreen wipers control. 14, Electric screen washer control. 15, Clock adjuster. 16, Ignition warning light. 17, Fuel warning light. 18, Headlamp warning light. 19, Trip reset. 20, Fresh air control 21, Heater control. 22, Ammeter. 23, Fuel gauge. 24, Lights switch 25, Oil pressure gauge. 26, Water thermometer. 27, Choke. 28, Choke warning light. 29, Rev counter. 30, Clock. 31 Direction indicator warning lights. 32, Speedometer 33, Handbrake and hydraulic fluid level warning light 34, Dip switch. 35, Boot lid control (see middle drawing)

The JAGUAR E-type

Roadholding and Handling to Match a Startling Performance

The characteristic Jaguar grille has gone and the functional elegance of the frontal treatment gives little encouragement to badge and spotlight collectors.

WHEN one of the finest engine designs of the present time, in its most highly developed production form, is installed in a fully independently sprung chassis which has been evolved well beyond the final development of a series of Le Mans winning cars, the result should be something of a landmark in sports-car progress. Three thousand miles at home and abroad in little more than a week have convinced us that this expectation is more than justified.

Curiously enough, its very close con-

nection in design and appearance with competition Jaguars gives people the impression that this is essentially a racing car with all the limitations for ordinary use that this implies. Nothing could be farther from the truth; admittedly it is quite easily the fastest car ever tested by *The Motor* but the roadholding is entirely capable of handling the power, the springing is more comfortable than that of many sober touring cars and the engine is extremely flexible and devoid of temperament. The ease and delicacy of control is such that 220 b.h.p./ton was no embarrassment at all on the packed snow and ice of Swiss mountain passes using ordinary racing tyres.

A good medium-powered family saloon will accelerate from 10-30 m.p.h. in top gear in about 10-11 sec. The E-type will do 110-130 m.p.h. in this time and, despite its very high top gear, 10-30 m.p.h. in half the time; on one occasion it climbed Birdlip hill (maximum gradient 1 in 6) in top, travelling quite slowly and using only part throttle. This initial rate of acceleration, about 4 m.p.h. every second, is maintained in one steady effortless sweep all the way up to 100 m.p.h., but for real exhilaration when emerging from a 30 m.p.h. speed limit, second gear will spin the speedometer needle round to the mid-

seventies in about 7 sec. to the accompaniment of a very subdued but delightfully hard exhaust hum and considerable strain on the neck muscles, whilst another 6 sec. in third brings up the hundred.

This exceptional combination of full-range torque and very high maximum output is complemented by smoothness and mechanical silence of a very high order. It should be said, however, that the engine in our test car used oil at the rate of about 1,300 m.p.g. when driven hard and that towards the end of a journey across London in the rush hour some fluffiness was noticeable due to sooting of the standard grade plugs. The 9 : 1 compression ratio caused a trace of pinking in the 2,000-2,500 r.p.m. band even with 100-octane fuel.

With the exception of bottom, the gears are quiet and the ratios extremely well selected, but the synchromesh is much less powerful than is now usual. With a clutch that has a fairly long travel and does not free perfectly, this means that really quick upward changes from first to second, and to a lesser extent, from second to third, cannot be made silently at high revs, whilst high-speed downward changes demand fairly accurate double declutching; the movement of the gearlever is rather heavy. "Heel and toe" operation of brake and throttle is possible but difficult.

In Brief

Price (as tested) £1,480, plus purchase tax £617 15s. 10d., equals £2,097 15s. 10d.
Capacity ... ... 3,781 c.c.
Unladen kerb weight ... 24 cwt.
Acceleration:
20-40 m.p.h. in top gear ... 5.6 sec.
0-50 m.p.h., through gears 5.6 sec.
Maximum direct top gear gradient 1 in 5
Maximum speed ... 149.1 m.p.h.
"Maximile" speed ... 136.4 m.p.h.
Touring fuel consumption ... 21.3 m.p.g.
Gearing: 24.8 m.p.h. in top gear at 1,000 r.p.m. (Based on tyre dia. at 100 m.p.h.) 35.6 m.p.h. at 1,000 ft./min. piston speed.

On the standard 3.31 to 1 final drive ratio the car proved undergeared for maximum speed. On our timed runs with the hood up it flattened out around 150 m.p.h., about 6,000 r.p.m. This is well beyond the engine speed for peak power, nominally 5,500 r.p.m. but probably less as installed, so that the optional higher axle ratio would produce an even higher maximum.

The Dunlop Road Speed RS5 tyres, which are standard equipment on the Jaguar, have been used by test drivers for short bursts up to 150 m.p.h., but it was considered highly desirable that maximum speed runs should be made on the R5 racing covers that are offered as optional extras. At 100 m.p.h. these give a rolling radius for the driving wheels some 4½% greater than that of the standard tyres.

Both bonnet and boot lid are spring counterbalanced in the open position and the former provides exceptional access to the engine and front suspension. The folded hood is normally enclosed by a neat cover. By undoing two thumb screws the central instrument and switch panel can be hinged down to expose the wiring and all the fuses.

Clearly it would be absurd to present a set of performance figures which could be obtained by using one type of tyre for top speed and fuel consumption and another of different size for optimum acceleration. All the figures in the data panel were therefore recorded on R5 covers, although a later check on Road Speeds showed slightly better initial acceleration which reduced the standing quarter mile to 14.7 sec.

The Jaguar has exceptional brakes, although despite the use of a vacuum servo, the pedal loads are fairly high, so that there is an initial impression of a lack of "bite" which the tabulated figures show

to be misleading. During a considerable part of the test the brakes were spoiled by a most obscure fault which gradually allowed air to leak into the rear hydraulic circuit giving excessive pedal travel.

Before we had driven the E-type very far it became clear that the new independent rear suspension was a major step forward which had put the road manners of the car into the highest category. The springing is quite soft and provides a most comfortable ride; at high speeds on bumpy roads very few touring cars can compete with it in this respect and certainly not in the tremendous feeling of security and stability with which it deals with sudden

Specification

Engine

Cylinders	...	6
Bore	...	87 mm.
Stroke	...	106 mm.
Cubic capacity	...	3,781 c.c.
Piston area	...	55.3 sq. in.
Valves	...	Overhead (twin o.h.c.)
Compression ratio	...	9/1
Carburetters	...	Three 2 in. S.U. H.D.8
Fuel pump	...	Lucas electric type 2FP
Ignition timing control	...	Centrifugal and vacuum
Oil filter	...	Tecalemit full-flow
Max. power (gross)	...	265 b.h.p.
at	...	5,500 r.p.m.
Piston speed at max. b.h.p.		3,820 ft./min.

Transmission

Clutch	...	10 in. Borg & Beck s.d.p.
Top gear (s/m)	...	3.31
3rd gear (s/m)	...	4.25
2nd gear (s/m)	...	6.16
1st gear	...	11.18
Reverse	...	11.18
Propeller shaft	...	Hardy Spicer open
Final drive	...	Hypoid bevel with PowrLok differential
Top gear m.p.h. at 1,000 r.p.m.		24.8
Top gear m.p.h. at 1,000 ft./min. piston speed		35.6

(based on racing tyre dia. at 100 m.p.h.)

Chassis

Brakes	...	Dunlop disc all round

Brake disc diameter:
Front	...	11 in. dia.
Rear	...	10 in. dia.
Friction area	...	31.8 sq. in. of friction material operating on 461 sq. in. rubbed area of discs

Suspension:
Front ... Independent by transverse wishbones, torsion bars and anti-roll bar
Rear ... Independent by lower wishbone, stressed articulated half-shafts and trailing link with coil springs and torsion anti-roll bar

Shock Absorbers:
Front ... ... Girling telescopic
Rear Twin Girling telescopic each side
Steering gear ... ... Rack and pinion
Tyres:
Dunlop RS5 6.40×15
or (as optional extra)
Dunlop Racing R5 6.00×15 front 6.50×15 rear

Coachwork and Equipment

Starting handle ... ... No
Battery mounting Under bonnet on left side
Jack ... Manual 3-stage screw jack
Jacking points One centrally each side
Standard tool kit: Adjustable spanner, screwdriver, pliers, plug spanner, 3 box spanners, 4 o.e. spanners, grease gun, hub mallet, tyre gauge, distributor screwdriver, feeler gauge, valve extractor.
Exterior lights: 2 headlights, 2 sidelights/flashers, 2 tail/stop lamps/flashers, number plate lamp.
Number of electrical fuses ... 8
Direction indicators ... Amber flashers
Windscreen wipers: 3 blade, two speed, self-parking electric
Windscreen washers: Lucas electric
Sun visors ... ... None
Instruments: Speedometer with total and trip distance recorders, combined rev. counter and clock, water temperature gauge, ammeter, oil pressure gauge, fuel contents gauge.
Warning lights: Direction indicators, fuel level,

brake fluid level and handbrake, headlamp main beam, choke.
Locks:
With ignition key ... ... Doors
With other keys ... ... None
Glove lockers: One (open) on passenger's side of facia
Map pockets ... ... None
Parcel shelves: One beneath rear window
Ashtrays ... One below centre of facia
Cigar lighters ... ... One
Interior lights: Map light under facia and light on rear bulkhead
Interior heater: Standard fresh-air heater/demister with two-speed fan
Car radio: H.M.V. Radiomobile (optional extra)
Extras available: Radio, R5 racing tyres, hardtop (detachable)
Upholstery material Vaumol leather hide
Floor covering: Carpet with felt underlay
Exterior colours standardized: 14 plus special colours at extra cost
Alternative body styles: Fixed head coupé

Maintenance

Sump: 11 pints, S.A.E. 30 (Summer), 20 (Winter) (13 pints, including filter)
Gearbox ... ... 2½ pints, S.A.E. 30
Rear axle ... 2½ pints, S.A.E. 90 (Hypoid)
Steering gear lubricant ... ... Grease
Cooling system capacity 22 pints (2 drain taps)
Chassis lubrication: By grease gun every 2,500 miles to 22 points
Ignition timing ... ... 10° b.t.d.c.
Contact-breaker gap ... .014 to .016 in.
Sparking plug type ... Champion N.5
Sparking plug gap ... ... .025 in.
Valve timing: Inlet opens 15° b.t.d.c. and closes 57° a.b.d.c. Exhaust opens 57° b.b.d.c. and closes 15° a.t.d.c.

Tappet clearances (cold): Inlet .004 in. Exhaust .006 in.
Wheel toe-in. Front $\frac{1}{16}$ to ⅛ in., rear 0 to ⅛ in.
Camber angle: Front, 0 to ½ deg. positive, rear ¼ to 1 deg. negative
Castor angle ... ... 1½ to 2 deg.
Steering swivel pin inclination ... 4 deg.
Tyre pressures:

	Normal use:		
Front RS5	23 lb.	Rear	30 lb.
Front R5	30 lb.	Rear	30 lb.
	Very high speed:		
Front RS5	30 lb.	Rear	35 lb.
Front R5	35 lb.	Rear	40 lb.

Brake fluid ... ... S.A.E. 70 R3
Battery type and capacity: 12 volt, 57 amp. hr.

colonial sections encountered at really high speed. Much softer damper settings can be used in the absence of an unruly live rear axle and this eliminates a lot of vertical motion.

Travelling fast across Northern France we discovered that the extra width of the R5 rear tyres was causing them to foul on the wheel arches and restrict the bump movement of the rear suspension. We understand that this will be corrected in future, but in any case it does not arise with the normal tyres; with these it was very difficult to bottom the rear suspension on its rubber stops in this country, except by travelling extremely fast over switchback sections.

Any idea that rack and pinion steering is suitable only for small, light cars is contradicted by the Jaguar. Despite high gearing (2½ turns of the wheel covers the not very good lock) there is practically no trace of kickback, and the characteristic virtues of precision, smoothness and lightness are present to an outstanding degree. Even manoeuvring needs only a moderate effort, and for directional stability at speed the car has few rivals.

A great deal of clever development must have been required to produce cornering characteristics which are not only outstandingly good but particularly well suited to the unusual power-to-weight ratio. It is basically very near to being a neutral steering car, but the driver is constantly astonished by the amount of power he can pile on in a corner without starting to bring the tail round; as with front-wheel drive, hard acceleration through a bend is the right technique, and lifting off suddenly gives a marked oversteering change. Naturally, the power technique can be overdone in the lower gears, but this merely increases the nose-in drift angle in a most controllable way. It is possible to go on increasing the sideways "g" value to a quite surprising level, because the E-type retains its balance far beyond the point at which most sports cars have lost one end. The very low build (we only realized how low when we

saw a small foreign GT coupé towering over it) and anti-roll bars at both ends keep the roll angles right down, and it seems natural to throw the car about in a manner usually reserved for smaller and lighter sports cars.

For this kind of driving we found that the highest recommended pressures (30 lb. front, 35 rear) gave the most pleasant feel with Road Speed tyres at the expense of only a little more harshness on bad roads. The structure is so rigid that there is no trace of the bonnet movement and scuttle shake which plague so many open cars, and the suspension is very effectively rubber insulated. As a result, even racing tyres at maximum speed pressures, which are notorious for their extreme harshness and noisiness, fail to destroy the pleasure of road motoring, and they enhance the cornering power even further.

Habitability

As a long-distance grand touring car, the open Jaguar needs further development before it reaches quite the same high standard. Luggage accommodation is limited by the shallowness of the boot, and the imperfect fit of the hood round the winding glass windows leads to wind noise but not to draughts. In fact, for a soft-top car the wind noise is low, but in relation to its tremendously high cruising speed it could well be lower still. Averaging some 400 miles a day for six days with over 500 miles packed into one or two, we found the seats unsatisfactory. The squabs are effectively concave where they should be convex to support the small of the back and the cushions are rather hard and flat so that one tends to slide forward. The positions of the pedals and of the very attractive wood-rimmed steering wheel on its telescopic column are such as to provide any driver up to about 5 ft. 10 in. with a good arm's-length driving position and excellent visibility over a bonnet which looks much shorter from inside than it really is. Seat adjustment is not adequate for most taller people and neither is the headroom with the rather upright sitting position.

Ventilation is also a critical factor for long-distance comfort. In cool or mild weather the fresh-air intake through the heater system is adequate but the inside of the car can become rather hot in warm sunny weather even when the very quiet two-speed fan is used. Opening either window between 40 and 60 m.p.h. causes a low-frequency pressure fluctuation which makes the hood drum very loudly, and if the tank is more than three-quarters full petrol fumes are drawn in.

One solution, of course, is to lower the hood, which is a very quick and easy operation involving only three toggle catches and giving reasonably draught-free motoring irrespective of whether the side windows are wound up or down. The central hood-fixing toggle is connected to a slender tension rod running down to the scuttle in order to relieve the screen top rail of aerodynamic loads and the rear-view mirror is mounted on this rod. When the hood is down the loss of tension allows the rod to flex and the mirror to shake about.

At night the Le Mans-type headlights were not really adequate for the performance. There was insufficient spread to illuminate the sides of twisty roads and the dipped beams seemed to cause considerable annoyance to other road users.

The car we tested was the first open model to be completed and it was assembled and tested in considerable haste as we stood by to snatch it away. It is not surprising therefore that many body details such as door and bonnet locks left something to be desired and much development is still going on. It is difficult to see, however, how this car can fail to be a tremendous success. The sheer elegance of line which Jaguar seem able to produce by total disregard for fashion trends is allied to a combination of performance, handling and refinement that has never been equalled at the price and, we would think, very seldom surpassed at any price.

THE NEW 3.8-LITRE JAGUAR E-TYPE G.T.

Sensational New 265-b.h.p. 165-m.p.h. Car with All-Round-Independent Suspension. Standing-start ¼-mile in under 15 seconds. Price with Purchase Tax £2,196 19s. 2d. Open Two-Seater Costs Under £2,098.

ON THE ROAD.—The Jaguar E-type which MOTOR SPORT *sampled last month was no hurriedly-contrived mock-up or worn-out prototype but a beautifully-finished car to production specification. To prove it we took this photograph of it in Newport Pagnell, after it had exceeded 150 m.p.h. along M 1.*

FOR many years now, indeed ever since before the war when the S.S.1 was conceived, new models from the company that is now Jaguar Cars Ltd. have each one been " a winner." This is particularly true of the sensational E-type Jaguar which was announced to the world on March 15th. When the first S.S.1 was released it caused a sensation not only because it had impressive lines and went very well but on account of its modest price. The same is true of the 1961 Jaguar E-type, but there all comparison ends.

What Sir William Lyons has done is to use all that was best in the race-bred and inspired C and D-type Jaguars, learn some useful lessons from the 3-litre Cunningham Jaguar built for the last Le Mans race, evolve stylish new bodywork and combine all these ingredients in a new British Grand Touring Jaguar that is about as fast as they come, immensely accelerative, endowed with extremely good road-holding, handling and braking characteristics, able to be driven by grandma at 15 m.p.h. or less in top gear, of returning some 20 m.p.g. of fuel under fast-travel conditions and which sells in G.T. coupé form, even after the Chancellor has had his levy of well over £618, for a mere £2,196 19s. 2d. Sir William Lyons has bred another winner!

The E-type project started some four years ago and to some degree carried on where the XKSS project, which the fire at the factory undermined, left off. Clearly, the Jaguar design team, under W. M. Heynes, realised that they had components and know-how derived from a great many successes in the sports/racing field, that would enable them to produce a G.T. car, in both open and coupé two-seater form, that would have a performance formerly associated only with the most costly and exotic Italian makes, while combining such speed, stability and acceleration with the commendable smoothness, silence and dependability that has for many years sold every Jaguar saloon that the Coventry factory could construct. It is typical that Jaguar should offer this sensational new road-burning 3.8-litre G.T. model at a price which makes the term " value-for-money " seem scarcely appropriate! For the E-type costs only about a third of the price of a G.T. Maserati or Ferrari of something like equivalent performance, and less than half the price of an Aston Martin DB4GT!

Jaguar would seem to have timed the advent of their E-type well—it is obviously intended for Britain's forthcoming new fast roads; it is just the stimulating very-high-performance car that cannot fail to increase Jaguar exports to the U.S.A. and other countries, and it is Britain's answer to German and Italian G.T. cars, thus ensuring continued prestige for Sir William Lyons' company at a time when it has (temporarily ?) turned its back on motor racing.

It is particularly stimulating to find that Jaguar have adopted independent rear suspension for their new E-type, proof, if such were needed, of the desirability of getting rid of the rigid back axle, however lightly constructed and well located. This is a pure i.r.s. layout, using universally-jointed drive-shafts, and was decided upon after exhaustive experiments with many different systems, including de Dion back axles. This self-contained suspension unit is mounted on rubber and 5° of movement relative to its sub-frame is deliberately permitted, controlled by trailing rubber-mounted torque links. Otherwise the construction follows D-type technique. Thus the Jaguar stressed-skin method is used, dispensing with a chassis frame, a body monocoque almost entirely of 20 g. sheet steel being welded up as a load-carrying structure to which front and back sub-frames of Reynolds 5H square-section steel tubing are bolted. The use of i.r.s. permits inboard disc-brakes and front suspension is very closely related to that devised for the D-type and 150S Jaguar models.

General Description

The Jaguar E-type is offered to the public in two forms : an open sports car—with or without detachable hard-top—and a coupé. In both cases, the cars are two-seaters and, except for minor items of detail, their chassis and body specifications are very closely related.

The front sub-frame is a built-up unit consisting of two triangulated side-members and a deep front cross-member. These are bolted together and replacement of any of the individual units does not necessitate removal of the whole assembly. The sub-frame carries the engine and all ancillaries, together with the front suspension and steering gear. These units are shrouded beneath a fabricated front section, which is hinged to the forward end of the sub-frame, and performs the same functions as do the bonnet and front wings on a car of more conventional design. This arrangement provides for accessibility for all major components.

The six-cylinder twin-cam XK engine is used in S-type 3.8-litre triple-carburetter form, developing 265 b.h.p. at 5,500 r.p.m. (b.m.e.p.= 172 lb./sq. in.) and 260 lb./ft. torque at 4,000 r.p.m.

Fuel is supplied by a submerged Lucas electric pump incorporated in the petrol tank. This pump is of entirely new design, and operates on the recirculation principle. Its main features are a high pumping capacity and an ability to prevent vapour locking in the petrol pipes. The carburetters have a common air cleaner, to which they are connected by a glass-fibre collector box.

The pressurised cooling system incorporates the new Lucas electric fan in place of the more conventional engine-driven unit. A thermostatic switch is employed which switches in the fan at 80° C. and switches it out at 72° C. The radiator is of the high-efficiency cross-flow type and is mounted on the front sub-frame.

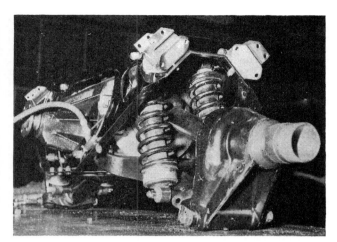

The independent rear suspension unit which is an important technical feature of the new Jaguar.

A separate header tank is used, mounted between the engine and the radiator.

Power is transmitted by a hydraulically-operated 10-in. Borg and Beck single dry plate clutch, to a Jaguar four-speed gearbox. This is manually operated by a centrally positioned gear-lever and has synchromesh on top, third and second gears. A short, stiff propellor shaft continues the drive to the hypoid rear axle which, together with the rear suspension, is mounted in a sub-frame. The axle unit is fitted with a limited slip differential. Axle ratios of 2.93, 3.07, 3.31 and 3.54-to-1 are available. Normally the 3.31-to-1 ratio is used, giving gear ratios of 11.17, 6.16, 4.25 and 3.3-to-1.

The front suspension utilises a system of independent suspension based on transverse wishbones and torsion bars. The front ends of the torsion bars are mounted in extensions of the lower wishbones, thus making it possible to remove the bars without disturbing the rest of the suspension. Telescopic dampers are fitted and an anti-roll bar links the two lower sets of wishbones.

The independent rear suspension is of completely new design. Location of the wheels in a transverse plane is achieved by the use of two tubular links of which the top link is the half-shaft—universally jointed at both ends. The lower link is also a tubular structure pivoted at the wheel carrier and at the sub-frame adjacent to the differential casing. To provide maximum rigidity in a longitudinal plane the pivot bearings at both ends of the lower link are widely spaced. The suspension medium is provided by twin coil-springs on each side, to Jaguar's own specification, enclosing telescopic hydraulic dampers, and these are mounted on each side of the differential casing. The whole assembly is carried in a fabricated steel sub-frame which is easily and quickly detachable from the body structure. This sub-frame is located in the body by four vee rubber blocks—and by a radius arm on each side of the car between the lower link and a mounting point on the body structure. The radius arm pivots are rubber bushed and, as a result, the whole suspension assembly, including the sub-frame, is allowed 5° of movement—the amount being controlled by the characteristics of the rubber used to make the vee blocks and radius arm pivots.

The E-type Jaguar is fitted with Dunlop disc-brakes on all four wheels, 11-in. at the front, 10-in. inboard at the back. The front brakes are mounted on the wheel hubs whilst the rear brakes are mounted inboard of the half-shafts and adjacent to the differential unit. The brakes themselves are of single pair pad design in which the friction pads are quickly replaceable. They are operated by a pedal actuating twin master cylinders through a compensating device which divides the system into entirely independent circuits to front and rear brakes. Each master cylinder has its own reservoir and low-level warning system, which operates a red light on the facia panel. A Dunlop bellows-type servo is fitted and operates direct onto the brake pedal, thus providing maximum retardation with low pedal pressures. The ratio of braking is 60/40, front/rear.

Rack-and-pinion steering is fitted, and a turning circle of 37 ft is provided with only 2¼ turns from lock-to-lock. The lightweight steering wheel is of polished alloy and has a wood rim. It is separately adjustable for both height and reach.

Centre-lock 72 spoke wire wheels normally carry 6.40×15 Dunlop RS5 tyres.

Rack-and-pinion steering is used, with the rack flexibly mounted on rubber, and the electrical equipment of this sensational new Jaguar is Lucas throughout. The fuel tank holds 14 gallons. The E-type is compact, having a wheelbase of 8 ft., a track of 4 ft. 2 in. and dimensions of 14 ft. 7 5/16 in. × 5ft. 5 in. × 4 ft. 0⅛ in., the last-named relating to height, so this car definitely belongs to the exclusive breed of G.T. coupé on which the proud owner can nonchalantly lean an elbow! Ground clearance is quoted as 5½ in. and dry weights as 22 cwt. for the two-seater, 22½ cwt. for the coupé.

The E-type body was designed and styled entirely in this country and will be made by Jaguar at their Coventry factory. A 1/10th-scale model was exhaustively tested in various wind tunnels. This proved the considerable upsweep of the tail to be correct. The twin exhaust pipes come out below the final-drive unit and up under the tail to secure the required extractor length and to enable additional expansion chambers to be fitted. From the back end, especially, the Jaguar E-type is a delightfully fierce-looking car, while the beautiful curves of the body are quite breathtaking at first sight. I felt glad to be an Englishman standing in Coventry viewing this amazing new British car!

Technical Appraisal

The basic structure of the body consists of two large-diameter longitudinal tubular members, which run the length of the main fuselage, and which are constructed from the outer skin panel and the inner rocker panel. At the front, two large vertical box sections are welded onto the top of the longitudinal members and these are built into a very deep box section cross-member which forms the scuttle of the body. At the rear, a deep box section cross-member is continued upwards to form a diaphragm between the rear wheel arches, whilst the panel across the top of the wheel arches is similarly boxed in for additional stiffness. The rear section of the body is built up as a stressed-skin unit with the addition of heavy-gauge stiffeners which comes up from the rear cross-member and form the base to which the rear suspension and drive units are mounted.

The main external panels are produced on a stretcher press, while most of the detail parts are made by normal presses or on rubber die presses. The all-welded construction calls for several new techniques in the welding processes, including the use of CO_2 wire-welding plant.

Already the E-type assembly line is coming into being and already the new car is in production. Incidentally, Jaguar now make their own gearbox gears and have installed a phosphating bath in the body shop since my last visit.

Reverting to the early stages of E-type evolution, the required performance was sought first and a refining process was then embarked upon, much of the testing being done at M.I.R.A., under Jaguar's head-tester, Norman Dewis.

When it is remarked that this fully-equipped, properly sound-damped docile Jaguar coupé has clocked 0-60 m.p.h. in 7.0 sec., 0-100 m.p.h. in 16.0 sec., and has covered a s.s. ¼-mile in 14.8 sec. *in the wet* at M.I.R.A., using the 9-to-1 compression-ratio and 3.31-to-1 axle ratio, my enthusiasm for it can, perhaps, be easily comprehended, especially bearing in mind the prices, which are :—

Coupé :

£1,550 + £646 19s. 2d. purchase tax = £2,196 19s. 2d.

Two-seater :

£1,480 + £617 15s. 10d. purchase tax = £2,097 15s. 10d.

Two-seater hard-top :

£54 + £22 10s. 0d. purchase tax = £76 10s. 0d.

The two-seater hard-top version of the new Jaguar, which you can buy for £2,174 5s. 10d. inclusive of purchase tax.

THE BUSINESS-LIKE LINES of the Jaguar E-type are nicely depicted in this view of the car outside the " White Hart " at Hockliffe. Mr. Marples may be pleased to know that we didn't drink at this hotel, because it was shut.

Incidentally, this new E-type, capable of 155 m.p.h. on the 3.31-to-1 axle ratio or 165 m.p.h. with the 3.07-to-1 ratio, does not replace any other Jaguar model, all of which—2.4, 3.4, and 3.8-litre Mk. II, Mk. IX, XK150 and XK150S—remain in production and full demand, the output being rather better than 500 cars per week.

The E-type on the Road

Just over a week before the announcement date of the new Jaguar I was allowed to sample it for a few hours on the roads near Coventry. I was aware that other motoring journalists had been permitted to venture as far afield as Italy in E-types but after many years' experience of the Motor Industry I have learnt to be thankful for small mercies, and thus I gratefully headed a coupé towards M 1—*a road, Mr. Marples, that was reduced to single-line traffic in several places* while men toiled to plough up and re-lay its so-called hard shoulders!

What followed was quite fantastic—remembering that an honoured British name and not one hailing from Modena, Marenello or Stuttgart graced our motor car. Getting the feel of the E-type and then encountering those aforesaid single-lane sections of the great Marples Motor Road, we nevertheless found ourselves as far away as St. Albans *within an hour of accelerating out of the gates of the Jaguar factory.* Put the E-type in top gear and it just goes faster and faster, until it is cruising along M 1 at 6,100 r.p.m., which we calculated to be a pretty genuine 155 m.p.h. At this speed it is possible for driver to converse with passenger in normal tones, wind-noise being low and little noise coming from transmission or final-drive—a fantastic experience! The E-type felt as if it would have been happy to go the length of M 1 at this speed—equal to a sutained 6,100 r.p.m.—had not vehicles crawling along the outside lane at 90/100 m.p.h. occasionally impeded its progress! After dropping to 4,000 r.p.m., or approximately 102 m.p.h., it was possible to accelerate to 5,000 r.p.m. (127 m.p.h.) in a mere eight seconds. . . .

It must be emphasised that, rapid as it is, the Jaguar E-type is a fully equipped, properly appointed, but strictly a two-seater motor car. You climb in a thought awkwardly, over the side-sill of the body, to sit in a racing-type bucket seat upholstered in Vaumol leather over Dunlopillo foam rubber. A valid criticism is that the seat might not go back as far as really tall exponents of the full-stretch driving stance would wish. The wood-rimmed wheel with triple drilled metal spokes is set low, adjustable for height and rake. The wide doors possess windows which wind almost fully down with three turns of the handle, but no quarter-lights. There is no sense of being within such a low car. Before the driver is a Smiths 160-m.p.h. speedometer and a tachometer reading to 6,000 r.p.m. with inset clock. On the central engine-turned panel are neat small dials recording water temperature

(which read just above 70° F.), oil pressure (40 lb./sq. in.), fuel contents and dynamo charge, with a quality lights switch between them. On the extreme left is the lamps dimming switch and a brake fluid low-level warning light. The engine-turned finish is carried on round the vertical radio panel and along the transmission tunnel, from which protrudes the normal short Jaguar gear-lever. On this l.h.d. coupé the hand-brake was inboard of the tunnel. By the side of the tachometer live the heater controls; matching on the opposite, cubby-hole panel, is a cold-start control with warning light. Along the centre panel below the dials are a line of flick-switches, etc., lettered on the bottom edge of the facia, from left to right, as follows : washers; wipers, fast, slow; map (light); starter (button); cigar (lighter); ignition (key); fan, fast, slow; panel, bright, dim; interior (light). The accelerator is of treadle-type and a left-hand stalk lever below the steering wheel controls the direction-flashers or, pulled upwards, looks after the very essential headlamp flashing.

Ahead of one the long, liberally-louvred bonnet has a big central " power bulge " which doesn't impair visibility. Behind the seats is a big area of luggage space with a lift-up panel to prevent suit-cases from sliding against the seats. Access to this is through the side-hinged rear-window panel. The shelf behind the windscreen is quite flat, not humped, which enhances forward visibility, and the screen itself, which has triple wiper blades, is more nearly vertical than on Continental G.T. cars, thus assisting side vision. The passenger has a neat grab-handle at the corner of the facia. The spare wheel lives under the floor of the luggage compartment.

The steering is very light and high-geared. The engine pinked slightly from around 3,000 r.p.m. in top gear but didn't run-on even after fast work on M 1. Further acquaintance of this Jaguar showed it to possess extremely good brakes, the Dunlop brakes retarding it from 130 m.p.h. to a crawl without deviation, and not only without any sign of fade but without so much as *smelling* hot. They are light to apply, the pedal action almost spongy under normal braking. The synchromesh can be beaten if the gear-lever is handled too rapidly but otherwise this is a precise, excellent gearbox, 100 m.p.h. in third gear soon being taken for granted! The speedometer actually read slow, indicating about a 100 m.p.h. at a genuine 110 m.p.h., while it didn't read above 135 m.p.h. even when the tachometer, and stop-watch checks, told us we were doing 155 m.p.h.

I have no reason to quote Jaguar's acceleration claims, because we obtained very similar figures—0-60 m.p.h. in 7.4 sec., 0-100 m.p.h. in 16.3 sec.—without practice. It was also possible to go from 10 to over 100 m.p.h. *in top gear* in 25 sec.!

The road-holding is of an exceptionally high standard, the car leaning on its outside wheels on really fast corners without any tendency to break away, while the ride is also outstandingly stable and comfortable. The quiet running has been emphasised previously and is most praiseworthy; slight resonance from the exhaust tail-pipes on the over-run will be rectified in production cars. Indeed, so safe to handle, even with the power turned on in second gear and the back wheels spinning, so well-braked even for stopping in a hurry from its top speed, is the Jaguar E-type, that anything below about 110 m.p.h. is loitering. Driven thus, I am told that petrol consumption does not fall below 20 m.p.g. The range, therefore, is about 280 miles, or under three hours of motorway driving. I would like a bigger fuel tank.

In my brief two-hour run in this remarkable car (it used three-quarters of a tank of fuel and covered something like 155 miles, by no means all of them on M 1, including several stops for photography and others in rush-hour Coventry traffic!) I was not able to assess it fully but I learnt enough to know that Jaguar have produced a G.T. car which fully deserves this honoured Gran Turismo designation. The E-type is a staggering motor car on all counts; safety, acceleration, speed, equipment, appearance—all are there, for a basic price of only £1,480. Staggering! I extend to Sir William Lyons, his design team, technicians and workers my humble congratulations.—W. B.

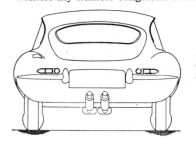

A view a great many drivers are soon going to have of the E-type, on road as well as circuit !

THE 'E' TYPE JAGUAR GT RANGE

A NEW SERIES WITH FABULOUS PERFORMANCE

JAGUAR have now added to their memorable alphabet with the 'E' type Grand Touring models. Shown for the first time publicly at the Geneva Show, where they are creating a tremendous furore, they are available as an open two-seater sports car—with or without detachable hardtop—and as a coupé.

Ever since the XK120 burst on to the motoring world Sir William Lyons has been setting the pace, in more way than one, and in no uncertain manner.

With the 'E' type it is already permissible to use that now much overworked word, fabulous. For here is performance unmatched by any other production car, a machine with a mean maximum of 150 miles an hour yet sufficiently docile for town shopping, well-finished in the tradition of the marque, and selling for what can only be described as a fantastic price.

The basic price of the open model is only £1,480, with Purchase Tax bringing it up to £2,097 15s. The fixed head coupé, with splendid luggage room behind the seats, and easy access to it from a large rear-opening door, sells for £1,550 basic, and £2,196 19s with tax. The detachable hardtop (available only on the open model) costs a total of £76 10s.

COMPETITION VERSION

This is obviously real performance for the money, and one can confidently forecast a terrific demand from the United States alone.

There is bound to be a long queue of customers anxious to race the 'E' type in competition. It is unlikely at the moment, however, that they will be seen at Le Mans this year, since the firm are naturally reluctant to see the new design thrown immediately into the world spotlight of the 24 hours race. But one can well imagine the eagerness with which some drivers will enter it for, say, the Tour de France. It would be logical to expect a competition version at a later date.

Despite its tremendous performance, the heart of the 'E' type is still the XK engine which, when it first appeared 13 years ago, was producing 160 horsepower. The 'E' type uses the 3.8 litre XK 'S' type engine, with three SU carburetters, a compression ratio of 9 to 1, and a maximum output of 265 horsepower at 5,500 rpm.

It is the combination of lower weight and better shape that have brought the increased performance. The open two seater weighs 22 cwt dry, compared with 28 cwt of the XK150, and the fixed head coupé 22½ cwt compared with 28¾ cwt of the parallel XK150 model.

The general concept of the car has been kept as closely as possible to the 'D' type, and in fact incorporates all the main 'D' type features of construction. The body is based on monocoque principles, with a stressed skin structure forming the main body shell.

A tubular steel front sub-frame carries the engine and its ancillaries, together with the suspension, and a fabricated steel rear sub-frame carries the rear suspension and final drive units. There is no chassis, all loads being taken by the body and sub-frame assemblies.

The body shell is made up almost entirely of 20 gauge steel sheet, and the rounded form

View from the front shows the sleek styling and bonnet bulge over the large engine.

of the panels—resulting from the streamlined shape of the car—makes a major contribution to the structural stiffness. In addition, the whole shell is welded up to form a single unit, and thus all panels—including the outer ones—are load carrying.

The model has been under development for over two years, and exceptional care was taken in arriving at the final body shape (which looks even more attractive in the metal than in any photograph).

EXTREMELY EXCITING

After deciding on the basic essentials, a body was designed with the minimum drag, an acceptable shape and a reasonable degree of luggage accommodation. Then a one-tenth scale model was built, and subjected to a long series of wind tunnel tests, using wind tunnels of various aircraft manufacturers and also Loughborough. Then modifications were carried out to improve further on the drag figure without radically altering the original requirements.

The result is extremely exciting in both versions, with the open model having perhaps an even more eager look than the coupé.

The front suspension follows the design used on the 'D' type competition cars, and based on transverse wishbones and torsion bars.

The front ends of the torsion bars are mounted in extensions of the lower wishbones, thus making it possible to remove the bars without disturbing the rest of the suspension. Telescopic dampers are fitted, and an anti-roll bar links the two lower sets of wishbones.

The independent rear suspension is of completely new design.

Location of the wheels in a transverse plane is achieved by the use of two tubular links, of which the top link is the half shaft (universally jointed at each end). The lower link is also a tubular structure, pivoted at the wheel carrier and at the sub-frame adjacent to the differential casing.

To provide maximum rigidity in a longitudinal plane, the pivot bearings at both ends of the lower link are widely spaced. The suspension medium is provided by twin coil springs enclosing telescopic hydraulic dampers, and these are mounted on each side of the differential casing.

The whole assembly is carried in a fabricated steel sub-frame which is easily and quickly detachable from the body structure. This frame is located in the body by four 'V' rubber blocks, and by a radius arm on each side of the car between the lower link and a mounting point on the body structure. The radius arm pivots are rubber bushed and, as a result, the whole suspension assembly, including the sub-frame, is allowed a carefully predetermined degree of movement—the amount being controlled by the characteristics of the rubber used to make the 'V' blocks and radius arm pivots. This not only insulates the whole assembly from the body structure, but eliminates transmission roughness and noise.

NEW LUCAS ACCESSORIES

Dunlop disc brakes are fitted on all four wheels, the rear ones being mounted inboard of the half shafts and adjacent to the differential unit. They are of single pair pad design in which the friction pads are quickly replaceable. They are operated by a pedal actuating twin master cylinders through a compensating device which divides the system into entirely independent circuits to front and rear brakes. In this way damage to one circuit does not result in a total loss of braking. Each master cylinder has its own reservoir and low-level warning system, which operates a red light on the facia panel. A Dunlop balloon-type servo is fitted, operating directly on to the brake pedal, with the aim of providing maximum retardation with low pedal pressures.

The steering is rack and pinion, and a turning circle of 37 feet is provided with 2½ turns from lock to lock. The lightweight steering wheel is of polished alloy, and has a wood rim; it is separately adjustable for both height and reach.

Three new Lucas accessories make their first appearance on the 'E' type—a new petrol pump, a cooling fan motor and a screen wiper with three arms.

The model 2FP fuel pump is located below the surface level of the fuel, as the most effective counter-measure to vapour locking. Thus no vacuum can occur on the intake side of the pump which, being gravity fed with liquid fuel, can maintain its rated pressure on the delivery side.

NOISE REDUCTION

The model 3GM motor driven cooling fan ensures a high rate of air flow through the radiator at low car speeds, and the temperature of the coolant can thus be maintained within close limits. A thermostatic switch is employed which switches in the fan at 80 degrees Centigrade, and switches it out at 72 degrees. Lucas say that advantages of the fan include a marked reduction of noise, increased power available at high speed, fuel economy, reduced belt wear, and quicker engine warm-up from cold. When the fan is operating the current consumption at 12 volts is between six and seven amps. The unit, including the two-bladed fan, weighs four pounds.

The screen wipers, model DL3, employ a link type transmission actuated by a two-speed, self-parking electric motor. To meet the special problem of cleaning a wide, shallow and acutely curved screen, the driving spindles of the outer arms protrude at

an angle to the front of the vehicle. They have proved effective on the 'E' type at speeds of up to 120 miles an hour.

The interiors of both 'E' type models have been specially studied from the viewpoint of the high speed driver. Large windows, combined with a wide wrap-round screen and thin screen pillars provide good all-round visibility.

A full set of instruments is provided, with the speedometer and rev counter positioned directly in front of the driver. The electrics are controlled by a row of clearly labelled tumbler switches. Panel illumination is provided by internal floodlighting controlled by a two-position dimmer switch. The long-range headlamps are controlled by a dip switch mounted on the facia, and a separate lever actuates the headlamp flasher equipment.

The interior layout is carefully designed for the high-speed motorist.

Principal Dimensions
Wheelbase, 8 feet. Track, front and rear, 4 feet 2 inches. Overall length, 14 feet 7¼ inches. Overall width, 5 feet 5¼ inches. Overall height, 4 feet. Ground clearance (laden), 5½ inches. Dry weight, open two seater, approximately 22 cwt; fixed head coupé, 22½ cwt.

The all-independent rear suspension showing the double coil springs including telescopic hydraulic dampers.

The bucket seats are upholstered in leather, and pile carpets with underfelt cover the floor. A fresh air heating and multi-point demisting system is provided.

On the open two-seater the door lights disappear completely when fully lowered. The hood is made of a specially damped material to reduce noise and vibration at high speeds, and the hood mechanism has been designed to permit single-handed erection and stowage. When down, the hood is concealed beneath a removable cover. The fibreglass hardtop, incorporating a large rear window, can be fitted without having to remove the stored hood. On this model luggage accommodation is provided in the tail, and the opening of the boot lid is controlled from inside the car.

REAL PERFORMANCE

In the coupé, the whole of the body to the rear of the front seats is available as luggage space. The flat floor is fitted with rubbing strips and at the front a hinged panel acts as a luggage retainer. If the maximum floor area is required, this panel can be lowered, a luggage retaining lip still being provided.

Access to the luggage compartment is provided by a large hinged panel which also incorporates the rear window; the release catch is operated from inside the car. In addition to the door lights which disappear completely when fully lowered, hinged quarter lights are also provided.

Driven at MIRA by Jaguar's chief test driver, Norman Dewis, the 'E' type coupé reached 100 miles an hour in 16 seconds, and covered the standing quarter-mile in 14 8 seconds.

This was using the normal 3.31 to 1 axle ratio. Optional ratios of 2.93, 3.07 and 3.54 are available. With the 3.07 ratio it is estimated that the car will be capable of 165-170 miles an hour.

The 'E' type is an addition to the Jaguar range, and does not supersede the XK150. It is obviously a very worthy successor to a series of models which have done much to uphold British prestige in motoring circles all over the world.

Above: The end most people will see!

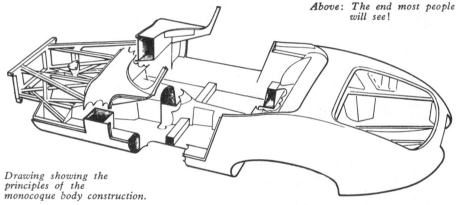

Drawing showing the principles of the monocoque body construction.

'E' Type on the road

One of our International Correspondents, Bernard Cahier, had the opportunity of driving an 'E' type coupé during a recent visit to Britain. Here are his impressions:

I WAS very fortunate in having one of those rare, beautifully sunny English days when I tried out the 'E' type towards the end of February.

The traffic on your narrow English roads is always quite heavy, but we still managed to find some country lanes with useful straights to carry out acceleration tests. I tested the maximum speed another day on a motorway.

I was most enthusiastic about the car, and particularly impressed by its superb road holding coupled with outstanding acceleration.

When driving fast on twisty roads the handling is quite neutral, with just a slight tendency to understeer. This is very easy to correct, and in the beginning it is quite amusing to find yourself in an oversteering car simply because at first the tendency is to correct too much.

This is fun in this car because of its marvellous power and the excellent responsiveness of the steering.

A car of this type often rides hard, but this is not the case with the 'E' type, and the Jaguar designers deserve credit for finding the right compromise between comfort and handling

The engine has terrific torque, and one of its best features is that the power starts to come in well very early—as low as 2,000 rpm—which makes the car very pleasant to drive whether on the open road or in town. Driving through town traffic did not seem to pose any problems, as the car behaved perfectly normally at all times.

Wind and road noise were surprisingly low, and that of the engine was most acceptable, though its healthy tone is loud enough to please the sporting type.

It would be exceptional to find a car with no points for criticism, and there were a number of these. The gearbox was hard to operate, and—most surprisingly—the brakes gave an impression of sponginess and did not seem to be responding quickly at first. This was perhaps due to an insufficient booster or wrong adjustment, and I am sure this can

be corrected. The bucket seats on the test car were not too comfortable, failing to give sufficient support, but the Jaguar people explained that this was being corrected in the production models.

As I said earlier, my road impressions were very favourable, and these were supported by the fine acceleration and speed figures. Among the figures were 0-60 mph in 6.4 seconds, and 0-100 mph in 16.2 seconds. The standing quarter took 14.7 seconds. Maximum speed was 149 mph

These are remarkable figures, comparing extremely favourably with most rivals at double the price. The acceleration figures are better than those of the normal GT Ferrari, and the 300SL Mercedes.

Fuel consumption was around 22 mpg.

For the record, the XK150S was a full second slower over the standing quarter, and 5 seconds slower up to 100 mph—quite an improvement considering that the same basic engine is used.

The clutch coped well with the fierce acceleration, and I appreciated the quality of the new rear suspension and transmission, which transmits the power smoothly with the minimum of wheelspin.

Jaguar have succeeded in developing an exciting, very fast GT at an unbeatable price.

Motor Racing are carrying out a fuller road test of the 'E' type, and the report of this will appear in the next issue.

SLEEK, low, powerful E-type is equally
at home in city traffic or on race tracks.

NEW STOCK JAGUAR DOES 150 m.p.h.

COUPE version looks even more
dynamic, weighs only 60lb. more
than open car. Trapdoor embracing
rear window helps luggage-loading.

UNTIL a few days ago, those who
fancied a Gran Turismo car of
any note had to shell out at
least £6000 to £8000.

Jaguar changed all that on March
15 by introducing their E-type G.T.
machine, available in either open or
closed coupe form.

It's at least equal to such paragons
as Ferraris and Aston Martins in looks
and all-around performance — and it
beats them hands-down when it comes
to price.

The open car costs £1480 stg. basic
in Britain, the coupe £70 more.
"Basic," of course, means before
Britain's stiff purchase tax is paid.

A comparison with the price structure of Jaguars already sold in Aus-

tralia suggests that, by the time exchange, freight, duty and sales tax
are paid, the two newcomers should
retail here for £3500 to £3700 in
our currency.

For this you will get:
● A magnificently streamlined body
of the kind people sigh for at specialist
coachbuilders' stands in European
motor shows;
● All-independent suspension, the
rear being carried on a combination
of transverse tubular lower links,
radius arms and twin coil springs enclosing telescopic hydraulic shock-
absorbers;
● Disc brakes all round, naturally —
the front ones being mounted on the
hubs of the centre-lock wire wheels

**Fabulous E-type
Gran Turismo model
is the first car
of its type offered
to the public at
a reasonable price:
about £3500 should
buy it in Australia**

and the rear ones inboard of the half-shafts, next to the differential;

● Luxury second to none and full competition-type equipment, plus a host of latest Lucas-developed innovations such as: three-blade screen-wipers; a thermostat-controlled electric fan that cuts in only after engine temperature rises above a certain point (claimed to save about 15 b.h.p.); a fuel pump that's safe from vapor lock because it is fully immersed in the petrol tank;

● Stressed-skin construction with a front subframe of immense rigidity, and rubber-cushioned mounting of engine and suspension assemblies that allows quick removal to simplify maintenance and repairs;

● And, of course, the powerful six-cylinder, twin-overhead-camshaft, 265 b.h.p. 3.8-litre S-type XK engine which Jaguar have developed over the past 12 years, and which has brought them so many victories in top-flight sports-racing events.

The E-type has an 8ft. wheelbase and 4ft. 2in. track (front and rear). Overall length is 14ft. 7¼in., width 5ft. 5¼in., height 4ft. (to top of coupe's roof or open car's hood). Minimum ground clearance is 5½in.

The open car weighs 22cwt., the coupe 22½. Both are two-seaters with good luggage room, the coupe having a side-hinged rear "door" to make loading easier.

Jaguar guarantee a top speed of 150 m.p.h. in straight-out "off-the-hook" form and say the car goes from 0 to 100 m.p.h. in 16 seconds flat and covers the standing quarter-mile in 14.8 seconds. Their claims are usually conservative, too.

This performance is achieved with the standard 3.31-to-1 rear end; optional ratios of 2.93, 3.07 and 3.54 are offered, and the engine can be hotted to give up to 170 m.p.h.

Despite all this, the E-type is incredibly flexible at low speeds, being able to dawdle at 10 to 15 m.p.h. in top gear — so it's at home in ordinary traffic as well.

Release of this car has led to speculations that Jaguar were returning to competition, since the Le Mans 24-hour race this year will be for G.T. cars instead of sports cars. Jaguar deny this, but admit they will "advise" a number of "private" entries — and privately entered C- and D-types had no trouble in scoring at Le Mans in recent years.

When will Australians see the E-type? — Sorry, no date set yet. ●

COCKPIT, with wooden racing wheel, short floor gearshift and battery of instruments, looks formidably purposeful. Photo at right shows the coupe's stressed-steel shell and extra-rigid front subframe.

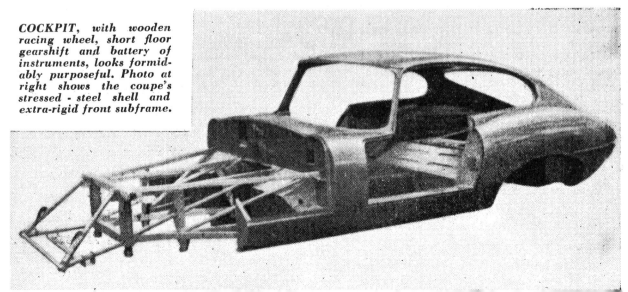

DRIVING THE FABULOUS
NEW JAGUAR TYPE "E"

by David Phipps

HERE IT IS at last, the E-type Jaguar. And to substantiate rumours that it was going to be: - 1, a road car, 2, a competition car, it turned out to be both - a Gran Turismo car in the truest sense of the word. It is available either as a coupe or as an open car with fabric hood and optional hardtop; in both cases it is purely a two-seater.

It is widely held that "racing improves the breed", and nowhere can this be more true than chez Jaguar. The famous XK engine has been developed, largely as a result of racing experience, to produce 265 bhp at 5500 rpm while retaining outstanding low speed flexibility. Disc brakes, first used on racing Jaguars many years ago, are now standardised - and fitted inboard at the rear to reduce unsprung weight. The chassis and front suspension of the E-type are directly descended from the sports/racing D-type and the independent rear suspension is of the kind introduced by other manufactures - Lola and Lotus - and tested on the prototype Jaguar which appeared at Le Mans last year. So all in all E-type Jaguar can be considered a very advanced car.

The basis of the design is a very stiff, stressed skin chassis/body structure, of 20 gauge sheet steel. As on the D-type, this is used in conjunction with a tubular steel front sub-frame - which supports the engine and suspension and takes out suspension loads into the main body shell - and a sheet steel rear sub-frame which provides mountings for the final drive unit and the rear suspension. The complete rear assembly is bolted to the main body shell via rubber blocks, which insulate the interior of the car from suspension and transmission noise.

The tubular front sub-frame is made up in three sections - two triangular side members and a deep front cross member - bolted together to facilitate manufacture and reduce the cost of repair in the event of damage. The front body section is hinged at the forward end of this sub-frame and lifts forward to provide access for servicing; it is secured by coach bolt-operated locks at either side. If necessary, the whole front body section can be removed in a matter of minutes.

As mentioned above, the front suspension is modelled on that of the D-type, and consists of unequal length double wishbones - the lower arms acting on longitudinal torsion bars. Steering is by rack and pinion gear, the wood-rimmed light alloy steering wheel requiring only 2½ turns from lock to lock. At the rear, where D-type had a live axle, suspension is by twin transverse links and a single radius arm at either side, together with co-axial coil damper units. The drive shafts act as the upper transverse links, while the lower members are pivoted at their inboard ends beneath the final drive housing and at their outboard ends on the wheel carrier. Anti-roll bars are used at both front and rear to mitigate the effects of using fairly low roll centres.

The power unit is the well-known six cylinder, twin overhead camshaft, 3.8 litre Jaguar XK "S" type, with three S.U. HD8 carburetors and a compression ratio of 9 to 1 (8 to 1 optional). It has a cast iron cylinder block, aluminum alloy cylinder head and pistons, and a counterweighted crankshaft carried on seven main bearings. Cooling is by cross-flow radiator, with separate header tank, and a thermostatically-operated radiator, with separate header tank, and a thermo-

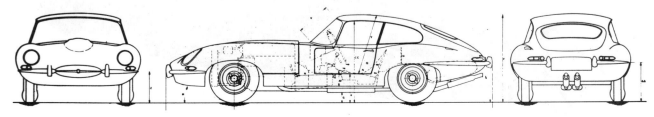

GT styling of E type enhances flowing lines of Coventry's sleek new offering.

statically-operated electric fan is fitted; it switches on when the water temperature reaches 80° C and goes off when it falls below 72° C.

Transmission is through a 10-inch hydraulic clutch and a four-speed, manually operated gearbox to a chassis-mounted final drive unit fitted with 3.31 to 1 ring and pinion gears and a limited slip differential. Alternative final drive ratios are 2.93.1, 3.07:1 and 3.54:1.

The body shape was decided after extensive wind-tunnel tests and its aerodynamic lines obviously play an important part in the car's high-speed performance. There is a reasonable amount of luggage space in the coupe, but this can hardly be said of the open car, on which the upward curve of the undertray - in the interests of aerodynamics - makes the trunk extremely shallow.

So much for the technicalities. What

do they all add up to for the potential owner? To assess this I went for a short run in a E-type coupe some time before the announcement date.

With a low roof line and fairly high door sill, the E-type is not the easiest of cars to get into. Once inside, however, the bucket seats feel extremely comfortable and the cockpit layout is most impressive, with wood-rimmed steering wheel, matching tachometer and 160 mph speedometer and a central console of clearly labelled instruments and switches. Leg room for tall drivers is rather limited - due partly to the long travel required by the clutch pedal. A fresh air heater is fitted as standard.

The hood stretches out ahead. The engine starts easily and at tickover burbles almost inaudibly; even at high speeds the exhaust note does not become obtrusive, and the general noise level remains remarkably low.

The E-type moves away from rest with all the docility of a limousine. It trickles through traffic without a sign of temperament, yet is ready at a moment's notice to accelerate away from around 10 mph in top gear if so required - and leave everything else on the road far behind. The engine's remarkable flexibility makes up, to some extent, for the rather widely spaced intermediate gear ratios and the long travel of the gear lever and clutch pedal.

For enthusiasts, one of the most important things about this car - the first Jaguar with all-independent suspension - will be its handling. First impressions, at moderate speeds, are that it is remarkably good. Its straight running qualities are also extremely reassuring. And very powerful braking is provided with moderate pedal pressures, thanks partly to the Dunlop bellows-type servo.

Stressed skin chassis/body and tubular sub frame give new Jaguar great strength

Some indication of the E-type can be gained from the following figures, obtained by Jaguar test driver Norman Dewis using a "fifth-wheel" speedometer. Maximum speed with the standard axle ratio is 150 mph, but over 160 mph should be possible with 3.07 to 1 gearing. However, perhaps the most impressive feature of all is the consistency of the top gear acceleration times throughout the range from 10-100 mph.

Acceleration through the gears —

0-60 mph	7.0 secs.
0-100 mph	16.0 secs
Standing ¼ mile	14.8 secs.

Top gear acceleration —

10-30 mph	5.7 secs.
20-40 mph	5.2 secs.
30-50 mph	5.3 secs.
40-60 mph	5.0 secs.
50-70 mph	5.4 secs.
60-80 mph	5.3 secs.
70-90 mph	5.5 secs.
80-100 mph	5.7 secs.
90-110 mph	6.3 secs.
100-120 mph	8.2 secs.

Fuel consumption is said to be in the region of 19 mpg, even when the car is driven fast, another tribute to its aerodynamic efficiency.

All in all, this new Jaguar is a very remarkable car. And at a basic price of less than $6,000 for both versions in Canada it is by far the least expensive car in the ultra-high performance GT class.

Principal Dimensions —

Wheelbase —	96 ins.
Track —	
Front	50 ins.
Rear	50 ins.
Overall Length —	175 5/16 ins.
Overall Width —	65½ ins.
Overall Height —	48 ins.
Ground Clearance (laden) —	5½ ins.
Dry Weight (approx.) —	
Open Two-Seater:	2464 lbs.
Fixed Head Coupe:	2520 lbs.

Big dials and busy-looking console give interior business-like look.

Tubular front sub-frame holds racing developed XK engine

Hard top is available for roadsters, blends with Jag's new smooth lines

RAVE NOTICE !
Jack Brabham Drives the 'E' Type

WOULD I like to try the 'E' type Jaguar? asked the Editor of MOTOR RACING. Would I! Trying hard to conceal a schoolboyish enthusiasm, I jumped at the chance.

Surely no one will disagree that the 'E' type range are most attractive cars, with the bonnet swooping away into the middle distance and everything hugging the ground.

The open two seater which I was loaned caused a furore wherever I went. In fact, the biggest problem about testing it was stopping. No, not brake trouble—they were jolly good—but every time I pulled up the car almost disappeared under a swarm of admiring sightseers.

BIG AND BEEFY

It is difficult to imagine how Jaguar's managed to pack the beefy 3.8 litre engine under the bonnet, and indeed it's a very tight fit. (The bonnet safety catch, too, is a tight squeeze, and calls for some knack at first).

There seemed a lot more car when I squeezed in through the quite small door. The high sills, by the way, easily get wet when the door is opened in rain, and it is almost impossible under these conditions to avoid picking up some of the moisture on entering or leaving.

The bulge along the bonnet looks very pronounced from driver's eye level, and I was intrigued to spot the working of the throttle control through the grille on the offside.

GOOD VIEW

Visibility is very good, as it should be with a car of such potential. There are blind spots caused by the rear sides of the hood, but of course this problem disappears when the hood is down, and does not exist at all on the coupé. The hood is a taut affair, easily taken down and erected—an operation taking an average of 30 seconds.

Though it is a lot of motor car, driving the Jaguar through the centre of London in the rush hour proved that it is very simple to place within an inch or two, and screen pillars help by being nice and thin.

PICCADILLY POTTERING

A tour round Piccadilly Circus in top gear demonstrated the amazing docility of this powerful beast. If you are feeling lazy it will go down to well nigh ten miles an hour in top and still pull away without much fuss, and the other gears are hardly needed. A lady driver could feel perfectly at home using this car for shopping—but it would not take much of her housekeeping money before the tiny boot was filled with groceries!

I was not entirely happy about the seating position. With the seat back as far as it would go I felt there was hardly enough leg or arm length. The steering wheel—a nice comforting affair with a wooden rim—has a telescopic adjustment, but when pushed hard towards the facia I tended to catch my knees on the lower edge of the rim.

WRONG ANGLE

The pedals, too, could I think be better. They are the pendant type, hanging rather high off the floor, with the pads at rather the wrong angle for me, and with a long throw on both clutch and brake. I wonder, in fact, whether 'conventional' pedals rather than the pendant variety might not suit the car better.

But that is enough of criticism, and indeed it is almost the lot.

The instruments and the rest of the controls are well placed for fast motoring, and I was glad to see the dip switch within easy reach of my right hand.

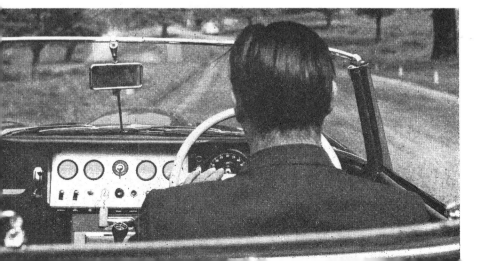

Above: The world champion looks very pleased to be at the wheel of the 'E' type. The lines of the open two-seater show to even greater advantage with the hood down. (The hood cover is not in position).

Left: Champion's view through the screen. Visibility is excellent and the instruments and controls are well placed.

The engine always sprang into life at the first touch of the button, and, as ever, I was amazed by the smoothness of this fine unit. The exhaust, though healthy, is not too rorty; if the throttle is used with discretion there never need be any danger of annoying old maids in urban areas.

The 9 to 1 compression ratio called for Esso Golden, and the fuel consumption worked out at just under 20 miles to the gallon.

SO SMO-O-TH

It was in fact the overall smoothness of the car that impressed me most of all. Once or twice I found myself going far quicker than I imagined. On one occasion my passenger nudged me and pointed out that I was cruising at 65 in a built-up area. After that I kept a closer watch on the speedo, because the performance is so terrifically deceptive. Eighty on the clock came up as often as fifty on a bread-and-butter saloon.

The mysterious factor about the terrific acceleration is that the car does not seem to be pushing you in the back or going places in a hurry. After over a hundred miles of acclimatisation I came to the conclusion that at 80 miles an hour the 'E' type is just trickling along, at 60 it is dawdling, and at 40 it is positively creeping.

GLUED TO THE ROAD

I have pretty strong views about driving really fast on public roads, and since I didn't find the opportunity of taking the car up M1 you will have to take the maker's claim that it is a 150 miles an hour machine; I have no doubt about it. But the 'ton' came up several times when the road was completely clear, and in one short burst we topped 130 mph with the greatest of ease.

At that speed the car sat the road most impressively. Jaguar's have done a wonderful job with the rear suspension. The limited slip differential and low unsprung weight, helped by inboard rear discs, gives splendid traction when the car is taking off like a bullet.

The ride is comparatively soft, and the car goes over rough stuff like a dream. Yet both ends are beautifully glued to the road, and I thought it fantastic the amount of power the car would take when it was at an angle—for example, round an island.

NO TYRE PROTEST

Around sharp corners there was less roll than I expected from a suspension so soft. Throughout all the time I drove the car I never once heard any protest from the Dunlop RS5's.

The steering gives real confidence. It is good to see a Jaguar with rack and pinion steering, beautifully responsive and high geared yet never heavy even at quite low speeds. The handling was almost neutral, with just a hint of understeer; in fact, just the job for spirited long distance motoring.

In the wet the 'E' type was just as impressive, creating lots of confidence, though naturally calling for a little discretion with the acceleration with 265 horsepower available.

My first feeling was that the brakes seemed a trifle spongy—they have some servo assistance—but the results were uniformly good. I couldn't help thinking that but for discs such performance would really not be possible, or safe, in a car built for public roads.

MCLAREN DROOLS

My impression was that the throw on the gear lever had been shortened compared with other Jaguars I have driven. But it is still a slow change, and the synchromesh is easily beaten. The clutch may have contributed towards this problem of making really rapid changes, because it had to be right at the end of the pedal travel before the clogs would slip in, and the last fraction of the pedal throw was rather heavy. But this is one of the problems in coping with so many horses under the bonnet; the clutch has a mighty job to do.

During my all-too-short 'ownership' of the car my Cooper team-mate, Bruce McLaren got to hear about it, and was round at my house like a shot. He took it out for a short run, and came back drooling with anticipation. (Bruce is eagerly awaiting delivery of one, and this only whetted his appetite further). He thought it the nearest approach to a formula car on the road he had ever experienced.

A FABULOUS MACHINE

The performance really is fantastic, and the way it is produced is just as astonishing. Given the right sort of roads, a hundred miles an hour is a very comfortable cruising speed. At that pace it feels rather like any normal car at 60 to 70 mph. I wondered what would happen when someone really got one tweaked up and started to use it for racing; my experience of it suggests it will have considerable success.

One point intrigued both Bruce and myself. The car I tried had a transfer number plate stuck fairly near the horizontal above the nose. If you want a normal metal plate at the front, where on earth do you put it?

By the end of my tryout I was fairly critical of the seats. They hold both driver and passenger very nicely against side thrusts, but for me at least the driver's seat had too much padding near the top and not quite enough lower down. I believe, however, that this is being altered on production models.

But all in all this is a car for superlatives, for it not only has exciting performance, but is well finished and packed with thoughtful features, such as the warning lights which announce when the handbrake has been left on or when petrol is getting low in the tank. And the price—just under £2,100—is yet another miracle wrought by Sir William Lyons.

It is not often that I use the word 'fabulous' about a car, but the 'E' type fully deserves that description.

It was a darned shame I couldn't have driven it for a week. Perhaps someone will take the hint?

Brabham enjoys himself throwing the Jaguar around an island. He was really moving when this picture was taken, but was very impressed with the way the car could be controlled. The rack and pinion steering he found delightfully light and responsive.

JAGUAR E-TYPE GT

BY BERNARD CAHIER *SCG European Editor*

Complete Details on Jaguar's Latest Tiger

FOR MANY LONG YEARS Jaguar fans, as well as sport enthusiasts all over the world, and particularly in America, have hoped that the Jaguar company would come out with something new, very fast and flashy, to replace the aging, 12 years old XK model. It was not that the latest XK version, the 150 S, was a bad car. On the contrary it was a good car in its field and price range, with a glorious background, but it was dating rapidly and its performance, although quite adequate for the average speed enthusiast, was now well overshadowed by those of such thoroughbreds as the GT Ferrari, Maserati and Aston Martin, without forgetting the very competitive Corvette in the States.

Change comes slowly in England and at Jaguar maximum efforts on their successful production model delayed the progress of the new model which would take the place of the XK.

A privately entered Jaguar, unofficially and erroneously called the E-Type, was seen at Le Mans in 1960. It aroused plenty of interest since nothing new had been seen from Jaguar at Le Mans since 1955. This suggested that Jaguar was either coming back into racing or that they had something new and exciting in their production department. As it turned out the first supposition was too premature, since Jaguar is still not racing today (primarily because they are against the limitation of displacement for sports car racing), but the second suggestion was well founded. Jaguar indeed had something new and big up its sleeve and the model entered at Le Mans by Cunningham last year was testing most of the elements of their latest battling tiger, the new E-Type Grand Touring which was officially presented on the neutral but very international soil of Geneva, Switzerland, on the occasion of their annual Automobile Show.

What is the new E-Type Jaguar? How does it look? What does it do? Thanks to Bob Berry of Jaguar and to Harry Mundy of the well-known English weekly "Autocar," SPORTS CAR Graphic was fortunate in being the first American magazine to try out this exciting new automobile With automobiles, as with women, that first contact is very important, and in our opinion Jaguar has succeeded in making this first rendezvous a striking one. Yes, the E-Type Jaguar GT is very striking indeed because it is very different from all its direct competitors and because it looks so fast just standing still. Its style is not Italian nor German nor, in a way, even English. It has its own Jaguar style, a style which caused quite a sensation in 1949 when the then-new, very slim and low XK-120 was presented. Whether it is the roadster or the coupe, both models have remarkably good streamlining for a GT car and both bear some of the unmistakable imprints of the great D Type sports car and, of course, of their E-Type prototype seen last year at Le Mans. It is obvious that Jaguar has used the important lessons they have learned throughout the years on the fast circuit of Le Mans where streamlining is so vital. They have succeeded in incorporating those years of research in streamlining into the final construction of this new GT car, giving a surprisingly good result. It is difficult to apply effective streamlining as well as styling to a production car.

The basic construction of the E-Type GT follows, there again, some of the components of the old D-Type and particularly those of the experimental Le Mans "E-Type" from which their new independent rear suspension was taken, among many other things. Once again solutions tested and proven in competition were used with success for the production models.

The E-Type is made of a monocoque body shell and chassis from the fire wall back. It is built of rigid sheet steel with welded joints throughout. Main load-carrying members are the rigid scuttle structures and a deep box section assembly just forward of the rear wheels. Bracing these two points is a deep box sill on each side. Midway along these sills is another hat-section cross member. There are also two additional longitudinal floor members running from the bulkhead to the rear cross member structure. At the rear a considerable degree of stiffness is obtained from the floor of the luggage compartment which braces the rear cross member of the main hull to the tail section. In the tunnel space thus formed there is a separate subframe carrying the final drive unit. The rear suspension assembly is separately attached at four points with rubber mountings to the main hull. The stiffness of such a type of construction is evident and no additional under-floor reinforcement was required, not even on the roadster, where it would normally seem needed.

Forward of the fire wall bulkhead there is a two part subframe on which the engine is mounted and to which steering and suspension are attached. This type of construction makes repair or replacement of parts much easier. This subframe is made of square tubes and box section members, with a separately attached forward section constructed of circular tubes to which the radiator is mounted and on which the counterbalanced, uplifting nose section hinges. The rear section of this subframe unit is attached by six points to the bulkhead, each with a four bolt flange, with a further attachment underneath on each side, coinciding with the longitudinal under-floor stiffening member of the hull.

The E-Type front suspension consists of forged wishbones with bolt pivots, top and bottom. The lower wishbone is connected to a longitudinal torsion bar anchored to the chassis. There is an inclined shock absorber on each side and a transverse anti-roll bar, each fixed to the lower wishbone near the wheel end. This suspension, as we can see, is directly derived from that of the D-Type on which it works very satisfactorily. As on previous Jaguars, the steering is of the rack and pinion type.

(continued on page 31)

Low height of the E-Type roadster makes it appear bullet-shaped and accents nose. The top is not the prettiest, but a hardtop will be an optional extra. The curb weight of the roadster is sixty-six pounds less than that of the fastback coupe.

Above: The sleek aerodynamic lines of the E-Type coupe will undoubtedly remain in style and popular as long as those of the XKSS. Long hood bubble allows cam cover clearance.

Below: Considered an outdated design by many, the 3.8-liter engine remains potent in both torque and horsepower, is able to push the one and one-quarter ton coupe to a clocked 149.

JAGUAR E-TYPE GT

Although quite common in countries such as Germany, France and Italy, the independent type rear suspension is still not common in England and it is very good to see it applied to the E-Type. The de Dion type rear end which was tested in the past on one of their competition cars was discarded in favor of the swing axle type and the one used on the new E-Type is a refinement of the prototype seen last year. This suspension incorporates, on each side, a lower transverse tubular link pivoted at the wheel carrier and subframe adjacent to the differential case and, above this, an unsplined halfshaft universally joined at each end. These serve to locate the wheel in a transverse plane. Longitudinal location is provided by the rubber mountings locating the subassembly in the body structure and by a radius arm between the lower link and a mounting point on the body structure. Twin coil springs, each enclosing a telescopic hydraulic damper, provide the suspension medium. The whole assembly, together with the differential unit, is carried in an easily detachable subframe which is located in the body structure by rubber mountings.

The E-Type uses the same gear box as the XK-150, with four speeds forward. The standard gear ratio is 3.31 to 1 but there are three other ratios available, the 2.93, the 3.07 and the 3.54. The Salisbury hypoid final drive, made of cast iron, incorporates a Powr-Lok limited slip differential as standard equipment. This interesting differential incorporates multi-plate clutches adjacent to the side gears to provide a torque bias between the two half shafts. By this means wheel spinning is controlled, since the internal frame forces have to be overcome before one wheel can slip.

Dunlop 12-inch disc brakes are used, front and rear. They are outboard in front and inboard on the rear, directly mounted on the output shaft of the differential. This arrangement results in the final drive casing dissipating more heat than normally and the oil seals are made of silicon rubber which is particularly resistant to high temperatures. These disc brakes, incidentally, have the same diameter as the ones used on the XK-150 and should be quite adequate for the new E-Type in spite of its superior performance since it is over 650 pounds lighter than the XK. Separate hydraulic circuits, with two master cylinders, are used which is a good safety factor. A booster completes the braking system but perhaps it is not boosting enough yet as the brakes gave a feeling of sponginess, a defect which should be easy to eliminate.

Although several types of engines were considered for this car, including the all aluminum one seen at Le Mans last year, it was an improved version of the well known 3.8 liter, used in the XK-150, which was adopted. This power unit is well known to our readers: it is the twin o.h.c. six-cylinder engine with a compression ratio of 9 to 1. Three HD-8 type S.U. carburetors with manual control have been selected rather than Webers, and the maximum hp is a real 265 bhp at 5,500 rpm, which brings it to the level of some of the latest Ferrari GT engines.

Getting into the E-Type is a relatively easy operation, that is if you are not a big 6-footer, but once installed you feel comfortable as the interior gives an impression of spaciousness, perhaps due to the excellent visibility and the large open trunk space behind the two seats. The driving position is excellent but unfortunately the seats on the test car were built too low, a point which will be corrected in the production models. Visibility, front and rear, is excellent and the two-way adjustable steering wheel can be fixed at just the position to suit your taste. The gear lever is well located and all the complete range of electrical

TEST DATA

VEHICLE	Jaguar	MODEL	E-Type GT
PRICE	$4500 (@ factory)	OPTIONS	—

ENGINE:

Type	6-cylinder, in-line, 4-cycle, water-cooled
Head	Aluminum, removable, hemispherical combustion chambers
Valves	DOHC and inverted tappets
Max. bhp	265 @ 5500 rpm
Max. torque	260 lbs. ft. @ 4000 rpm
Bore	3.43 in. 87 mm.
Stroke	4.17 in. 106 mm.
Displacement	230.6 cu. in. 3781 cc.
Compression Ratio	9 to 1
Induction System	3 HD-8 SU carburetors on Y-branch, individual manifolds
Exhaust System	Cast headers, 6-into-2, dual pipes and mufflers
Electrical System	12-volt Lucas single distributor ignition

CLUTCH:	Borg & Beck single-disc	**DIFFERENTIAL:**	Salisbury hypoid with limited-slip
Diameter	10 in.	Ratio	3.31 to 1
Actuation	hydraulic	Drive Axles (type)	Open ½-shafts, 2-joint rigid tube

TRANSMISSION: 4-speed, full-synchro, alloy case

		STEERING: Rack & Pinion, adjustable steering column
Ratios: 1st	3.377 to 1	
2nd	1.861 to 1	Turns Lock to Lock .... 2 & ¾
3rd	1.28 to 1	Turn Circle .... 37 ft.
4th	1 to 1	**BRAKES:** Dunlop caliper discs with booster
		Drum or Disc Diameter ..... 12 in.
		Swept Area .... 561 sq. in.

CHASSIS: Monocoque, steel

Frame	Integral with body, partial, space frame with sub-assemblies
Body	Unitized, stressed steel
Front Suspension	Unequal, forged A's, torsion bar and tube shock
Rear Suspension	Independent with lower transverse arms and axles forming upper members
Tire Size & Type	6.40 x 15 Dunlop RSS, optional sizes

WEIGHTS AND MEASURES:

Wheelbase	96 in.	Ground Clearance	5.5 in.
Front Track	50 in.	Curb Weight	2520 lbs.
Rear Track	50 in.	Test Weight	n.a.
Overall Height	48 in.	Crankcase	6½ qts.
Overall Width	65.2 in.	Cooling System	n.a.
Overall Length	175.3 in.	Gas Tank	17 gals

PERFORMANCE:

0-30	2.8 sec.	0-90	13.3 sec.
0-40	4.5 sec.	0-100	16.1 sec.
0-50	5.6 sec.	0-110	19.5 sec.
0-60	6.4 sec.	0-120	23.4 sec.
0-70	8.6 sec.	0-130	37.1 sec.
0-80	11.0 sec.		

Standing ¼ mile 14.6 sec. @ 95 mph

Speed Error	30	40		Top Speed (av. two-way run) 148.8 mph
			50 60 70 80 90 130
Actual	30	41		51 61 72 82 92 135

Fuel Consumption Test	n.a.
Average	18 mpg

Recommended Shift Points:

		RPM Red-line	6000 rpm
Max. 1st	42 mph	Speed Ranges in gears: Using 5500 rpm as maximum:
Max. 2nd	77 mph	1st .... 0 to 42 mph
Max. 3rd	112 mph	2nd .... 35 to 77 mph
		3rd .... 57 to 112 mph
		4th .... 65 to top mph

REFERENCE FACTORS:

BHP per Cubic Inch	1.1
Lbs. per bhp	9.87
Piston Speed @ Peak rpm	3820 ft./sec.
Swept Brake area per lb.	0.2222 sq. ft.

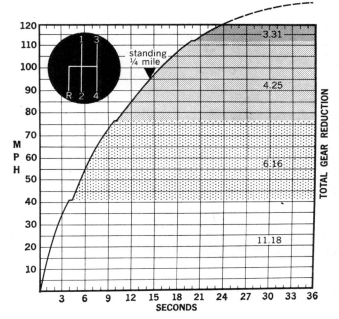

31

Using some access-design techniques from David Brown's Aston coupe, the E-Type is handy to load, enter and service.

Enjoying rare English sunshine and discussing the merits of Jaguar's latest are tester Cahier, H. Mundy, Tony Brooks.

Instruments and controls are well-located and the new wood-rimmed steering wheel is adjustable to suit any arm-length desired. While entry is a bit tight, interior of the new coupe is very roomy. Seat height will be increased in the production models.

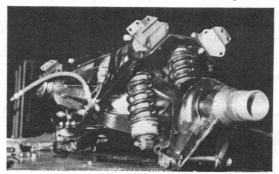

Two views above show the extremely clean lines of coupe's body and how the square-tube frame is integrated with the rigid, monocoque shell. Thin roof supports and "dog-leg" in the door opening are necessary compromises in the design.

The unique rear suspension is bolted in a subframe and fixed to the body with rubber mounts. Dual coil-shocks attach to each lower arm. The clean front suspension utilizes forged control arms, torsion bar springing plus an anti-sway bar.

JAGUAR

instruments are very visible, and happily old fashioned. There is a good space for your foot to rest on the left but the pedals will probably be too close together for men with big feet. Thick upholstering comfortably trims the entire interior, and...could be easily removed to save weight for competition! The E-Type is strictly a two-seater but there is a large space for baggage in the back which is easily accessible as the whole back window raises.

I just said that the car is strictly a two-seater but the day I was driving it I had the opportunity of seeing that much more could be done than the designers ever dreamed of when we were forced to go to lunch with four grown people plus a two year old child. I personally tried out the rear window location and I can assure you that you remember it the next day upon awakening. It is fine for baggage but not recommended for passengers.

When we tried out the E-Type we were very fortunate in having one of those rare beautiful sunny English days, and it was February, truly incredible. The traffic on the narrow English roads is always quite heavy but we still managed to find some country lanes where we found some good straights to do the acceleration figures, while the maximum speed was done on a freeway another day. We were most enthusiastic about driving the Jaguar and particularly impressed by the superb handling of this car, combined with the outstanding acceleration. When driving fast on curvy roads the comportment of the E-Type is quite neutral with a slight tendency to understeer. This is very easy to correct and in the beginning it is quite amusing to find yourself in an oversteering car simply because the tendency is to correct too much. This is fun in this car because of its marvelous power and the excellent responsiveness of the steering which at all times makes things comfortable and safe. Often a car of this type, with such remarkable handling, rides hard. This is not the case of the E-Type and much credit must be given to the Jaguar people for finding the right compromise between comfort and road holding. The 265 hp

engine has terrific torque and one of its best features is that its power starts to come in well very early, as low as 2,000 rpm, which makes the car very pleasant to drive whether you are on the open road or in a town. Driving through the traffic in towns didn't seem to pose any problems as the car behaved perfectly normally at all times. Wind and road noise were surprisingly limited. The noise of the engine was most acceptable, and fortunately its healthy tune is loud enough to please a sportive ear. While watching the car drive by at a good speed I did appreciate the round Jaguar sounds coming from its two generous exhaust pipes.

It would be too exceptional to find a car with no bad points and in the case of the E-Type there were several such things. I found, first, the gear box was a little hard to operate and I truly think it is outdated in a period when so many other fine gear boxes are available. The second thing we were surprised not to find right was the brakes. They gave an impression of sponginess and didn't seem to be responding quickly at first. This was perhaps due to an insufficient booster or to wrong adjusting and undoubtedly this can be corrected in the future. The bucket type seats we had on the car tested were not very comfortable, not giving enough support and when we were explaining this to the Jaguar people they told us that this is being corrected. For a car of such prestige, the general inside finish could have been better, although our test car *was* one of the first ones made.

As I mentioned earlier, road impressions of the car were very favorable and these impressions were well substantiated by the very good acceleration and speed figures attained by this new E-Type. Indeed, among many others recorded, (see spec tables), 60 mph in 6.4 seconds, 100 mph in 16.2 seconds, the standing quarter mile in 14.7 seconds, are remarkable figures comparing extremely favorably with most of its competitors for double the price. Just for the record, the XK 150 S was a full second slower on the standing quarter mile and 5 seconds slower on the 0 to 100 mph figure, quite an improvement when you think that it is the same basic engine being used. The clutch withstood the acceleration tests well

and once more we appreciated the quality of the new rear-end suspension and transmission which transmits the power smoothly with no jerking and with a minimum of wheel spin.

The good weather during the test prevented us from checking the weather sealing of the car but we were pleased to notice that the car was equipped with three wipers propelled by a strong electric motor. The air ducting of the car seemed very adequate and simple to operate.

Certainly not long enough for our tastes, this first acquaintance with the new E-Type was altogether a very favorable one. Jaguar has succeeded in developing an exciting, very fast Grand Touring car at an unbeatable price. As it is, the Jaguar should be able to please a large and demanding clientele looking for something better than a regular GT car. The E-Type, Jaguar says, is no competition car and no speed kits except gear ratios are available for it. Still, in its present form, it should do fairly well in competition against the reigning Ferraris, especially on the fast circuits. The E-Type is basically not too heavy (2,460 pounds for the roadster and 2,520 for the Coupe, dry weight) and it should be easy to lighten it quite a bit without forgetting that after all it is made of steel. As it is offered now to the public the E-Type is a good compromise between a racing GT machine and a normal touring GT, and yet it has the advantage over its competitors of having that exciting fast sports car allure which you usually don't find in a conventional GT car.

Long awaited but now here, the E-Type is assured of a fine career, especially if the Jaguar people are willing always to look into the future and to make the changes necessary to cope with the fast moving competitors. I say this because in the past too many manufacturers have come out with something good and then left it unchanged for too long. I hope that this will not apply to the new exciting E-Type, especially when I think that the five-times Le Mans-winning firm will be on the starting line there again in 1962 for their racing come-back. Watch out for Jaguar. They still have some surprises in reserve for us, including an all aluminum injection 340 hp engine!

JAGUAR XK-E

Sensational is the word for this Coventry cat

PHOTOS BY POOLE

IF A NEW CAR ever created greater excitement around our office than the new Jaguar XK-E, we can't remember it. And to sum up this car in the third sentence of a report may be unusual for us, but it is easy to do. "The car comes up to, and exceeds, all our great expectations." The car itself was fully described in our May issue, but, briefly, it has a 96-in. wheelbase monocoque chassis, a 3.8-liter double-over-head-camshaft 6-cyl engine developing 265 bhp, and a curb weight of just over 2700 lb. Two body types are available, a coupe and a roadster—the latter being actually a true convertible, also available with a very neat removable hardtop.

This report is a compendium of experiences involving three people, four cars and two countries. However, we must say that the longest time at the wheel (by one driver) was only two hours and in this respect we were at a disadvantage, as cars were made available to the British Press early in March. Our test data, therefore, are limited to a top speed of 100 mph and the fuel consumption range, given as 15 to 21 mpg, must be considered tentative.

As is well known, the genuine top speed of the showroom-stock Jaguar XK-E is 150 mph. Actually, this speed has been slightly exceeded and, though the fastback coupe looks more aerodynamic than the roadster, there appears to be very little difference in drag, or concomitant top speed. In this connection, our coasting tests from 80 mph were made in a roadster and reference to the performance graph will show that lowering the top shortens the coasting times and distances.

The standard axle ratio specified for the XK-E is 3.31:1. In our opinion this is a perfect choice, completely satisfactory and ideal for 99% of all owners, or prospective purchasers. This ratio gives almost exactly 150 mph at 6000 rpm, with an allowance for tire expansion. However, ratios of 2.94, 3.07 and 3.54 are available and it will be interesting to see what can be done in a speed run with the lowest ratio; we would expect something close to 180 mph under favorable circumstances. The axle ratio in our test car, however, gives a somewhat misleading comparison with the older, heavier XK-150-S. Similar gearing in the two cars should result in a striking performance difference.

While such speeds are largely academic, the acceleration figures are factual and useful. Our test car, which, as we said, was a roadster, had a modest speedometer error, being 3% fast at an indicated 100 mph. Thus, we got 0 to 100 mph in 16.0 sec, but the time to 103 mph was 16.7 sec, achieved, by the way, without using 4th gear. One of the most frequent questions we hear regarding the Jaguar's performance is "Does it outperform the Corvette?" The answer is a qualified no. A showroom stock fuel-injection Corvette will just "nip" the acceleration times of the Jaguar, but it won't go as fast at the top end. This, of course, indicates that a Jaguar with the optional 3.54 ratio might just equal the Corvette and, as the Corvette has a 3.70 axle ratio, a similar ratio (though not available) would give the Jaguar a definite margin. However, here we must remember that the hot Corvettes running in competition have a 4.10 axle and turn 7000 rpm. Thus, the Corvette has a definite advantage "on-paper" over the XK-E, but a well-tuned "E" may produce a few surprises when it gets into competition in this country, despite its much smaller displacement.

As is well known, the engine is the same unit as used last year in the XK-150-S model. In 13 years of development, the XK engine has remained fundamentally unchanged, except for a larger cylinder bore introduced two years ago. Yet, minor revisions have provided a power increase of 65%, from 160 bhp in 1948 to 265 bhp at present. The three-carburetor version, as applied to the XK-E, seems even smoother and quieter than before, possibly because there is no engine-driven fan. During the test runs for acceleration data the engine temperature never went above 73° C, with the outside temperature at the same reading in Fahrenheit. Because the electric fan comes on only at 80° C, it is obvious that it will seldom run, and when it does it draws only 7 amps, about the same as one headlight.

Despite the three large carburetors (2-in. size), the powerplant is extremely flexible and will accept full throttle at 1500 rpm without bumbling. Thus, while 3rd gear would normally be used for cruising through 35-mph zones, it is possible to drive at 15 mph in 4th gear without jerking or back-lashing. The unit doesn't like full throttle at this low speed, but it will accelerate smoothly and briskly if a little initial care is exercised. The tachometer has a caution zone from 5500 to 6000 rpm. While the engine is designed for 6000 rpm, this speed is really a bit harsh for a unit having a stroke of over 4 in. Our test results are all based on a revolution limit of 5500 rpm, though the maximum speeds in the gears are given for 6000 rpm. (See data panel; true speeds will be slightly higher because of tire expansion, particularly in 3rd gear.)

When the XK-E was announced, it was stated that the designer's goal was to achieve family sedan-type comfort with sports car handling qualities. In driving the car for the first time, the superb riding qualities do indeed make an immediate impression. In fact, the ride is so good we will say without equivocation that only one other sports car has a comparable ride, and it also has independent suspension on all four wheels. The Jaguar ride may not equal the soft boulevard characteristics of our prestige-type sedans, but we do not think it should. The XK-E has soft, yet extremely well controlled springing.

But what is even more remarkable is the car's uncanny adhesive characteristics. A car of this power-to-weight ratio can be a real handful, even dangerous, if a heavy foot is used on the accelerator. But this car is very difficult to "break loose." Of course, in 1st gear, which is very low (or high, numerically), it is possible to spin the rear wheels on dry pavement, but even here the limited slip differential (standard equipment) makes all the difference—there is no tendency to go sideways at take-off unless the driver deliberately sets

up wild wheelspin of the type that gets nowhere.

In normal driving 1st gear is seldom used except for a short initial start, because this gear is so low, slightly noisy, and not synchronized. Another reason for this is that 2nd gear is so handy and useful, despite the fact that its synchromesh unit is not very effective. This gear, at 6.16:1 overall, is just a fraction too high for normal starts from a standstill—it can be done, but it's not recommended. But once underway, 2nd gear is a very useful ratio and, with a speed range of from 5 to 76 mph, it can provide magnificent cornering over and around twisting mountain roads. If you get over-exuberant the rear wheels break loose, but control is excellent and you can hold a "tail-out" attitude with very little practice. In general, the steering characteristic is just a trace of understeer at all times, with the possibility of induced oversteer if an indirect gear is engaged and throttle applied.

In this connection, the steering also rates as very close to, if not actually, the best we have experienced. There is just the right amount of road feel, no kickback, moderate parking effort, and a ratio that is quick without being too sensitive or tricky at high speed. (The number of turns lock to lock, at 2.6, sounds very quick, but the turning circle is not too good.) We might also mention that the Jaguar's weight distribution is somewhat unusual; 50/50 at the curb or 49% front, 51% rear, with driver and full tank. This gives a basically neutral-steering car, in which only very slight compro-

mises in suspension geometry are necessary to give modest understeer and high speed stability. The net result has to be experienced to be believed.

As with the steering, the disc brakes just can't be criticized. It is virtually impossible to feel the booster come in, and the pedal pressure is moderate without being overly sensitive. These are disc-type brakes, so the problem of fade is non-existent and, incidentally, there was no sign of the squeals or squeaking sometimes encountered with metal-to-metal brake pads.

While there has been some criticism of the interior seating space, we liked the layout very much, particularly the way the steering wheel (which is adjustable over a range of 3 in. in and out) is placed well forward. At the same time, the interior dimensions are not satisfactory for over-6-footers, and the present brake and clutch pedal angles are a little awkward. We understand this is being changed and that the seats are to be redesigned so that they will move farther aft (present adjustment range is only 3 in.).

Instrumentation is very complete and the white-on-black numerals are strictly functional, as they should be. A heater and defroster are standard equipment, but we had no opportunity to try them. The heater includes a fresh-air vent, but this appears to let in warm air only and ventilation might be a bit of a problem in a summer rain storm. When the side windows are lowered, a windbeat noise is very noticeable, and the cockpit is too drafty for long distance touring with top down, at least if speeds of over 80 mph are contemplated for any length of time. The fast-back coupe is better in this respect, for its hinged quarter windows can be used to give an extractor effect.

An unusual feature is the provision of three windshield wiper blades. These are driven by a 2-speed electric motor and are said to be adequate for driving in the rain at slightly over 100 mph.

The over-all appearance is, of course, what attracts most people and we have yet to hear a detractor, though the roadster's soft top isn't as attractive as the optional hard top. Sheet metal protection front and rear is minimal for American parking conditions; the front parking lights, in particular, look vulnerable and the rear bumper is located very high, exactly 6 in. higher than the front bars, in fact. This exposes the twin mufflers and tail pipes. The plastic headlight covers are also vulnerable.

Obviously, the Jaguar XK-E is one of the most exciting sports cars ever produced. While it is unfortunate that a strike at the body plant has delayed production, this lull may prove to be beneficial, in that Jaguar can make the few obvious corrections that are needed before real production commences.

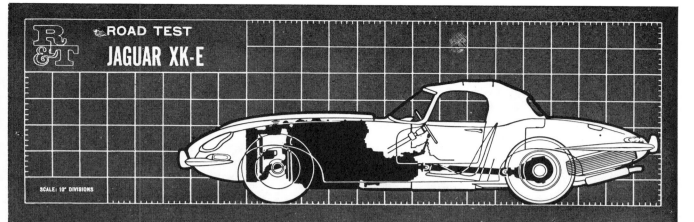

ROAD TEST
JAGUAR XK-E

SCALE: 10" DIVISIONS

DIMENSIONS

Wheelbase, in	96.0
Tread, f and r	50.0
Over-all length, in	175.3
width	65.2
height	48.1
equivalent vol, cu ft	318
Frontal area, sq ft	17.5
Ground clearance, in	5.5
Steering ratio, o/a	n.a.
turns, lock to lock	2.6
turning circle, ft	38.4
Hip room, front	2 x 20
Hip room, rear	n.a.
Pedal to seat back, max.	41.0
Floor to ground	8.0

CALCULATED DATA

Lb/hp (test wt)	11.3
Cu ft/ton mile	114
Mph/1000 rpm (4th)	23.6
Engine revs/mile	2550
Piston travel, ft/mile	1770
Rpm @ 2500 ft/min	3600
equivalent mph	84.7
R&T wear index	45.1

SPECIFICATIONS

List price	$5595
Curb weight, lb	2720
Test weight	2990
distribution, %	49/51
Tire size	6.40-15
Brake swept area	461
Engine type	6 cyl, dohc
Bore & stroke	3.43 x 4.17
Displacement, cc	3781
cu in	230.6
Compression ratio	9.0
Bhp @ rpm	265 @ 5500
equivalent mph	130
Torque, lb-ft	260 @ 4000
equivalent mph	94.1

GEAR RATIOS

4th (1.00)	3.31
3rd (1.28)	4.25
2nd (1.86)	6.16
1st (3.38)	11.2

SPEEDOMETER ERROR

30 mph	actual, 29.2
60 mph	57.0

PERFORMANCE

Top speed (4th), mph	150
best timed run	n.a.
3rd (6000)	110
2nd (6000)	76
1st (6000)	42

FUEL CONSUMPTION

Normal range, mpg	15/21

ACCELERATION

0-30 mph, sec	3.1
0-40	4.6
0-50	5.7
0-60	7.4
0-70	9.2
0-80	11.6
0-100	16.7
Standing ¼ mile	15.2
speed at end	94

TAPLEY DATA

4th, lb/ton @ mph	330 @ 60
3rd	450 @ 53
2nd	640 @ 40
Total drag at 60 mph, lb	100

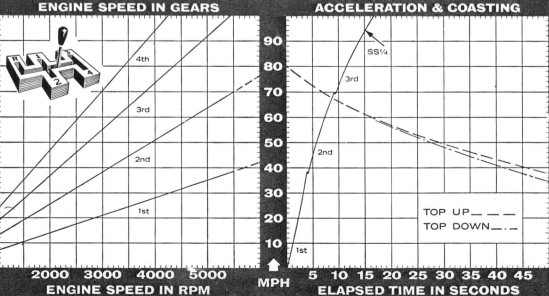

ENGINE SPEED IN GEARS

4th
3rd
2nd
1st

2000 3000 4000 5000
ENGINE SPEED IN RPM

ACCELERATION & COASTING

MPH

SS¼
3rd
2nd
1st

TOP UP _ _ _
TOP DOWN _ . _

5 10 15 20 25 30 35 40 45
ELAPSED TIME IN SECONDS

GRAND TOURING

Awestruck by the scenery (the 5,085 ft. Col de Pillon) or the car (an E-type Jaguar)? Tommy Wisdom (above) and his wife "Bill" enjoyed both. Right: Rallyists Peter Riley and Ann Wisdom after a spell in the snow. Verdict: Quite a car.

Expedition by E-type

By Tommy Wisdom

THE Wisdom Winter Expedition to the Swiss Lakes provided a chance to discover how that superb example of the car makers' art—the Jaguar E-type coupé—performed under Grand Touring conditions.

Mrs. W., despite fond memories of stark T.T. Rileys and M.G. Magnettes at Brooklands, is nowadays only interested in high performance cars so long as their speed is achieved in comfort and silence. Ann is more used to tough rally cars that resemble to a certain degree the old-type sports models on which I cut my competition teeth.

Britain leads the world in the variety of sporting cars it produces; 32 makers offer no less than 18 models capable of more than 100 m.p.h. Many of these new cars, because they are so quiet and comfortable, and hold the road so well, need a new approach to driving. Though these modern cars are intrinsically safer, they can, in inexpert, inexperienced hands, be more dangerous than the old-type sports car. Think back to the Vauxhall 30/98, the 3-litre Bentley, the M.G.s, the S.S.100 and other great machines of the 'thirties. Their noise, both exhaust and mechanical, the harsh suspension, uncertain brakes, heavy, direct steering, the very rush of wind at a mere 80 miles an hour made you concentrate—mentally and physically—on handling them. The rattling, jarring, bouncing machine really kept you on the job.

(Those who sigh for those good old days "when craftsmen built cars" should listen to W. O. Bentley, who says: "Everything made more noise in those days—permitted tolerances and the fact that the standard of machining, gear-cutting and general quality of design were all vastly inferior to what we expect today.")

The faster, quieter, safer machines of today can easily lull you into a false sense of security. Unless you "Drive on instruments" you may be chatting away to your passenger with little appreciation of the speed at which you are proceeding. It's too easy. Stirling Moss once said that concentration is the hardest lesson to absorb in the whole manual of driving instruction, and the very effortlessness of the modern fast car makes this more difficult.

Why are sports cars unpopular with the insurance companies? Because they have a lot of accidents. Why do they have a lot of accidents? Because drivers (some of them anyhow) are not concentrating. The designers have done their part, the drivers do not. This is a pity, because to acquire advanced technique is no more difficult than taking the first steps in motoring. It can be done just as easily as the *ab initio* pilot of a Tiger Moth converts to a twin-engined machine.

On our winter run to Switzerland the journey south-east through France was naturally over main roads—my favourite short cuts are inadvisable in the winter and, in any case, traffic is relatively light. Including stops for petrol and the frontier crossing the Jaguar averaged 49½ m.p.h. to Montreux. And this was dawdling, for we were changing drivers (we had Peter Riley's Volvo as tender car) to give everyone an opportunity of sampling the E-type under winter conditions.

The journey back was made under more pressure. The same route was followed—from Montreux round the Lake to Lausanne, over intermittent ice to Vallorbe, where the sun shone on the skiers on the nursery slopes of Mont d'Or, then rain through the Jura, and by way of Pontarlier, Chaumont, Chalon-sur-Saône, Rheims and Arras to Dunkirk, the last 100 miles being in that wet mist so typical of northern France. Our best hour was just after St. Dizier to Rheims—71 miles. The overall average was 60.3. This involved frequent cruising at 100 m.p.h. and three times the speedometer needle exceeded 120 m.p.h. This statement should shock no one, for the car was under complete control at all times; genuinely I took no risks. But I could not rid myself of the recurring thought—the racing Jaguar 3½-litre S.S.100 at Brooklands before the war was not as fast as this. (Then we managed a lap at 118 m.p.h.)

Pleasant surprise—the round trip of 1,378 miles was covered at an average petrol consumption of 21.2 m.p.g.

The atrocious weather convinced us once again that a wind-screen washer is essential. In fact the E-type reservoir is not really big enough for a Continental day's run. It needs either a bigger bottle or arrangements for an outside filler orifice so that replenishment can be made easily at a petrol stop.

All four of us were impressed by the easy pace of the Jaguar, its quietness and comfort; in the favourite phrase of the motor testers, it fairly eats up the miles.

On the open roads of France, despite rain and snow, fog and ice in turn, it put 60 miles into the hour with almost contemptuous ease. The car was as steady as a rock at three-figure speeds; the pronounced camber of some of the northern *routes nationales* had no effect on the steering wheel. It is at these touring speeds that the driver must keep alert; there is no physical effort required. On the open road, with its 20 m.p.h. to maximum in top gear, there is no need to change gear in the Jaguar—and therefore the mind must be attuned to the possible emergency.

Maximum speed? I don't know. But I can say from experience that this E-type will do exactly 100 m.p.h. in third gear at 5,500 r.p.m. What I do like is the ability to trickle quietly and smoothly through traffic at less than 20 m.p.h. and then accelerate away into the three-figure regions.

Brakes? Deceptive—for they are very much more effective than they feel at first. The brake meter proves this to those who miss the old-fashioned " grab " of the drum brake.

Luggage accommodation? It is ample on the coupé, not so on the open model. But it is only older folk who raise this question; the modern motorist travels light. The cabin trunk and the Gladstone bag went out with the aspidistra. Air transport has brought this about. Today the younger people set off to the South of France with a couple of hold-alls, but it is difficult for the middle-aged to appreciate the change. A wine merchant friend in my age-group who complained about the lack of space on the E-type needed to be reminded that 30 years ago he set off blithely on 3,000 miles of Alpine Trial in an open M.G. with his grip lashed to the spare wheel.

Un-witch-like (or should it be Un-*Which?*-like) the female side of the expedition was quite uncritical; they *were* persuaded to say the apparatus to provide audible means of approach was not really up to the standard of the rest of the machine: the E-type really deserves a Fulgor to awaken the more somnolent of the *camion* pilots. My own slight criticism is that the lights are adequate: no more. *Cockpit Comments*—Bill Wisdom: " Surprisingly comfortable car." Ann Wisdom: " It's smooth and it steers like a dream." Peter Riley: " A genuine grand tourer—I can think of nothing more desirable for Continental touring." My own: " Here is a car which, like a pedigree gun or a green-heart trout rod, is so worth learning to use properly."

P.S. . . .

The Cheval Blanc at Sept-Saulx, a favourite of the Rheims Grand Prix " circus," is comfortable and warm out of season and its magnificent table is still unsurpassed in Northern France.

*   *   *

The Auberge Franc-Comtoise (the Ferny family still runs it impeccably) at Champlitte is more than a good pull-up for car-men.

*   *   *

The Swiss are building their first autoroute—from Geneva round the Lake to connect with the St. Bernard tunnel. Last year's plebiscite to inquire whether it should be paid for by an increased tax on petrol was turned down. The Swiss, in effect, said, " We've heard that story before—let's have the road first then we'll pay." (Shades of our Road Fund!)

*   *   *

Swiss drivers rarely disobey their involved traffic rules. Failure to halt at a STOP sign in view of a gendarme results in the immediate and physical loss of the driving licence which is not returned for at least a month.

By E-Type To Monaco

A Tough Continental Test of the Fastest Model in the Jaguar Range

PAUSE FOR MEDITATION.—The Editor looks down from the Jaguar E-type on that part of the Col de Restefond which he has already driven over, during MOTOR SPORT'S *2,800-mile road-test of this enthralling 150-m.p.h. British sports car.*

WHEN the Jaguar E-type was announced at last year's Geneva Show it aroused World-wide admiration and was an immediate success. So naturally, everyone wanted to try it. But, apart from brief acquaintance with an early specimen down M 1 and up A 5, we had to exhibit patience, partly because certain teething troubles required sorting out—such as the rear wheels fouling the body, oil-loss from the chassis-mounted final-drive unit, brake troubles, etc.—and because there were too few E-types to share amongst a great number of motoring correspondents.

MOTOR SPORT could, nevertheless, have published a road-test report on this 150-m.p.h. Jaguar before now but we preferred to recount our experiences after a testing journey on the Continent rather than drive such a fast and powerful car in the thraldom of English traffic. Thus it was that plans discussed with Bob Berry, Jaguar's P.R.O., at the London Show last October came to fruition late in May, when a 2-seater " soft-top " Jaguar E-type was delivered to our offices, its ignition and carburation suitably adjusted to enable French octane-ratings and 9-to-1 pistons to enjoy some degree of compatability.

Early Impressions

The evening prior to enplaning from Southend for Bàsle we tried the car on the journey home and over local roads. This first re-acquaintance with this fastest of production Jaguars was entirely reassuring. In pouring rain, we had not gone farther than the Bank before feeling entirely at home behind the wheel of this 265-b.h.p. sports car. The 3.78-litre engine, for all its power, high-compression pistons and twin o.h. camshafts, will run contentedly down to 1,000 r.p.m. in 3rd gear, even in top, with the standard 3.31-to-1 axle-ratio. From such modest crankshaft speeds acceleration was clean and instantaneous, with never a cough, splutter or flat-spot. On the Embankment a pedestrian stepped on to a crossing and on the rain-slippery road the servo-actuated Dunlop disc brakes on all four wheels retarded progress surely, in a straight line, without any need to back-off on the pedal.

Past the derestriction signs the performance could really be used, 100 m.p.h. became common-place, and the engine proved willing to rush up to 5,500 r.p.m., although when the Jaguar, to which all eyes seemed to turn, was lolloping along at 95 m.p.h., the revs in top fell to a modest 4,000.

Experiments on still-wet twisty roads showed that the rear-end is extremely reluctant to breakaway, even when the power and torque (260 lb./ft. at 4,000 r.p.m.) were turned on hard in 2nd gear, such is the grip of the Dunlop RS5 tyres. The steering, by rack-and-pinion with no lost motion and good stops at full-lock, is pleasantly light and quick, being geared 2½ turns, lock-to-lock. The suspension of the E-type is soft enough to give an excellent ride over rough roads, yet is fully in keeping with the car's phenomenal performance, for there is very little roll, it is possible to " dodge " unexpected obstructions with alacrity, and, apart from a trace of " tail-happiness," there are no vices whatsoever. The steering characteristic is, indeed, virtually neutral. At the front torsion bars and wishbones are used, at the back the new Jaguar i.r.s. with stressed articulated drive-shafts, lower wishbones and trailing links with coil-springs. We have always advocated properly-designed i.r.s. and the Jaguar E-type and Mk. X endorse our views!

This preliminary canter certainly whetted the motoring appetite and made us eager to shake the traffic congestion of England from our chunky 6.40 × 15 tyres.

Since the earliest versions foot-wells have been provided and the pedals have been re-positioned. Although six-footers still find the E-type impossible or exceedingly uncomfortable to drive, as average-height mortals we were very nicely accommodated and found the driving position ideal, although it came as a mild surprise to discover that it is not possible to " heel-and-toe " on these race-bred cars. The adjustable and low-set wood-rimmed steering wheel, with its three drilled metal spokes, is particularly commendable.

The minor controls, too, are not only impressive to look at but are sensibly laid-out. A r.h. stalk works the direction-flashers and the full-beam signal flasher. The headlamps are dimmed

ON ITS WAY.—These pictures show the Jaguar being hoisted into the hold of the 4-engined Carvair and Capt. Tootill at the controls of this new aircraft—if you consider your instrumental-panel is well stocked. . . . !

by a r.h. flick-switch on the facia, the matching tachometer and speedometer (reading to 6,000 r.p.m. and 160 m.p.h., respectively) are immediately before the driver, there is the usual Jaguar warning-lamp for handbrake-on or brake fluid at a dangerously low level, and, of course, the normal warning lights, including one as a reminder that refuelling is due. The central instrument panel carries four matching dials, comprising ammeter, fuel gauge, oil gauge and water thermometer, and a row of six flick-switches, divided by ignition key, cigar igniter and starter button, which look after the various services. These switches are sensibly located, for the left hand goes out naturally to washers and 2-speed wipers switches and, moving one place to the left, selects the map light. The other three switches, reading from l. to r., control interior lamp, panel lighting (which can be bright or dim), and 2-speed heater fan. The engine always commenced promptly, the vertical quadrant control of mixture-strength being operated from cold—a warning light reminds the driver to push this down as temperature rises. Oil pressure is normally approximately 60 lb./sq. in. and water temperature 70° C.; if the latter rises towards boiling point, in traffic or low-gear mountaineering, the electrically-driven fan comes into operation. When the E-type was introduced one weekly contemporary said this happened at 80° F. and its opposite number quoted 80° C., but on the test car this happened, to the accompaniment of some subdued shuddering, at just under 90° C.

The bonnet is easily released by turning toggle-handles on each side of the bulkhead sill and operating a safety-catch at the rear end of the " power bulge." The boot is released by pulling a knob behind the driver's seat; this was hardly a one-man operation, because it was also necessary to press down the trailing edge of the lid. More serious, on several occasions, as 120 m.p.h. on a rough piece of road came up, the lid would open of its own volition, a fault not confined to this particular E-type. Fortunately the lid is spring-loaded, so attention to probable loss of luggage is drawn by it blanking the view in the mirror, but this does not exactly contribute anything to *Gran Turismo !*

The heavy bonnet stays open on its own and there is then excellent accessibility of the beautifully-finished power unit and entire front of the chassis. The rear-view mirror tended to vibrate and shift, but otherwise no criticism of the Jaguar's detail arrangements is called for, except that the horn-push in the wheel-centre sounded a rather unpleasant horn which became erratic for a few miles on our return to England. The hood has a big rear window, stows easily, and is covered by a hood bag; there still remains space behind the seats for a brief-case and oddments. The spare wheel lives under the floor of the boot, which contributes to the limited luggage space.

The lights-switch is reminiscent of that on a pre-war Derby-Bentley and a specially pleasing feature is the labelling of each of the controls in clear lettering along the base of the panel, illuminated, to two degrees of brightness, at night.

The Smiths clock resolutely refused to tell the time (like our Smiths travelling clock) but everything else functioned with precision. A big tunnel separates the two bucket seats, central gear-lever and handbrake are located conventionally, the stayed windscreen has triple wipers, there is a small open cubby-hole, you get in and out over wide chassis sills (if you aspire to a boy-friend or sugar-daddy with an E-type, girls, you will need slacks) and the doors have glass windows wound up fully with 3 turns of the handles.

So much for a preliminary look round this most impressive Coventry-built motor car. Impressive the Jaguar E-type most certainly is, in action for obvious reasons, at rest in appearance, from its long all-enveloping front-hinged bonnet with its big bulge over the cam-boxes flanked by louvres, those on the off-side covering the triple 2-in. S.U. HD8 carburetters, to its low hood (or hard-top) and its cocked-up tail beneath which the twin tail-pipes and silencers sneak upwards.

We had elected to take the open 2-seater *sans* hard-top, in the hope of sweltering weather in the South of France. In this we were disappointed, but this did not occasion any worry, for the easy-to-erect, high-quality hood (made in Jaguar's own trim-shop, each one individually tailored), braced truly rigid and drum-free by triple toggles on the screen-frame, is fully weather resistant, and the heater very effective. Indeed, let us here and now offer the highest praise for a sports car into which not a drop of water penetrated, or so much as dripped from under the dash, even in thunderstorms of tropical intensity—no mean achievement at the customary high cruising speeds of the E-type!

That this 2-seater is not a true *Gran Turismo* car was evident when we had to pack our evening suits into one case, supplemented only by a soft-bag, although the coupé version naturally carries far more luggage. Moreover, the fact that petrol fumes penetrated into the boot so that confectionery carried therein had to be thrown away, a passenger was sick and one's clothes, even those carried in a bag, reeked of petrol is hardly compatible with the meaning of the letters G.T.!

Channel Air Bridge

One object in making this journey to Monte Carlo was to sample the new Channel Air Bridge service from Southend to Basle; the others, quite obviously, were to submit the Jaguar to a searching and revealing test and to watch the Monaco G.P.

The new Southend-Basle service, which is complementary to similar services now in operation to Geneva and Strasbourg, is flown in four-engined aircraft, known as Carvairs, which are Douglas DC-4s modified by Channel Air Bridge to carry 5-6 cars and 23 passengers. The cars are hoist-elevated into the forward hold and the passengers occupy the spacious fuselage. In this fashion we were flown smoothly by Capt. Tootill, a keen reader of MOTOR SPORT since he discovered it in R.A.F. messes during the war, at 9,000 feet, the 450 miles to Basle occupying 2 hr. 20 min. The Carvair is appreciably quieter than the Bristol Superfreighter 170s of the cross-Channel routes and during the flight sandwiches and drinks are served by attractive Stewardesses.

There is little need to emphasise the excellent start to a Continental holiday that flying like this to Basle, Geneva or Strasbourg provides. The heavy bookings for these flights, which were inaugurated earlier this year, are a tribute to the motorists' approval. The Jaguar E-type was, of course, the least suitable car with which to prove our point, for it would have disposed of this dull part of the journey at about a quarter the speed of the Carvair but in any normal car the drive across France entails hour after hour of boring travel over roads excellent but largely devoid of good scenery. The cost of taking an E-type thus is £17 and as petrol would, at a very rough estimate, cost in the region of £14, what possible excuse could there be for *not* going *via* Channel Air Bridge, apart from the great saving in time, nervous strain and fatigue? Motorists using these Carvair long-distance flights find themselves well placed for entry into Switzerland, or travel to the South of France either over any of the usual Passes or down the more straightforward N 7 route.

That morning, on our way to the office, we had encountered Lord Montagu's 1907 120-h.p. Itala on its trailer, going back to Beaulieu after its Monza outing. Sure enough, said our charming dark-haired Chief Stewardess, it had been flown out and back from Basle by Carvair.

The Basle and Geneva services operate in the afternoon, enabling Midlands' motorists to travel easily to Southend Airport in the morning, and so at tea-time, with the burbling exhaust-note of our dark green E-type once again in our ears, we found ourselves driving along that "no-man's-land" that is a reminder that Basle is half in Switzerland, half in France. After an easy passage through the frontier there followed a rapid drive into the setting sun (the last time it shone in earnest!) for an adequate dinner and bed at the Grand Hotel et Bains in Bescancon.

On the Thursday morning we set off in high spirits, the sun growing warm in the early morning and the Jaguar devouring the pleasant road towards Bourge, where we paused for fuel and oil and the E-type was much admired by the French mechanics.

CURIOUS!—As we were going to Monte Carlo we naturally followed the signposts saying " Nice " but the road got rougher and rougher and eventually we came to a snowdrift . . . .

In a car which, without exceeding 5,000 r.p.m., goes to genuine maxima of 34 m.p.h. in the 11.18-to-1 bottom gear, 63 m.p.h. in the 6.16-to-1 2nd gear, 92 m.p.h. in the 4.25-to-1 3rd gear (with a maximum in this cog of 113 m.p.h. at 6,000 r.p.m. and a usable 103 m.p.h. at 5,500!), and which will leap to "the ton" in 16 sec., nothing comes up, even on French roads, to challenge it. A comfortable corrected top speed is 122 m.p.h. at 5,000 r.p.m. but 5,500 r.p.m. can be held if you back-off occasionally, and that equals 138 m.p.h.

We lunched, appropriately enough as the Editor had been driving, at Corpse, and that afternoon were in the rally country of Gap and Sisteron. Indeed, innocently following some signposts to Nice, we took to the Col de Restefond, and ignoring the alarming unguarded drops to the valley far below and the appalling road surface, wound the Jaguar round innumerable hairpins, lowered it gently over gulleys, steered it with inches to spare past huge fallen rocks, until—we came to a snowdrift There was no alternative but to retrace our route. The rocks and boulders had opened up a small crack at the front of the unprotected sump through which Shell X-100 30 began to seep and both exhaust pipes were considerably flattened. Whether exotic cars with Italian names would go over such terrain without damage we do not know but in our opinion a Grand Touring car should be able to do this, and the E-type thus proved that it is not a rally or G.T. car. Eventually we crossed by the Col de la Cayolle, meeting a good deal of traffic and pausing at a *garage* to put up the hood against the rain that was to persist for the whole of our stay on the "sun-drenched" Côte d'Azur.

In driving for some 300 miles over continually twisting roads fatigue was obviated by the lightness and predictability of the E-type's steering and the reassuring power and certainty of those entirely excellent Dunlop disc brakes, which the vacuum servo rendered light to apply and which remained entirely vice-free, squeaking only slightly under mild applications of the pedal.

In climbing the *cols* the gearbox was in continuous use, and it is the least-pleasant feature of the car. The synchromesh is almost useless for rapid changes and causes jarring at the lever, and it is necessary to fully depress the heavy clutch pedal to effect quiet changes, which, with its excessive movement, is tedious. This is a pity, because the gears are quiet, the little rigid central lever nicely placed, and the engine unconcerned about being revved to 5,500 or used for long periods in the lower ratios. Long spells in 2nd gear cause the transmission tunnel and handbrake lever to get surprisingly hot, however.

As we wound the car for ever upwards and round corner after acute corner, the long bonnet nosing to the sky-line, and then dropped it swiftly downwards round hairpin upon hairpin bend, the enjoyment of 265 obedient horses and impeccable road-holding endowed by all-round independent suspension was marred only by a persistent tapping noise that suggested something amiss in the valve gear.

At last level roads were regained and we approached Nice in a traffic stream, being passed for the only time in the entire 2,800 miles of the test, by a Simca Sport that slipped past in a 50-k.p.h.

speed limit that we thought it prudent to observe, in view of the interest the French motorcycle police were displaying in our fierce-looking English " racing-car "! The driver felt tired only in the final congested miles, when traffic was diverted in Nice to accommodate an International Coach Rally, competitors' numbers in which ran into the 300s!

So to Monte Carlo. Next day British Motors Ltd. proved to be busy repairing exhaust systems and body dents in Jaguars that were taking part in a Jaguar D.C. Rally but on the Saturday morning they put the travel-stained E-type up on a hoist, drained out all the new oil with which we had just filled the sump, repaired the crack with Mr. Holt's well-known cement and some black paint, and pronounced the tap in the valve gear as unimportant—we had previously checked the tappet settings and found them correct. They had also found a universal joint for Bruce McLaren and this he was fitting to his personal Jaguar E-type, prior to winning the Monaco G.P. so calmly and convincingly in the V8 Cooper-Climax.

Incidentally, the run down had served as a reminder that 2 c.v. Citroëns still swarm the roads and lanes of France in spite of the new Renault 4s and Citroën Ami 6s, and that the Simca 1000 is now frequently encountered.

Strolling round the Principality we encountered Edward Eves, who reminded us that there is yet another satisfactory way of travelling to Monte Carlo—he had flown from Bagington (Coventry) to Cannes in his pre-war Miles Whitney Straight, hitched a lift to the *gare*, and come on by train!

Although Monte Carlo was crowded with cars, E-types competing for the attention of the passers-by with the Ferraris of the G.P. team, the cosmopolitan motoring atmosphere nicely emphasised when we looked from our window in the Hotel de Palmiers to see a 2 c.v. Citroën cheekily hiding behind a Mercedes-Benz 220SE (later we had a good view of Princess Grace leaving a Red Cross reception in her Rolls-Royce, from the same window), it is possible, once a parking space has been found, to leave a car there for several days without being molested. So for much of our stay the E-type sat brooding to itself, while we got drenched to the marrow watching the 5-a.m. practice on Friday, watched more practice on the Saturday and an extremely interesting race on the Sunday. However, the Continental Correspondent did " have a go " up La Turbie, and over the Turini and Col de Braus. He was impressed, but declared the Jaguar large, noisy and heavy as to steering and gear-change after a Porsche.

All good things terminate eventually, the pessimists remind us, and at 4 a.m. on post-race Monday we stowed our luggage and pointed the long nose of the E-type towards the Nice *autoroute* (toll approximately 10s.) *en route* for Calais. There was no intention of making a particularly fast run but on the other hand we didn't mean to hang about. As the route followed, up N 7 to Lyon, N 6 to Chalon and along N 44 from the other Chalon to St. Quintin, is a much-used one, we append our times, as they may be of interest and stimulus to others who traverse this road in good motor cars.

Monte Carlo	..	4.00 a.m.	Reims	..	..	1.55 p.m.
Aix en Provence		5.41 a.m.	**St. Quintin**		..	2.47 p.m.
Avignon..	..	6.30 a.m.	**Cambrai**		..	3.12 p.m.
Valence ..		7.48 a.m.	**Arras**	..	..	3.30 p.m.
Lyon	..	8.51 a.m.	**Bethume**		..	3.50 p.m.
Dijon	..	10.59 a.m.	**St. Omer**		..	4.16 p.m.
Longres ..		11.50 a.m.	**Calais-Marck**			
Chaumont	..	12.09 p.m.			**Airfield**	4.41.5 p.m.
St. Dizier	..	12.55 p.m.				

Distance for each full hour, inclusive of stops :

1st hour :	69.5 miles		7th hour : 62.3 miles (petrol)
2nd hour :	68.1	,,	8th hour : 59.5 ,,
3rd hour :	68.9	,,	9th hour : 60.0 ,,
4th hour :	53.5	,, (petrol)	10th hour : 59.5 ,, (petrol)
5th hour :	52.7	,,	11th hour : 70.0 ,,
6th hour :	57.0	,,	12th hour : 60.6 ,,

Petrol stops : 21 minutes at rest.

Average speed overall for 12 hours : 61.4 m.p.h.

We had started from the far side of Monte Carlo in the dark and driven comparatively slowly to Nice Airport to deposit a third passenger, an accurate time allowance being made for the detour. On the Nice *autoroute* the cruising speed was an indicated 110 m.p.h. at 4,500 r.p.m., we never exceeded 135 m.p.h., which was reached but once, and naturally there were the usual impedi-

On the right road at last. The Jaguar descending the Col de la Cayolle.

ments—difficulty in finding the way onto the *autoroute* at Nice, a good deal of lorry and tourist traffic, various pauses at red traffic lights, market day and many lorries in Villefranch, a long detour along N 460 and D 28 between Dijon and Longres, where the vineyards give place to agricultural scenery, and a very slow deviation in Reims. There is a motor-road of sorts from Avignon to Valence but it is two-way, there is a semi by-pass at the latter town but the real one is under construction, *pave* and traffic-lights slowed us in Cambrai with its rail-like tramcars, and a level-crossing bar fell, but rose again at the sight of the speeding Jaguar, ere we scented coffee beans being ground in Bethume. Also, there were three stops for fuel, totalling 21 min., and a brief pause to shut the boot-lid, which had again sprung open, either because the catch rattles free or due to chassis distortion over bad surfaces. Food—we had it with us! The need for three fuel stops was a bit depressing, for I consider a G.T. car should require refuelling only once, at lunchtime, on a coast-to-coast blind across France (I note that the Aston Martin DB4GT has a 30-gallon petrol reservoir, the Ferrari 250GT Berlinetta and the G.T. Maserati each have 22-gallon tanks, compared to the Jaguar E-type's 14-gallon tank. . .)

However, as a sports car there is no denying that the E-type is a superlatively rapid and enjoyable means of crossing Continents. Always the speed seems to be between 90 and 120 m.p.h., " the ton " comes up along any piece of clear road, and a drop into 3rd lifts speed from 50 to 70 m.p.h. in less than 4 sec., from 80 to 100 m.p.h. in under 5 sec. In sober fact, 0–50 m.p.h. occupies 5.7 sec., 0–60 m.p.h. takes 7.0 sec.! Let us emphasise again that this was a normal run by a normal driver, that we had no thought of establishing a " record," that the brakes never once went on hard. Yet twelve hours after leaving Monte Carlo we were beyond the *pave* of Lillers, the odometer indicating 736.6 miles, and the total distance of 777.7 miles took 12 hr. 41½ min., or 12 hr. 20 min. running time. Although the tapping noise in the valve gear was still with us the car otherwise showed no sign of distress. The brakes were as powerful as ever, oil pressure steady at 60 lb./sq. in., and the engine as responsive to the throttles as at the start, although pinking badly even on Azur petrol below 3,000 r.p.m.

To be able to average over 61 m.p.h. across France in daylight traffic in comfort and security is really something; in a normal car the long straights of N 7 can be tedious and thoughts would have turned enviously to those returning per Carvair. The bucket seats, not outstanding, nevertheless remain comfortable on such a journey, and we found the rather spongy front of the cushions and that ill-placed trim-rib under our bottoms acceptable on long acquaintance. In any case, any small faults that this 150-m.p.h., disc-braked, all-independently sprung, 0–120 m.p.h. in 24¼ sec. sports car may possess are entirely excused by its astonishingly competitive price—£1,480, or £2,036 0s. 3d. when purchase tax has been met. A hard-top is available for £68 and the coupé version of the E-type is priced at £2,123 5s. 3d. inclusive of purchase tax.

Tailpiece

Two days later we took the car to Coventry for Jaguars to re-set the ignition for English fuel, whereupon pinking was virtually
CONTINUED ON PAGE 57

A
RACING
E-TYPE
JAGUAR

Ken Baker's
successful car
is tested on road
and track by
PATRICK McNALLY

WHEN the E-Type was announced early in 1961, its specification was so advanced, people actually considered racing standard cars, and indeed early on several cars were successfully raced in an unmodified state. Since that time, however, much work has been done on this marque and the present racing E-Type bears little resemblance to its standard predecessor.

The subject of our test was Ken Baker's car which is, perhaps, one of the most modified of the racing E-Types seen around the circuits. The car was first used in competition with only 50 miles on the clock, when it won its class at the Thames Estuary A.C.'s Stapleford Sprint in September 1961. At this time it was running with radio, heater, and white-wall RS.5's. Since that date, the car has competed in no fewer than 24 meetings and has scored 19 wins, being placed in the remaining five races, and also holds records at Castle Combe and Brands Hatch. Ken has also won the 1962 B.R.S.C.C. "500" Trophy, and the West Essex Car Club President's Trophy and the Howarth Trophy.

Before going out to order your E-Type for the 1963 season, perhaps it would be a good idea to digest certain of the transformations this car has gone through until it was in race-winning form!

The bodywork has been extensively lightened by using aluminium for the bonnet and boot, as well as in the doors, the latter items being fitted with perspex windows without winding equipment. The steel bumpers, too, have been replaced by aluminium replicas. For all this, the car is outwardly a standard-bodied vehicle. Further weight has been lost by the use of seats fabricated in aluminium, which have deep seat wells to give extra height to the sloping back-rests; these are beautifully made, but as they are tailored for Ken Baker, they were of little benefit to the writer. All this has reduced the weight to just over one ton dry-weight. The interior has been attractively retrimmed in leather to give a business-like appearance.

The 3.8-litre power unit of this car, with its 9 : 1 compression ratio, is stated to produce 265 b.h.p. at 5,500 r.p.m. There-

fore, with such a good power/weight ratio and the excellent torque of the Jaguar engine, it might be argued that improvements to this part of the car were the least important. This is definitely not so. The standard E-Type block, pistons and con rods are retained, after being balanced and crack-tested. A D-Type cylinder-head with a 10 : 1 compression ratio has been added after seeing a lot of work in the hands of Messrs. Fred Warnell Motors Ltd., of Walthamstow. Fred Warnell's technique when it comes to gas-flowing, needs no introduction. The head has enlarged ports, the valve-seats being cut down to one-eighth of an inch, and many other secrets, along known to Fred, are to be found in the preparation of this "very special" cylinder head. Fuel is supplied by three 45 DCO Webers but a standard petrol pump, coil and distributor are retained.

Transmission improvements include a lightweight steel flywheel which mates to a Borg & Beck competition clutch, the union effected by courtesy of Ferodo. Close-ratio gears are to be found in the normal Jaguar box, but it is hoped that this will be replaced by a full D-Type unit by next season.

The suspension and brakes have undergone continuous development throughout the racing life of this car. The front suspension is standard except for Armstrong adjustable shock absorbers and altered torsion bars to allow for the difference in weight between the aluminium and steel bonnet, this having the effect of lowering the car. The back-end is where the work lies. The camber of the rear wheels has been increased from ¼ degree to 2 degrees negative, this being made possible by removing all the shims and machining the disc flanges. Special Armstrong shockers have also been fitted to the rear. The springs and the anti-roll bar are standard, but the rubber mountings between the diff-carrier and the body have been removed and replaced by solid steel blocks to prevent axle twist and also to cut out rear wheel steering. The axle ratio used throughout the season, for all circuits other than Brands Hatch and Crystal Palace, was a 3.45 : 1, at these circuits, a 3.77 : 1 was found more suitable.

That E-Type bugbear, the brakes, seem

to have been conquered. The front brakes are 10 ins. with $\frac{1}{2}$ in. competition discs; the rear too are of 10 ins. diameter, again with $\frac{1}{2}$ in. discs. Both front and rear are fitted with Ferodo DS.11 pads—$2\frac{1}{8}$ ins. on the front and $1\frac{3}{4}$ ins. on the rear. The ordinary servo has been removed and replaced by a Mark III Ford system. Cooling ducts, fabricated in aluminium, blow on the rear discs, the front discs being kept cool by ducting in the front apron.

Prior to fitting the Ford servo system, it was found that all other servos produced braking too fierce or too inefficient. Fitted with the Ford servo the car completed 110 laps of Club Silverstone during the Six Hour Relay Race, finishing with the brakes as efficient at the end as they were at the start; this would seem to suggest that the very difficult braking problem has been solved.

Having described work done on the car, the resulting performance has proved that the E-Type really benefits from these detailed attentions.

The acceleration must be described as almost incredible—100 m.p.h. is reached in 11.2 secs. and the rest of the acceleration figures are just as impressive: 0-30 m.p.h. in 2 secs., 0-50 m.p.h. in 4.2 secs., 0-60 m.p.h. in 5.2 secs., and 0-80 in 8 secs. These figures were taken in far from ideal conditions and great care was taken not to overstress engine or transmission as this was a privately owned car. There is no doubt that all these figures could be bettered under improved conditions.

The quarter-mile was covered, with very little fuss, in 13.3 seconds.

Gearing controlled the speeds through the gears and, of course, the maximum. First gear gave 47 m.p.h., second 70 m.p.h. and third 106 m.p.h., if one used 6,000 r.p.m., but in all cases, including acceleration tests, changes were made at 40 m.p.h., 60 m.p.h. and 100 m.p.h. Maximum speed using 6,000 r.p.m. in top was 128 m.p.h.

On the road, this car proved extremely tractable, the engine never being temperamental or oiling up—throughout the period of testing the plugs were never touched. The engine pulled well at all revs and didn't just have top-end performance. Maximum power was found between 3,000-5,500 r.p.m., and the close-ratio gearbox allowed the driver to keep within this rev-band. Fast take-offs were helped by a Powr-Lok differential and the fixed rear-carrier, these two coping with take-offs at 4,000 r.p.m., providing the driver was capable of holding the car in a straight line.

Not a cheap car to run, at 10 m.p.g., but it certainly gave value for money. The consumption was increased by the low axle

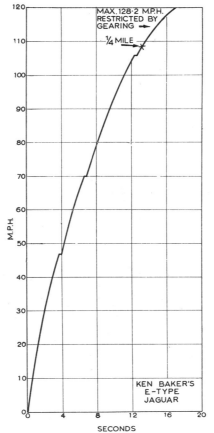

ACCELERATION GRAPH

ratio and the rich mixture setting of the carburetters. Oil consumption was quite low at one pint per 100 miles. Oil temperature and pressure never gave any worry, whilst the water temperature, if anything,

ran too low, despite the fact that the radiator was half blanked-off.

The brakes were very good indeed with medium pedal pressure, and never locked up, an amazing improvement over standard. The steering, although heavy at low speeds, was stable when really motoring, and the lock was as good as ever. In fact, for a car of this size the steering must be described as superlative.

The less said about the gearbox the better, for although the ratios were close and need no criticism, the gear change was as slow as ever, and the movement between gears just as great. The clutch was very heavy, but made up for this by its efficiency and its smooth take-up. As Ken Baker doesn't bother to "heel-toe", the controls were set to make this manoeuvre impossible, as one's knee was tight under the steering wheel. By adjusting the wheel, it was possible to lift the leg to encompass both accelerator and brake, but not without adopting a Nuvolari-type driving position.

The ride was firm, to the point of being hard, this resisting any attempt by the car to pitch or roll. As expected, the roadholding was of a very high order. The tendency to understeer, with such power available, was no problem, and power-induced oversteer could easily be brought about—ideal handling qualities indeed.

We took the opportunity of exercising 300 h.p. around Silverstone and the impressions we had already gained on the road were borne out in 40 or so laps of the circuit. Unfortunately, we could only use the short circuit but, surprisingly enough, it was possible to exceed maximum revs in top before braking for Woodcote. Through Becketts, the car could be made to do more or less anything, being extremely manageable and, needless to say, as with the other corners, the car was controlled on the throttle.

Once or twice it was a question of who was taking who for a ride as we were shod with half-worn D.9s. Together the combination proved very satisfactory, for the superb handling qualities took care of any over-enthusiasm on my part.

One of Ken Baker's own firms, D.R. Fabrications, Ltd., of Gidea Park, made all the alloy bodywork, whilst Fred Webster prepared the car throughout the season—the car is a credit to both.

ACCELERATION

		(Modified)		(Standard)
0–30 m.p.h.	..	2 secs.	—	2.6 secs.
0–50 m.p.h.	..	4.2 ,,	—	5.6 ,,
0–60 m.p.h.	..	5.2 ,,	—	6.8 ,,
0–80 m.p.h.	..	8.0 ,,	—	10.8 ,,
0–100 m.p.h.	..	11.2 ,,	—	15.8 ,,
Standing quarter-mile	13.3 ,,		—	14.8 ,,

SPEEDS IN THE GEARS
1st—47 m.p.h. 2nd—70 m.p.h. 3rd—106 m.p.h.

Jaguar E-type 3,781 c.c.

TWO years have elapsed since we published the first full test of an E-Type Jaguar G.T. coupé, then making its startling maiden appearance at the Geneva Show of 1961. Although the latest model today looks almost exactly the same as that left-hand drive prototype, in fact, a number of improvements have been made. The 1963 coupé now tested differs in one important mechanical respect; it has a high ratio back axle of 3·07 to 1 in place of the 3·31 to 1 of the early car. As a result it is a few m.p.h. faster, because the engine r.p.m. for maximum power are reached at a higher road speed. The earlier car was well over its peak at 150 m.p.h.

The extra 5 m.p.h. of top speed is rather academic, a slight reduction in acceleration is insignificant when so much remains, but top gear now gives 24·4 m.p.h. instead of 22·9 m.p.h. per 1,000 r.p.m., and this makes for more restful and economical cruising at very high speeds. For example, a 100 m.p.h. average over 60 miles of motorway was sufficiently quiet for a radio to be enjoyed, and the fuel consumption was at the rate of 16·2 m.p.g.

With a 14-gallon tank, safe range between refuellings is normally 230 miles. There is a yellow warning light to show when fuel is getting low. Owners will normally get 18 to 20 m.p.g., which is remarkably good for a powerful 3·8-litre engine. Oil consumption is now much reduced at about 1,800 m.p.g.

Other modifications made by Jaguar in the past year concern additional body insulation from both noise and heat, and although engine, exhaust and transmission noises are still heard as would reasonably be expected on a G.T. car of such performance, they are more remote and now seem outside rather than in the car with you. Wind noise around the body continues to be very slight; the airstream pattern as seen after driving fast in rain is interesting to study. Streamlining is obviously very good and the whole top of the long nose remains completely clean. Door and boot lid sealing has been improved. A thermostat-controlled electric fan now replaces the engine-driven kind, with saving in power and reduction of noise.

This E-type is a truly remarkable car in several respects: it is deceptively fast (the speedometer is very accurate) yet its handling is so good and natural that drivers used to speeds 20 or 30 m.p.h. less are not embarrassed by the unaccustomed rate of progress.

No special impression is gained of the steering behaviour

PRICES	£	s	d
Fixed head coupé	1,583	0	0
Purchase Tax	330	7	1
Total (in G.B.)	1,913	7	1
Extras (including P.T.)			
Electrically heated rear window	16	18	9
Smiths 620T radio	43	14	11

Make • JAGUAR   Type • E-type Fixed Head Coupé

Manufacturers : Jaguar Cars Ltd., Browns Lane, Coventry

Test Conditions

Weather ... Dry, overcast, with 5-10 m.p.h. wind
Temperature ... 11 deg. C. (52 deg. F). Barometer 28·5in Hg.

Dry concrete surfaces

Weight

Kerb weight (with oil, water and half-full fuel tank)
25·0cwt (2,800lb–1,270kg.)
Front-rear distribution, per cent F, 49·5; R, 50·5.
Laden as tested 28cwt (3,136lb–1,423kg.)

Turning Circles

Between kerbs .... L and R, 39ft 1in.
Between walls .... L and R, 40ft 7in.
Turns of steering wheel lock to lock .... 2·6

Performance Data

Top gear m.p.h. per 1,000 r.p.m.............. 24·4
Mean piston speed at max. power ... 3,480ft/min.
Engine revs. at mean max. speed ...... 6,200 r.p.m.
B.h.p. per ton laden .... 189 (gross)

FUEL AND OIL CONSUMPTION

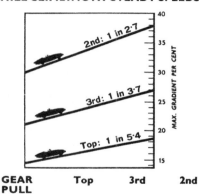

FUEL .... Super Premium Grade
(100 octane RM)

Test Distance .... 1,274 miles

Overall Consumption .... 18·6 m.p.g.
(15·3 litres/100 km.)

Normal Range ....13–23 m.p.g.
·(21·7–12·3 litres/100 km.)

OIL: S.A.E. 30 ... Consumption 1,800 m.p.g.

MAXIMUM SPEEDS AND ACCELERATION (mean) TIMES

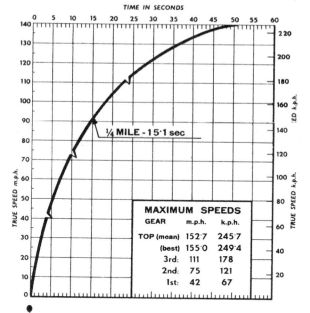

¼ MILE - 15·1 sec

MAXIMUM SPEEDS		
GEAR	m.p.h.	k.p.h.
TOP (mean)	152·7	245·7
(best)	155·0	249·4
3rd:	111	178
2nd:	75	121
1st:	42	67

TIME IN SECONDS											
2·5	3·6	5·5	7·2	9·0	12·1	15·1	18·0	22·7	29·6	36·5	50·6
0	30	40	50	60	70	80	90	100	110	120	130	140	TRUE SPEED m.p.h.
	29	39	49	59	69	79	89	100	110	121	132	142	CAR SPEEDOMETER

Speed range and time in seconds

m.p.h.	Top	3rd	2nd	1st
10—30	—	5·9	2·8	2·3
20—40	7·4	5·6	3·8	2·3
30—50	7·0	5·4	3·6	—
40—60	7·2	5·3	3·5	—
50—70	7·9	5·4	3·8	—
60—80	7·8	5·8	—	—
70—90	8·0	6·0	—	—
80—100	7·9	5·9	—	—
90—110	8·0	7·0	—	—
100—120	9·9	—	—	—
110—130	11·9	—	—	—
120—140	21·0	—	—	—

BRAKES

	Pedal Load	Retardation	Equiv. distance
(from 30 m.p.h. in neutral)	25lb	0·30g	100ft
	50lb	0·44g	69ft
	75lb	0·60g	50ft
	100lb	0·78g	39ft
	115lb	0·98g	30·8ft
	Handbrake	0·46g	66ft

CLUTCH Pedal load and travel—50lb and 6·3in.

HILL CLIMBING AT STEADY SPEEDS

2nd: 1 in 2·7
3rd: 1 in 3·7
Top: 1 in 5·4

GEAR PULL	Top	3rd	2nd
(lb per ton)	410	590	765
Speed range (m.p.h.)	94–100	75–80	48–52

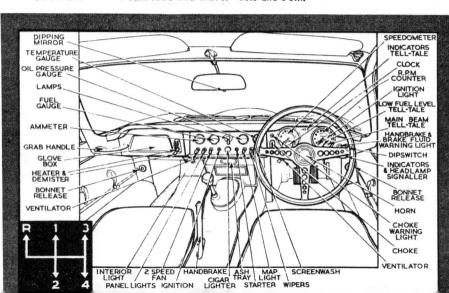

Surrounded by equipment, and occupying most of the available space, the impressive looking twin camshaft engine is accessible—and it keeps clean

Jaguar E-type . . .

through bends because the driver is not conscious of using special skill or effort. The characteristics are neutral and it is a rack-and-pinion system. The car responds to guidance round bends as if it knew what was wanted of it. However, experienced drivers soon discover that it is better to drive out of a corner, because a touch of power obviously helps the car round.

If it is necessary to cut power or even brake in the middle of a fast bend the car behaves normally and properly, tending to run a little wider than it would otherwise have done. Too much power when leaving a corner on a wet road will, of course, result in the tail starting to slide. Adhesion is extremely good in wet or dry conditions, and the moment power is eased, a slide is checked and there is quick steering—only 2·6 turns from lock to lock—to correct the car's heading. The independent, coil-spring rear suspension contributes a great deal to the combination of good handling and relatively soft ride.

One of the safety factors of the E-type is the quickness and ease with which a slow vehicle can be overtaken.

Using second or third gear, any given speed can be increased by 20 m.p.h. in under 4 seconds up to 70 m.p.h. Thus there is never any temptation to take a chance because you have been held back for mile after mile.

When a good clear stretch presents itself, the car can surge up to 100 m.p.h. from a crawl in a few hundred yards and in well under 20 seconds. Its speed at the end of a standing ¼-mile is just about 90 m.p.h. Directional stability at high speeds is good. Gusts have little effect up to 120 m.p.h., above which figure guidance becomes more sensitive.

Improved Brakes

There was some criticism of the brakes of earlier E-types —not that they were inferior, but because they were matched to the high-speed end of the car's performance. As a result, pedal pressures for stopping from low speeds were too high and the sudden bite needed for a crash stop in traffic was absent. Modifications have taken care of these points. They involve increased servo assistance, altered pedal linkage to give greater mechanical advantage and different material for the disc pads.

The servo unit is of the bellows-type operating directly on to the brake pedal. There are twin master cylinders and twin reservoirs to give completely independent systems front and rear. There is also a common warning lamp for the brake fluid reservoirs, should the levels fall dangerously low.

Now a pedal load of 25lb gives 0·30g retardation, as compared with 0·20g previously. At heavy pedal pressures stopping power is also increased, 115lb giving a mean maximum figure of 0·98g (as compared with 0·87). The Dunlop RS 5 tyres take some credit for this high figure. The brake pedal travel is quite long, but increase in effect is pleasantly progressive and hard braking at high speed produces no snaking. Above 115lb pressure, which is quite high by accepted road car standards, the front wheels lock. During acceleration testing we made the brakes hot but did not detect any increase in pressure for a given response.

To obtain good standing-start acceleration figures, a driver has to be rather hard on the car. On advice from Jaguar we let in the clutch with the engine turning at about 2,000 r.p.m. as compared with 3,000-3,500 with the previous test car. We were asked to observe the start of the r.p.m. red sector in the intermediate gears. This meant changing up at 5,500 r.p.m. The clutch, which is more gentle than before, spins for a second or two and produces a strong smell, but it comes to no harm. It is not the car's

Minor but important changes have been made inside recent E-types; in particular there is more room for feet and for stretching long legs. The well-equipped interior is both attractive and functional

This is roughly the angle from which most people see the E-type

best feature, and its pedal still has too long a movement and too high a pressure—a full 6in. and up to 50lb. Women, if not men, find this tedious, particularly as it needs full movement to disengage completely for a clean gear selection. A limited-slip differential is standard equipment.

We have expressed our views on the gearbox on several occasions; it remains unchanged and unworthy of the car. Very slow, deliberate changes have to be made to avoid a crunch—particularly up into second gear. Bottom is without synchromesh and at high r.p.m. sounds like that of a vintage car.

When standing still, as at red traffic signals, it was often very difficult to select bottom gear from neutral, and sometimes second also. One could not be sure of obtaining reverse when it was wanted, but in the embarrassment of holding up a honking line of traffic while seeking bottom, it was all too easy to find reverse by mistake. We got into the way of dropping first gear in just before the car came to a standstill in traffic, so as to be able to move off normally, even though this meant riding the clutch—which is a bad habit.

For some hundreds of miles of our test we ran with the tyres at the recommended pressures for sustained high speeds, namely 35 p.s.i. front, 40 p.s.i. rear. The ride was firm and stable but remained surprisingly shake-free. At the normal pressures of 25 p.s.i. front, 30 p.s.i. rear, the ride is exceptionally comfortable and restful for such a car.

Perhaps the attribute that should be stressed is that of grand tourer; by using only a part of the terrific performance available, two occupants can make a relaxed, satisfying and quite economical journey, and still be much quicker and at the end less tired than in almost any other car.

More Leg Room

The interior of the coupé now seems much roomier, largely because the seats can move farther back on their slides into newly provided recesses. There are also shallow wells beneath the pedals to give more foot room. The clutch and brake pedals themselves are still set too horizontally, as one may confirm by the wear on the near edge of their pad rubbers and the mint appearance of the remaining area. The flimsy pendant accelerator pedal is some 3in. lower than that of the brake, which is inconvenient and bad in an emergency. The new footwells, just visible under the car, do not improve the pedal attitudes.

This is not the easiest car to get into and out of, but the doors swing wide and have a firm stay-open catch. If one has to park close on the offside it is a struggle to climb across to get out of the passenger door.

Few could find fault with the driving position of the

latest car, and virtually gone is the earlier knees-up and splayed attitude required of long-legged drivers. The steering column length is adjustable as well as the seat positions, but the backrests are fixed.

Considerable shaping in back and cushion makes the support and location of the bucket seats unusually good. The rolls in the upholstery are rather hard but they suit most people's contours. The seats are faced in leather, trim is in matching leathercloth. Elsewhere there is thick carpeting and in the roof, wool pile attached directly to the insulating material on the roof panel.

There is a full complement of instruments and equipment laid out systematically and attractively; they are labelled in our drawing. Close to the driver's right hand is the headlamp dip switch which he can flick up or down without taking his fingers off the wheel's wooden rim.

The full beam of the lamps is good and penetrating, apparently unhindered by the toughened glass covers to the lamp wells. On early cars these were of transparent plastic material. One occasionally feels the need for something

Such is the area of the luggage shelf that a number of bags and smaller items can be accommodated without stacking. The car being very low, loading through the rear door is not difficult

Jaguar E-type . . .

between full and dipped heads; from experience with our own E-type we know that a pair of small lamps can be mounted in its main air intake. A reversing lamp is now standard.

Because of its pronounced slope the rear window restricts vision *via* the rear view mirror, but sufficient is seen for safety without the aid of wing mirrors, which are a little out of place on the E-type's sleek nose. Triple wipers clear a wide strip of the screen, but the offside blade, which curves with the screen edge, lifts too readily and leaves a blurred view in rain or spray from about 70 m.p.h. upwards. In a cross-wind the critical speed may be lower. Vision through the flatter central area of the screen is kept clear up to higher speeds.

The heating and fresh air system has been altered in detail. A pair of levers in vertical quadrants control the volume of fresh air and the degree of heat. In addition there are two hinged flaps under the scuttle which must be shut to obtain full air delivery to the screen. A quiet, two-speed fan placed behind the near-side front wheel, in effect balancing the engine air filter on the offside, provides a reasonable blast, but mainly through the central slits at the base of the screen. More flow still needs to be diverted to the sides of the screen to keep them clear. Built-in electric demisting for the rear window is optional.

E-type Jaguars, of course, are two-seaters with no practical possibility of squeezing in a third person. Luggage space is rather limited, but two suitcases can be laid on the wide platform under the sloping rear roof and other soft luggage tucked around them. If luggage is to be stacked higher, retaining straps would be needed and rear vision would be lost. Loading is quite easy through the large rear door, which has a stay and a prominent latch with a safety catch, operated from inside the car.

Covering the luggage shelf is plastic-topped carpeting properly bound and with rubbing strips attached to it. Press fasteners hold a large, square section beneath which is a wooden floor panel covering the spare wheel recess. Rolls of tools lie in the wheel.

Interior safety has been watched; there are anchorage points for safety straps, the steering wheel is sprung and flat, the vizors are of soft padded felt and the rear-view mirror has a metal frame; the edge of the coaming is softer and rounder and there are padded rolls round the door openings. The only sharp projections we would like altered are the heater and air control levers. A grab handle is provided for the passenger. The quality of the fittings, and of the finish both inside and out, is mainly high.

Like other Jaguars this E-type coupé represents outstanding value for money. It is obviously built for a special kind of motoring and its tremendous, effortless performance, with which slow speed docility is also combined, is for the connoisseur of grand touring.

Specification

Scale: 0·3in. to 1ft.

Cushions uncompressed.

ENGINE
Cylinders	...	6 in-line
Bore	...	87mm (3·43in.)
Stroke	...	106mm (4·17in.)
Displacement	...	3,781 c.c. (230·6 cu. in.)
Valve gear	...	Twin overhead camshafts
Compression ratio		9·0 to 1

OVERALL LENGTH 14' 7·3"
OVERALL WIDTH 5' 5·25"
19", 49", 6·5", 49", 38·5", 35", 39"
26·5-28·5"
28"
29"

OVERALL HEIGHT 4' 0·1"
38"
24"
30·5"
13·5-21", 22-25·5", 9·5", 39·5", 49"
5·5"
15-20", 26"
10"
GROUND CLEARANCE 5·5"
WHEELBASE 8' 0"
FRONT TRACK 4' 2"
REAR TRACK 4' 2"

Carburettors	...	Three 2in. S.U. HD8; manual controlled cold starting
Fuel pump	...	Lucas Type 2FP, submerged in tank
Oil filter	...	Tecalemit full-flow
Max. power	...	265 b.h.p. (gross) at 5,500 r.p.m.
Max. torque	...	260 lb. ft. at 4,000 r.p.m.

TRANSMISSION
Clutch	...	Borg and Beck single dry plate, 10·0in. dia.
Gearbox	...	Four speed, synchromesh on upper three ratios. Central floor-mounted lever.

Overall ratios	...	Top 3·07, 3rd 3·93, 2nd 5·71, 1st and reverse 10·38
Final drive	...	Hypoid bevel, ratio 3·07 to 1. Powrlok limited slip differential

CHASSIS
Construction	...	Monocoque stressed steel body

SUSPENSION
Front	...	Independent wishbones and torsion bars with Girling gas-cell telescopic dampers
Rear	...	Independent; lower wishbones and fixed length drive shafts, longitudinal radius arms. Twin coil spring and Girling gas-cell telescopic dampers at each side
Steering	...	Alford and Alder rack and pinion. Wheel dia. 16in.

BRAKES
Type	...	Dunlop discs, outboard F, inboard R, with Kelsey-Hayes vacuum servo. Separate hydraulic circuits F and R.
Disc diameter	...	11·0in. F, 10·0in. R.
Swept area	...	461 sq. in. total (370 sq. in per ton laden)

WHEELS
Type	...	Centre-lock, wire-spoked, 5·0in. wide rim
Tyres	...	6·40—15in. Dunlop RS5 with tubes

EQUIPMENT
Battery	...	12-volt 57-amp. hr.
Headlamps	...	Lucas, 60-60 watt
Reversing lamp	...	1 standard
Electric fuses	...	10
Screen wipers	...	Triple blades, two-speed, self-parking
Screen washer	...	Standard, Lucas electric
Interior heater	...	Standard, fresh air with two-speed booster
Safety belts	...	Extra, anchorages provided
Interior trim	...	Leather seats, cloth roof lining
Floor covering	...	Pile carpet, felt underlay
Starting handle	...	No provision
Jack	...	Manual screw type
Jacking points	...	Central each side
Other bodies	...	Open Roadster

MAINTENANCE
Fuel tank	...	14 Imp. gallons (no reserve)
Cooling system	...	32 pints (including heater)
Engine sump	...	15 pints SAE 30 (summer), SAE 20 (winter). Change oil every 2,500 miles; change filter element every 5,000 miles
Gearbox	...	2·5 pints SAE 30. Change oil every 10,000 miles
Final drive	...	2·75 pints SAE 90. Change oil every 10,000 miles
Grease	...	9 points every 2,500 miles
Tyre pressures	...	F. 25; R. 30 p.s.i. (normal driving up to 120 m.p.h.). F. 35; R. 40 p.s.i. (fast driving)

JAGUAR "E" TYPE

EVERY SO OFTEN one comes across a car which is so superior to the others in so many respects that it provides a kind of motoring of which few people, but for a fortunate minority, have ever dreamed. Such a car is the Jaguar "E" type; certainly one of the fastest series-production cars ever built, equally certainly one of the safest, and quite possibly one of the finest. The car will cruise effortlessly at a speed far greater than that achieved by the ordinary car when absolutely flat out: its acceleration is almost astonishing, its roadholding faultless and its brakes smooth, progressive and powerful. Yet for all this colossal performance, it remains a quiet, refined car: it possesses that "small" feeling which only the really good big cars have.

It need scarcely be said that the power unit for this superb car is the six-cylinder, twin overhead-camshaft unit of 3,781 c.c. which has powered so many fine Jaguars: for the "E"-type it breathes through three huge S.U. carburettors, and develops 265 b.h.p. This big, lusty engine is smooth and effortless, as well as being practically inaudible at all speeds: only when the car is travelling at something over 130 m.p.h. does it make its presence felt. The engine always started easily throughout the test, with no signs of "temperament": it is flexible, allowing town driving in top gear at speeds down to around 25 m.p.h., while the exhaust note is quiet and unobtrusive, even outside the car. Idling is smooth, silent and reliable.

It is rather difficult to find fault with this splendid car, but a feature which does not perhaps measure up to the high standard of the rest of the machine is the gearbox.

The ratios are well-chosen, but the lever movement is rather long and the change itself very slow: weak synchromesh does not assist matters, and the acceleration of the car suffers if one is concerned with clean gear changes. Downward changes require double declutching with a very precise judgment of engine speed. The box is,

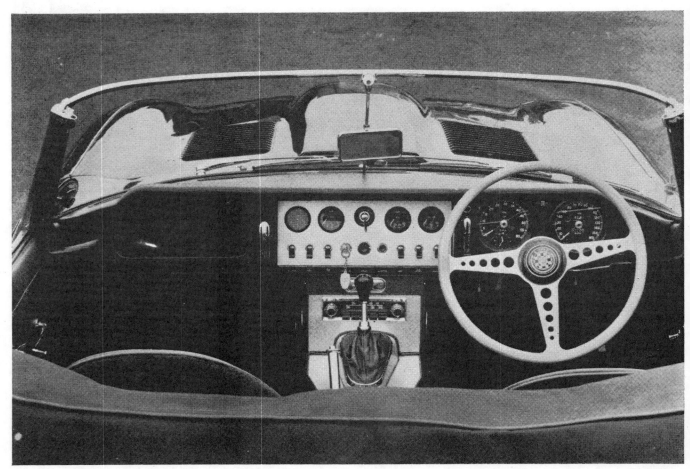

however, quiet in operation, and engagement of first gear from rest is always easy, although no synchromesh is employed on this gear. The clutch is light and progressive, with no fierceness as it takes up the drive positively and surely.

The "E" type's all independent suspension is of the well-known Jaguar pattern, with semi-trailing wishbones and coil springs enclosing telescopic dampers at the front: stub axles and carriers are carried on widely-spaced, self-adjusting ball joints. Rear suspension is also fully-independent, transverse location of the rear wheels being achieved by means of two tubular links, of which the upper link is the half-shaft; the suspension medium is twin coil springs, mounted on either side of the differential casing.

This provides a smooth ride, ironing out all bumps yet retaining sufficient stiffness to prevent rolling and pitching on uneven surfaces, and providing the driver with a feel of the road which is essential in a car with such glorious performance.

The interior is less "plush" than in the saloon Jaguars, yet retains and multiplies the impression of being definitely a driver's car. The steering is precise and lighter than we have

found on other, non-power assisted Jaguars: it provides a pleasant and direct control over the car's movement, and the wheel is free from road shocks. The seats, of bucket type, do a perfect job of positioning driver and passenger, and although some passengers complained of discomfort, arising from a seam in the upholstery across the small of the back, the writer found no fault with them at all. The pedals are well-placed, making heel-and-toe gear-changing easy, and all three pedals are light to operate. With plenty of adjustment in the seats fore-and-aft range, and with a steering wheel which is adjustable vertically as well as fore-and-aft, an ideal driving position can be found. Instrumentation is full, the rev. counter and matching speedometer—which reads to 160 m.p.h.—being set immediately in front of the driver. In a panel in the centre of the dashboard are located oil pressure, fuel contents and water temperature gauges and an ammeter, with hand controls and switches placed below them in usual Jaguar style. All the instruments are easy to rear, and have steady, well-damped needles. The speedometer is remarkably and unusually accurate except at the upper end of the scale, where it is actually slow.

All-round visibility from the driving seat is good, with no blind spots in front or at the sides. Rearwards, however, the gentle slope of the coupé's rear window causes some distortion to be reflected in the mirror, which in fact "looks" only through the upper few inches of the window. Relocating the mirror lower down would improve this, but rearward vision might then be impeded by luggage in the boot. The test car had covered some 14,000 miles at the start of our test, and remained rattle-free and watertight throughout. The body has a sleek, exciting appearance which, although the model has been seen on the roads for some time, continues to cause crowds of admiring spectators to gather wherever it is parked.

Following the Jaguar tradition, Dunlop disc brakes on all four wheels are assisted by a powerful servo, giving extreme lightness of operation of the pedal. Their performance is well up to that of the car, and extremely fast motoring can be enjoyed with complete confidence in the car's ability to stop as well as to go.

When one considers the performance, one must be prepared to set new standards. The car's mean maximum speed was timed at 149.8 m.p.h., and

for less-skilled motorists to be shy of it, and one's wife could take it shopping and find that it behaves in a docile and altogether gentlemanly manner. On the open road, it is one of the least tiring cars for fast cruising: with the 3.07 final drive ratio fitted to the test car, 100 m.p.h. is achieved at an effortless 3,800 r.p.m., and this can be maintained for as long as road conditions permit with surprisingly little wind noise and practically no fuss from the power unit.

All this, however, can be expected from a Jaguar: the really surprising aspect of the car is its economical running. During the period it was in our hands it covered over 1,100 miles, including day-to-day commuting, thick traffic, high-speed cruising on the open road, with full use of the acceleration and, of course, the always thirsty business of taking performance figures. The overall fuel consumption worked out at just 22 m.p.g., or little worse than a medium-sized family saloon under the same conditions.

For night driving, the headlights are powerful, combining beam and spread to permit fast motoring after dark, while in wet weather the triple windscreen wipers clear a wide area of the windscreen. The car's own airstream keeps the shallow rear window clear, and visibility is almost unimpaired. Heating and demisting equipment is powerful, while fresh-air ventilation in the car in warm weather is easily arranged individually for driver and passenger. Luggage space on the fixed-head coupé is generous, and access is easily gained through the opening rear panel of the car. The space can be illuminated at night.

in one direction 150 m.p.h. was exceeded, although this, in fact, caused the needle of the rev. counter to edge its way into the "red". If full acceleration is used, considerable delicacy in the use of the clutch is required if wheelspin is not to leave long black marks on the road from a standing start. On the move, the car's acceleration is equally impressive: third gear will encompass well over 100 m.p.h., while even in top the manner in which the car goes on accelerating up to around 140 m.p.h. causes surprised comment from even experienced passengers. With such acceleration and third gear performance, overtaking can be carried out almost as though the obstacle was not there, while the speed with which one can return to the "home" side of the centre of the road is a valuable safety feature. On wet roads, one must be careful to remember that the right foot can release a great deal of power, but provided common sense is used no problems arise: there is absolutely nothing "savage" about the "E"-type.

Roadholding is excellent, although the car is somewhat sensitive to tyre pressures. Using the Jaguar recommended pressures for high-speed driving, however, the car is endowed with just the right amount of understeer, while there is plenty of power

available for steering with the throttle. Directional stability is without fault, even at very high speeds, and the car can be driven "hands-off" at around 140 m.p.h. without deviating from its chosen path. On corners, it adheres to its line like a thoroughbred. Obviously, this is very much a car for the experienced driver: unlike many cars of similar type, however, there is no reason

SPECIFICATION AND PERFORMANCE DATA

Jaguar "E" type fixed-head coupé. Price: £1,583, plus £330 7s. 1d. purchase tax=£1,913 7s. 1d.

Engine: Six cylinders, 87 mm. × 106 mm. (3,781 c.c.). Compression ratio: 9 : 1; 265 b.h.p. at 5,500 r.p.m. Triple S.U. carburettors. Twin overhead-camshafts.

Transmission: Four-speed and reverse gearbox with synchromesh on upper three forward ratios and central floor-mounted control.

Suspension: Front, independent with semi-trailing wishbones and coil-spring damper units. Rear, independent, with transverse tubular links and twin coil springs. Tyres: 7.50 × 14.

Brakes: Dunlop disc brakes on all four wheels with servo assistance.

Equipment: 12-volt lighting and start-

ing. Self-parking, two-speed windscreen wipers. Electric windscreen washers. Speedometer, rev. counter, oil pressure, fuel contents and water temperature gauges, ammeter. Electric clock. Cigar lighter. Headlamp flasher unit. Flashing direction indicators. Built-in reversing light. Map-reading lamp. Heating, demisting and ventilating equipment, with separate ducts to front seats. Combined brake fluid and hand-brake warning light. Radio.

Performance: Maximum speed 149.8 m.p.h. mean; 151.2 m.p.h. best one-way speed. Speeds in gears (at 5,500 r.p.m.): 1st, 40 m.p.h.; 2nd, 72 m.p.h.; 3rd, 108 m.p.h. Acceleration: 0–30, 3.0 sec.; 0–40, 4.0 sec.; 0–50, 5.9 sec.; 0–60, 7.5 sec.; 0–70, 9.3 sec.; 0–80, 12.3 sec.; 0–90, 14.5 sec.; 0–100, 17.6 sec.; 0–110, 21.2 sec. Standing quarter mile: 15.4 sec. Fuel consumption: 22 m.p.g.

JAGUAR

E

TYPE

LIFE with an E-type Jaguar is just one long, hard shove in the back — even after you change up into top (at 111 m.p.h.) and push close to 150.

The test car had the now standard (unless otherwise specified) 3.07:1 back axle. There were, of course, obvious limitations to this test: road space, and my ability to deal with power in quantities I'd not before experienced.

The picture you'll get is what the average sort of driver would be able to do with a sports car that knows no peer except for the Ferrari 250 GTO. But the GTO is not a car that anybody with the money can buy off the showroom floor.

The incredible thing about the E-type's mechanics is not that the 3781c.c., twin o.h.c. six-cylinder engine can produce 265 b.h.p. at a modest 5500 r.p.m. on an equally modest 9:1 compression: It is that this is basically an engine designed in 1948, which first appeared in the XK120. In between, it has powered the D-types to a record number of victories in the Le Mans 24-hour classic — and the damn thing's still going in company with the best.

But don't get the idea that there's anything unmannerly about this machine. Jaguar simply label it a Grand Touring car — meaning that it is not only fast, safe and properly equipped, but also meant to be driven on ordinary roads and in ordinary traffic conditions without getting awkward. And the E-type lives up to this claim:

● It will walk off 10 m.p.h. in top gear without ticking a tappet; and do it without so much as a suspicion of a hiccup from its three SU carbies.

● It doesn't ping or snatch — and it doesn't get half as hot and bothered in a traffic crawl as I do.

● Then, look at the performance at the other end: it's just as happy at 140-150 m.p.h.

Who dares say that racing doesn't improve the breed?

Sure, there are people who say

Tops on speed-for-money basis, the sensational E-type Jaguar coupe has more power than most people would ever use, great handling—and a few shortcomings, reports Bryan Hanrahan

this sort of speed is crazy. They would be right if their brand of motor-car had E-type power and they abused that power.

Under the right conditions of road and traffic, I felt safer in the Jag in the early hundreds than I've felt in many cars at fifty. I will confess that I got a bit nervous when the tacho needle began to nudge the 5000 mark in top — but I'm not used to piloting a personal rocket.

The car will give over 150 m.p.h. with the new higher axle ratio (old one was 3.31:1, and the engine was well past peak revs before you got to 150 on the speedo), but the problem's to find the road for this sort of travel. Best I could cater for was 148.2 m.p.h. It is a bit academic, of course, to worry about a leeway of 5 or 6 m.p.h. in 150.

I have been told by people who know that my acceleration figures are not bad for a mug road-tester. The experts can sneak up to a fifth of a second some places, they say.

Much-improved Brakes

The big changes in the model now on sale are the back axle (helps a lot to keep the car quiet at high speed: top gear now gives 24.4 m.p.h. per 1000 revs instead of 22.9) and the brakes.

The higher axle also helps fuel consumption. Over the 140 miles of our test, this was a very modest 19.1 m.p.g. — and with 14 gallons in the tank, that's not much short of 300 miles with hard driving.

Earlier models had a much-too-fierce brake action at low speeds, yet needed a diving boot to get any effect at the top end of the speed range. In other words, the worst features of disc brakes were emphasised.

Layout is the same — outboard discs up front and inboard at the back — still with a servo unit, but now with a sort of two-stage effect. The manifold-vacuum-aspirated

unit is made by Kelsey-Hayes. So far as I can find out, it doesn't produce full effort when the brake pedal trips the valve, as do all normal units of this type. Instead, it gives low power at low revs and high power at high revs.

The pedal linkage has also been revised, to afford a little more mechanical aid for the leg muscles.

However hard I put the brakes on at speed (and this was as hard as I dared), those four sets of pads gripped the steel discs absolutely evenly. You never had to back off the pedal to stop the car crabbing —it just put its nose down and kept right on line.

Fade? — not a trace.

These Dunlop brakes are also self-adjusting. Apart from cutting out the need for adjustment at all wheels, they allow the handbrake a better go. With non-self-adjusting discs you only had to use the handbrake a dozen or so times, and the pads would no longer engage the discs: this meant re-setting the back pads.

There are, of course, twin master-cylinders, giving independent front and back braking systems. A dash warning lamp lights up if the brake-fluid level falls low.

Another mechanical mod is the engine fan: The belt-driven type has been superseded by an electrically-driven fan, thermostatically controlled. This saves power and, again, cuts down noise, because it only works when the engine needs cooling air.

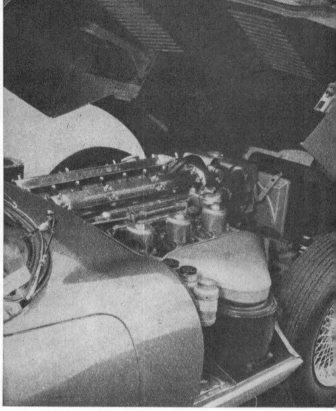

CONTROLS *could not be better laid out or labelled. However, the gearlever to the poorly synchronised four-speed box requires lon throw.*

MASSIVE *twin-cam engine is fed by three big SU carburettors. Fat aircleaner helps to crowd things but bonnet opening provides reasonable access.*

More body insulation is used, which cuts down both noise and heat inside the car. You can still hear the engine and gearbox when they're stirred up — but what else would you expect in a GT car of this kind?

Controls and Handling

The rack-and-pinion steering can't be considered separately from the handling — it is part of the car's near-perfect progress.

No conscious effort is needed at the wheel, and it's delightfully quick at 2.6 turns lock-to-lock. Sounds as if it could be oversensitive, but it isn't. The car seems to know where to go.

Suspension on test was set up to be dead neutral. In this condition it was possible on a fast corner to cut off the power, or even hit the brakes, with no more effect than causing the car to run slightly wide. Perhaps this is the Jag's most fantastic characteristic.

But she handles best with power on, out of a corner; and she is also sensitive to wheelspin up to speeds at which you'd imagine it would be impossible.

Any spin, of course, is equally distributed between the back wheels by the Powr-Lok limited-slip differential. Likewise, you get even power through any corner.

The ride is softish, even at low speeds. The independent back end allows this, while still sticking hard to the road in cornering attitudes.

You get a fair idea of the Jag's performance if you realise that for overtaking purposes it will get up to 100 m.p.h. from rest, in only a few hundred yards and in less than 16 seconds, speed at the end of a flying quarter-mile is almost bang on 90 m.p.h.

A share of the credit for this must go to the RS5 Dunlop tyres. They are round-shouldered, quiet in most antics —and whether it's acceleration or deceleration you want, the grip on the road is terrific.

I used 35lb. pressure in the front tyres and 40lb. at the back (as recommended) for the speed tests: Normal — and much more comfortable — pressures are 25lb. front, 30lb. back.

The two worst features of the car, are the clutch and gear change.

The clutch pedal is set very high

MAIN SPECIFICATIONS

ENGINE: 6 cylinders, d.o.h.c.; bore 87mm., stroke 106mm., capacity 3781c.c.; compression ratio 9:1; maximum b.h.p. 265 (gross) at 5500 r.p.m.; maximum torque 260lb./ft. at 4000 r.p.m.; triple SU carburettors, electric fuel pump; 12 volt ignition.

TRANSMISSION: Single dry-plate clutch; four-speed gearbox with synchromesh on upper three; ratios, 1st, 10.38; 2nd, 5.71; 3rd, 3.93; top 3.07; final drive 3.07:1.

SUSPENSION: Independent all round by coils with wishbones at the front and lower transverse tubular links at rear. Telescopic shockers all round.

STEERING: Rack and pinion; 2½ turns lock to lock, 37ft. turning circle.

WHEELS: Centre lock wire type with 6.40 by 15in. tyres.

BRAKES: Hydraulically actuated discs all round, servo assisted; 461 sq. in. of swept area.

DIMENSIONS: Wheelbase, 8ft. 0in.; track, front and rear, 4ft. 2in.; length, 14ft. 7½in.; width, 5ft. 5½in.; height, 4ft. 01/8in.; ground clearance, 5½in.

KERB WEIGHT: 23½cwt.

FUEL TANK: 14 gallons.

PERFORMANCE ON TEST

CONDITIONS: Fine and cool with cross breeze; two occupants, premium fuel.

MAXIMUM SPEED: 142.3 m.p.h.

BEST SPEED: 148.2 m.p.h.

STANDING quarter mile: 15.3s.

MAXIMUM in indirect gears: 1st 43 m.p.h.; 2nd 75 m.p.h.; 3rd 111 m.p.h.

ACCELERATION from rest through gears: 0-30, 2.6s.; 0-40, 3.7s.; 0-50, 5.5s.; 0-60, 7.1s.; 0-70, 9.0s.; 0-80, 12s.; 0-90, 15.2s.; 0-100, 17.8s.; 0-110, 22.5s.; 0-120, 30.0s.; 0-130, 37.1s.

ACCELERATION in top (with third in brackets): 20-40, 7.4s. (5.8s.); 30-50, 7.1s. (5.3s.); 40-60, 7.2s. (5.3s.); 50-70, 7.9s. (5.5s.); 60-80, 7.8s. (5.8s.); 70-90, 8.1s. (6.0s.); 80-100, 7.9s. (5.8s.).

ACCELERATION in second gear (with first in brackets): 20-40, 3.8s. (2.3s.); 30-50, 3.6s.; 40-60, 3.5s.; 50-70, 3.8s.

BRAKING: 30ft. 2in. to stop from 30 m.p.h. in neutral.

FUEL CONSUMPTION: 19.1 m.p.g. over 140 miles.

SPEEDO: accurate throughout range.

PRICE: £3380 including tax

off the toe-board, and needs hefty legwork. Travel is very long.

Best accelerative results are to be had by letting it in at about 2200 revs. It slips a bit, and soon gets to smelling, but I must say that it didn't show any signs of packing up.

The gear-change — in the manner of all Jaguar changes — is abominable. The synchro is slow and crunchy, particularly going into second gear.

There's no synchro on first, which also makes a terrible racket.

Nearly always, first is very hard to select from neutral; second is often difficult, too. Reverse is too close to first, and so badly protected by a weak spring that you can easily find yourself in backward trim instead of forward.

You don't need a great deal of imagination to realise what can happen if 265 b.h.p. start to propel you in the wrong direction.

These two things are appalling, when you think that the car has been in production for well over two years.

Other Points

I have no complaints about the interior economy, except that the brake pedal is much higher than the accelerator. It is very hard to heel-and-toe, and it's a long foot movement from accelerator to brake.

The body and chassis are something of a minor miracle. Ready for the road, fully watered and fuelled, the car weighed in at 24 cwt. — that's a bit over 220 b.h.p. per ton. The secret is in the monocoque construction, based on a rigid pan at the bottom.

However much you may like the lines, they were not developed to tickle a rich man's fancy: a wind tunnel decided them. As a result, the car is quiet enough for normal conversation at around the century mark.

Superb comfort is provided for two people. Seats are firm and give good support. Layout of instruments and minor controls could hardly be better. The adjustable wheel is set just right, and the fly-off handbrake is mounted handily on the transmission tunnel.

The space behind the back seats is strictly for parcels, or a couple of flattish suitcases. There's plenty of depth — but if you use it, you block your backward vision. I personally would prefer not to break the beautiful body line with an outside mirror.

The big, sideways-opening back door is not very handy in a breeze.

All-round vision is good, even through the steeply sloping back window. The rear-vision mirror blocks out too much of the screen — it should be mounted on the dash.

Finish is good. Seats are faced with leather, and there's good-quality carpet on the floor. Both heating and ventilation are efficient, but the demister doesn't clear the outer edges of the screen.

This is rather odd when triple-blade, two-speed wipers are fitted outside to cover the biggest possible glass area. Incidentally, the blade in front of the driver is inclined to lift off the curved glass at around 60 m.p.h.

Headlights have terrific penetration and spread, but cut off rather abruptly. I suppose the ideal would be to have some auxiliary medium-range lamps, because you can use all the penetration you can get. Problem, though, is where to mount them.

A fragile little reversing lamp, set right above the exhaust tailpipes, is now standard equipment. It's not very bright — and neither was the bloke who decided to put it there.

Minor acrobatics are needed to get in and out — but who would care?

There's only one thing you care about when you get hold of a car like this — hanging on to it until you're forced to give it back. A lot of detail improvements could be made, but as I said just now, who would care if they weren't? ●

CONTINUED FROM PAGE 43
eliminated on Esso Golden and the fantastic performance still further enhanced. Jaguar saw no reason to fit new tyres, change the sump or replace the brake-pads after this tough 2,000 miles. A check on fuel consumption showed this to be an overall 17.6 m.p.g., which is excellent for a very hard-driven 3,781-c.c. engine. In the 1,060 miles since the crack in the sump had been repaired 9 pints of oil were required to replenish the level, equal to 920 m.p.g.

At the Coventry factory the E-types are line-assembled in a separate shop, from which they emerge at the rate of 150 a week. Every Jaguar engine is bench-tested, after which the sump is dropped for inspection of the bearings, and as aforementioned the hoods are individually tailored. A slave hard-top is applied to every body to ensure a sound fit should one be ordered subsequently. Every Jaguar is road-tested before final inspection, some 35 test drivers being employed on these tests.

The Jaguar is a splendid example of good Coventry workmanship and the E-type is in every way an outstanding example of the highest conception of British race-bred sports car. Although its performance, acceleration and speed-wise, naturally constitutes its primary attraction, its astonishing docility, the more surprising because it is unexpected, the comfort allied to stability of the suspension, the excellent brakes and its eye-able appearance combine to make the Jaguar E-type one of the World's great motor cars.

We would dearly like one, not only for getting effortlessly and very quickly about Europe, but for shopping and going to the post, especially when only a few minutes remain before the last collection!

Following its return from Coventry the E-type remained in our hands for some days longer, covering in all 2,800 miles without incident or further trouble of any kind. Used as transport to Mallory Park on Whit-Monday, the Jaguar cruised up M 1 very comfortably at 4,800 r.p.m. (117 m.p.h.) and held 6,000 r.p.m. (153 m.p.h.) for a mile, although taking a considerable distance to attain this impressive maximum speed. On the return run an average speed of 104 m.p.h. was achieved for the full length of the Motorway, during which, according to a log kept by the passenger, over 900 cars, all but one keeping to their own lanes, were overtaken—but by then the Editor was rolling quietly about the Hampshire lanes in a Rover 80! During this further mileage another 6 pints of oil had to be added to the engine, and at the conclusion of the test the tyres were pretty well due for replacement.

One matter completely baffles us. Insurance brokers cannot be unintelligent, for it takes intelligence, allied perhaps to a certain low cunning, to make oodles of money and the insurance business makes it all right—just look at the " marble halls " from which they issue policies and the liveried commissionaires who guard their portals. How then, as intelligent beings, can they demand high premiums to insure that " dangerous " car, the Jaguar E-type. I can only conclude that they have never seriously driven one. For no car could be safer, more docile, instil greater confidence, than this stupendously clever 150-m.p.h. Jaguar, that is priced so modestly.—W. B.

JAGUAR XK-E

"The greatest crumpet collector known to man"

ALTHOUGH IT CAN be criticized from certain aspects, the Jaguar XK-E is among the very few really exciting cars on the market at the present time and, at less than $6000, it represents an amazing amount of car for the money. This, of course, is the history of the Jaguar Company from the earliest SS days, and the XK-E certainly upholds the long tradition.

The car is available either as a coupe or as a roadster with removable hardtop, and we chose the coupe for our test car. Opinions differ regarding the general appearance of the car, but it is certainly striking from any angle, particularly from the rear. Unfortunately, the body design makes it most vulnerable and no attempt has been made to fit anything other than minimal bumpers which are more decorative than functional. In keeping with Jaguar's policy, considerable attention has been paid to the appearance of the engine compartment, which features polished valve covers and a touch of chrome here and there. The right side of the engine is dominated by three 2-in. SU carburetors of the diaphragm type, and it is pleasant to notice that a manual choke is used rather than the electric starting carburetor that was always a potential source of grief to XK-120 owners. Another improvement is the electric radiator fan, which should eliminate any tendency toward overheating.

The engine is the tried and true Jaguar unit which first appeared 15 years ago in the original XK-120. At that time, the power output was 160 bhp and this has gradually been raised to the 265 bhp of the "E" type. To obtain the additional 105 bhp, the capacity of the engine has been increased from 3.4 liters to 3.8 liters by boring, the valve size has been increased and the timing altered, the compression ratio has been stepped up from 8:1 to 9:1, and the number and size of carburetors increased from two 1¾-in. SUs to three 2-in. SUs. These are the major steps and, surprisingly enough, the extreme docility which was such a characteristic of the XK-120 remains unimpaired and the car has a top gear performance more in keeping with a big V-8. Critics of the Jaguar are inclined to say that the company needs a new engine, but it must be remembered that this power unit was an extremely advanced design when it was introduced and it incorporated all the goodies which are normally only associated with pure racing engines. Among the more important features is the crankshaft, which is held in seven main bearings to provide extreme rigidity, and the twin overhead camshafts, which permit a hemispherical combustion chamber. At 4.17 in., the stroke is comparatively long by today's standards but it does help the low-speed torque of the engine and also permits an efficient combustion chamber shape with the 9:1 compression ratio.

If Jaguar does not need a new engine, it certainly does need a new transmission, because the present unit is totally archaic by today's standards. In 1964 one can expect synchromesh on first in a $6000 car and, furthermore, one can expect synchromesh that really synchronizes on the other three, but in the case of the Jaguar, this is not so. However, as far as first is concerned, it is only a starting gear and second will do the job as long as the car is rolling.

With the exception of the transmission, the Jaguar is basically a very advanced piece of engineering. The steel body is of monocoque construction with a front subframe of box section to support the engine and front suspension. The rear suspension is independent, giving a very soft ride by sports car standards, and also exceptional adhesion under all conditions. In the past, one has tended to approach independent rear suspension with some trepidation because it has usually been associated with rear engines and swing axles, which can so easily lead to disaster under certain conditions. However, the Jag design gives no cause for alarm at any time, and is a fine example of the handling qualities to be expected from a good IRS layout.

Jaguar was one of the first companies to use disc brakes on all four wheels and, if one or two problems were encountered to start with, these have now been eliminated to the extent that the Dunlop brakes on the XK-E are as good as any brakes we have ever encountered. A bellows type servo is used on the brake pedal, and twin master cylinders permit two entirely separate hydraulic systems to the front and rear brakes. The pedal requires firm but not excessive pressure, the action is progressive, and the brakes and suspension system complement each other under all conditions.

In keeping with the brakes and suspension, the steering cannot be faulted although it is inclined to be heavy by today's standards around town. However, it is positive and with plenty of feel throughout the speed range.

The interior and seating position have been altered since the car was first introduced, with a considerable improvement in driving comfort. The car is still hard to get in and out of, but there is sufficient adjustment on both the seat and the steering wheel to accommodate all shapes and sizes of drivers. Strangely enough, we found the driver's seat to be considerably more comfortable than the passenger's, and we can only assume that this was due to a "breaking in" process which it had undergone during the 6000 miles the car had been driven.

The Jaguar is a complex automobile, and therefore difficult and expensive to service, and the prospective purchaser would be well advised to bear this in mind before putting his money down. The factory is well aware of the service problem confronting it in the American market, and has always strived to build up efficient and well-trained service

Hood, and grille guard, barely clear ground when open.

Luggage is protected against damage from rear lid hinges.

organizations throughout the country. However, one feels that Jaguar itself has on occasions compounded the problem by launching a new model on the market before it has been thoroughly tested under American conditions. A case in point is the 2.4 and the early 3.4 sedans, both of which left a lot to be desired when first marketed, and both of which had to be modified to some extent before any degree of reliability was achieved.

We receive a considerable amount of correspondence

JAGUAR XK-E

AT A GLANCE...

Price as tested	$5908
Engine	6 cyl, dohc, 3781 cc, 265 bhp
Curb weight, lb	2900
Top speed, mph	150 (mfr)
Acceleration, 0-60 mph, sec	7.4
Passing test, 50-70 mph, sec	4.4
Overall fuel consumption, mpg	17

Driver comfort has been improved considerably.

Beauty is more than skin deep—and it's well proven.

JAGUAR XK-E

from owners of all types of car, but a preponderance of letters from Jaguar owners concern the problem and expense of servicing their cars. At $6000, the "E" type is within the reach of a surprising number of people but, because of the complex nature of the car, potential owners should make sure that there is still some money left after making their monthly payments to pay for routine servicing and repairs. This is particularly true when buying a used car, which may be close to the point of needing a valve job, a clutch replacement or other major service operations.

The performance of the car on the road is nothing short of formidable. The maximum speed is nearly 150 mph, although circumstances prevented us from attaining this velocity, and it is in the higher speed ranges that the car really comes into its own. The standing ¼ mile was covered in 15.6 seconds (accompanied by audible complaint from the transmission), and while this is not an exceptional

time, the car had just got well into its stride at 90 mph when we crossed the line.

The appearance of the car and its potential performance give the impression that it would be difficult to drive. Actually, this is far from the case because it is a model of docility, tractability, easy starting and general good behavior, and well within the capabilities of the average woman driver. It is not the best vehicle for city traffic and it was not designed for that purpose but, once one gets out on the open road, the car immediately inspires confidence by its effortless handling and ability to maintain a high cruising speed. On the other hand, for the experienced sports car driver it is a wolf in sheep's clothing and a perfect tool for practicing the art of fast driving.

The Jaguar XK-E offers the ultimate in performance, matched by superb road holding and braking, at a remarkably low price. This has been achieved by very clever and advanced engineering, and the efficient limited mass production methods used at the factory. Since the introduction of the XK series, this is what the Jaguar owner has come to expect, and this is what he gets in the "E" type. 🐾

Interior appointments are well placed and easy to use.

Luggage compartment is spacious and accessible.

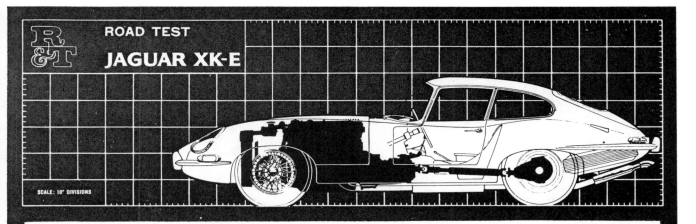

PRICE

List, West Coast POE......$5685
As tested, West Coast.....$5908

ENGINE

Engine, no. cyl, type......6 dohc
Bore x stroke, in......3.43 x 4.17
Displacement, cc..........3781
  Equivalent cu in........230.6
Compression ratio...........9:1
Bhp @ rpm.............265 @ 5500
  Equivalent mph...........130
Torque @ rpm, lb-ft..260 @ 4000
  Equivalent mph...........94.1
Carburetor, no., make.....3 SU
  No. barrels--diameter....1-2 in
Type fuel required......premium

DRIVE TRAIN

Clutch, diameter & type: 10 in.,
  single plate, dry
Gear ratios, 4th (1.00).......3.31
  3rd (1.28)...............4.25
  2nd (1.86)...............6.16
  1st (3.38)..............11.2
Synchromesh.........2, 3 and 4
Differential, ratio...........3.31
Optional ratios....2.93, 3.07, 3.54

CHASSIS & SUSPENSION

Frame type: Monocoque body with
  front subframe
Brake type..................disc
  Swept area, sq in..........461
Tire size & make..6.40 x 15 Dunlop
  Wheel revs/mi............770
Steering type.....rack and pinion
  Overall ratio.............n.a.
  Turns, lock to lock........2.6
  Turning circle, ft........37.0
Front suspension: Independent,
  with unequal-length A-arms and
  torsion bars.
Rear suspension: Independent with
  transverse links, radius arms, and
  coil springs.

ACCOMMODATION

Normal capacity, persons........2
Occasional capacity............2
Hip room, front, in........2 x 19
  Rear......................
Head room, front............36.5
  Rear......................
Seat back adjustment, deg...none
Entrance height, in..........44.5
Step-over height............16
Floor height.................8.5
Door width, front...........22

GENERAL

Curb weight, lb............2900
Test weight................3245
Weight distribution
  with driver, percent...47.4/52.6
Wheelbase, in..............96.0
Track, front/rear..........50
Overall length, in..........175
  Width....................65.2
  Height...................48.1
Frontal area, sq. ft........17.5
Ground clearance, in.......5.5
Overhang, front............37
  Rear.....................44
Departure angle, no load, deg.13.5
Usable trunk space, cu. ft....15.8
Fuel tank capacity, gal.......16.5

INSTRUMENTATION

Instruments: 160-mph speedometer, tachometer, clock, water
  temp, oil pressure, ammeter, fuel.
Warning lamps: parking brake,
  ignition, fuel, high beam, turn
  signals, choke.

MISCELLANEOUS

Body styles available: coupe as
  tested and roadster. (Removable
  hardtop also available.)

ACCESSORIES

Included in list price: wire wheels,
  heater, back-up lights, leather
  upholstery, cigar lighter, limited-
  slip differential.
Available at extra cost: chrome
  wire wheels, seat belts, grill
  guards, electric antenna, air
  conditioning, radio.

CALCULATED DATA

Lb/hp (test wt).............12.2
Cu ft/ton mi.................104
Mph/1000 rpm (4th).........23.6
Engine revs/mi.............2550
Piston travel, ft/mi........1770
Rpm @ 2500 ft/min.........3600
  Equivalent mph...........84.7
R & T wear index...........45.1

MAINTENANCE

Crankcase capacity, qt.........9
  Change interval, mi.......2500
Oil filter type...........full flow
  Change interval, mi......5000
Lubrication grease points.......9
Lube interval, mi..........2500
Tire pressures, front/rear,
  psi.....................25/30

ROAD TEST RESULTS

ACCELERATION

0-30 mph, sec.................2.9
0-40 mph.....................4.2
0-50 mph.....................5.7
0-60 mph.....................7.4
0-70 mph.....................9.4
0-80 mph....................12.2
0-100 mph...................19.0
Passing test, 50-70 mph..... 4.4
Standing ¼ mi, sec..........15.6
  Speed at end, mph.........91

BRAKE TESTS

Max deceleration, ft/sec/sec....27
  2nd stop..................26

FUEL CONSUMPTION

Normal range, mpg........14-20
Cruising range, mi.......231-330

TOP SPEEDS

High gear (6300), mph...150 (mfr)
  3rd (6000)...............110
  2nd (6000)................76
  1st (6000)...............42

GRADE CLIMBING

(Tapley Data)

4th gear, max gradient, %.....16.0
  3rd gear.................22.0
  2nd gear...........off scale

SPEEDOMETER ERROR

30 mph indicated.....actual 29.0
40 mph....................38.5
60 mph....................57.7
80 mph....................76.3
100 mph...................96.5

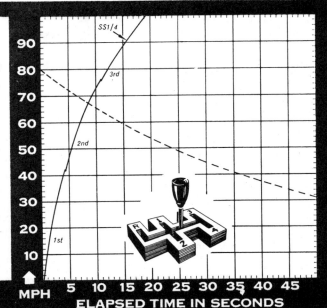

SLEEPING BEAUTY. The Jaguar E-type at rest beside a lake near Spa, Belgium.

Classic Moderns — No. 1

THE MAGIC OF AN E-TYPE

By GREGOR GRANT

SINCE the middle 1930s, when the SS90 was introduced, Jaguars have always produced a sporting two-seater. In the immediate pre-war period the SS100 had a large following, and this machine, with its six-cylinder 3½-litre engine and individual body styling with flared wings, has now become something of a collector's piece. After the war the name SS disappeared and the cars simply became known as Jaguars.

In 1948 the sensational XK 120 Jaguar appeared, with twin-o.h.c., 3½-litre engine. This car marked the end of an era during which the company had little or no interest in competitive motoring, and heralded the start of a policy which was to bring the name Jaguar into the headlines. Encouraged by the demand for a competition version of the XK 120, and by the many successes in the hands of private owners, notably by the late Leslie Johnson, the late Johnnie Claes, Stirling Moss in the Tom Wisdom-entered machine, and the original Ecurie Ecosse team, Sir William (then Mr.) Lyons instigated serious factory participation in international racing with the famous C-type. This car, in the hands of Peter Walker and the late Peter Whitehead, won the 1951 Le Mans 24-Hours race, at a record average speed of 93.5 m.p.h.

The C-type was an immense success, but was made completely obsolete in 1954 when Chief Engineer Bill Heynes and his men produced the fabulous D-type. This had the now well-proved engine stepped up to over 250 b.h.p., semi-monocoque construction and an entirely "new look" in body profile. With this car, Jaguars won Le Mans in 1955; and in 1956 and 1957 the D was again victorious, entered in both cases by Ecurie Ecosse.

Along with the competition cars were produced a splendid series of normal road two-seaters, the XK 140, the XK 150 and XK 150S models. Race-proved components were incorporated in the production cars, for example Dunlop disc brakes which had been pioneered by Jaguars, and rack-and-pinion steering.

In 1957 the extremely purposeful XK SS convertible was announced, based on the D-type and mainly intended as an ultra-high-performance Grand Touring machine. Unhappily, a disastrous fire all but destroyed the Jaguar factory, and in the need to produce more orthodox closed and XK models the XK SS series had reluctantly to be abandoned.

Nevertheless, the lessons of the D-type were not forgotten by Sir William Lyons, and there was quietly produced in the experimental section a car which is now known as the E-type. Many thousands of miles went into the testing of the new car, and when it was announced in 1961 in open and fixed-head coupé form the E created a tremendous sensation—not only because of its appearance and specification, but for its remarkably moderate price.

As a high-performance touring car there are few machines to equal the E-type, and none at all in its price bracket. Effortless is the correct word to describe it, for it is a real mile-eater and also one of the least-fatiguing cars to drive on the market at the present time. In addition, it carries prestige value, for it is regarded by the most discriminating customers as the best buy in its category which it is possible to acquire.

Having done a considerable mileage, both in this country and abroad, I feel that criticism of the E-type is both unjust and undeserved, and I fully believe that this stems from the opinions of the unknowledgeable, many of whom have never driven an E, far less been a passenger in one. Driven intelligently, it is easily one of the safest vehicles on the road: it has superb steering and road-holding, the brakes on the latest versions are as smooth and powerful as one could wish, and the acceleration is so vivid that overtaking can be done with the greatest confidence. As is usual with thoroughbreds, in the wrong hands the E-type can become a danger both to the inexperienced driver and, it follows, other road-users.

High average speeds are purely automatic with this Jaguar, and such is the potential performance that at no time is it necessary to use other than a fraction of the available horse-power. The absence of fuss is one of its major attractions, whether it be pottering around in traffic or cruising up the M1 at around two miles a minute. With the standard 3.31 to 1 axle fitted, this represents about 5,200 r.p.m. Maximum power is developed at "five-five", so there is plenty left!

One cannot drive an E-type without having at least one try to "see what she will do". The venue chosen was a splendid stretch of road between Le Mans and Angers, with little or no traffic around. I felt very guilty pushing the tachometer up to 6,200 r.p.m., but even at that rate the engine felt delightfully smooth. The speedometer needle was swinging towards its 160 m.p.h. stop, and at all times the car was as steady as a rock. True speed is getting on for 152 m.p.h., so the E-type is certainly no sluggard. I once tried an earlier model which was fitted with a 3.07 axle, but could not exceed 5,800 r.p.m. John Bolster, who first road-tested the car when it was announced, did a timed 148 m.p.h. with the 3.31 axle, but owing to side winds found that six-thou was not quite there.

One reason for the increase in maximum could be some extra b.h.p. due to the absence of an engine-driven fan, this now being dropped in favour of a thermostatically controlled electric unit. There have been detailed improvements in the engine itself during the past three years, not the least being the remarkable reduction in oil consumption. Over 2,000 miles of really rapid Continental motoring caused a scarcely measureable drop on the dipstick measure. I well recall a very early edition which used oil at the rate of 600 m.p.g.!

As regards the much-maligned gearbox, one learns to live with it, and becomes quite jaunty when a whole day's motoring caused a scarcely measurable single "s-scrunch" in the lower ratios. It is no box for the impatient driver, and the absence of synchromesh on bottom ratio is to be regretted—particularly on those unexpected hairpins in Alpine regions. The clutch is much lighter than before, but still requires a fairly long pedal travel before it disengages freely. On occasion, bottom and reverse gears are difficult to find.

Braking has been improved beyond all recognition, and the discs are as effective at low and medium speeds as they were the opposite on earlier models. The former excessive pedal pressure has been eliminated with the adoption of a bellows-pattern servo system, and one has not the slightest hesitation at using their maximum effort from high cruising speeds. The hand brake works really well, and will hold the car on the steepest of gradients.

Faced with a seemingly impossible average speed between Spa and Paris (Le Bourget), the Jaguar did it with plenty of time in hand. Parts of the route taken (via Bouillon) are very twisty indeed, but with the immense reserve of power, the immaculate handling and the effective all-independent springing, this was a truly enjoyable trip. Many British cars have trouble with the inevitable Peugeots and Citroëns, but the only thing that might live with the Jaguar would be another E-type or a sports-racing car. I did manage to have a brief tussle with a Ferrari Berlinetta, but just when it was getting interesting the man decided to fill up at a petrol station.

I cannot say that the E-type is the easiest of cars to get into—or out of for that matter. However, by increasing the travel of the seats, the manufacturers have finally acknowledged the existence of long-legged folk. The driving position is first-rate, and I did not hear any complaints from passengers. Instrumentation is restrained, yet very expensive-looking, and the air ventilation system receives full marks. The electrically heated rear window is a worthwhile fitment, and I understand that it is available as an extra at £19 8s. 9d.

The exhaust system is quieter than of yore, but this may be due to the noticeably improved sound-proofing in the interior. Nevertheless, these twin tail pipes are inclined to be troublesome, and the low-level silencers do ground on hump-backed bridges and on some of the ramps used on the Channel air-ferries. Anyway, no doubt Jaguar technicians have ideas of getting the system more out of harm's way.

The six-cylinder engine is undoubtedly one of the most reliable in-line power-units available. The E is fitted with three HD8 SU carburetters. Standard compression ratio is 9 to 1, but 8 to 1 is available if required.

Taking it by and large, the E-type Jaguar is a sound investment for the owner who prefers two-seater motoring, and, in the case of the fixed-head coupé, can carry a vast amount of luggage. It is remarkably economical for a machine with a 265 b.h.p., 3.8-litre engine, and after 2,000 miles of typical E-type motoring this worked out at rather better than 21 m.p.g. So with a 14-gallon tank there is quite a useful range. Really rapid motoring naturally pays its price in increased consumption, and can come down to around 14 m.p.g. if that pedal is pressed too far down for too long. Incidentally, even at over 100 m.p.h. on the motorways it is possible to listen to the radio—a tribute to the more efficient interior sound-proofing.

One can become rather tired of proffering the old cliché about how Jaguars can do it at the price, and so on. The value goes without saying, but the main consideration is that the E-type is a superb machine in its own right, and merely because Sir William Lyons and his associates decided to market it at a realistic price does not mean that there is any cheeseparing in its conception, or any lowering of engineering standards in order to produce it at a price. I unhesitatingly nominate the E-type Jaguar as an outstanding example of the classic modern motor-car, and a notable instance of how a planned motor racing programme can influence eventual production vehicles.

SNEAK VIEW. The purposeful-looking prototype E-type photographed by the Managing Editor at Silverstone in 1960 (above and below).

Number
42
MOTOR TESTED
3020
MILES

JAGUAR E-type 4·2

PRICE
£1,648 plus purchase tax of £344 17s. 11d. ·
equals £1,992 17s. 11d.

How they run ...

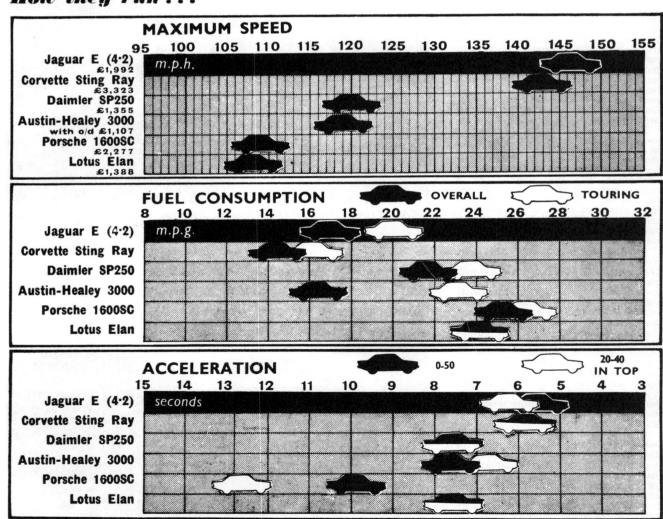

MAXIMUM SPEED

	95	100	105	110	115	120	125	130	135	140	145	150	155
Jaguar E (4·2) £1,992											145 (m.p.h.)		
Corvette Sting Ray £3,323										140			
Daimler SP250 £1,355						120							
Austin-Healey 3000 with o/d £1,107						120							
Porsche 1600SC £2,277				107									
Lotus Elan £1,388				107									

FUEL CONSUMPTION ● OVERALL ○ TOURING

	8	10	12	14	16	18	20	22	24	26	28	30	32
Jaguar E (4·2)					16 (m.p.g.)		20						
Corvette Sting Ray				14		18							
Daimler SP250								22	24				
Austin-Healey 3000					16				24				
Porsche 1600SC									24	26			
Lotus Elan									24	26			

ACCELERATION ● 0-50 ○ 20-40 IN TOP

	15	14	13	12	11	10	9	8	7	6	5	4	3
Jaguar E (4·2)									7 (seconds)	6			
Corvette Sting Ray									7	6			
Daimler SP250								8	7				
Austin-Healey 3000								8	7				
Porsche 1600SC		14				10							
Lotus Elan							9	8					

THERE have always been a handful of exotic cars built throughout the world which, by their very cost and scarcity, inspire a detached awe from ordinary mortals who cannot afford them. On every count but cost, the E-type would be an obvious choice for the current *corps d'elite* but at £2,000 it creates its own unique position among the world's desirable cars with a combination of performance, handling, looks and refinement that, even after 3½ years' production, is still unequalled at the price. Development of this remarkable vehicle has never stopped and numerous detail improvements have been made since its debut at the Geneva Show in March, 1961. Now, a bigger 4·2-litre engine, new all-synchromesh gearbox, better brakes and seats, and other details, mark the first major change; the latest car supplements, rather than replaces, the unaltered 3·8.

The new 4·2-litre supersedes the earlier 3·8 as the fastest car *Motor* has tested, with a mean maximum of exactly 150 m.p.h.; this marginal increase (less than 1 m.p.h.) stems from a higher axle ratio rather than more power, which remains at 265 b.h.p. (gross). The 10 per cent increase in capacity is reflected lower down the rev band by a corresponding increase in torque (from 240 to 283 lb. ft.) which, despite the higher gearing and greater weight, gives almost identical acceleration to our previous test car: with the lower (3·31 : 1) axle used before, there would be an appreciably greater strain on one's neck muscles which is severe enough now, 100 m.p.h. being reached from a standstill in well under 20 seconds. Using the lowest axle ratio, Americans will benefit from a better low-end performance while British and Continental buyers have improved steady-speed fuel consumption and even more relaxed cruising (100 m.p.h. corresponds to 4,060 r.p.m.) without any sacrifice in speed or acceleration.

The biggest improvement is the all-new, all-synchromesh gearbox. Gone is the tough, unrefined box that had accumulated a certain notoriety, in favour of one that will undoubtedly establish a correspondingly high reputation: although the lever movement is still quite long, it is fairly light and very quick, the synchromesh being unbeatable without being too obstructive. A good box by any standards and excellent for one that must transmit so much power.

Handling, steering and brakes are of such a high order that sensible drivers will never find the power/weight ratio of 220 b.h.p. per ton an embarrassment: indeed, this is one of those rare high-performance cars in which every ounce of power can be used on the road. The new seats are a big improvement but lack sufficient rake adjustment to make them perfect for all drivers. Nevertheless, 3,000 test miles (many of them on the

Continent) confirm that this is still one of the world's outstanding cars, its comfortable ride, low noise level and good luggage accommodation being in the best GT tradition.

Performance

PRECONCEIVED ideas about speed and safety are apt to be shattered by E-type performance. True, very few owners will ever see 150 m.p.h. on the speedometer but, as on any other car, cruising speed and acceleration are closely related to the maximum and it is these that lop not just seconds or minutes, but half hours and more, off journey times. Our drivers invariably arrived early in the E-type and the absurd ease with which 100 m.p.h. can be exceeded on a quarter mile straight never failed to astonish them: nor did the tremendous punch in second gear which would fling the car past slower vehicles using gaps that would be prohibitively small for other traffic.

From a standing start, you can reach the 30 m.p.h. speed limit in under 3 seconds, or the 40 m.p.h. mark in under 4 seconds, so it needs a wary eye on the instruments to stay inside the law. In either case, these speeds can be doubled in little over twice the times to whisk the car clear of other traffic at a derestriction sign. From 30 m.p.h., it takes under 15 seconds to reach 100 m.p.h. and there is still another 15 m.p.h. to go before top must be engaged. Up to 90 m.p.h., any given speed can be increased by 20 m.p.h. in 4–5 seconds using third, and in 5–7 seconds using top. Low-speed torque and flexibility are so good that you can actually start in top gear, despite a 3·07 : 1 axle ratio giving 24·4 m.p.h. per 1,000 r.p.m. Driving around town, this fascinating tractability can be fully exploited by starting in first or second and then dropping into top which, even below 30 m.p.h., is sufficiently lively to out-accelerate a lot of cars. Before the plugs were changed half way through our test for a similar set of Champion N5s, prolonged low-speed town work caused misfiring when higher speeds were resumed, but a short burst of high revs in second gear would usually cure this fluffiness.

Motorway cruising speeds are governed by traffic conditions rather than any mechanical limitations: on lightly trafficked roads we completed several relaxed journeys at over 110 m.p.h. on the Italian Autostrada and Belgian Autoroutes. Not unexpectedly, hill climbing is remarkably good, top gear pulling the car up slopes (up to 1 in 5·2) that reduce many another to a second gear crawl. First copes easily with a start on a 1-in-3 hill.

New bucket seats have generous adjustment for reach, very small adjustment for rake. Most drivers found them a little upright but comfortable. Central armrest conceals a useful box for stowing odds and ends.

JAGUAR E-type 4·2

All this performance is accompanied by astonishingly little fuss, the engine remaining smooth and mechanically quiet at all times. The electronic rev counter is an essential instrument, for the human ear could not detect that 5,500 r.p.m. was anywhere near the suggested limit of this magnificent engine. Even 6,100 r.p.m.—corresponding to 150 m.p.h.—does not sound unduly strained.

Unlike other Jaguars, the E-type has a hand choke: cold starts are instant after a night out in the open and the engine pulls without hesitation or coughing, though on full choke (which is only needed momentarily) idling speeds are high. The new pre-engaged starter is much smoother and quieter than the old Bendix gear.

Running costs

AT FIRST sight, 18·5 m.p.g. overall sounds heavy, but in relation to the performance this is an excellent consumption: many smaller-engined cars with nothing like the same performance can barely match it. Gentle driving will obviously improve the figure but not by any significant amount, as there is less than 4½ m.p.g. difference between the consumptions at a steady 30 m.p.h. and a steady 80 m.p.h. Good aerodynamics, high gearing and an efficient engine account for this unusually flat consumption curve. Only the very best British 100 octane petrol will prevent pinking at low r.p.m.; on the best Belgian, French and Italian brands, it would knock loudly if the throttle was not eased down progressively. At 5s. 1d. a gallon, fuel bills work out at £13 14s. 6d. per 1,000 miles at the overall consumption, and £11 8s. at the touring consumption of 21·5 m.p.g.

M.p.g. over several typical journeys worked out like this:—

45 miles of motorway, average 107 m.p.h. ..	17·1 m.p.g.
8 miles through London's northern suburbs, average 22 m.p.h.	19·2 m.p.g.
50 mile cross-country journey, hard driving over various roads; 58 m.p.h. average	16·7 m.p.g.
Comparatively gentle cruising over quiet roads; 46 m.p.h. average	26·0 m.p.g.

At one time notoriously high, oil consumption has been checked by new oil control piston rings to around 400 miles per pint.

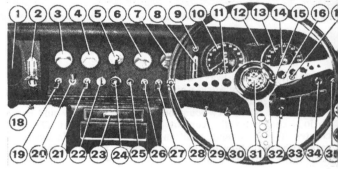

1, cubbyhole. 2, heater controls. 3, ammeter. 4, petrol gauge. 5, lights switch. 6, oil pressure gauge. 7, water thermometer. 8, choke. 9, choke warning light. 10, rev counter. 11, clock. 12, direction indicator warning light. 13, speedometer. 14, mileage recorder. 15, ignition light. 16, low fuel level warning light. 17, main beam warning light. 18, ventilator. 19, interior light. 20, panel light. 21, heater fan. 22, ignition key. 23, ashtray. 24, cigar lighter. 25, starter. 26, map light. 27, wipers. 28, screen washer. 29, clock adjuster. 30, ventilator. 31, horn. 32, trip re-set. 33, indicators and flasher. 34, handbrake on (and low fluid level) warning light. 35, dip switch. 36, bonnet.

Performance

Test Data: World copyright reserved: no unauthorized reproduction in whole or part.

Conditions: Weather: Dry and sunny, 12–18 m.p.h. breeze. (Temperature 54°–64°F, Barometer 30·07–30·02 in. Hg.) Surface: Dry tarmacadam. Fuel Super Premium grade pump· petrol (101 octane by Research Method).

MAXIMUM SPEEDS

Flying kilometre	
Mean of four opposite runs ..	150·0 m.p.h.
Best one-way time equals ..150·0	
" Maximile " Speed: (Timed quarter mile after 1 mile accelerating from rest)	
Mean of four opposite runs ..	136·2
Best one-way time equals ..	137·0
Speed in 3rd (at 5,500 r.p.m.)..	107
Speed in 2nd	78
Speed in 1st	51

ACCELERATION TIMES

From standstill

0-30 m.p.h.	..	..	..	2·7 sec.
0-40	..	..	..	3·7
0-50	..	..	..	4·8
0-60	..	..	..	7·0
0-70	..	..	..	8·6
0-80	..	..	..	11·0
0-90	..	..	..	13·9
0-100	..	..	..	17·2
0-110	..	..	..	21·0
0-120	..	..	..	25·2
0-130	..	..	..	30·5
Standing quarter mile	..			14·9

On upper ratios

			Top sec.	3rd sec.
10-30 m.p.h.	..	..	5·8	4·3
20-40	..	..	5·5	4·4
30-50	..	..	5·4	4·2
40-60	..	..	5·3	4·0
50-70	..	..	6·0	4·4
60-80	..	..	6·6	4·7
70-90	..	..	6·6	4·8
80-100	..	..	7·3	5·9
90-110	..	..	7·3	6·9
100-120	..	..	7·8	—
110-130	..	..	10·2	—

Overtaking
Starting at 40 m.p.h. in direct top gear, distance required to gain 100 ft. on another car travelling at a steady 40 m.p.h.=437 ft.

HILL CLIMBING

Max. gradient climbable at steady speed

				lb./ton
Top	..	..	1 in 5·2 ..	(Tapley 420)
3rd	..	..	1 in 4·1 ..	(Tapley 535)
2nd	..	..	1 in 2·8 ..	(Tapley 745)

BRAKES

Deceleration and equivalent stopping distance from 30 m.p.h.

0·4 g with 25 lb. pedal pressure ..	75 ft.
0·75 g with 50 lb. pedal pressure ..	40 ft.
0·97 g with 60 lb. pedal pressure ..	31 ft.
Handbrake	
0·44 g deceleration from 30 m.p.h. ..	68½

Brake Fade
TEST 1. 20 stops at ½ g deceleration at 1 min. intervals from a speed midway between 30 m.p.h. and maximum speed (=90 m.p.h.)

Pedal force at beginning	..	25 lb.
Pedal force for 10th stop	..	35

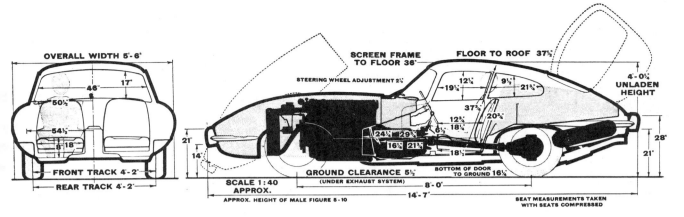

OVERALL WIDTH 5'-6"
46" 17"
50½"
54½"
8 18"
FRONT TRACK 4'-2"
REAR TRACK 4'-2"

SCREEN FRAME TO FLOOR 36"
STEERING WHEEL ADJUSTMENT 2½"
FLOOR TO ROOF 37½"
12½" 9½" 21¾"
19½"
37½"
4'-0½" UNLADEN HEIGHT
12¾" 20¼"
18¼"
24¼" 29¾" 6½"
16½" 21¾"
18½"
28"
21"
21"
14"
SCALE 1:40 APPROX.
APPROX. HEIGHT OF MALE FIGURE 5·10
GROUND CLEARANCE 5½"
(UNDER EXHAUST SYSTEM)
BOTTOM OF DOOR TO GROUND 16¼"
8'-0"
14'-7"
SEAT MEASUREMENTS TAKEN WITH SEATS COMPRESSED

Released by two inside catches, the enormous bonnet tilts forward to reveal the whole of the engine and front suspension; an alternator and new induction manifolding are obvious changes. Accessibility for routine maintenance is excellent.

Transmission

WITH THE new gearbox in the 4·2, the slow deliberate change, weak synchromesh, and awkward engagement of first are things of the past. Instead, a lightweight lever can now be whisked into any gear as fast as the hand can move, without beating the new inertia-lock baulk-ring synchromesh. First gear still whines but not nearly so loudly and it can now be used to advantage for quick overtaking; the other ratios emit only a faintly audible hum. The new Laycock diaphragm clutch is much lighter than before and pedal travel reduced; although the movement is still quite long it is no longer essential to press the pedal to the floorboards when engaging first or changing gear. The clutch bites smoothly when moving off and will accept the brutality of racing changes without slipping and such is the low-speed torque that there is never any need to abuse the clutch for rapid take-offs, quick engagement at 2,000 r.p.m. giving the optimum results. High revs merely produce long black lines on the road, although we were always astonished at just how much power could be turned on without spinning the wheels.

Jaguar have reverted to the high 3·07 : 1 axle ratio as standard equipment for the home and European markets since it gives the fast, relaxed cruising speeds that are legally possible on our motorways, autobahns and autostradas. North American cars, restricted in top-end performance by low speed limits, have a much lower ratio that gives a lower maximum but considerably better acceleration.

Handling

ENORMOUS power in a relatively light chassis demands impeccable road manners. Developed from a famous line of Le Mans cars, it is not surprising to find the E-type's monocoque chassis and all-independent suspension are more than adequate for the power. The best technique is to accelerate round corners, weight transfer making the steering lighter and forcing the back down onto Dunlop RS5 tyres which have excellent adhesion on both wet and dry roads. They are, however, not really suitable for prolonged speeds above 140 m.p.h. and racing tyres were used for our maximum speed runs.

Cornering on an open throttle, even in a low gear, merely increases the drift angle as the car accelerates. Ultimately, the back will break away but in the dry it does so controllably and well beyond the point at which you think it should. In the wet, the accelerator must be treated with greater discretion. Even under severe cornering like this, the low build and anti-roll bars at each end keep roll angles to a minimum.

Positive medium-weight rack and pinion steering transmits plenty of feel through the wood-rimmed steering wheel, and some kick-back, too, on poor roads. High gearing—2½ turns from poor lock to lock—and absence of understeer gives unusual responsiveness and swervability (especially on racing tyres which are otherwise rather harsh for normal motoring) and unlike some powerful cars, the E-type can be thrown about with confidence on twisty roads. At speed in a straight line, it is completely stable.

FUEL CONSUMPTION

Overall fuel consumption for 3,020 miles, equals 18·5 m.p.g. (15·4 litres/100 km.) Touring fuel consumption (m.p.g. at steady speed midway between 30 m.p.h. and maximum, less 5% allowance for acceleration) .. .. 21·5 m.p.g.
Fuel tank capacity (maker's figure) 14 gals.

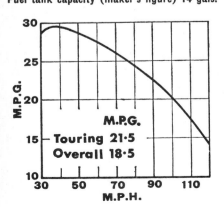

M.P.G.
30
25
20
15 — Touring 21·5
10 Overall 18·5
30 50 70 90 110
M.P.H.
M.P.G.

Pedal force for 20th stop 35
TEST 2. After top gear descent of steep hill falling approximately 600 ft. in ½ mile increase in brake pedal force for ½ g stop from 30 m.p.h.=nil.
Waterproofing
Increase in brake pedal force for ½ g stop from 30 m.p.h. after two runs through shallow watersplash at 30 m.p.h.=5 lb.

CLUTCH

Free pedal movement .. .. .. 1 in.
Additional movement to disengage
clutch completely .. .. .. 4 in.
Maximum pedal load .. .. .. 45 lb.

STEERING

Turning circle between kerbs: ft.
Left 35¾
Right 38¼
Turns of steering wheel from lock
to lock 2½
Steering wheel deflection for 50 ft.
diameter circle .. .. 0·9 turns
Steering force (at rim of wheel) to
move front wheels at rest .. .. 33 lb.

Steering force to hold car on 100 ft. diameter circle at 15 m.p.h. (=0·3 g approx.) .. ..10½ lb.

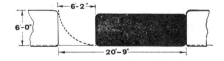

6'-2"
6'-0"
20'-9"

SPEEDOMETER

Speedometer at 30 m.p.h. .. 1½% fast
Speedometer at 60 m.p.h. .. 1½ %fast
Speedometer at 90 m.p.h. .. 2% fast
Speedometer at 120 m.p.h. .. 2½% fast
Distance recorder .. .. accurate

WEIGHT

cwt.
Kerb weight (unladen, but with oil, coolant and fuel for approximately 50 miles) 25·1
Front/rear distribution of kerb weight
49½/50½
Weight laden as tested .. .. 28·8

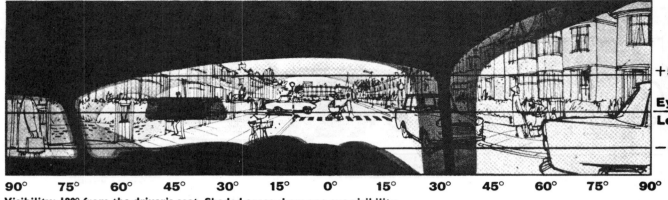

90°   75°   60°   45°   30°   15°   0°   15°   30°   45°   60°   75°   90°

+5

Ey
Le

-5

Visibility: 180° from the driver's seat. Shaded areas show one-eye visibility.

JAGUAR E-type 4·2

Brakes

RETAINING the safety of twin master cylinders, the braking system now has a bigger servo which greatly reduces pedal effort. Our first E-type test car needed a 100 lb. push to record 0·96 g: 60 lb. is sufficient on the 4·2 for 0·97 g. There is also better progression and feel in the pedal, the disconcerting sponginess we recorded at low speeds before being completely absent in the latest car. A slight tendency to pull to one side marred high-speed stability under braking but otherwise the Dunlop discs on all four wheels felt immensely powerful and reassuring.

Although a severe Alpine test descent made the discs glow bright red, there was always plenty of braking in reserve to stop the car easily without snatch or unevenness, if at rather higher pedal pressures. So long as the brake fluid is in sound condition and of the right type, heat soak will not boil the hydraulics causing a complete loss of braking. This we confirmed after our standard brake fade test of 20 ½g stops at one minute intervals from the touring speed—a punishing 90 m.p.h. for the E-type. Pedal pressures increased a mere 10 lb and pedal travel was slightly longer towards the end of our test. Otherwise, the brakes were still true and very powerful—as we expected for Jaguar's own acceptance test is even more severe than ours at 30 stops from 100 m.p.h., again at one minute intervals.

The handbrake, working on the rear discs, is quite powerful and will hold on a 1-in-3 hill.

Comfort and control

THE E-TYPE belongs to the (happily) growing ranks of modern sports and GT cars in which outstanding handling has been combined with the ride of a comfortable saloon. There is none of the harsh, vertical bouncing that was once an inherent part of high performance cars, and even unexpectedly severe bumps taken at speed are smothered without unpleasant jarring, soft damping of the independent rear end reducing vertical movement. The structure feels immensely stiff, an impression strengthened by the way the whole car rides with any irregularities, like a block of wood in a stream, when travelling too slowly for the suspension to be wholly effective.

We found the entirely new bucket seats a big improvement on the old, especially now that deeper foot wells and greater seat movement (two modifications made some time ago) have greatly improved leg room for tall people. A small swivelling distance piece at the base of the folding squab gives two rake positions but most of our drivers would have liked to recline still further: the backrest is rather upright and tends to support the back at shoulder height rather than the base of the spine unless you push well back into the

Unaltered bodily, the E-type retains the impressive lines of a classic GT. Wrap-round bumper and overriders protect the well finished paintwork, but the front air intake is still vulnerable to clumsy parkers (below).

The spare wheel is stowed beneath a large luggage platform which carries the boxes shown (total 7·2 cu. ft.) without obscuring the driver's visibility; the big rear door is released by a catch in the driver's side door pillar. A well-stocked tool kit lives with the spare wheel (bottom).

soft, deep cushions. Even so, the driving position is generally good and one of our testers completed a one-day solo drive from Italy without any aches or discomfort.

An open throttle in the lower gears produces that characteristically hard, healthy snarl, yet cruising at 100 m.p.h. with the windows shut this is a particularly quiet and fussless car, wind and engine roar being unusually subdued. On a hot day sufficient cooling air can only be admitted through open side windows which disturb the quietness at speed. Better heat insulation round the gearbox and transmission tunnel have lessened the problem of overheating in the cockpit, but some form of cold air ventilation that by-passes the heater would still be a welcome refinement. Flaps above each foot well direct the heater's adequate output, two levers projecting from the passenger's side of the facia controlling the volume and temperature. Front hinged rear extractor windows can improve ventilation at the expense of some wind whistle.

Most drivers found the pendant pedals awkwardly placed for heel-and-toeing (curiously, they often are in sports cars), and both clutch and throttle have fairly long movements but very smooth and easy linkages. The gearlever—a short stick surmounted by a large round knob—is easily reached well forward on the massive transmission tunnel above which a glove box lid provides an arm rest without getting in the way.

Despite the low build and long bonnet literally bulging with power, the driver has a good view of the road immedi-

ately ahead and, except in busy town traffic, the projecting (invisible) ends and absence of an effective width gauge are of little handicap.

Tall people found the top edge of the large rear window (its effective size reduced by the slope) obscured any distant view through a mirror which itself can form a blind spot, mounted as it is in the centre of the screen. Shorter drivers did not find it troublesome.

New sealed beam lights improve dip and main beam intensity but it is still essential to keep the covers clean, for their acute slope exaggerates any film of bugs and dirt which high-speed motoring inevitably collects. On a very good road, we found the lights just good enough for 100 m.p.h., but generally they are inadequate for fast driving after dark.

Fittings and furniture

THE COCKPIT layout remains practically unchanged, with a comprehensive set of instruments set neatly into a padded facia panel, the large speedometer (reading to 160 m.p.h.) and rev counter being viewed through a three-spoke steering wheel. Some people thought the wooden rim would be easier to grip if it were a little thicker and it was slippery to hot hands. As in other Jaguars a row of identical minor switches are lined across the centre where they are easy to confuse (and locate) until the positions are memorized.

A very small facia cubbyhole is supplemented by a more useful lidded box on the central transmission tunnel, and a map/book shelf behind the seats. The large flat luggage platform, protected by metal strips with plastic inserts, can be reached through the rear door which opens well out of the way and is secured by a chrome stay. The forward edge of the platform hinges upwards to prevent luggage from sliding forward under braking. Like the outside door handles, petrol filler hole and central bonnet release, the rear door release is irritatingly small for man-sized hands.

Excellent handling and roadholding are the E-type's best concessions to safety. Inside, the projecting heater controls on the passenger's side are potentially dangerous but comfortable seat belts fitted to our test car minimized any risk of being thrown forward.

1, front suspension. 2, heater. 3, windscreen washer bottle. 4, alternator. 5, oil filler cap. 6, radiator cap. 7, coil. 8, distributor (far side of engine). 9, SU carburetter (one of three). 10, clutch and brake fluid reservoirs. 11, oil dip stick. The raised bonnet restricts headroom (especially at the front) but accessibility is generally excellent.

MAKE Jaguar ● MODEL 4·2-litre E-type ● MAKERS Jaguar Cars Ltd., Coventry, England

ENGINE
Cylinders	..	6
Bore and stroke	..	92·07 mm. × 106 mm.
Cubic capacity	..	4,235 c.c.
Valves	..	Twin o.h.c.
Compression ratio		9 : 1 (8 : 1 optional)
Carburetter(s)	..	Three S.U. HD8
Fuel pump	..	S.U. AUF 301 electric
Oil filter	..	Tecalemit full flow
Max. power (gross)		265 b.h.p. at 5,400 r.p.m.
Max. torque (gross)		283 lb. ft. at 4,000 r.p.m.

TRANSMISSION
Clutch	..	Laycock Haüsserman 10 in. diameter diaphragm
Top gear (s/m)	..	1 : 1
3rd gear (s/m)	..	1·27 : 1
2nd gear (s/m)	..	1·74 : 1
1st gear (s/m)	..	2·68 : 1
Reverse	..	3·08 : 1
Final drive	..	Hypoid bevel with limited slip diff., 3·07 : 1
M.p.h. at 1,000 r.p.m. in:—		
Top gear	..	24·4
3rd gear	..	19·4
2nd gear	..	14·05
1st gear	..	9·1

CHASSIS
Construction	..	Monocoque with space sub frame at front

BRAKES
Type	..	Dunlop discs with servo assistance
Dimensions	..	11 in. diameter front, 10 in. diameter rear
Friction areas	..	461 sq. in. rubbed area

SUSPENSION AND STEERING
Front	..	Independent by wishbones and torsion bars
Rear	..	Independent by lower wishbones with radius arm and twin coil springs; upper location by half shafts
Shock absorbers:		
Front and rear	..	Girling telescopic
Steering gear	..	Alford and Alder rack and pinion
Tyres	..	Dunlop RS5 6·40—15 with tubes

COACHWORK AND EQUIPMENT
Starting handle	..	No
Jack	..	Screw pillar
Jacking points	..	One each side
Battery	..	12 volt under bonnet
No. of electrical fuses	..	8
Indicators	..	Self-cancelling winkers
Screen wipers	..	Self-parking 2-speed electric with three blades
Screen washers	..	Twin jet electric
Sun visors	..	Two
Locks:		
With ignition key		Both doors
Interior heater	..	Fresh air system with temperature, volume and distribution controls
Upholstery	..	Leather
Floor covering	..	Pile carpet over felt
Alternative body types	..	Open two-seater

MAINTENANCE
Sump	..	15 pints S.A.E. 30
Gearbox	..	2¼ pints S.A.E. 30
Rear axle	..	2¾ pints S.A.E. 90 EP
Steering gear	..	Multi purpose grease
Cooling system	..	32 pints (2 drain taps)
Chassis lubrication		Every 2,500 miles to 6 points (additionally, 6 more at 5,000 and 2 more at 10,000)
Ignition timing	..	
Contact breaker gap	..	0·014–0·016 in.
Sparking plug type		Champion N5
Sparking plug gap		0·025 in.
Tappet clearances (cold)	..	Inlet 0·004 in., Exhaust 0·006 in.
Front wheel toe-in		$\frac{1}{16} \pm \frac{1}{32}$ in.
Castor angle	..	$1\frac{1}{2} \pm \frac{1}{2}°$
Tyre pressures	..	23/30 p.s.i. for normal driving, 30/35 for sustained fast driving

THE well-known E-type Jaguar two-seater remains in production in its 3.8-litre form. This advanced ultra-high-performance car, it will be remembered, is of monocoque construction and has independent suspension of all four wheels, the rear end employing the articulated shafts as locating members and having inboard disc brakes.

Now an additional 4.2-litre version of the car has been announced, having a

JOHN BOLSTER

Tests the latest of a

famous line—the

4.2-LITRE JAGUAR E-TYPE

new engine and gearbox and a redesigned braking system.

The whole object of the larger engine is to make greater torque available in the middle ranges, the maximum power being similar to that of the 3.8. An output of 265 b.h.p. is achieved at 5,400 r.p.m. on a compression ratio of 9 to 1, while the torque is 283 lbs. ft. at 4,000 r.p.m. The construction of the engine follows previous Jaguar practice, with twin overhead camshafts and three SU-type HD8 carburetters, the dimensions being 92.07 mm. x 106 mm. (4,235 c.c.).

To transmit the increased torque, a Laycock 10 ins. diaphragm clutch is fitted. The new gearbox is perhaps the most important feature of the car. It has synchromesh on all four speeds and is used in conjunction with a higher rear-end gear of 3.07 instead of 3.3 to 1. A Powr-Lok limited slip differential is installed.

A new copper cross-flow radiator of robust construction is used, with a thermostatically controlled electric fan. An alternator now looks after the battery charging, giving a high output even in slow-speed traffic.

The brakes have quickly replaceable friction pads and a tandem master cylinder divides the front and rear circuits to give independent operation. A new and much more powerful servo gives lighter and more progressive pedal operation.

Inside the car, entirely new seats are much more comfortable than the old ones, though a very tall driver might still ask for more leg room. The steering wheel may be adjusted for position in both planes—a most valuable feature—and all the other controls are well placed.

I was able to test the new Jaguar on a trip which included plenty of fast Continental motoring. I also used it as my town carriage during the Paris Salon and associated functions. Let me say, straight away, that it is a superb car, a veritable magic carpet, which can make haste unobtrusively and automatically achieves fantastic averages. I had a most dramatic drive to catch a boat when an aircraft was grounded by fog, and I was able to motor disgracefully fast in congested areas without exciting the fury of the *gendarmes* or the populace.

The 4.2-litre engine seems even smoother than previous Jaguar units. It is quite happy at 20 m.p.h. in top gear and overtaking can be done rapidly without changing down. If desired, one can go quickly up to 140 m.p.h. on any reasonably straight stretch. The ultimate maximum is of little importance, but on the standard gear it is possible to exceed 150 m.p.h., though a fairly long straight is then desirable. The needle of the rev-counter has by then invaded the red section of the dial, but the engine is just as smooth as in the medium speed range, and that means very smooth indeed.

In spite of the great flexibility of the engine, it is delightful to have a fully synchronized gearbox which permits really rapid changes. As 40 m.p.h. can be comfortably exceeded on first speed, it is handy to be able to engage this ratio at any time in city traffic. Second and third speeds are well arranged, giving about 70 m.p.h. and 105 m.p.h. respectively. The E-type is fundamentally a safe car because it is on the wrong side of the road for such a short period when overtaking.

Many of the roads of northern France are still very bumpy and steeply cambered. This is just the sort of terrain that demonstrates the advantages of independent rear suspension. So often, the drivers of cars with rigid axles dare not go down the camber to permit overtaking. The Jaguar suspension works particularly well here, the comfort of the occupants being remarkable while the directional stability is first class. A slight understeer is at once deleted when the big engine is put to work, the car cornering fast even on bumpy roads. One has a wonderful sense of control on wet surfaces, the absence of wheelspin being also remarkable. Incidentally, the triple windscreen wipers are very effective.

The brakes are very much better than those of previous E-types. It might still be necessary to give them some attention before racing, but on the road they stand up to hard driving very well indeed. The clutch is smooth and grips well but the pedal pressure is fairly high.

Having a streamlined shape, the car slips easily through the air, the resulting absence of wind noise being very restful. As with previous E-type Jaguars, the cockpit tends to become rather warm in hot weather during hard driving. A bit more heat insulation around the transmission tunnel, or more ventilation, would probably eliminate this defect.

The machine is quite remarkably economical of fuel. It will do 16 m.p.g. during very hard driving and considerably better than this when used normally. The big six-cylinder engine is superior to a V8 in this respect. The test car used some oil when driven hard.

The new 4.2-litre Jaguar is a very great car indeed. Almost unbelievably smooth, quiet, and flexible, it is comfortable on good and rough surfaces alike. Yet it has a tremendous performance instantly on tap, but will idle for

hours in city traffic without complaint. Add to all this a new gearbox, which Jaguar enthusiasts will regard as the greatest improvement of all, and you have a car worth £4,000 for £1,992 17s. 11d.

ACCELERATION GRAPH

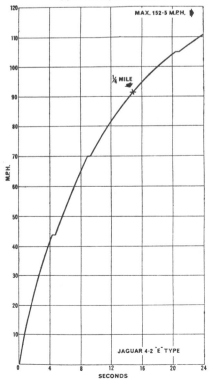

MAX. 152·5 M.P.H.

¼ MILE

JAGUAR 4·2 'E' TYPE

SECONDS

SPECIFICATION AND PERFORMANCE DATA

Car Tested: Jaguar 4.2-litre E-type fixed head coupé. Price £1,992 17s. 11d., including P.T.

Engine: Six-cylinder 92.07 mm. x 106 mm. (4,235 c.c.). Twin overhead camshafts driven by two-stage roller chain. Compression ratio 9 to 1. 265 b.h.p. at 5,400 r.p.m. Three SU type HD8 carburetters. Lucas coil and distributor.

Transmission: Laycock 10 ins. diaphragm clutch, four-speed all-synchromesh gearbox with short central lever, ratios 3.07, 3.90, 5.34, and 8.23 to 1. Hypoid final drive with "Powr-Lok" limited slip differential.

Chassis: Combined steel body and chassis. Independent front suspension by wishbones, torsion bars and telescopic dampers. Rack and pinion steering. Independent rear suspension by lower wishbones, upper half-shafts, radius arms and anti-roll bar. Twin coil spring and damper units at each side. Duplop self-adjusting brakes with

(front) 11 ins. (rear) 10 ins. discs, inboard at rear. Dunlop knock-on wire wheels, fitted 6.40–15 ins. tyres.

Equipment: 12-volt lighting and starting. Speedometer. Rev. counter. Ammeter. Water temperature, oil pressure, and fuel gauges. Triple windscreen wipers and washers. Heating and demisting. Flashing direction indicators. Cigar lighter.

Dimensions: Wheelbase, 8 ft.; track, 4 ft. 2 ins.; overall length, 14 ft. 7 ins.; width, 5 ft. 5¼ ins.; weight 1 ton 2½ cwt.

Performance: Maximum speed, 152.5 m.p.h. Speeds in gears, third 105 m.p.h.; second, 70 m.p.h.; first, 44 m.p.h. Standing quarter-mile, 14.9 s. Acceleration: 0-30 m.p.h., 2.5 s.; 0-50 m.p.h., 5.8 s.; 0-60 m.p.h., 7.4 s.; 0-80 m.p.h., 11.5 s.; 0-100 m.p.h., 18 s.

Fuel consumption: 16-19 m.p.g.

JAGUAR E-TYPE

Convertible

ENGINE CAPACITY 231.25 cu in, 3,781 cu cm
FUEL CONSUMPTION 19 m/imp gal, 15.8 m/US gal, 14.9 l × 100 km
SEATS 2 **MAX SPEED** 150 mph, 241.5 km/h
PRICE list £ 1,513, total £ 1,829

ENGINE front, 4 stroke; cylinders: 6, vertical, in line; bore and stroke: 3.42 × 4.17 in, 87 × 106 mm; engine capacity: 231.25 cu in, 3,781 cu cm; compression ratio: 9; max power (SAE): 265 hp at 5,500 rpm; max torque (SAE): 260 lb/ft, 35.9 kg/m at 4,000 rpm; max number of engine rpm: 6,000; specific power: 70.1 hp/l; cylinder block: cast iron, dry liners; cylinder head: light alloy, hemispherical combustion chambers; crankshaft bearings: 7; valves: 2 per cylinder, overhead, Vee-slanted at 70°, thimble tappets; camshafts: 2, overhead; lubrication: mechanical pump, full flow filter; lubricating system capacity: 14 imp pt, 16.70 US pt, 7.9 l; carburation: 3 SU type HD carburettors; fuel feed: electric pump; cooling system: water; cooling system capacity: 22 imp pt, 26.42 US pt, 12.5 l.

TRANSMISSION driving wheels: rear; clutch: single dry plate, hydraulically controlled; gearbox: mechanical; gears: 4 + reverse; synchromesh gears: II, III, IV; gearbox ratios: I 3.376, II 1.859, III 1.282, IV 1, rev 3.376; gear lever: central; final drive: hypoid bevel, limited slip; axle ratio: 3.31.

CHASSIS integral, front tubular frame; front suspension: independent, wishbones, longitudinal torsion bars, anti-roll bar, telescopic dampers; rear suspension: independent, wishbones, semi-axle as upper arm, longitudinal trailing lower radius arms, anti-roll bar, 4 coil springs, 4 telescopic dampers.

STEERING rack-and-pinion; turns of steering wheel lock to lock: 2.50.

BRAKES disc (front diameter 10.75 in, 273 mm, rear 10 in, 254 mm), separate front and rear circuits, servo.

ELECTRICAL EQUIPMENT voltage: 12 V; battery: 57 Ah; ignition distributor: Lucas; headlights: 2.

DIMENSIONS AND WEIGHT wheel base: 96 in, 2,438 mm; front track: 50 in, 1,270 mm; rear track: 50 in, 1,270 mm; overall length: 175.31 in, 4,453 mm; overall width: 65.25 in, 1,657 mm; overall height: 48 in, 1,219 mm; ground clearance: 5.50 in, 140 mm; dry weight: 2,520 lb, 1,143 kg; distribution of weight: 49.6% front axle, 50.4% rear axle; turning circle (between walls): 39.4 ft, 12 m; width of rims: 5"; tyres: 6.40 × 15; fuel tank capacity: 14 imp gal, 16.9 US gal, 64 l.

BODY convertible; doors: 2; seats: 2.

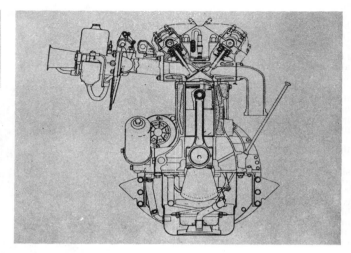

PERFORMANCE max speeds: 42.2 mph, 67.9 km/h in 1st gear; 77.6 mph, 124.9 km/h in 2nd gear; 116.2 mph, 187.1 km/h in 3rd gear; 150 mph, 241.5 km/h in 4th gear; power-weight ratio: 9.5 lb/hp, 4.3 kg/hp; carrying capacity: 441 lb, 200 kg; acceleration: standing ¼ mile 14.7 sec, 0 — 50 mph (0 — 80 km/h) 5.6 sec; speed in direct drive at 1,000 rpm: 23 mph, 37 km/h.

PRACTICAL INSTRUCTIONS fuel: 95-100 oct petrol; engine sump oil: 10.80 imp pt, 12.89 US pt, 6.1 l, SAE 20 (winter) 30 (summer), change every 2,500 miles, 4,000 km; gearbox oil: 2.50 imp pt, 2.96 US pt, 1.4 l, SAE 30, change every 10,000 miles, 16,100 km; final drive oil: 2.75 imp pt, 3.38 US pt, 1.6 l, SAE 90, change every 10,000 miles, 16,100 km; greasing: every 2,500 miles, 4,000 km, 15 points, every 5,000 miles, 8,000 km, 6 points, every 10,000 miles, 16,100 km, 4 points; tappet clearances: inlet 0.004 in, 0.10 mm, exhaust 0.006 in, 0.15 mm; valve timing: inlet opens 15° before tdc and closes 57° after bdc, exhaust opens 57° before bdc and closes 15° after tdc; tyre pressure (medium load): front 30 psi, 2.1 atm, rear 35 psi, 2.5 atm.

VARIATIONS AND OPTIONAL ACCESSORIES 8 compression ratio; 2.93 3.07 3.54 axle ratios; competition tyres 6.00 × 15 front, 6.50 × 15 rear; hardtop.

CAR and DRIVER ROAD TEST

JAGUAR XK-E 4.2

No Jaguar was ever perfect,
yet no other make has ever
fired the enthusiast's imagination
to quite the same extent

A cursory glance at the automobile market in this country offers proof-aplenty that there are lots of citizens who like lots of performance, and prefer it in two-seater packages. The startling acceleration and high-speed cruising capabilities of American sedans have forced higher standards of acceptable performance upon the manufacturers of sports and GT cars, and there is a substantial group of potential buyers who feel insecure about the limited "go" of the small-displacement imports.

There aren't very many two-seater sports or GT cars around that will meet that set of requirements, but the few makes that *do* fill the bill are, understandably, pretty impressive machines.

Ferrari has some superb cars in this class, as do Maserati and Aston Martin. Unfortunately—for most of us—their prices are very steep. There's the Cobra at something over $6000, but the Cobra's spartan accommodations and race car ride will only appeal to the most red-blooded of enthusiasts. That probably leaves about three possibilities—three makes that have the necessary performance and creature comfort at something like a moderate price. They are the Corvette

JAGUAR XK-E 4.2

(*C/D January*), the Sunbeam Tiger (*C/D November*), and our test car, the newest Jaguar XK-E roadster.

No Jaguar was ever perfect, and yet no other make has ever fired the enthusiast's imagination to the same degree, or over such a sustained period of years. The XK-120 overheated regularly but it electrified the keen-types of the late Forties and earliest Fifties. The XK-120M was too fast for its brakes, but nobody cared—it was beautiful and it made the most purely-sexual noise ever emitted by an automobile. The XK-140 and XK-150 were fat, overdecorated versions of the lithe, taut XK-120, but they were Jaguars, by God, and that was enough for the men that bought them.

Then came the XK-E. It had been predicted by the "experts" ever since the waning days of the XK-120 series. Everybody *knew* that Jaguar was going to produce a street machine based on the fabulous D-Type racing car. And finally, after more than one false start, it came. Who cared if it still had the old Moss transmission? Who cared if there wasn't any room inside and the seats weren't comfortable? Who cared if it didn't have proper fresh air ventilation? Nobody, that's who.

It was a new Jaguar!

The automobile magazines mewed lamely about the flaws mentioned above, but even those criticisms were washed away in the euphoric flood of exultant prose that accompanied the announcement of the new XK-E.

A man six-foot-six could wedge himself into the driver's seat, acknowledge the fact that he could not possibly drive the car, and still want one worse than he'd ever wanted anything in his life. An old hand, an ex-Jaguar owner, could say that he'd had bad luck with his previous Jaguar and that he'd never own another one, only to rush pell-mell to the Jaguar showroom the first time an XK-E droned past.

There's something so sensual, so elemental in the appeal of that car that few men can resist its siren song. It's like that woman you used to love, the one you'd never waste another minute on. You can avoid her for months, but one night she calls and you'd crawl naked across three-hundred yards of flaming gasoline and broken bottles to get to her. Obviously, a car that can excite such primitive urges is bigger than a non-synchro first gear or bad oil-consumption.

So let's suppose that you want a quiet, powerful two-seater that will hold its own in any company and look absolutely stunning from any angle . . . *Voilà!* You discover that the Jaguar XK-E you loved so well has taken a whole new lease on life. It has a revised 4.2-liter version of the tried-and-true dohc six-cylinder engine, a completely new all-synchro transmission, a new clutch, a new exhaust, and more comfortable seats. While you're digesting all that you'd better stop by the bank, because you may be about to buy another Jaguar.

The new XK-E is a pleasant blending of go and show, capable of 15-second quarter-miles and a maximum speed of 150 mph. It will cruise all day with the speedometer needle stuck well into the three-figure bracket. It is not really suitable for road racing, nor does it claim to be, but it *looks* racy as all-get-out even when sitting in a dentist's parking lot. Its performance is not the explosive, spine-jarring kind one experiences in an American super-stock. It has that English quality of tasteful understatement—it's obviously capable of going terrible fast, but it would rather not tell everybody.

What about the old complaints? Jaguar has been accused of ignoring its owners' anguished pleas in the past, but this time they listened intently and fixed virtually everything.

New oil-control rings (standard on all Jaguars since

STANLEY Z. ROSENTHALL

AL. FRANCEKEVICH

late '63) cured the oil consumption problem, and a completely new four-speed transmission was designed for the 4.2-liter engine. It has faultless, crashproof synchronizers (baulk-ring type) on all four speeds, and the constant-mesh gears run in needle roller bearings. An oil pump in the transmission housing provides positive lubrication. The short lever can be banged into first at 40 mph without a qualm, although it's sometimes a little sticky when selecting the same gear at rest. This transmission is easily the Number One improvement on the new Jag.

The 4.2-liter engine dovetails nicely with this vastly improved transmission. By virtue of a fatter torque curve it requires considerably less shifting. No attempt was made to get more power—the aim was to improve mid-range torque and fourth gear flexibility. The success of that gambit is best demonstrated by the car's locomotive-like ability to pull smoothly away from anything over 500 rpm in any gear.

The new seats are very comfortable, but they still don't go back far enough for tall Americans, because the rear suspension members block their way. The only real fix for this would be lengthening the wheelbase, and Jaguar was naturally reluctant to do that. However, people of short to medium stature have been known to reach new heights of joy in the XK-E, and have accomplished 500-mile journeys in a single day's driving stint without discomfort. Limited luggage capacity in the XK-E roadster makes this sort of travel problematical, but it's noteworthy that the car makes you want to do it. (Fortunately, the AMCO people sell a luggage rack that will solve this problem.)

Excepting the steering, the controls of the old XK-E used to be the he-man type. Now the vacuum brake servo of earlier models has been replaced by a new Lockheed actuation system, giving lighter pedal pressures and quicker stopping bite. Also, the old clutch has been replaced by a new Laycock diaphragm type with a smooth, progressive action. No special provision has been made to help the driver depress the accelerator pedal, but normal enthusiasm seems more than adequate for that task anyway.

The increase from 3.8 to 4.2 liters resulted from respacing the cylinders within the block, and at the same time the crankshaft was reworked for greater stiffness and the water passages and circulation were improved. It's a thoroughly reliable engine and it enjoys the benefits of all the development work that's gone into the old 3.4 (and its descendants) since 1948.

The electrical system has also received a little subtle attention: it now sports a Lucas alternator that delivers a full charge from 910 rpm up, a pre-engaged starter, and a thermostatically-controlled electric fan.

Paralleling these efforts to match American electrical practice, Jaguar has also made a first step toward some simplification of the maintenance schedule. The lubrication interval for the steering and suspension ball joints has been extended from 2500 to 12,000 miles through the use of protective polyurethane boots, and the life expectancy of the mufflers has been increased about 400% by fabricating them from aluminized sheet steel that offers greatly-increased rust protection.

Driving the 4.2-liter XK-E is little different from driving its 3.8-liter predecessor. The driver sits proudly behind the same comprehensive—and comprehensible—instrument panel and bends the eager beast to his will. If he's tall, he may also have to do a little bending of his less-than-eager legs, but that's a subject for another meeting.

The short shift lever is just about where you'd put it yourself, and the throws are short, quick, and accu-

AL FRANCEKEVICH

rate. The steering wheel is placed at a nice angle for those who like to affect the Stirling Moss-Hero Driver style, and the steering is amazingly light for such a big car. It goes where it's pointed without fuss or surprises, and the handling is the kind that forgives the most ham-fisted cretin. The ride is sedan-like, and although the car isn't small the driver soon loses any apprehensions he might have had about that long nose and where it's going.

The XK-E costs more than a Corvette (approximately $5500 for the roadster and $5700 for the coupe), but not enough to take it out of the GM product's class. As competitors, the two cars are admirably suited to one another—similar, yet different enough to give the prospective buyer a choice. We're really very impressed by all the improvements that have been made to the XK-E, but we must be completely honest and admit that the things that really get to us are the looks and the noise. It's a Jaguar. It reeks of purest automotive erotica, and that ain't bad, Jim. **C/D**

JAGUAR XK-E SERIES II

Importer: Jaguar Cars, Inc.
32 East 57th St.
New York, N.Y.

Price as tested: $5525

ACCELERATION

Zero to	Seconds
30 mph	2.1
40 mph	3.2
50 mph	5.0
60 mph	6.5
70 mph	8.5
80 mph	11.1
90 mph	14.0
100 mph	17.4
Standing ¼-mile	98 mph in 15.0

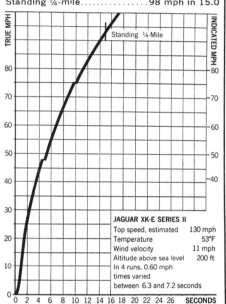

Standing ¼-Mile

JAGUAR XK-E SERIES II

Top speed, estimated	130 mph
Temperature	53°F
Wind velocity	11 mph
Altitude above sea level	200 ft

In 4 runs, 0.60 mph
times varied
between 6.3 and 7.2 seconds

ENGINE

Water-cooled 6-cyl.-in-line, cast iron block, 7 main bearings
Bore x stroke....3.625 x 4.17 in, 92 x 106 mm
Displacement.................258.4 cu in, 4235 cc
Compression ratio.................9.0 to one
Carburetion.................3 SU Type HD-8
Valve gear.. Twin chain-driven overhead camshafts
Power (SAE)..........265 bhp @ 5400 rpm
Torque..........283 lbs-ft @ 4000 rpm
Specific power output......1.03 bhp per cu in, 67.7 bhp per liter
Usable range of engine speeds 500—6000 rpm
Electrical system..12-volt, 16 amp-hr battery
Fuel recommended.................Premium
Mileage.................16–22 mpg
Range on 15.7-gallon tank.....270–370 miles

DRIVE TRAIN

Clutch.................10-inch single dry plate
Transmission.........4-speed all-synchromesh

Gear	Ratio	Over-all	mph/1000 rpm	Max mph
Rev	3.08	10.88	7.0	-42
1st	2.68	9.48	8.1	48
2nd	1.74	6.15	12.4	75
3rd	1.27	4.50	17.0	102
4th	1.00	3.54	21.5	130

Final drive ratio.................3.54 to one
Unit construction, all-steel body.

CHASSIS

Wheelbase.................96 in
Track.................F 50 R 50 in
Length.................175.5 in
Width.................65.5 in
Height.................48 in
Ground clearance.................5.5 in
Dry weight.................2465 lbs
Curb weight.................2515 lbs
Test weight.................2800 lbs
Weight distribution front/rear........49/51 %
Pounds per bhp (test weight).............10.6
Suspension F Ind., unequal length wishbones and torsion bars
R Ind., twin transverse links and radius arms, dual coil springs and stabilizer bar
Brakes.. Dunlop 11 in. discs front, 10 in. discs rear, 461 sq in in swept area
Steering.................rack and pinion
Turns, lock to lock.................2.5
Turning circle.................37 ft
Tires.................6.40–15
Revs per mile..................788

CHECK LIST

ENGINE

Starting	Good
Response	Excellent
Noise	Good
Vibration	Excellent

DRIVE TRAIN

Clutch action	Very Good
Transmission linkage	Very Good
Synchromesh action	Very Good
Power-to-ground transmission	Excellent

BRAKES

Response	Excellent
Pedal pressure	Good
Fade resistance	Excellent
Smoothness	Excellent
Directional stability	Excellent

STEERING

Response	Excellent
Accuracy	Excellent
Feedback	Good
Road feel	Excellent

SUSPENSION

Harshness control	Very Good
Roll stiffness	Very Good
Tracking	Excellent
Pitch control	Excellent
Shock damping	Very Good

CONTROLS

Location	Very Good
Relationship	Good
Small controls	Poor

INTERIOR

Visibility	Fair
Instrumentation	Excellent
Lighting	Very Good
Entry/exit	Fair
Front seating comfort	Good
Front seating room	Poor
Rear seating comfort	—
Rear seating room	—
Storage space	Good
Wind noise	Good
Road noise	Very Good

WEATHER PROTECTION

Heater	Fair
Defroster	Good
Ventilation	Fair
Weather sealing	Fair
Windshield wiper action	Excellent

QUALITY CONTROL

Materials, exterior	Good
Materials, interior	Excellent
Exterior finish	Excellent
Interior finish	Excellent
Hardware and trim	Excellent

GENERAL

Service accessibility	Excellent
Luggage space	Good
Bumper protection	Poor
Exterior lighting	Excellent
Resistance to crosswinds	Very Good

JAGUAR E-TYPE 4·2 LITRE

Extreme in ferocity or docility, responsive to the mood. It's lithe, gorgeous body stirs emotions which are refreshing as morning frost or whole as a yacht on motionless water.

IT should be said instanter that the E-type Jaguar is the sexiest damn car on the road. You can use all your best adjectives: Lithe, libidinous, lascivious; but none of them is worth considering as doing justice to the car. Just sitting there, mutely pleading to be taken out on the open road where it belongs, it kind of grabs you under the rib cage. Kind of.

This is perhaps because the E-type is all things to all men. Charles J. Gerard-Lascivio can use it as a boulevard cruiser for impressing the birds and making all the early-model Holden owners throw up, but you can also hack it to the track and take out a class win in marque sports cars. Above all this, of course, it is essentially a 3 am car that you drive not because you have to go someplace but because right at that moment you can think of nothing else you'd rather do than get in and point it.

Our test car came from Sydney's Capitol Motors prestige car division, via Colin Gilltrap, one of the inner circle enthusiasts who was going through a phase at this stage; he was driving a GTO Pontiac with slush box and was heard to say out loud that he preferred it to the E-type. At this stage there just wasn't another 4.2 E-type for test anywhere in the country.

There were a few 4.2 litre E-types sold in Australia before this one, but the Capitol car was a little more special in that it carried a magnificent coat of red paint with a special all-black interior trim option. It was less a head-turner than a vertebrae-dislocator, but we never did quite work out whether it was the color or the small 4.2 script on the rear deck. Or perhaps it was the darkly handsome good looks of the driver.

It has been said several times already that the 4.2 E-type is an infinitely better car than the 3.8; what has not been said is why. It got a new all-synchromesh gearbox simply because the old one was slow, noisy and rapidly approaching premature senility. But it got the 4.2 engine not because it wasn't quick enough but because Jaguar conceded to American dealer's demands for more poke for the Mark X.

The big Jaguar is quite competitive with the large Detroit iron except in traffic-light GPs, where the 3.8 engine had to drag with almost two tons of car and an automatic box. The 4.2 was

78

Seeing double: We give you two looks at the flowing, sexy lines of the E-Type Jaguar, unchanged externally though now in 4.2 litre form. Note how the windscreen bends the armco.

The boy-Fangio's dream home: Luxurious seating, wheel at arm's length, heel-and-toe pedals, all-four synchromesh and more switchgear than you can operate with 12 arms.

At work the bigger E is a contrast of lithe beauty and fearful aggressiveness.

invented to give it more torque low down, and was donated to the E as well only because it runs on about the same production scheduling. The 4.2 is not yet available for the Mark II or S-type sedans, and hasn't there been some wailing and gnashing of teeth over that!

The effect of the 4.2 is that the extra 454 ccs and the 10 percent more torque right through the range is far more significant than the minor step-up in power. While acceleration figures have been improved slightly, top speed with the tallest rear end (fitted to the test car) is about the same. The most noticeable thing is the infinitely smoother running at all engine speeds and the way the long-stroke engine will spin to 6000 where before 5500 was a little hard on the nerves. All this, of course, makes the E even more remarkably docile around town; it can be accelerated away from rest in third gear with a minimum of clutch slip. However, the new gearbox is so good that a 4.2 driver will certainly use it more than he ever used the 3.8 gearbox.

The main changes for the 4.2 are that torque goes up from 240 lb/ft to 283 lb/ft through the engine changes, there is the new gearbox, plus a Lucas AC alternator, an electro-thermostatic fan with a copper cross-flow radiator, an improved starter motor, a new diapragm spring clutch by Laycock, an improved brake servo, and careful attention to the seating. The engine is still very

much the XK unit, but has a new block, in which the centres of cylinders 2 and 5 stay the same, 3 and 4 are moved together, and 1 and 6 spaced out slightly; this is to make possible the 5 mm increase in bore. The water-jacketing has been re-arranged slightly, and with the new block comes a torsionally more rigid crankshaft with thicker webs and rearranged balance weights. These and a new vibration damper all help to lower bottom end loadings. The engine also has new pistons and rings, an aluminium inlet manifold, with cast-in balance pipe to take three SU HD8 carburettors, and a redesigned exhaust system with aluminised muffler.

The new all-synchromesh gearbox has a cast-iron casing which goes a long way toward reducing reflected teeth noise. It has inertia-lock baulk ring, large ball bearings in all the important places and is pressure lubricated by a rear-mounted pump. The brakes, while unchanged in caliper and pad design, have a more powerful servo which is mounted remotely, while still retaining the "fail-safe" tandem master cylinder.

The cockpit is now a pleasant place to live, and much better tailored to the exacting business of driving such a fast car. The seats have been remedied — they were one of the 3.8 car's worst features—and now have quite sensitive adjustment for rake and reach and are extremely comfortable. The backs now tilt forward for

You never know what came down in the last shower — water pool yields a second chromie.

access to the rear deck. The dashboard is unchanged except for small details, but is finished in matte black, which seems to give a much better background for the excellent instruments.

Of course, driving an E is quite unreal, almost to the point of madness. Here is this gorgeous thing, perfectly comfortable bumbling along at nought rpm in top around town, with you perfectly frantic at all the Sydney cabs crowding around with their cast-iron bumper bars and the engine temperature dead steady and oil pressure ditto ditto. If you have time, in between dodging the car in front which shazams into the back of the car in front of him because everybody's looking at YOU, you remind yourself that it will run from 30 to 150 mph in top, although the tall gearing which makes the interesting feat possible is not terribly marvellous when you're playing Don Garlits and Ol' Swamp Rat at the lights.

The E is very sensitive (perhaps overly so) to tyre pressures, and we fiddled with them for some time before settling at 28 front, 30 rear for normal work and 34 front, 38 rear for the quick bits. This did not have any marked effect on the ride, which itself is not very much changed from the 3.8. That is to say that the independent rear end produces a soft, well-controlled ride that is ridiculous in a sports car and quite acceptable for a Rolls-Royce. Joining strips in concrete roads do produce a slight thump, but the car does not lurch over potholes or bumps. One of its most incredible characteristics is the way it strides over hump-backed crests or through sudden dips without any change in attitude. It feeds back most of the information you need about the road under you without impressing on you the fact that it is really there.

Despite the aforesaid long bottom, the E accelerates quite hard, with no real noise from valve gear or gearbox such as is standard equipment in almost every sports car. There is some boom from the exhaust system, but it is very pleasant. The new gearbox is extremely fast and sure, with short throws between gears; reverse has been moved to alongside second instead of up next to first. This is a more natural movement. The gear-

It almost hurts to look. Under the forward hinged complete front section lies this dazzling arrangement of chromed cam covers, inlet manifolds and SU bells. This little lot manages to produce 150 mph plus — anyone for three dual throat Webers?

shift is close enough to the rim of the wheel to enable the driver to make those snap shifts from third to top and top to third that light small bonfires behind your eyes if done properly. It is, to be colloquial, a real beaut box.

You can, of course, drive an E-type as slow or as fast as you want. Driving it fast produces some fairly real problems on our apologies for main roads. You can cruise it calmly and quietly (as we did) at between 110 and 120 mph, and give nobody any trouble, but only if you make large allowances for your closing speeds and for the human frailties of other occupants of the Queen's Highway. It would be very easy to stuff this gorgeous motor car under the tray of a semi-

GENERAL INFORMATION:

Steering type	Rack and pinion
Brake type	Discs, 11 in. front, 10 in. rear
Swept area	461 sq in.
Weight (kerb)	2520 lbs
Tyre size	6.40 by 15
Make of tyre on test vehicle	Dunlop RS5
Fuel tank capacity	15 gals
Cruising range	270-300 miles
Fuel requirement	98-100 octane
Oil system capacity	7½ qts

SUSPENSION:

Front —
Independent, wishbones, torsion bars, anti-roll bar

Rear —
Independent, lower wishbones, radius arms, coils and anti-roll bar

Shock Absorbers .... Telescopic

ENGINE:

Cylinders	six, in line
Bore and Stroke	92.07 mm by 106 mm
Cubic capacity	4235 cc
Compression Ratio	9 to 1
Valve operation	Inclined, by twin overhead camshafts
Piston speed at maximum rpm	4175 ft/min
Maximum torque	283 lbs/ft at 4000 rpm

PERFORMANCE:

Top Speed Average	148 mph
Maximum, first	54 mph (6000 rpm limit)
Maximum, second	86 mph (6000 rpm limit)
Maximum, third	117 mph (6000 rpm limit)
Maximum, fourth	148 mph (6000 rpm limit)
Standing quarter mile average	15.5 secs
Fastest run	15.2 secs
0-30 mph	2.7 secs
0-40 mph	3.4 secs
0-50 mph	5.5 secs
0-60 mph	7.4 secs
0-70 mph	9.0 secs
0-80 mph	11.4 secs
0-90 mph	14.2 secs
0-100 mph	18.8 secs
0-110 mph	21.6 secs
Fuel consumption, cruising	17-18 mpg
Fuel consumption, overall	15 mpg

TRANSMISSION:

Overall ratios —	
First (synchro)	8.22
Second (synchro)	5.34
Third (synchro)	3.89
Fourth (synchro)	3.07
Final drive	3.07 to 1

Please close the door after use. Station-wagon rooflid lifts for good access to the car's only luggage space. Below, squat sections give the car a road hugging look befitting its lines.

trailer just through blinking an extra once a second.

Not that the car isn't safe. It is. But it accelerates so effortlessly and quietly that you must keep a tight reign on your boy-Fangio leanings. It has more than enough brakes for any situation, but the best brakes in the world aren't of much help when you find your closing speed is 50 mph more than you thought. Braking effort is very low, with good servo and good fore-and-aft balance. However, near 1g stops from 100 mph and more did tend to make the car weave as one wheel or another tended towards momentary lock-up. This may have been peculiar to the test car, but we sensed a marked point in the pedal pressure where one seemed to be able to induce lock-up, particularly in the rear.

The 3.8 car has in some circles a reputation for being a little twitchy; this is in the way of being an unwarranted slander, which we think stems more from the way the car attains such high velocities effortlessly than from any bad handling habits. In other words, the car may seem twitchy only because you're going faster everywhere. Certainly, we found no fault with the handling, except the ultra-sensitivity to tyre pressures. On dry surfaces, with correct pressures, the car understeers and does in fact feed back a bit more wheel movement than necessary because of this. On severe provocation this turns into roll oversteer, which is generally correctable with a combination of wheel and power. You find yourself steering the E-type with the throttle everywhere possible, because the steering is so light and accurate that it becomes very pleasant to set up a corner with a certain amount of lock, apply a lot of power as you start the exit, and then correct the car out of the corner with a touch of opposite lock and a lot more power. The resultant exits are quite fast, as you can imagine.

I certainly did not approach the car's limits at any time. Understand me, this was not because I was suffering from an advanced case of tester's twitch but simply because the levels of adhesion required to completely unstick this car are higher than most normal mortal's ability to control what happens. On corners that could be taken at up to 90 mph you could play Merry Andrew as much as you liked, but over that you leave it to the boy wonders.

But — we seem to have said this before — you can have enormous fun with the car at any level of its gargantuan performance scale.

Even thundering through the countryside at 70 mph, pulling third for snap overtakes and second when you get held up, is quite exhilarating. It must be one of the few cars in the world which is just as exciting at 60 at it is at 135 mph.

And you enjoy it more in the 4.2. The cockpit changes, though small, have improved the habit-

CONTINUED ON PAGE 91

JAGUAR E-TYPE 2+2

Technical description and road impressions of the latest Jaguar

By JOHN BOLSTER

THE E-type Jaguar has gained a wonderful and well-deserved reputation as an extremely high performance car of great refinement. Only its lack of interior space has been criticized by some prospective buyers. Now, an additional E-type model, 9 ins. longer in the wheelbase, has been announced.

The 2+2 has a wheelbase of 8 ft. 9 ins. and the overall length has been increased from 14 ft. 7½ ins. to 15 ft. 4½ ins. The windscreen is 1½ ins. deeper and the roof 2 ins. higher while the floor is lower. The width of the doors has been enlarged by 8½ ins. and the dry weight is 24½ cwt. Having regard to this slight increase in weight and to the extra passengers or luggage that may be carried, the gearbox has wider ratios.

With the standard 3.07-to-1 final drive, the manual box gives 4.07 to 1 on third gear, 6.06 on second, and 9.33 on first. For the first time on an E-type Jaguar, a Borg Warner automatic transmission may be specified, in which case the final drive ratio is 2.88 to 1. In other respects, the new car is mechanically similar to the existing two-seater, having a steel monocoque body shell with front and rear insulated sub-frames.

The new body has many detail refinements. Most important is the incorporation of more effective heat shields, for earlier E-types tended to fry their occupants in hot weather. There is an improved heating and ventilation system with variable direction outlet nozzles and the rear window is electrically heated for demisting. There is a lockable cupboard in the facia and a full-width shelf beneath, the wider doors having "burst proof" catches. The outer pair of the three wiper blades are now longer to give more complete coverage of the screen.

The front seats can be adjusted to suit the tallest driver or passenger. Behind them, a pair of extra passenger seats can be used if the front seats are not too far back. Ideal for children, and with ample head room, these seats can be occupied by adults, but not perhaps for extended journeys. The seat squab can be instantly moved forward to give a longer luggage deck—a most useful feature.

To my mind, the car is better looking than the two-seater, the deeper screen and windows giving it almost an Italian look. It is also easier to enter, thanks to the wider doors and slightly higher roof. The improved heat shielding seems to act as sound insulation, there being remarkably little engine noise inside the car. The gearbox is audible when the indirect speeds are in use, but not aggressively so.

As the car is no wider than its predecessor, the maximum speed is similar. The 4.2-litre engine is not supposed to rev quite so freely as its 3.8-litre brother, but it remains smooth during brief excursions into the red portion of the rev counter dial. One can attain 130 m.p.h. without visiting this territory, so that speed could be maintained indefinitely. I permitted myself a short burst at 140 m.p.h., which the car attained surprisingly quickly. I have no doubt that it could do a little more than this, but the warning needle was deep in the red section and my conscience called a halt.

Third speed gives a useful 94 m.p.h. and second is good for 61 m.p.h., while first allows 40 m.p.h. to be touched. The acceleration figures were excellent, in spite of a suspicion of clutch slip on occasion. They were: 0-30 m.p.h., 3.2 secs.; 0-50 m.p.h., 6 secs.; 0-60 m.p.h., 7.6 secs.; 0-80 m.p.h., 13.9 secs.; 0-100 m.p.h., 21.6 secs. The gearchange is really splendid, very fast changes being possible without a sound. I assert that anybody who criticizes this box just can't drive, and should specify the automatic alternative! With the giant torque of the big six-cylinder engine, there is little need to use the gear lever at all if the driver feels lazy.

Both the roadholding and riding comfort seem to benefit from the longer wheelbase of the 2+2. It took me some hours of driving before I felt that I was able to extend the car to its absolute limit, after which I seemed part of the machine and supremely confident. The brakes of the E-type have been criticized in the past, but although they naturally got well warmed up on the Snetterton circuit, they seemed fully up to the hardest driving on the road. The car can be drifted beautifully through 100 m.p.h. curves and is not too long for the sharper corners.

The new heating and ventilation system works well and is easy to control. This is just as well, for driving with the window partly open causes exhaust fumes to collect inside the car. Perhaps a slight change in the exhaust pipe angle would eliminate this fault. As there are no front quarter lights and the screen panels are slim, one gets a very good view.

An impressive feature of the car is its relatively modest fuel consumption. Quite hard driving on the road, and many flat-out laps of Snetterton, failed to bring the average below 17 m.p.g. Certainly, quite a few owners will regularly record at least 20 m.p.g. Perhaps the best characteristic of the 2+2 is the wonderful ease with which it covers long journeys. Acceleration is the finest safety feature that a car can have, and the Jaguar has this in abundance, whether the gearbox is used to full advantage or not. Just a gentle pressure of the right toe sends the speedometer needle rushing round the dial with no sense of effort at all.

The unusually long bonnet might daunt some drivers, but it is less noticeable from behind the wheel than might be expected. However, the long nose and rather large turning circle render parking a bit of a chore on occasion. On the open road, the car feels quite small and it is as easy to drive as any bread-and-butter saloon.

The E-type 2+2 Jaguar is as practical as it is exciting, and many people will consider it to be the best Jaguar yet. I enjoyed every moment of my "ownership" and I am greatly looking forward to a much longer test which I shall be making in the not too distant future. This is one of the few really great cars.

Last week at a press conference held by Jaguar's Sir William Lyons announced the prices of the 2 + 2. The manual gearchange model costs £2,245 including purchase tax, and the automatic model is £2,386 with tax.

Above is the new 2 + 2 and below the normal E-type.
The differences in silhouette are very subtle but the bright
flash under the side windows is an "instant recognition" point.

E-type
Extended

*A Jaguar 2+2
with optional automatic
transmission. Two
seater continues*

SOME people say that two-seaters are selfish; others think them intimate but anti-social. The real truth is that two-seater travel represents motoring at its best, but most restricted. It cuts out the family man with children, it inhibits the driver who likes to be able to give his friends

a lift and it makes life difficult for the cluttered tourist who takes the kitchen sink as well.

All this has been very much in the minds of Sir William Lyons and his directors at Jaguar in relation to the E-type. The outcome is a 2+2 model with extra accommodation at the cost of a little more weight, a few inches on the wheelbase and a slight increase in frontal area.

Compared with the normal fixed-head coupé the 2+2 is $1\frac{1}{4}$ cwt. heavier at 27 cwt., 9 in. longer in the wheelbase at 8 ft. 9 in., 2 in. higher at 4 ft. 2 in. and has 5 per cent more frontal area at 17.36 sq. ft. Extra weight roughly equivalent to carrying another passenger will obviously cause some slight loss in acceleration but it is doubtful if the added height will make much difference since the aerodynamic shape is probably better.

Apart from the 9 in. increase in both wheelbase and overall length, mechanical changes are confined to appropriately higher rear spring rates and damper settings, more effective heat shields between the exhaust and the lowered floor of the body, and a shield (now applied to all E-types) to guard the alternator fan and armature.

In addition—and for the first time on an E-type the 2+2 is available with automatic transmission as an optional extra. The Borg-Warner Model 8 has D1 and D2 ranges to enable the driver to decide whether to use first or second-gear starts according to his personal hurry/leisure factor of the moment; the D1 position also gives kickdown changes into low or intermediate

*Well-padded space for the family. The back of
the seat can be folded forwards, estate car
fashion, to give a bigger luggage area when only
two people are aboard. See diagram overleaf.*

instead of into intermediate only, as with D2. The transmission is controlled by a stubby control lever with bristles in the gate as a draught-and-dirt excluder.

For the home market, the final-drive ratio with automatic transmission is 2.88:1 (compared with 3.07:1 for manual transmission) which torque-multiplication turns into a top range of 2.88 to 5.76:1. For the U.S. market (where getaway is more important than sheer maximum) the "automatic" top is 3.3-6.62:1 compared with the manual ratio of 3.54:1.

The fully upholstered rear seats are frankly "occasional" and in no way comparable with the rear-compartment accommodation of an S-type or Mark II; but they will seat a couple of adults tolerably for a few miles or take two children in comfort on long runs. Our photograph shows a 5 ft. 10½ in. passenger sitting behind a 5 ft. 10½ in. driver.

Access is by tipping a front seat and the rear squab is split horizontally with the upper section mounted on toggle levers so that it can be swung bodily forward when the rear seats are not required. Attached to the back of this section of the squab is an extension piece for the rear luggage floor, which can thus be lengthened by 11 in. at the point where the luggage space is at its greatest width and depth. For two-up, long-distance touring, the arrangement should be a boon.

In the course of re-planning the body for this extra luggage/passenger space in the rear, several detail improvements affecting the front passengers have been made. The increase of 1½ in. in the height of the front screen gives better upward vision for driver and front passenger and the higher roof line

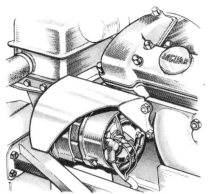

All E-types now have a protective shield for the alternator.

The 2 + 2 is the first E-type to have automatic transmission. A handy lever on the transmission tunnel has opposing sets of bristles to seal the slot against dirt and draughts.

necessary to give 33 in. of headroom in the rear has also resulted in front headroom being increased slightly—by ½ in. to 35½ in. The extended body also makes it possible to slide the front seat back far enough for very tall drivers.

The doors have been widened 8½ in. to

3 ft. 5 in. and are now fitted with "burst-proof" locks which prevent them from flying open through body distortion in an accident.

Other improvements include a deeper glove compartment with lockable lid in the facia panel with a full-width parcel shelf below, and better (green) instrument lighting. The heating system now has variable-direction outlet nozzles (as in the S type), and longer blades have been fitted to the outer wiper arms. In common with all Jaguars, this model can be supplied for the U.S. market with the American "hazard" arrangement by which all direction indication lamps can be flashed simultaneously.

Finally, to anticipate a possible question, the 2+2 is available only as a fixed-head model; an open version is not contemplated.

* * *

Driving the new E-type

AT least seven children (three at a time) rode in the back of the new 4-seater E-type we sampled for a brief weekend before its announcement. They all loved it. Junior's assessment is of course very important because it effectively turns the E-type into a family grand tourer and will therefore extend Dad's youth for at least another seven years. Eight-year-olds and over will probably complain that there is not enough space for their legs unless the front seats are pushed well forward; but there is plenty of headroom. The large platform behind—reached as before through a big side-hinged rear door—leaves sufficient room for holiday luggage.

Increasing the car's length and weight has not in any way spoilt the superb ride and handling and the engine feels even smoother when coupled to the torque converter of an automatic gearbox. Although most of our drivers would prefer the excellent four-speed manual transmission for such a sporting car, the Borg-Warner automatic (presumably aimed at the North American market—hence the left-handed lever markings) can be manually controlled with "holds" for the three ratios. Even in the fully automatic range, the acceleration is still formidable and the gearchanges reasonably smooth except when they occur on full throttle. A road test report on the new E-type will appear shortly.

R.K.B.

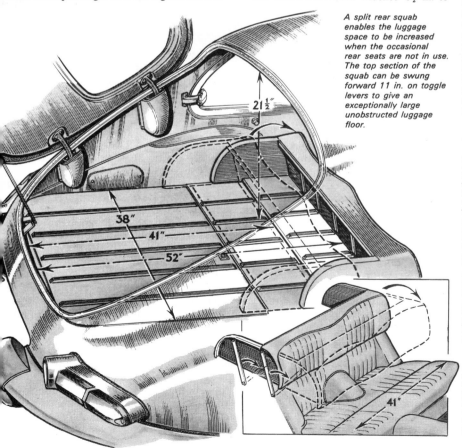

A split rear squab enables the luggage space to be increased when the occasional rear seats are not in use. The top section of the squab can be swung forward 11 in. on toggle levers to give an exceptionally large unobstructed luggage floor.

21½"
38"
41"
52"
41"

In brief

Engine: 6-cyl., 92.07 mm. x 106 mm., 4,235 c.c.; o.h. valves (twin overhead camshafts); three S.U. carburetters; 265 b.h.p. gross at 5,400 r.p.m.; 283 lb/ft. torque at 4,000 r.p.m.

Transmission. *Manual:* 4-speed gearbox with synchromesh on all forward gears; ratios, 3.07, 4.07, 6.06 and 9.33; reverse, 9.45. ***Optional automatic:*** Borg-Warner Model 8 fully automatic system including torque converter and 3-speed epicyclic gearbox giving D1 and D2 ranges; ratios 2.88/5.76, 4.2/8.4 and 6.92/13.84; reverse, 5.76/11.52.

Running gear: Dunlop disc brakes all round with Lockheed dual line vacuum servo; independent front suspension (torsion bars and wishbones); independent rear suspension (coil springs); rack-and-pinion steering; Dunlop 185-15 Sp41 HR tyres.

Dimensions: Wheelbase, 8 ft. 9 in.; track 4 ft. 2 in.; length, 15 ft. 4⁷⁄₁₆ in.; width, 5 ft. 5¼ in.; height, 4 ft. 2⅛ in.; kerb weight (less petrol), 27 cwt.

Prices
- Manual transmission: £2,245 8s. 9d.
- Automatic transmission: £2,385 12s. 1d.
- *Both prices include purchase tax.*

XK-E PLUS TWO

Big brother to the XK-E coupe, the 2+2 offers two extra seats,
an automatic transmission and grand touring, family-style.

BY BILL GAVIN

With the introduction of the XK-E 2+2, Jaguar has given every married man the rationale he's always dreamed of. We can hear it now: "Sure, honey, it looks racy, but see, it's got two seats in the back just like a *big* car." The craftsmen in Coventry, England, have given the XK-E coupe nine more inches between the wheels, two extra inches of headroom and two seats in the rear, and best of all, they have tacked only $700 onto the coupe's $5500 price tag, thereby keeping the 2+2 within reach of family-minded buffs.

Moreover, Jaguar seized the opportunity to do a little more than mere roof-raising and base-stretching. They've added an automatic transmission option and have tidied up the interior. But the most striking aspect of the 2+2 lies not in any radical differences—rather, it's noteworthy for its similarity to the XK-E coupe. In fact, the two are almost indistinguishable. Look at it from all sides, from the front, from the rear—even from above—and you'll detect almost no styling departures. Put it nose-to-nose with the coupe and the differences will still be unexaggerated. A longer door, a bigger windshield and a chrome strip to break up the possible topheavy effect of the taller 2+2 are the only obvious changes. Jaguar could see no reason to change the

XK-E's looks. Neither can we. It's been a runaway best-seller since its introduction. (In fact, back-orders of the regular coupe are frantically being filled, delaying the 2+2's debut by several months.)

A considerable amount of engineering went into those extra inches of wheelbase, particularly in the rear. The box-sectioned transverse chassis member behind the seats of the original XK-E has been eliminated. The longer-wheelbase version features an inverted channel section member to which the rear suspension is attached, and this more compact structure allows extra cockpit space. Jaguar has chosen to retain the 265-horsepower six-cylinder engine (though we've heard rumors concerning a V-12), and the baulk ring, all-synchromesh gearbox is still available with a 3.54 rear axle for a top speed of 130 mph. The 3-speed automatic transmission available on the 2+2 has a slightly higher 3.31 final drive. This is a Borg Warner Model 8 transmission with a torque converter coupling between the engine and the hydraulically-operated 3-speed planetary gearbox. The selector and quadrant are mounted on the transmission tunnel. The two forward drive positions give the driver fairly effective control of what gears are engaged. In D_1, the car starts in first gear and changes up automatically; a kickdown enables the driver to select intermediate or low gear appropriately. The D_2 gear will start the car in the intermediate range and change to top; from top, kick-down will select only the intermediate gear, which has an effect ratio range from as low as 9.67 up to 4.83.

The "+2" part of the New Jaguar is reasonably effective. The short rear seat squab and restricted leg room limit forward-facing passengers to children or very small adults. Engineers have allowed for the possibility of one adult sitting back there—but he'd have to ride sideways with his feet in the foot well on the opposite side of the car. Nevertheless, Jaguar feels that the success of the 2+2 is assured—not only in the family market, but also with its present clientele, for the 2+2 offers extra room to those who will continue to use it as a two-seater. With the driver's seat pushed back to the limit, even an over-six-footer has ample leg room, and as he pulls the adjustable steering wheel towards him, it rises enough for him to operate the accelerator and brake pedals without his thighs fouling the bottom of the rim. The back of the rear seat folds forward to extend the luggage platform and provides much more storage space than the standard coupe.

There's been a little face-lifting around the dash-board too. The glove compartment has been enlarged and given a lockable lid, and a useful new addition is a two-part shelf beneath each side of the dashboard. It's not much use for parcels, but has sufficient depth to accommodate a stereo tape deck as well as the motorist's personal bric-a-brac.

The 2+2 weighs a couple of hundred pounds more than the standard XK-E, but this affects the accelera-tion only slightly. Likewise, the increased frontal area has little effect on maximum speed. The nine inches added to the wheelbase and overall length have, of course, broadened the diameter of the turning circle—you need 41 feet to get the 2+2 around compared with 37 for the normal XK-E. This could have been an excuse to list power steering as an option, but purists will be pleased to hear that Jaguar hasn't even con-sidered that so far. Roadholding is said to be unim-paired by the tailoring, and the ride is now a little flatter—a decided improvement.

The XK-E was greatly improved two years ago with the installation of a torquey 4.2-liter engine, a better clutch, lighter brake petal and all-synchromesh gear-box. It became, at that point, a suitable car for ladies, including your timid maiden aunt. With the 2+2, Jaguar is offering the family man the ideal wish-fulfillment package. Men will tell their wives it's a family car, and all kinds of nice, young mothers will be hoodwinked by those two rear seats and the automatic transmission. They'll stow little Dick and Jane in the back and before they know it, they'll be Grand Touring in the finest European fashion. There are, to use the British under-statement, worse ways to be hoodwinked.   **c/D**

NEW JAGUAR E-TYPE 2+2

It's an E-type with an additional 9 inches spliced in

BY TONY HOGG

PHOTOS BY GEOFFREY GODDARD

RUMORS OF A new 2+2 Jaguar have been circulating for so long that we were much relieved when we finally received the summons to attend at Coventry and inspect the beast. Anticipating something rather radical, we were at first a little disappointed on being confronted by an XK-E coupe that evidently had been put on the rack and stretched a little. However, a closer look reassured us that the new 2+2 will be a worthy addition to the Jaguar range.

Jaguar builds 525 cars a week, of which 120 are E-types. The biggest single market for the E's is America and the 2+2 has been produced to widen the appeal of the XK-E range with the American demand for a 4-place sports car particularly in mind. Because the distinctive shape of the E-type lends itself to 2+2 treatment, it was decided merely to lengthen the wheelbase of the existing model without making any other major changes. Therefore the general specifications remain the same, except that an optional automatic transmission is offered for the first time and the following dimensional changes have been made.

—Wheelbase increased 9 in. from 96 to 105 in.
—Overall length increased 9 in. from 175.5 to 184.5 in.
—Overall height increased 2 in. from 48 to 50 in.

There is no change in the width of the body and with the exception of half an inch, the increase in length has all been made at the door aperture. This means that the front and rear portions of the car are exactly the same as previously and the method of construction has not been changed. In order to retain the line of the top panel, the total height has been increased by 2.0 in. and the windshield height increased by 1.5.

The resulting effect on the appearance of the car depends to some extent on the angle from which it is viewed. Generally speaking, the wheels now appear to be smaller, which is of course an illusion, and the rear wheels give the impression of being at the extremity of the car. From certain angles the increase in height accentuates the flat hood line and gives the windshield a more upright appearance, although the angle of the windshield has not been altered. These changes are not necessarily for better or for worse, and they are noticeable only because the shape of the car is slightly different from what one has become accustomed to.

As is the case with most 2+2s, the 2 in the front fare much better than the 2 in the back. In fact, the rear seats in the Jaguar are quite inadequate for two adults although they will accommodate two children. One adult can be carried in reasonable comfort sitting sideways, and one wonders if a 2 + 1 would not be a better arrangement with the additional seat placed across the car so that the 1 could be carried for long distances in complete comfort.

If the available space is sufficient only for two children or one adult, it can at least be used to the fullest extent for either passengers or luggage. The back of the rear seat is constructed rather ingeniously as two sections and the upper half can be pulled forward over the seats, when they are not in use, so that the luggage compartment is increased in length by nearly a foot. When the rear seats are in use, the luggage accommodation is virtually the same as in the standard XK-E coupe so that the car has a dual role and is considerably more practical in 2+2 form.

Apart from body changes, one or two detail improvements have been made for the comfort and convenience of the driver. The heating and ventilating system is now similar to that of the S-type and includes variable-direction outlet nozzles, the glove compartment has been enlarged, and a full-width parcel shelf has been added below the instrument panel. For additional safety, the door catches and locks are now of the burst-proof type, and a "Hazard" warning system is installed which enables all the direction indicators to be flashed at once.

Other welcome improvements, which were actually introduced with the 4.2-liter engine, involve the electrics—never a very strong point in European cars. The generator has been replaced with a Lucas alternator which reaches full charge at 910 engine rpm and has the other advantages of an alternator such as self-regulation of current, although a conventional vibration contact voltage regulator has to be employed. To insure easy starting in below-zero weather, the starter is now of the pre-engaged type.

Unfortunately, we were not permitted to extend the car in that critical area over 100 mph where one should judge the handling qualities of 150-mph cars. But some fairly brisk driving did not indicate any appreciable difference in the handling characteristics of the long wheelbase car compared with the shorter one. When traveling in a straight line there did seem to be a tendency for the car to pitch slightly less, although this has never been a criticism of Jaguar models. The overall impression is one of smooth, silent power and speed combined with superb roadholding derived from comparatively soft suspension. This is all part of Jaguar's policy, which dates back to 1948 when the company revolutionized sports car design with the introduction of the XK-120. As far as acceleration is concerned, the car is handicapped slightly by an additional 220 lb, but with so much performance to spare you hardly notice the difference.

One of the peculiarities of the XK range of cars is that the engine has been gradually developed from an initial 160 bhp to its present 265 bhp, but seems to have gotten more flexible instead of less along the way, which is decidedly unusual. The last engine modification was a big one which involved increasing the engine capacity from 3.8 to 4.2 liters, and it was done specifically to improve the torque in the low and middle speed ranges rather than to increase the maximum power output. The result is that the current model, despite its twin overhead cams and three carburetors, can be driven like a Detroit car and the engine is most suitable for coupling to an automatic transmission.

While we were in the area, we raised the question of the rumor surrounding the introduction of a V-12 engine, but the rumor does not appear to have reached as far as the Jaguar factory yet. Actually, the whole situation has changed radically in the last few years because Jaguar has absorbed Daimler (luxury cars and buses), Coventry Climax (engines), Henry Meadows (light engineering), and Guy Motors (trucks and buses), which means that the availability and requirements for engines are somewhat different.

The 2.4-liter V-8 Daimler unit is of course offered as an option in the 3.8 Jaguar, but apparently the very fine 4.5-liter Daimler V-8 is not much of a success when installed in the Mark 10, because it does not match the performance of the 4.2 Jaguar engine. Furthermore, it won't go into the other cars in the Jaguar range without excessive modification to the steering, suspension, and engine compartment. Anyway, Daimler limousine sales are at a peak so there is plenty of de-

Rear seat makes room for 4 as demanded by most Americans.

NEW JAGUAR E-TYPE 2+2

mand for the big V-8. The acquisition of Guy Motors in 1963 for $2.3 million is timely because the British trucking regulations have been liberalized recently. Meanwhile, Jaguar has negotiated an arrangement to build Cummins Diesel engines so that Jaguar, through Guy Motors, should soon become a power in the trucking industry.

These developments mean that Sir William Lyons is no longer just a specialist car builder, but a big industrialist in his own right with much greater resources for design, development and expansion than he had previously.

Jaguar and Coventry Climax engine design is combined in the Group Power Units Department, which employs such ace engine men as Wally Hassan, Harry Mundy and Claude Baily. Exactly what they are working on remains to be seen,

but we were informed that the present twincam six Jaguar engine has another three to four years development left in it, in which case it should go out in a blaze of glory around 1970 producing some 320 bhp. Of course, this will probably depend on the success of Jaguar sales over the next two or three years.

For the first time on an E-type, the new 2+2 is offered with a choice of manual or automatic transmission. The manual is the recently introduced all-synchromesh unit which is positively lubricated from a pump at the rear of the case. It is a vast improvement over the previous transmission and its ease of operation is enhanced by the Laycock 10-in. diaphragm clutch. The automatic is the Borg-Warner Model 8, which is basically similar to the Model 35 but designed for heavier duty. The transmission fluid temperature is controlled by a heat exchanger in the cold water return pipe from the engine cooling system. Selection is by a quadrant on the transmission tunnel and there are D2, D1 and L positions.

Although not the most sophisticated of automatics, the Model 8 suits the Jaguar well, and there are one or two tricks that can be used to get the most out of it. For instance, if one starts in L and then moves the lever into D1 the transmission will shift into 2nd, but immediately moving the lever back to L will cause it to stay locked in 2nd until D1 or D2 are selected. Similarly, apart from the usual kickdown arrangement, it is possible to shift down from 3rd to 2nd by selecting L, and from 2nd to 1st if the car is traveling at less than 16 mph.

At present, the price of the 2+2 has not been announced, but we are assured that it will be under $6500. How Jaguar can produce so much car for so little money is one of the mysteries of the automobile business, but one good reason is that old Sir Bill rules his empire (and those of his suppliers) with an iron hand. It is often suggested that Jaguar should charge more for its cars, but the answer is that a good profit can be made by selling them at about $6000 provided there is sufficient volume. If the price were raised to $8000, the volume would drop off and the cars would cost $8000 to produce.

Anyway, at under $6500 the Jaguar 4.2-liter XK-E 2+2 is excellent value for the money, and the basic model has been around long enough for Jaguar to have gotten the bugs out of it, which is an important consideration when buying these cars. For the family with not more than two children it offers ample accommodation, and for young married couples planning weekend trips it is a much more practical proposition than the conventional 2-place model because of the extra luggage space—and in any case, the stork is never very far away.

New model is also offered with Borg Warner automatic.

Even with new seat there is still much luggage space.

Ultimate versatility

*. . . people who prefer 'automatics' . .
(can now) . . sample the pleasure of safe, fast
motoring in a car superbly designed to give
just that . . .'*

PUBLIC images of the unattainable are often in sharp contradiction to facts. Unusually, the E-type is every bit as good as the image of a name synonymous with the ultimate in high performance road cars, and the Jaguar reputation of good value for money keeps this car in the attainable range for quite a number of people.

As a sports car or Grand Tourer the E-type Jaguar offers all that the discerning and enthusiastic motorist requires for a fast interesting road car with completely vice-free handling, outstanding performance and the ability to cover long distances with a minimum of driver fatigue. Petrol consumption is reasonable for this sort of car (around 20 m.p.g. is possible) and as a grand tourer it has some space for luggage even in the open 2-seater cars. Unfortunately some disadvantages accrue from the shape which, although both aerodynamically and aesthetically good, is difficult to park between other cars; this sort of short term annoyance, however, does nothing to mar the long lasting pleasures of open road driving.

The original E-type design had one more obvious drawback; a carrying capacity limited to two people, preferably under six feet tall. With the addition of the 2 + 2 to the range, Jaguar have stilled this complaint; you can now have an E-type for six footers who can also extend the ownership for at least seven years of family ties, or more with a family of one trained to sit transversely. Two adults would be decidedly uncomfortable in the occasional rear seat but one and a child is quite feasible. Further, an automatic transmission—the Borg-Warner Model 8—is now offered

with the 2 + 2, and it was in this form that our test car arrived.

It is obviously not as fast as with the manual transmission or the lighter two-seater body that we tested in October 1964, and the automatic transmission is not as smooth as Americans might expect nor as versatile as English enthusiasts might want. There are many people, however, who prefer "automatics" for their own brand of motoring ease and who have so far been unable to sample the pleasure of safe, fast motoring in a car superbly designed to give just that. With both the 2 + 2 and the automatic option, the E-type has broadened its field successfully without losing its attraction in whatever form you buy it.

Performance and economy

With a little choke and a touch on the separate starter button six cylinders of Jaguar burst into muffled song; from the start there is a hint of something more than just motive power. After a mile or so of part choke, during which the engine can stall or occasionally hesitate, spitting through the S.U.s if insufficient choke is used, it reaches running temperature and is ready to give its customary smooth and powerful output. Although by current standards this unit, designed originally during the war, has a long stroke, it is still very free revving and is happy to start delivering its power from around 1,500 r.p.m., a necessary attribute when a lot of time is spent in the torque conversion range of top gear. During our acceleration runs, we tried three different systems of gear selection, each quicker than the last by a useful amount. If you start in D2—that is without first gear—you reach 60 m.p.h. in a "leisurely" 12.3 seconds; if you start in D1, the time is reduced to 9.1 seconds compared with the "manual" lighter coupé which needed only 7.0 seconds. The third way involved

---

**PRICE £1,973 plus £412 12s. 11d. equals £2,385 12s. 11d.
Basic price without automatic £1,857. Total £2,245 8s. 9d.**

From most angles, it is difficult to spot the higher roof-line of the 2+2 E-type but the chrome flash under the windows gives it away. With commendable restraint Jaguar have not written 2+2 and Automatic on the back.

Interior of the 2+2, showing the transmission tunnel gear selector. The seats are in extreme positions with the driver's one raked back at the alternative, but very similar, angle. High door sill tends to get dirty as people step up over it.

Jaguar E-type 2 plus 2

holding on to the intermediate gears so that first was used up to nearly 60 m.p.h.—reached in 8.9 sec.; using up to 6,000 r.p.m., with some trepidation as the noise rises considerably beyond 4,500 r.p.m., the car reached 100 m.p.h. in under 20 seconds—fast by any standards and quicker than any other automatic yet tested.

Compared with our previous 4.2-litre coupé, this version with a maximum at 136.2 m.p.h. is some 14 m.p.h. slower—about 10 per cent. Such a difference is predictable and will be the subject of a future article, but briefly the increase of frontal area, power loss in the automatic transmission, a probable increase in drag coefficient with the more abrupt roof slope, and the use of radial ply tyres instead of the racing Dunlop R6s used previously, all combine to absorb more power than before. Such a figure is largely academic, particularly in this country, but a spell in Holland where we timed the maximum speed reminded us how useful is a truly effortless cruising speed over 100 m.p.h. To all motorists, however, acceleration is the most important facet of this type of car, and the E-type is particularly well endowed; with the automatic, acceleration is instantly on tap for the heavy-footed.

The consistency of the fuel consumptions recorded at various stages of our test mileage was surprising. At worst with testing and many miles of unrestricted motorway we recorded 18 m.p.g.; at best, which inevitably included London and weekend traffic where hard acceleration but lower crusing speeds are used, we approached 20 m.p.g., a figure which most owners will be able to better, particularly with more frequent use of the D2 range. With a 14-gallon tank you get around 250 miles between stops.

Oil consumption, which had started at a very reasonable 400 miles per pint, increased to 100 miles per pint during the trip to Holland where the engine had to work rather harder, but this did not drop with lower cruising speeds on our return; we would expect nearer the 400 per pint of our previous road test car to be the norm.

Transmission

The Borg-Warner Model 8 automatic transmission is used in the Jaguar saloons for which it is well suited as a natural complement to power steering. But the enthusiast may express surprise that someone who buys an E-type, presumably for pleasure motoring, could possibly want to remove one of driving's keener pleasures. How well does automatic transmission go with sporting performance? It has three ratios instead of four; it has some over-riding control over their selection, though not as much as with a manual box; it will change up or down almost instantaneously; there is some power loss; and the automatic transmission is combined with a higher final drive—2.88 instead of 3.07—which gives wider speed ranges for the three gears.

Select D1 for starting and the car moves off very smartly in bottom gear with some whine as if with subdued straight cut gears; if you keep your foot flat on the floor the upward changes occur with a forward surge at 5,100 r.p.m. and 4,800 r.p.m. respectively. If mechanical sympathy forces you to ease the throttle you should get second gear but may get top if you release the throttle too far; there is an appreciable jerk when changes occur above 3,000 r.p.m.

In D2 you start in second gear, so there is one less opportunity for a surging change but acceleration is correspondingly leisurely. L for lock-up can be selected at 80 m.p.h. on the overrun when approaching a corner, but the unit does not change into second gear until about 65 m.p.h. unless you press the accelerator first. This is the smoothest and most satisfying change in the "box". Below 15 m.p.h. in L, first gear comes in automatically with an unpleasant jerk or it can come in when just accelerating hard at 20 m.p.h. without actually treading on the kickdown switch.

For the person who wants an automatic E-type, this unit will

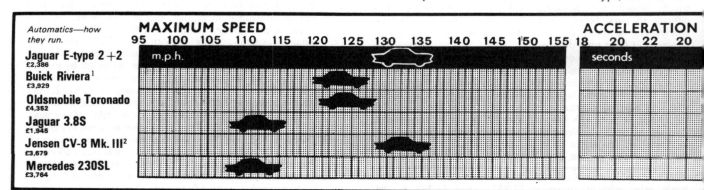

Automatics—how they run.	MAXIMUM SPEED												ACCELERATION			
	95	100	105	110	115	120	125	130	135	140	145	150	155	18	20	22	20
Jaguar E-type 2+2 £2,386	m.p.h.													seconds		
Buick Riviera[1] £3,929																
Oldsmobile Toronado £4,352																
Jaguar 3.8S £1,945																
Jensen CV-8 Mk. III[2] £3,679																
Mercedes 230SL £3,764																

fulfil all needs except the complete smoothness associated particularly with American units; in time you learn to help the transmission but this should not be necessary, and the installation does not seem as naturally smooth as other Borg-Warner units. A period of driver adjustment is necessary before the progress through the gears will be as smooth to a passenger as a well driven manual transmission.

Apart from the distant sound in bottom gear and a slight wheeze as the gears change, there is little noise from the gearbox, and only a faint whine at steady speeds on light throttle from the back axle.

On the test hills, D1 was needed for a start on a 1-in-3 slope, but a 1-in-4 hill was surmounted in D2.

Handling and brakes

The effect of automatic transmission on the E-type's handling is more pronounced than in other cars. Without the drive line rigidity, it is impossible to vary the attitude of the car on the

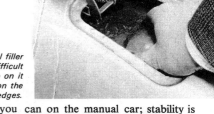

If the petrol filler cap is on at all tight, it is difficult to get an adequate grip on it without barking knuckles on the sharp edges.

throttle in the way that you can on the manual car; stability is considerably enhanced by the use of SP 41HR tyres which further limit slip angles until final rear end breakaway, now rather more sudden but at very high cornering forces.

Up to this point the handling remains neutral and the car goes just wherever you aim it, but if you prefer a more obvious final oversteer and want to corner fast, you can brake sufficiently

Continued on the next page

Performance

Test Data: World copyright reserved; no unauthorized reproduction in whole or in part.

Conditions

Weather: Occasional drizzle, light winds 10-15 m.p.h.
Temperature: 42°F, Barometer 29.28 in. Hg.
Surface: Damp at times.
Fuel: Premium 97-octane (R.M.)

Maximum speeds

	m.p.h.
Mean of opposite runs	136.2
Best one-way run	138.0
Intermediate (at 4,800 r.p.m.)	87
Low (at 5,100 r.p.m.)	56

"Maximile" speed: (Timed quarter mile after 1 mile accelerating from rest.)
Mean 126.0
Best 127.8

Acceleration times

m.p.h.	Man. cont.	D1	D2
0-30	4.2	4.2	5.7
0-40	5.7	5.7	7.9
0-50	6.8	6.8	10.2
0-60	8.9	9.1	12.3
0-70	11.0	11.2	14.2
0-80	13.1	13.8	17.0
0-90	15.2	17.9	21.1
0-100	19.1	21.3	24.5
0-110	24.4	26.6	29.8
0-120	30.0	32.2	35.4
Standing quarter mile	16.4	16.6	18.5

	Kickdown D1	Kickdown D2
m.p.h.	sec.	sec.
20-40	2.7	4.3
30-50	2.6	4.5
40-60	3.4	4.4
50-70	4.3	4.0
60-80	4.7	4.7
70-90	6.8	6.9
80-100	7.5	7.5
90-110	8.7	8.7
100-120	10.9	10.9

Fuel consumption

Touring (consumption midway between 30 m.p.h. and maximum less 5% allowance for acceleration) . . . . 21.8 m.p.g.
Overall . . . . 18.3 m.p.g.
=15.4 litres/100 km.
Total test distance . . . . 2,390 miles
Tank capacity (maker's figure) . . . . . 14 gal.

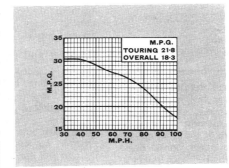

Brakes

Pedal pressure, deceleration and equivalent stopping distance from 30 m.p.h.

lb.	g	ft.
25	0.36	83½
50	0.96	31
55	0.98	30½
Handbrake	0.25	120

Fade test

20 stops at ½g deceleration at 1 minute intervals from a speed midway between 30 m.p.h. and maximum speed (=83.1 m.p.h.)

	lb.
Pedal force at beginning	32
Pedal force at 10th stop	35
Pedal force at 20th stop	38

Speedometer

Indicated	10	20	30	40	50	60
True	10	20	30½	40½	50	60½
Indicated	70	80	90	100	110	120
True	70½	80½	89½	99	109	119
Distance recorder					1½% fast	

Steering

	ft.
Turning circle between kerbs:	
Left	37½
Right	40½
Turns of steering wheel from lock to lock	2.9

Steering wheel deflection for 50 ft. diameter circle = 1.2 turns

Weight

Kerb weight (unladen with fuel for approximately 50 miles)	27.7 cwt.
Front/rear distribution	50/50
Weight laden as tested	31.4 cwt.

Parkability

Gap needed to clear a 6ft. wide obstruction parked in front

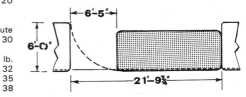

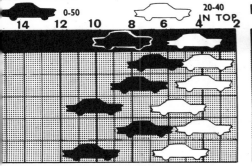

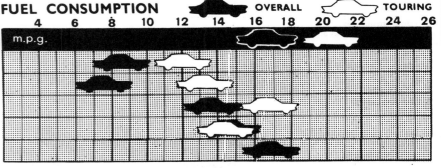

Five foot nine sits with difficulty behind a six-foot driver (one from last notch on sliding adjustment). There is not room for two knees between the front seats, but if the front passenger's seat is pushed forward you could just get another adult in. Headroom is adequate.

Jaguar E-type 2 plus 2
continued

deep into the corner to provoke the tail and use the extreme sensitivity of the steering to warn you that this is about to happen; when it does you can release the brakes, put power on and balance the car on the throttle. This is smoother if you use left foot braking so that releasing the brakes and starting to accelerate appears to be one continuous movement; considering the size of the pedal, Jaguar must surely have had left foot braking in mind.

At near track speeds it is possible to reach final power over-

Safety check list

1	**Steering assembly**	
	Steering box position	Ahead of front "axle" line.
	Steering column collapsible?	Universally jointed—yes.
	Steering wheel boss padded?	No
2	**Instrument Panel**	
	Projecting switches, etc.	Switches, heater and radio controls protrude.
	Sharp instrument cowls etc?	None
	Effective padding?	Scuttle top hard but would yield. Parcel shelf padded on edge of fibre board.
3	**Ejection**	
	Anti-burst door latches	Yes
	Child proof door locks	No, but no rear doors.
4	**Windscreen**	Laminated
5	**Door structures**	
	Interior door handles and window winders	Project
	Front quarter light catches	None
6	**Back of front seats**	Tubular frame well padded with no projections
7	**Windscreen pillar**	Rounded and firmly padded
8	**Driving mirror**	
	Framed?	Rounded metal frame
	Collapsible	No
9	**Safety harness**	
	Type	3-point
	Pillar anchorage	Good, well back without obstructing rear passengers
	Floor anchorage	Well placed

steer but the car comes back under control as soon as the throttle is eased, albeit with a bit of a lurch which is the only thing to tell you that there has been any roll at all. Most of the time the car stays very flat and the handling is always very safe with upper limits that few will ever explore. With a limited slip differential it is difficult, even in the wet, to provoke tail slides until you kick down into bottom gear when the increased power available is sufficient to break adhesion; this too is easy to control, but it would be even easier if the steering were higher geared, not requiring so much arm twirling, particularly in town.

Little effort is required for steering but there is quite a lot of kickback—we suspect a fair amount of this is gyroscopic in origin due to the considerable changes of camber as the offset wheels move up and down on bumps or potholes—but we should not like to lose any of the delightful feel and sensitivity just for a reduction in kickback.

In Europe it is fortunately an accepted fact that if you endow a car with the ability to go really quickly, it is an essential social duty to make it stop too, not just once from high speed but repeatedly, and in the braking department all Jaguars are very well equipped. Large disc brakes with twin circuit systems and a good servo give powerful effortless stopping; in our fade test there was little rise in pressure during our 20 stops from around 85 m.p.h. at minute intervals, and only a slight increase in pedal travel which returned to normal as the brakes cooled down again.

On the Continent we travelled many miles on motorways in very heavy downpours without touching the brakes; when they were applied, they required considerably increased pressure and it took two or three applications to bring them back to normal. Two trips through the watersplash give much the same effect and again the E-type required higher pressures than before for the same efficiency. The handbrake could just hold the car on a 1-in-4 hill and provide a 25 per cent stop when one rear wheel locked.

Comfort and control

Even with independent suspension all round the balance of ride and handling is always a compromise which Jaguar have mastered to give the E-type very good handling and a ride which, though obviously not so good as that of the S-type, is very good by sports car standards. At out-of-town speeds the suspension takes sharp bumps as if they were rather longer undulations, and generally smooths out progress very comfortably but still retains the taut feel that is so reassuring at high speeds. Side winds have more effect on the 2 plus 2 than on the smaller car, but not enough to call for speed reduction or even directional correction; hump-back bridges have to be taken with caution to keep the rear wheels on the ground.

With the addition of the 2 plus 2 to the range, all sizes of people can now own an E-type because of increased room for knees and head; the steering column can be adjusted for rake (with a spanner) and driver reach altered to make anyone at ease. The seats are well shaped and give sufficient side-support to get the better of the difficult compromise between good support and easy access; they have ample sliding adjustment as well as an alternative position for rake, and are high enough to give even small

With the back seat forward, we installed 7.8 cu. ft. of our test luggage without obstructing the mirror view at all. More could safely go in, if tied down. The rear compartment is 38½ in. wide and the longest diagonal, with the seat in the 2+2 position, is 50 in. The comprehensive toolkit is housed in the spare wheel well under the floor. The jack has a ratchet lever.

people a commanding view over the bonnet. Getting over the high body still tends to discourage the use of tight skirts.

The rear seat is pretty occasional for adults; *one* can sit in fair comfort tranversely but two would find it rather confined, even if the front seat had been pushed well forward until the passenger's knees were touching the parcel shelf rail. At most the rear would accommodate one adult and one seven-year old for longish distances with a shortish driver, but the big advantage is the extension that this grants to the family man's E-type ownership.

Unfortunately the heating and ventilation of the E-type are rather below par; the main trouble is that the airflow to the screen is inadequate for good demisting. Sliding levers at the passenger's end of the facia control air flow and temperature but at speeds up to 50 m.p.h. or so you need a booster fan. With the two duct control knobs twisted to warm the feet the output is good, but it takes practice to sort out the best combination. The system needs a positive outlet rather than open and noisy rear quarterlights, with fresh cold air at face level.

Comfort in a grand tourer is not complete unless the car is quiet at grand touring speeds; in this our test car was not as good as some E-type coupés, having rather poor sealing on the passenger's door, but even at speeds over 100 m.p.h. it was still impressively quiet and completely relaxing for long journeys; the combination of good seats, good ride and little noise make this an ideal travelling companion, and it is not until you are travelling at over 4,500 r.p.m. that the engine becomes at all obtrusive when the subdued hum becomes more of a hard working throb.

The general effect of good forward visibility is maintained all round with an adequate view of following traffic through the rear window—Triplex heated as an option on the test car—and a

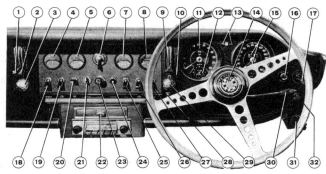

1, heater volume control. 2, heater temperature. 3, L.H. heater direction control. 4, ammeter. 5, fuel gauge. 6, light switch. 7, oil pressure gauge. 8, water temperature. 9, choke. 10, choke tell-tale. 11, rev. counter. 12, clock. 13, indicator tell-tales. 14. horn. 15, total and trip mileage recorders. 16, handbrake and low fluid level warning light. 17, headlamp dipswitch. 18, interior light. 19, two setting panel light. 20, two-speed heater fan. 21, ignition key. 22, ashtray. 23, cigar lighter. 24, starter button. 25, map light. 26, two-speed wipers. 27, electric washers. 28, clock adjustment. 29, R.H. heater direction control. 30, indicator/flasher. 31, R.H. bonnet release. 32, trip zero. Warning lights for ignition (red), low level fuel (amber) and main beam (blue) are housed in the bottom of the speedometer (right hand dial).

Specification

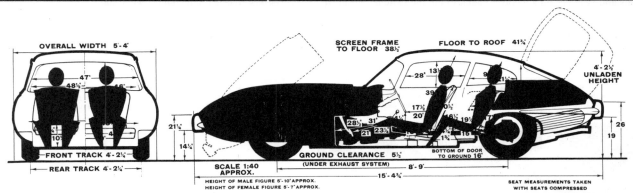

Engine

Cylinders	6
Bore and stroke	92.07 mm. x 106 mm.
Cubic capacity	4,235 c.c.
Valves	Twin overhead camshafts
Compression ratio	9:1 (8:1 optional)
Carburetters	Three SU HD8
Fuel pump	Electric SU AUF 301
Oil filter	Tecalemit full flow
Max. power (gross)	265 b.h.p. at 5,400 r.p.m.
Max. torque (gross)	283 lb. ft. at 4,000 r.p.m.

Transmission

Clutch	Borg Warner Torque Converter
Top gear	1.0
Intermediate	1.46
Low	2.40
Reverse	2.00
Final drive	Hypoid bevel 'Power-lok' differential 2.88/1

M.p.h. at 1,000 r.p.m. in:—

Top gear	26.4
Intermediate	18.1
Low	11.0

Chassis

Construction	Unitary with space frame ahead of bulk-head and sub-frame for rear suspension

Brakes

Type	Dunlop disc brakes with twin circuits and vacuum servo
Dimensions	11 in. front 10 in. rear discs.
Friction areas:	
Front	15.9 sq. in. of lining operating on 242 sq. in. of disc
Rear	15.9 sq. in. of lining operating on 219 sq. in. of disc

Suspension and steering

Front	Independent: wishbones and torsion bar, anti-roll bar.
Rear	Independent: trailing arms and lower transverse link with drive shaft serving as upper link. Twin coil spring/damper units. Anti-roll bar.
Shock absorbers:	
Front	Girling telescopic
Rear	Girling telescopic
Steering gear	Alford and Alder rack and pinion
Tyres	Dunlop SP 41 HR 185–15
Rim size	5K–15

Coachwork and equipment

Starting handle	No
Jack	Ratchet screw type
Jacking points	One peg for each wheel between axles.
Battery	12 volt negative earth 57 amp. hrs. capacity
Number of electrical fuses	8
Indicators	Self cancelling flashers
Screen wipers	Lucas triple arm two speed.
Screen washers	Electric
Sun visors	Two
Locks:	
With ignition key	Both doors
With other keys	Glover locker
Interior heater	Fresh air type
Extras:	
Fitted to test car	Safety harness, heated rear window, radio, chromium plated wire wheels.
Available	White side wall tyres, alternative axle ratios.
Upholstery	Vaumol, leather and pvc
Floor covering	Carpets
Alternative body styles	None for 2 + 2

Maintenance

Sump	15 pints S.A.E. 30 or Shell 10W/40
Gearbox	16 pints Automatic transmission fluid
Rear axle	2¾ pints S.A.E. 90
Steering gear	Grease of recommended type
Cooling system	32 pints (drain taps 2)
Minimum service interval	3,000 miles
Ignition timing	10° b.t.d.c.
Contact breaker gap	0.014–0.016 in.
Sparking plug gap	0.025 in.
Sparking plug type	Champion N5
Tappet clearances (cold)	Inlet 0.004 in.; Exhaust 0.006 in.
Valve timing:	
inlet opens	15° b.t.d.c.
inlet closes	57° a.b.d.c.
exhaust opens	57° b.b.d.c.
exhaust closes	15° a.t.d.c.
Front wheel toe-in	$\frac{1}{16}$–$\frac{1}{8}$ in.
Camber angle	0–$\frac{1}{2}$°
Castor angle	1$\frac{1}{2}$–2°
Kingpin inclination	Not given
Tyre pressures:	
Up to 130 m.p.h.	Front 23 p.s.i. Rear 25 p.s.i.
Over 130 m.p.h.	Front 30 p.s.i. Rear 35 p.s.i.

Jaguar E-type 2 plus 2

good view sideways around the thin screen pillars. The triple wipers sweep a very good area of windscreen and stay in place at all reasonable speeds, except in certain side wind conditions when the windward blade lifts on part of its stroke.

A disadvantage of aerodynamic priorities is that the headlights have to be faired in behind sloping glass covers which cut out a lot of light; on main beam, 90 m.p.h. is about the limit on straight roads; fast enough though this may be, it is not surprising that owners are tempted to fit spot lights inside the radiator intake.

Fittings and furniture

When the 2 plus 2 is being used as such, the room behind the rear seat is the same as with the ordinary coupé, and you can get a surprising amount of luggage in without obstructing the rear view. With the "plus 2" part converted into luggage space by moving the top half of the rear seat forward on toggle levers, the capacity is even greater and more than adequate for two people. Our 7.8 cu. ft. of square luggage stayed below the natural line from the mirror to the rear window, but more could be accommodated without obscuring all the vision, although it would probably need to be anchored securely. Access is through the rear door, released by a small lever behind the door pillar and finally opened by pressing a safety catch inconveniently mounted on the wrong side of the partly open door.

The rear compartment is covered in pvc with rubber-faced strips, matching the colour of the rest of the interior and the leather seats. Tradition is evident in the facia layout—many dials and switches on a wooden background; the switches, grouped

Triple wipers sweep a very good area of the new taller screen. Headlamp covers are shaped toughened glass

in threes, need learning and switch on upwards, aircraft fashion, but the most used wiper and electric washer switches are paired together at the right hand end of the line.

Only something very flat can fit into the shallow glove locker, but more oddments can go in the central arm rest or on the passenger's parcel shelf with its padded rail limiting the movement of the passenger's knees.

Servicing and maintenance

Servicing is needed every 3,000 miles but this is not beyond the scope of the private owner armed with the 22-item tool kit supplied and a syringe to fill the back axle. You can get a wall chart with all servicing points on it or follow the driver's handbook.

Underbonnet accessibility to anything not in front of the engine is good, but the bonnet does not open very far. It is released by sliding levers at either end of the bulkhead, which is rather inconvenient for a driver on his own, particularly as it is often necessary to lean on the bonnet when sliding the lever back in again.

Maintenance chart

A Engine. Every 3,000 miles—check radiator level, drain oil, clean oil filter and renew seal, top-up carburetter dampers, check slow running adjustment. Every 6,000 miles—renew oil filter, clean fuel line and carburetter filters, adjust timing chain. Every 12,000 miles—renew air filter, check exhaust system.

B Steering and front suspension. Every 6,000 miles—grease all nipples, check front wheel alignment. Every 12,000 miles—lubricate and check end-float of front wheel bearings.

C Transmission and rear suspension. Every 3,000 miles—check levels of rear axle and gearbox (manual or automatic). Every 6,000 miles— lubricate suspension nipples. Every 12,000 miles—drain rear axle, drain manual gearbox (only), lubricate and check rear wheel bearings.

D Wheels and brakes. Every 3,000 miles—check tyre pressures, check fluid levels in clutch and brake reservoirs. Every 6,000 miles— examine brake pads.

E Electrical. Every 3,000 miles— check battery level and connections, lubricate distributor and check points, clean and test sparking plugs. Every 6,000 miles—check alternator belt for wear. Every 12,000 miles— renew plugs, check headlamp alignment.

1, alternator. 2, radiator cap. 3, coil. 4, oil filler. 5, triple HD8 SUs. 6, brake fluid reservoir. 7, heater fan. 8, second circuit brake fluid reservoir. 9, washer reservoir. 10, dipstick. 11, automatic transmission dipstick.

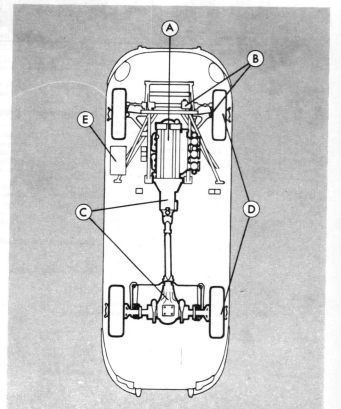

THE JAGUAR E Type 2+2

THE Jaguar E-type ranks as one of the greatest cars of all time and an extremely valuable British export commodity. Some owners find themselves in need of enough space to carry their children or to give an occasional lift to a second passenger, and for this reason, and to increase its dollar-earning capacity, a longer-wheelbase 2+2 coupé version was put in hand, the floor re-formed to enable a Borg-Warner automatic gearbox to be fitted, if desired.

Production plans were unavoidably retarded, so instead of being released at last year's Earls Court Motor Show the new 2+2 E-type was first shown at Geneva last month. To celebrate this important new model's imminent appearance, Sir William Lyons threw a cocktail party on the top floor of Henlys' Piccadilly showrooms the week before the Geneva Show opened. Afterwards coaches took the bulk of the party off to lunch at Whyte's, while a smaller select number of guests were taken in a fleet of dignified Daimler Majestic Major limousines to lunch with Sir William at Grosvenor House. After Richard Bensted-Smith had wished the new E-type well, Sir William rose to thank all those present for agreeing to try the new car before its release and make helpful comments as to how it appealed to them, and give suggestions for possible improvements. In fact, we were not included in this scheme and had not driven the car, so we are free from blame in respect of any complaints it may occasion! In any case, we prefer to leave such matters in the capable hands of Bill Heynes and his design team. . . .

* * *

An opportunity was given to us later to try the new E-type for one full day's motoring. E-types are not for Editors, or not for this one at any rate, and I derive what pleasure I can from rather mediocre small cars. But the Continental Correspondent has been running a staff 4.2 E-type 2-seater for more than 20,000 trouble-free miles, so it seemed logical to ask him to compare this car with the new 2+2.—W. B. D. S. J. writes :—

When the Editor produced the new 2+2 Jaguar E-type for me to try, in view of my having had a year's experience with a 4.2-litre E-type 2-seater coupé, the first thing to do was to get mine out and put it alongside the new one to see how they differed. At a casual glance the 2+2 could be taken for a normal E-type, just as the 4.2-litre E-type can easily be mistaken for the earlier 3.8-litre E-type, but putting them side by side and running a rule over them showed just how cleverly the Jaguar designers have achieved

the new car without losing the classic E-type lines. The scuttle height is the same, but the windscreen is $1\frac{1}{8}$ in. taller, measured in the centre (though many handouts and write-ups quote $1\frac{1}{2}$ in.). This very small increase is the start of some clever and subtle alterations, for it allows the roof line to go on upwards as it goes rearwards so that when it starts to fall into the sloping tail it has got beyond the seating compartment. The wheelbase is increased from 8 ft. to 8 ft. 9 in., and this nine inches is in the seating compartment, so that the altered roof line gives headroom in the rear. This raising of the roof line, together with doors that are $8\frac{1}{2}$ in. longer than the normal E-type, gives easier access, the vertical height of the opening going up from $27\frac{3}{4}$ in. to $29\frac{3}{4}$ in. This extra space inside the car has allowed the front-seat runners to be raised by half an inch and an inch or two lower floor line allows foot room under the front seats for the rear passengers. The longer wheelbase and a redesign of the rear compartment provides sufficient room for a seating space behind the front seats, thus solving one of the tiresome things about the normal E-type, which is the impossibility of taking a third person with you, even for a short distance. Two small people who know each other intimately can squeeze into the passenger seat of the normal E-type, and I have often had to resort to this method in order that someone's wife or girl friend isn't left behind. The rear quarter-lights are half an inch shorter in length on the 2+2, but the rear window, electrically heated as on the normal 4.2-litre E-type, is unchanged.

The rear seat is shaped into two small ones and is very well padded and for one person, even a six-footer, it is completely practical to sit sideways across the rear compartment, when space and comfort are such that a long journey could be contemplated. The instrument layout is unchanged but a useful improvement is the addition of a shelf across the scuttle under the instrument panel and glove locker; this last item has a lockable lid and is ridiculously small. Instead of the hinged flaps under the scuttle on the normal 4.2-litre E-type, for allowing hot or cold air to blow down on the feet, there are now two knobs on the instrument panel that do this by remote control. Between the front seats is a useful odds and ends box, with a padded lid to act as an armrest, but on the 2+2, due to space being needed at the rear of the seats, this box is $3\frac{1}{2}$ in. shorter which is a pity as it now barely takes maps. The handbrake has a knob on the end to press for release, instead of the button on previous E-types. The interior width of the car is unchanged, but the luggage space in the rear is smaller; if the rear seat space is not in use the seat squab can be slid forwards on two swinging links, and at the base of the squab and behind it is a length of flooring that in the forward position fills in the gap that would appear, providing luggage space equivalent to the normal 2-seater E-type. The rear door that hinges about its left side, to permit easy access to the luggage space, now has a fixed linkage to prop it open, instead of having to pull a prop out of a rubber grommet.

On the 3.8-litre E-type the motif on the rear door merely says "Jaguar," while on the 4.2-litre E-type it says "4.2-litre Jaguar." The new 2+2 has the same motif and I feel it is a pity that the job was not completed by a motif reading "2+2 Jaguar." Apart from the longer side doors and windows the only outward addition is a chrome strip on each side from the base of the windscreen along the top of each door.

Opening the two bonnets, which appear to be identical, the first thing I noticed was that the alternator now has a cover over it to protect it from engine heat and road dust, while the windscreen washer fluid is now in a plastic container instead of the vulnerable glass bottle used previously. Most important is an extra strip of spongy rubber added to the bonnet along the line where it is supposed to seat on the lower rubbers when in the closed position. On my 4.2-litre the sealing around the front-wheel arches when the bonnet is closed is very inadequate and road muck covers the air filter, carburetters, battery and other under-bonnet items. When the hinged bonnet closes down it is supposed to make a seal with various lengths of rubber, but like the household refrigerator light that goes out when you shut the door, the E-type bonnet sealing cannot be seen to be working, or not, until dirt and grit appear in the engine compartment. The 2+2 has improved sealing, but the method of attachment is still poor; thin steel strips clamp the

rubber to the body panels by means of aluminium pop-rivets and a ridiculously thin coat of black paint covers everything. In 25,000 miles the paint has given way to rust and the aluminium rivets have corroded and become unpopped so that the rubber sealing strips have fallen off. Even on the 2+2 test car, with 5,000 miles on the odometer, there was far too much rust and corrosion appearing on bolts and small things under the bonnet. It is agreed by everyone that Jaguar do a remarkable job in producing the E-type for a comparatively low price (for the price of a Ferrari you can have *three* E-types!), but it would appear to be done by skimping on detail finish in places where it does not show. The external finish of the body and the cockpit are beyond criticism, but when you start delving down into the mechanism you get a bit depressed after a year of hard use. A pampered E-type that spends most of its life in a heated garage and is never driven in bad weather or on bad roads, would no doubt not give cause for despair, but cars should be built for use.

My 4.2-litre engine has given no cause for criticism, apart from heavy oil consumption until 10,000 miles had been done, and the 2+2 uses an identical power unit, the test car using oil as mine did in its early days. It now has the legend "Use only Super Shell 10W/40" on the filler cap on the exhaust cambox, whereas my engine is prepared to accept any make of oil. As the test car was fitted with a Borg Warner automatic transmission there is an additional dip-stick alongside the engine oil dip-stick. There are improvements to the heat shields between the engine compartment and the cockpit, but until one drives a 2+2 in really hot weather its effectiveness cannot be judged. While motoring in Italy and Sicily last year the cockpit heat in my car became unbearable, most of the heat being from the handbrake, which soon becomes too hot to touch, and from the gear-lever. It is like having a two-bar electric fire switched on in the cockpit, and the only way for the heat to get out is by opening a side window or a rear quarter-light. This is impracticable if you are motoring fast, as the wind noise becomes impossible. With all the windows closed the wind noise at 100 m.p.h. is impressively low, so one is reluctant to spoil this in order to get rid of the cockpit heat. The answer at the moment seems to be to remove more and more clothing! Porsche or Mercedes-Benz-type extractor slots in the rear of the roof would seem to be the answer.

Driving this nearly new 2+2 E-type immediately after my own 2-seater E-type coupé with 25,000 hard miles on the clock made me realise how mine had gradually worn itself out in small ways. Everything on the new car was that much tauter, the doors did not rattle, and the rear door did not flutter and the suspension did not give out knocks and tappings. It is not that my car has reached the point of needing everything renewing, but it was interesting to feel the difference between a taut E-type and a loose E-type. From the driving seat you are not conscious of any difference between the 2-seater and the 2+2, but with the Borg Warner automatic transmission the method of driving was very different. The Borg Warner is controlled by a lever on the floor between the front seats that moves fore and aft in six positions, reading from front to back, P-R-N-D₂-D₁-L, and they are Parking, Reverse, Neutral, Drive for High and Intermediate gear, Drive for High, Intermediate and Low gear, and Lock position for locking the transmission in any one gear, thus frustrating the automatic selection. By pressing the accelerator pedal down to full throttle a kick-down switch is operated that will cause the transmission to change into a lower ratio, depending on the r.p.m. and the lever position. You can either put the lever in D_1 and let the automatic mechanism do all the changing up and down using Low, Intermediate and High gear, or in D_2 when it uses only Intermediate and High, so you can play tunes on a combination of the kick-down switch and the lever position, but by the time you have done all that you might just as well have a proper manual gearbox, except that the Borg Warner has no clutch pedal to operate. Personally I am not sold on the Borg Warner automatic gearbox, for if you are going to drive the car properly it is anything but automatic, relying on a lot of stirring about by the driver. The ZF all-syncromesh gearbox on the 4.2-litre E-type, which is also available on the 2+2, is more than adequate, being quite pleasant to use, though not a gearbox in the Porsche 911 sense of gearboxes. With only three ratios in the Borg Warner the E-type does not give of its best, even though the hydraulic torque converter is supposed to fill in the gaps. With this transmission the final drive is 2.88 to 1, as against 3.07 to 1 with the ZF manual gearbox, and this was the first noticeable difference I experienced, for the 2+2 Automatic did not feel anything like so lively between 90-110 m.p.h. as my own car. I find with the 3.07 to 1 axle that the gearing is about spot-on and 100 m.p.h. comes up on any short straight without recourse to third gear and peak r.p.m., but

the higher axle ratio with the automatic transmission gave a feeling of being slightly over-geared.

The only noticeable difference in handling was a feeling of understeer on long fast bends with the 2+2, compared to a very neutral-steer on the 2-seater, presumably brought about by the longer wheelbase and consequent moving of the c. of g., but I found this a rather desirable change. The 2-seater will oversteer at speed but you have got to be very brave (or foolhardy) to reach this point on the public roads and for all normal high-speed motoring the steering is very neutral. Outstanding was the reduction in noise level, by means of sound-damping, for the 2-seater coupé is quiet anyway but the 2+2 was noticeably quieter from both engine noise and road noise aspects. One disadvantage I found in using the 2+2 was that it was impossible to open or shut the rear quarter-lights from the driving seat, and adjustment of these is vital to interior temperature, especially to get the heater flowing properly in cold weather. In the 2-seater it is a simple matter to reach backwards and open or close the hinged quarter-light while driving along, but on the 2+2 it meant stopping, unless you had someone in the back. The front seats are unchanged and still have the ridiculous little hinged distance pieces at the back of the runners for altering the rake of the seat-back. Not only do you have to get out to do this, but there are only two positions for the seat-back and I defy anyone to notice the difference, the range of adjustment being so infinitesimal. However, the seats themselves are good, and give excellent support in all directions and are very comfortable. I did two short 25-mile journeys sitting in the back of the 2+2 while the Editor drove, and discovered a depressing feature. With either of the rear quarter-lights open exhaust fumes were sucked into the rear of the car and five miles would have been more than enough. Quite why this should happen is hard to explain, but by the blue haze on the rear bumpers and over-riders it would seem that the slight alterations to the body shape have set up some peculiar aerodynamics. In the front seats these fumes cannot be sensed, and it does not appear to happen on the 2-seater coupé, as my bumpers and over-riders are un-blemished. Sitting in-line in the rear, with my feet under the passenger's, seat was all right except that I could not move and

25 miles was too much, but sitting in the left hand part of the rear seat with my legs across and into the well behind the driver proved very comfortable, the back and sides of the rear compartment being nicely padded, so that 25 miles was no hardship at all.

To talk of the 2+2 as a 4-seater E-type is all wrong I feel, unless you intend to carry two small children, but as a 2-seater with more than adequate room to take one or two extra persons down to the pub, or out to the circuit from town, it is excellent and does away with one big criticism that I have of the 2-seater coupé E-type. This 2+2 arrangement is what I specify for a usable GT car; not that the E-type is a true GT car even in 2+2 form. The handling of all E-types does not come up to my specification for a GT car, and you only have to rush down a twisty, bumpy, mountain-like descent to see what I mean. The E-type becomes a big, gormless car when you do this. However, with 265 b.h.p. you do not have to rush madly round corners, and up mountain passes, you proceed in a series of shattering squirts from hairpin to hairpin, using 2nd gear. To my mind the E-type Jaguar is a very nice, refined, touring car for Touring in the Grand manner, and that does not mean Gran Turismo.

This new 2+2 Jaguar E-type is going to be the answer for a lot of people, and unless you have just parted with a 2-seater E-type coupé, you would not know the difference when driving it, and I feel that Sir William Lyons' engineers have once again done a splendid job. Jaguars are not necessarily the World's best cars, but they do represent value-for-money and the company does not produce bad ones. The prices for the 2+2 in this country, which includes Purchase Tax for the Government, is £2,245 8s. 9d. for the manual gearbox model and £2,385 12s. 1d. for the Borg Warner transmission model, and if the Coventry craftsmen had got on with their work instead of going on strike this new Jaguar model would now be selling in great numbers, for it would have been on show at Earls Court last October. In his annual statement Sir William had cause to reprimand his workers for being the cause of the delay in the appearance of this new model. Now that it is in production, as a supplement to its classic brother, let us hope that the workers will build the 2+2 model with all speed, for there are bound to be a lot of buyers.—D. S. J.

··

JAGUAR E-TYPE

CONTINUED FROM PAGE 81

ability of the car no end. The seats locate very well, and with a telescoping steering wheel and multi-position squab adjustment the car will fit almost any size of driver. There is good leg room, the wheel — slightly dished *away* from the driver — is in just the right position, and all the instruments can be clearly read.

I have always been made slightly giddy by Jaguar dashboards, as they are so complete and so absolutely pro-driver that even flicking a tumbler switch makes you a King of the Road. The tumblers are massed in a neat row along the lower edge of the instrument panel, with their function labelled clearly in white lettering. The usual ploy about having to learn their positions in the dark does apply, but if you haven't the desire to memorise your switches then you're not fit to own an E-type.

The tachometer and speedometer sit squarely before the driver, very clearly marked, with the speedometer carrying a trip odometre and tenths mileage recorder. The other gauges are in a row in the centre above the tumbler switches, two each side of the headlight switch which is still that old-fashioned turn-toggle that Jaguar have used for years. It looks fine in a post-war classic but not so hot in 1965. The tumbler switches — with the ignition switch and starter button in the centre — control panel lights (two positions), heater blower (the heater system is quite poor, with low output), wipers and washers. Below the switches are an ashtray with padded lid and a blank (also padded) for the radio. The choke control runs in a vertical slide on the right of the centre panel, and is matched by dual slides on the left that govern the heater/demister. An open glovebox with shaped Holy Cow handle complete the facia.

Getting in and out of the car is not easy, as you have to step over high door sills formed as part of the monocoque structure, but once in you're there to stay. Behind the seats the forward 5 ins. of the luggage platform hinges up to reveal a small compartment, while a section of the platform floor also lifts to reveal spare wheel and tools. The rear deck lid is unlocked by an awkward latch behind the driver's right shoulder. Shifting luggage around the platform is not easy, even though the rear door props open at a big angle. The roof line cramps you somewhat, and it is hard to pack soft luggage from the front seats, for instance.

Oh, there are disadvantages. Rearward vision is not good, because of the steep angle of the rear window, and the dual exhaust pipes, exiting in the centre of the bumper below the reversing lamp, look quite vulnerable to steep driveways.

We didn't get a chance to use the three windscreen wipers in heavy rain, but they cleared the screen beautifully when used with the washers. The headlights are good up to about 110 mph; over that they seem to lose a lot of penetration because of diffusion through the clear hoods that cover them. It is not an easy car to park, as the lower extremities fall away with the body styling and the "power bulge" of the hood cuts down forward view a little. And it is impossible to gauge the position of the rear bumper bars.

But never mind. Even though you can't leave it in parking stations because you don't trust the attendants and you can't park it in the city because people will lean all over it and dent the bodywork, who's complaining? An E-type isn't meant to stand still. Take it out on the open road where it belongs.

Go on. Get!   #

Compare the two coupes: dotted lines show bigger door, glass, longer roofline and chrome sill-strip.

On the draftboards of the world has appeared a new equation for automotive design: Jaguar has launched into the future with a bold new formula for high performance motoring....

$4\sqrt{E\ TYPE} = WILL\ GO$

Somewhere in the middle of that complicated machine known as the E Type, the Coventry firm found room for an extra two people. This is the 2 plus 2.

IF you thought no car could set you further back on your heels than an E Type you were wrong: meet the E Type 2 plus 2 coupe. Look hard at the pictures here and marvel, for Jaguar has done it yet again, and (to form) even better than before.

The 2 plus 2 E Type was released in America on March 8. It will be produced in coupe form only, and will have a three speed automatic gearbox as optional equipment (for two seaters as well). No price has been named to date.

The Coventry firm claims the car will seat four in luxurious comfort, with many of the driver/fatigue factors eliminated, and the safety aspect increased — yet without any significant reduction in performance, styling, handling and so on. The model is outwardly unidentifiable except for a chrome ledge under the windows and along the top of the door ledge. This strip is very similar to the chrome sill on the roadsters. From a distance the car might be almost indistinquishable as the 2 plus 2 if a two seater were not in the vicinity. But a quick comparing glance will show the slightly longer roofline in the centre, bigger wind-up windows, and longer doors.

The car has gained its four-place status by a synonymous extension of wheelbase and overall length by 9 ins. This was executed by sectioning the centre section and extending. Weight gain is said to be negligible although there must be some 200/300 lb involved in additional trim, metalwork, seating etc. The all-steel monocoque body is a new pattern for the extra length, and is not made simply by modifying existing two seater shells.

The basic mechanicals remain virtually identical with previous E Types. Suspension is still the four wheel independent coil-spring set-up that

Auto-shift retains the sportif flavor while reducing the driving effort. Unit is three speed with manual hold.

Two-seater was extended nine inches in overall length and wheelbase to make room for two more.

has been used since the first 3.8s were produced. The engine is the same massive 4.2 twin ohc unit that was introduced to both coupe and roadster last year.

Front and rear tracks, ground clearance, overall width and height and even turning circle remain unchanged, according to our latest information.

However, the fabulous big four wheel disc brakes (11 in. front, 10 in. rear) have gained a twin hydraulic system to minimise chances of total brake failure. This system has also been adopted for the other E Types. The rack and pinion steering has been retained with its delightfully light and precise ratio of 2.5 turns lock to lock.

Seating arrangements have been carefully designed to provide an optimum combination of passenger accommodation and luggage space. The rear seat cushion is a bench-type seat — though separated into two distinct buckets by the suspension hump in the centre. The squab is well canted back for a relaxing position but can also be folded down on top of the cushion to extend the parcels area to 52½ ins. in length. (The nor-

Where they fit: Two pictures show two section squab, tunnel intrusion in rear seats. Legroom is good.

Luggage room options — picture one with rear seats in use, picture two with maximum luggage space.

mal huge-hinged rear deck lid is retained to provide access to the luggage compartment.) The squab itself is pleated heavily in the centre for easier folding. There are no armrests for rear seat passengers. The front of the rear seat cushion is just level with the door pillar, so access to the rear seats seems much easier than might be expected.

The front seats are fully adjustable for rake and length, and the squabs fold forward for access to the rear. All seats are leather covered.

After the four seats, the automatic gearbox option is the most significant addition. It has not been officially released by Jaguar, but it seems certain the automatic will also be available for the coupe two seater and roadster versions as well. The key to this reportedly smooth unit is a centre-console-mounted short stubby sportshift. The box provides for low and two ranges of drive as well as the normal reverse, park and neutral positions. Any gear can be manually held in with the lever.

The handbrake lever has been re-located on the edge of the leather-padded console and slightly more to the rear than on the previous models. There is a centre armrest with parcels bins below it. Additional oddments space is provided

in a new and enlarged lockable glovebox and full-width parcels shelf. The normal comprehensive instrumentation and switch gear is retained.

For those who have a short memory, here is a brief refresher course on E Type performance in the key scales as taken from our own SPORTS CAR WORLD road test of last year:

Top speed achieved on test was 148 mph, although some overseas magazines have claimed a figure as much as 10 mph higher. With the tall rear axle ratio, available top speed can be upped to 170 mph.

Acceleration times are in the drag strip class: 0-50 mph takes 5.5 secs, 0-60, 7.4 secs. The ton comes up in under 20 secs — 18.8 to be precise — and the best quarter time we turned was around 15.2 secs. Gears are useful to 54 mph (first), 86 mph (second) and 117 mph (third).

Although the 2 plus 2 coupe may be heavier than the car which turned in these figures, times should be only marginally altered.

While we don't suggest for a moment that hundreds of thousands of average Australians can now buy E Types because there is room for the kids, it must be remembered that on the Continent and in the United States the E Type is still a cheap motor car — a car which the

E-TYPE 2 PLUS 2

CHASSIS AND BODY DIMENSIONS:
(Two-seater shown in brackets)

Wheelbase	8 ft 9 ins. (8 ft)
Track, front	4 ft 2 ins. (4 ft 2 ins.)
Track, rear	4 ft 2 ins. (4 ft 2 ins.)
Ground clearance	5.5 ins. (5.5 ins.)
Turning circle	37 ft 3 ins. (37 ft 3 ins.)
Turns lock to lock	2.5 (2.5)
Overall length	15 ft 4¼ ins. (14 ft 8¼ ins.)
Overall width	5 ft 5¼ ins. (5 ft 5¼ ins.)
Overall height	4 ft 0⅛ in. (4 ft 0⅛ in)

GENERAL INFORMATION:

Steering type	Rack and pinion
Brake type	Discs, 11 in. front, 10 in rear dual hydraulic system

Swept area	461 sq in.
Weight	Increase unknown (2520 lb)
Tyre size	6.40 x 15
Fuel tank capacity	15 gals
Cruising range	270 - 300 miles
Fuel requirement	98 - 100 octane
Oil system capacity	7½ qts

SUSPENSION:

Front:—
Independent, wishbones, torsion bar, anti roll bar

Rear:—
Independent, lower wishbones, radius arms, coils and anti-roll bar

Shock absorbers	Telescopic

ENGINE:

Cylinders	six, in line
Bore and stroke	92.07 mm x 106 mm
Cubic capacity	4235 cc

Despite car's overall weight increase the massive dohc 4.2 litre engine needs no additional power to haul auto box.

above-average businessman can afford. The sales record overseas is little short of astounding and with this double-bunger introduction of four seats and automatic transmission option, Jaguar Coventry can expect to collar a big new section of the American market.

You would almost swear the car had been designed specifically as an escape route for the bachelor-with-means who suddenly finds himself with a wife and family. To our way of thinking it is the swiftest, most desirable escape route available.   #

Door-top chrome strip from this 4.2 roadster is key to the 2 plus 2 identification.

From some angles the 2 plus 2 is indistinguishable from two-seater car: rear and front views can be particularly deceiving.

Compression ratio	9 to 1
Valve operation	Inclined, by twin overhead camshafts
Piston speed at maximum rpm	4175 ft/min
Maximum torque	283 lbs/ft at 4000 rpm

TRANSMISSION:

Type: Four speed, all syncro manual

Ratios overall:—

First	8.22	Fourth	3.07
Second	5.34	Final Drive	3.07 to 1
Third	3.89		

Optional: Three speed, automatic. Gear ratios and final drive ratio not available

INTERIOR:

Seating: Fully adjust for buckets. Bench rear (fold-down squab).

Upholstery .... Leather seat coverings. Fully carpeted floor

Luggage compartment .... Max depth 52½ ins.

Instruments: Speedo, tacho, oil psi, water temp, fuel gauge, ammeter, Warning lights: Fuel low level, ign, high beam, trafficators.

MAKE: **JAGUAR**
TYPE: **E-type 2+2**

Speed range, gear ratios and time in seconds

m.p.h.	Top (3·07)	Third (4·07)	Second (6·06)	First (9·33)
10—30	6·6	5·0	3·3	2·3
20—40	6·6	4·6	3·3	2·3
30—50	6·5	4·7	3·2	—
40—60	6·1	4·5	3·0	—
50—70	6·1	4·5	3·7	—
60—80	6·5	4·7	—	—
70—90	6·9	5·4	—	—
80—100	7·4	7·1	—	—
90—110	8·6	—	—	—
100—120	11·4	—	—	—

WEIGHT
Kerb weight (with oil, water and half-full fuel tank): 27·4 cwt (3,067lb-1,396kg)
Front-rear distribution, per cent F, 49·1; R, 50·9
Laden as tested .. 30·4 cwt (3,403lb-1,550kg)

TURNING CIRCLES
Between kerbs .. L, 43ft 9in.; R, 39ft 9in.
Between walls .. L, 45ft 5in.; R, 41ft 5in.
Steering wheel turns lock to lock .. 2·8

PERFORMANCE DATA
Top gear m.p.h. per 1,000 r.p.m. .. 24·8
Mean piston speed at max. power 3,750 ft/min
Engine revs. at mean max. speed 5,600 r.p.m
B.h.p. (gross) per ton laden 174

OIL CONSUMPTION
Miles per pint (SAE 10W/30) 150

FUEL CONSUMPTION
At constant speeds
30 m.p.h. 29·0 m.p.g.   70 m.p.h. 26·0 m.p.g.
40 ,, 29·0 ,,   80 ,, 24·2 ,,
50 ,, 27·6 ,,   90 ,, 22·6 ,,
60 ,, 26·2 ,,   100 ,, 20·4 ,,
Overall m.p.g. .. 18·8 (15·0 litres/100km)
Normal range m.p.g. .. 18-22 (15·7-12·8 litres/100km)
Test distance (corrected) .. 1,885 miles
Estimated (DIN) m.p.g. 23·6 (12·0 litres/100km)
Grade .. Super Premium (98-100 RM)

TEST CONDITIONS
Weather .. Dry, overcast with 5-10 m.p.h. wind
Temperature .. .. 18 deg.C (64 deg.F.)
Barometer .. .. .. 29·8in. Hg.
Surfaces .. .. Dry concrete and tarmac

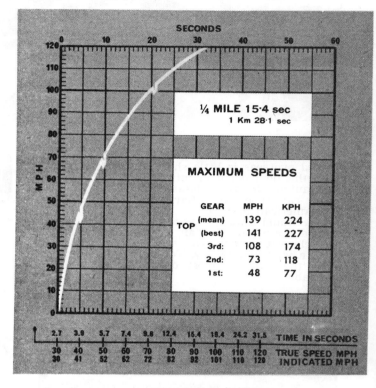

¼ MILE 15·4 sec
1 Km 28·1 sec

MAXIMUM SPEEDS

	GEAR	MPH	KPH
TOP	(mean)	139	224
	(best)	141	227
3rd:		108	174
2nd:		73	118
1st:		48	77

TIME IN SECONDS	2.7	3.8	5.7	7.4	9.6	12.4	15.4	19.4	24.2	31.5
TRUE SPEED MPH	30	40	50	60	70	80	90	100	110	120
INDICATED MPH	30	41	52	62	72	82	92	101	110	120

BRAKES
(from 30 m.p.h., in neutral)	Pedal load	Retardation	Equiv. distance
	25lb	0·25g	120ft
	50lb	0·65g	46ft
	70lb	1·0g	30·1ft
Handbrake		0·25g	120ft

CLUTCH Pedal load and travel—40lb and 5in.

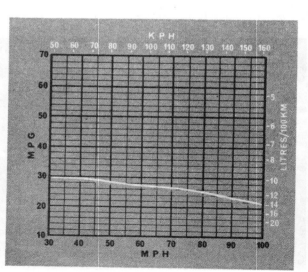

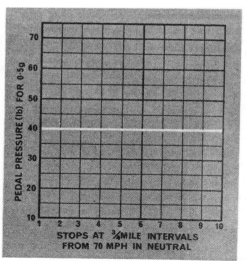

Jaguar E-type 2+2 4,235 c.c.

AT A GLANCE: Latest four-seater version of Jaguar's famous sports car. Superb brakes, steering and road-holding. Better tyres. Slightly lower gearbox ratios improve flexibility and acceleration. Interior extensively revised. Usual excellent Jaguar value for money, and outstanding economy for the performance available.

MANUFACTURER:
Jaguar Cars Ltd., Browns Lane, Coventry.

PRICES

Basic	..	..	..	£1,857	0s 0d
Purchase Tax	..	..	£388	8s 9d
Total (in G.B.)	..	..	£2,245	8s 9d

EXTRAS (INC. P.T.)

Chrome wheels	..	..	£51	7s 1d
Heated backlight	..	..	£19	18s 9d
Radiomobile 980T	..	..	£43	15s 5d
Seat belts (pair)	..	..	£12	1s 8d

PERFORMANCE SUMMARY

Mean maximum speed	.. 139 m.p.h.
Standing start ¼-mile	.. 15·4 sec
0-60 m.p.h.	.. 7·4 sec
30-70 m.p.h. (through gears)	7·1 sec
Overall fuel consumption	.. 18·8 m.p.g.
Miles per tankful	.. 263

ONE can argue that a car like the E-type is wasted in Great Britain with a blanket speed limit of 70 m.p.h., and it's true that we were forced abroad to appreciate it to the full. Yet as recently as the Whitsun weekend, when all thoughts of fast driving must give way to disciplined pottering with the stream, we enjoyed considerable pleasure and satisfaction merely by being behind the steering wheel of this Jaguar and sensing its responses to the controls.

This 2+2 version is the latest of a series introduced five years ago hard on the heels of the famous XK range. It must have been some intelligent market investigation and, no doubt, some pretty hard lobbying of the factory by family men, that prompted Jaguar even to consider expanding the E-type coupé to take two in the back. It cannot have been an easy task either, as the original two-seater has near-perfect lines that could not be spoilt, yet the project went ahead and despite delays has turned out remarkably well.

In the back of the standard two-seater E-type there could be no rear legroom because of the transverse box section immediately behind the seats. It was therefore necessary, as a first step, to extend the wheelbase by 9in. and rejuggle the structure. Next, the roof was raised 2in. for headroom in the back and to permit the front seats to be lifted for footroom under their cushions. Doors were stretched 8½in., glass heights increased to fit, and the 2+2 emerged still looking just like an E-type, but without quite the same flowing lines from nose to tail-pipes; it's as if the artist lifted his brush for a moment in painting the profile.

Jaguar thinking also decreed that several developments should be incorporated into this latest model, and those familiar with the two-seater will notice lots of little changes. For example, the tiny glove locker (it really is only big enough to take a pair of gloves) now has a lid with locking push button and there are shallow shelves each side under the facia. A padded armrest between the seats covers another tiny storage box and there are now additional armrests on each door. Control of the heater has been simplified by fitting swivelling outlets to direct air either to the screen for demisting or progressively backwards from the feet to the body.

All this and the extra metal in the larger body have added nearly 2cwt to the kerb weight which, together with a substantial increase in frontal area, reduce the performance compared with the two-seater. Just how much is not easy to determine, as the indirect gearbox ratios have been lowered very slightly for better acceleration and there has been a tyre

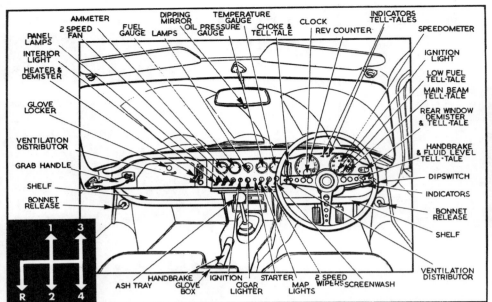

change on all E-types since our last test. Dunlop SP41 HR radials with a constant rolling radius (radials do not grow at speed like cross-ply tyres) equivalent to 24.8 m.p.h. per 1,000 r.p.m. have replaced the RS5s which grew from 25.1 m.p.h. per 1,000 r.p.m. at 30 m.p.h. to 25.9 at 100 m.p.h.

This lower overall gearing makes the 2+2 slightly quicker getting away than the two-seater we tested a year ago, but by 100 m.p.h. it has lagged behind by just under 2sec. Even so it still makes 100 in comfortably under 20sec from rest. From 20 to 80 m.p.h. in third takes 13.8sec in the 2+2 compared with 14.2sec in last year's two-seater, so it is really a case of gaining on the swings and not losing very much on the roundabouts. Maximum revs are reached at lower speeds in each gear, but the differences are never more than a few per cent and third still runs to well over 100 m.p.h.

Top speed is affected by the extra drag and the lower gearing so our mean figure was 139 m.p.h. with a best in one direction of 141 m.p.h. At this speed the rev counter on the test car was reading 5,950 r.p.m. (a true 5,650) and the needle was well into the red sector which the handbook says should not be entered "under ANY CIRCUMSTANCES." We had previously cleared this point with the factory, but it does look as though the maximum of the car (either two-seater or 2+2) on the latest tyres should be only the 137 m.p.h. which corresponds with the safe rev limit of 5,500.

This speed is, of course, quite fast enough for all conditions and the lower gearing is appreciated much more than a possible (and rather academic, especially in this country) ultimate 10 m.p.h. Flexibility is better as well, and we were able to pull smoothly from only 10 m.p.h. in top and still reach over 110 m.p.h. in less than a mile.

ON THE CONTINENT

In order to experience true Jaguar performance within the law and measure maximum speed, we flew the 2+2 to Geneva and drove south-east into Italy. On *autostrada* the car settles to a natural gait at about 4,500 r.p.m. (110 m.p.h.) and literally eats up the kilometres at a fantastic rate. To drive 400 miles in a day is no strain, and there is still time to stop for meals and arrive at a hotel early for a wash and change before dinner. Even when twisting through the slower roads of the Alps we were surprised at the distances covered in such short intervals, and at how often the speedometer flicked over 100 m.p.h. even when climbing the main road passes.

One has every right to expect impeccable brakes on such a car, and here the E-type did not disappoint. Sensitivity has improved immeasurably since the early 3.8 cars, and it now takes less than 100lb. on the pedal for a 1g stop from 30 m.p.h. From 70 m.p.h. only 40lb. is needed for 0.5g, and this value never varied during our 10 repeated stops at ¼-mile intervals. In the Alps we proved the point conclusively, as often going up the mountains as when descending the other side, with never the slightest sign of fade nor any feeling of overworking the anchors.

Once or twice we made a complete descent in top gear as an additional test of brakes and engine flexibility. The only difference was extra heaviness on the steering, as no engine torque was being used to transfer

This is as far as the nose section lifts, but most of the vitals are not too difficult to reach. The top of the dipstick can be seen in its clip by the exhaust manifold at the back of the engine, where it gets too hot to touch

Back seats are well padded round the edges to make it comfortable to sit half sideways. The top half of the backrest pulls forward to increase the luggage space behind

Jaguar E-type 2+2 . . .

weight off the front wheels and power was not helping the back of the car round the tight turns.

The handling of the E-type is of the highest order and bends become a treat for driver and passengers alike. One can sight along the huge power bulge in the centre of the bonnet and line the car up for the turn with supreme confidence. Without much power on, the car understeers a trace with perfect feel of the cornering forces coming back through the steering. As more throttle is used the balance becomes more neutral until at the right speed and with a steady foot there is perfect cornering balance back and front. Towards the limit the angle of the tail drifts out progressively in an easily controlled manner, and after only two or three laps of the M.I.R.A. road circuit we were performing tidy four-wheel drifts through each of the turns.

Steering loses none of its precision at speed and the driver can relax his grip on the slim woodrim wheel knowing the car will do nothing sudden or strange. Stability is exemplorary, and the E-type runs true as an arrow "hands-off" at 140 m.p.h.

With its longer wheelbase the 2+2 seems to ride bumps and undulations even better than the two-seater, although some of our testers thought the front plunged up and down rather more. Certainly the ride over deformed Continental roads is most impressive and one can storm along at three-figure speeds with barely a thought for what the wheels are up to. There is one limitation, however, as we discovered when struggling up a track in a French ski resort, in that the extra distance between the front and rear wheels reduces the effectiveness of the 5in. ground clearance and we bottomed the exhaust system several times. Sitting higher, one does not bridge the humps with quite such a blind view, but one still needs to remember the extra three feet of bonnet out of sight up front.

Another snag with the longer car is that turning circles have increased from about 38ft between kerbs to a mean of 42ft, with a very poor left lock on the test car of 44ft. This means that turning into driveways can be tricky and one often uses the full lock to the limit stops in narrow back streets.

One of the poor features of early E-types was the gearbox, which, although very precise in its movements, had lazy synchromesh on the upper three ratios and none at all on first. This was remedied 18 months ago when the new all-synchro box was introduced with the 4·2 engine, and it now functions faultlessly. If the clutch isn't quite floored, movements can be stiff and notchy, but normally the lever can be snatched between positions very fast and silently. The gears themselves whine quite noticeably, but this is not an unpleasant noise and it seems well subdued.

The handbrake is a big pull-up lever between the seats and it now has a much larger and easier-to-use release button. Despite a self-adjusting mechanism its performance seemed to vary throughout our rather prolonged test mileage, and at its best it managed only a 0·25g stop from 30 m.p.h.

Left: Shelves above knee level are special to the 2+2 and the handbrake now has a larger release button. The glove box has a lockable lid and is big enough inside for passports. Right: This is the luggage space at its maximum capacity. The platform, which covers the space wheel and tools, makes an excellent grandstand for watching races from

Our dusty test car pauses for a moment on the descent of the Col de la Forclaz near Chamonix. Only the more upright windscreen gives away the 2+2, although the whole roof is 2in higher

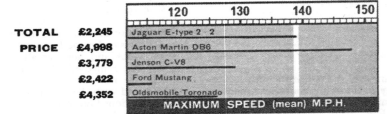

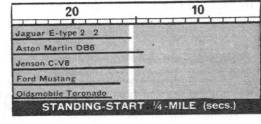

HOW THE JAGUAR E-type 2+2 COMPARES:

TOTAL	PRICE
£2,245	
£4,998	
£3,779	
£2,422	
£4,352	

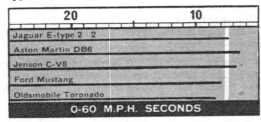

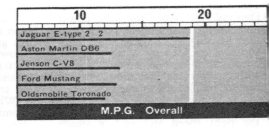

on a wet surface. It just held the 2+2 on a 1-in-4 when applied with two hands, but failed on anything steeper.

Dunlop SP radials are renowned for their wet road grip, and they lived well up to their reputation on the E-type. On a very wet track they howled through the water and gave an astonishing amount of adhesion. A Powr-Lok limited-slip differential is standard and allied to these tyres it helps to eliminate wheelspin almost completely.

There has been no change to the E-type instruments on the 2+2, except in their lighting, which has reverted to that pale kind of fluorescent blue-green used by Jaguar until a few years ago. It proved very restful on the eyes and illuminated the dials as clearly as daylight. The driver has two very large instruments directly under his eyes to tell him road and engine speed, with a row of

supplementary gauges on a central panel. This section can be released in a moment by undoing two thumbscrews and hinging it forwards to reveal all the instrument wiring and fuses; it proved very useful for replacing a faulty rectifier which sent the fuel and temperature gauges on to half power. One very surprising thing we discovered when a wire came adrift on the alternator is that the ignition lamp is simply an " ignition circuit live " indicator and not a lack of charge warning. This has now been changed, but owners of earlier 4·2 cars should keep a wary eye on their ammeters.

The occasional rear seat in the 2+2 has been particularly cleverly contrived, and the top half of its back can be pulled forwards on over-centre links when not required to give 4ft. 3½in. of flat floor behind it. A lot of odds and ends can still be stowed behind the front seats with the back

one in this position. With the back seat in use the floor space behind reduces to 3ft. 5in., and the sloping back always limits the height of luggage that will fit.

We found an adult could manage to get quite comfortable in the back if he sat half sideways with his feet under the passenger seat and his trunk behind the driver. This also meant that only the passenger needed to slide forwards from the normal position and the driver could retain his relaxed armstretch from the wheel. Two adults can be carried easily for short journeys, but the driver has to sit right up over the pedals and move the wheel back on its adjustment to clear his thighs. Two children, of course, pose none of these problems and tumble straight in without a thought.

Looking at the E-type, there doesn't seem to be a square angle on it anywhere and all corners are well rounded. This helps provide the body with an unusually low drag co-efficient, and it seems to coast for ever when slipped into neutral at speed. This must to some extent account for the very creditable fuel consumption of 18·8 m.p.g. overall, with separate figures of 19·5 m.p.g. for 1,150 miles driven in England and Wales and 18·2 over 735 miles of faster Continental driving. One remarkable thing is that the E-type has one of the flattest steady-speed fuel graphs of any car, and still betters 20 m.p.g. at 100 m.p.h.

To sum it up, the E-type is impressive from its exciting looks to its performance, which few can match. Yet as much, it is the easy and efficient way it goes about its tasks that gives the satisfaction. One's standards of driving often reflect the character of the car, and in the E-type we all felt obliged to try to live up the excellence of the machinery. This 2+2 extends the scope of what is a truly grand tourer to those with families, or bachelors with more than one friend. As such it has become slightly less of an E-type and rather more of a Jaguar. ■

SPECIFICATION : JAGUAR E-type 2 + 2, FRONT ENGINE, REAR-WHEEL DRIVE

ENGINE
Cylinders	.. 6, in-line
Cooling system	.. Water; pump, electric fan and thermostat
Bore	.. 92·1mm (3·63in.)
Stroke	.. 106mm (4·17in.)
Displacement	.. 4,235 c.c. (258 cu. in.)
Valve gear	.. Twin overhead camshafts
Compression ratio 9·1-to-1; Optional 8·0
Carburettors	.. 3 SU HD8
Fuel pump	.. SU electric
Oil filter	.. Tecalemit full-flow
Max. power	.. 265 b.h.p. (gross) at 5,400 r.p.m.
Max torque	.. 283 lb. ft. (gross) at 4,000 r.p.m.

TRANSMISSION
Clutch	.. Laycock-Hausserman disphragm-spring 10in. dia.
Gearbox	.. 4-speed, all synchromesh
Gear ratios	.. Top 1·0; Third 1·33; Second 1·97; First 3·04; Reverse 3·07
Final drive	.. Hypoid bevel with Powr-Lok limited-slip differential, 3·07 to 1

CHASSIS AND BODY
Construction	.. Integral steel body with separate front and rear sub-frames

SUSPENSION
Front	.. Independent, torsion bars, wishbones, telescopic dampers
Rear	.. Independent, coil springs, wishbones, telescopic dampers, radius arms, anti-roll bar

STEERING
Type	.. Alford and Alder rack and pinion Wheel dia. 16in.

BRAKES
Make and type	.. Dunlop disc front and rear
Servo	.. Lockheed vacuum type
Dimensions	.. F. 11in. dia., R. 10in. dia.
Swept area	.. F, 242 sq. in., R. 219 sq. in. Total 461 sq. in. (304 sq. in.) per ton laden)

WHEELS
Type	.. 72-spoke centre-lock wire type, 5in. wide rim
Tyres	.. Dunlop SP41HR tubed—size 185—15in.

EQUIPMENT
Battery	.. 12-volt 60-amp. hr.
Alternator	.. Lucas 11AC
Headlamps	.. Lucas sealed beam 75-60-watt
Reversing lamp	.. Standard
Electric fuses	.. 8
Screen wipers	.. 2-speed, self-parking
Screen washer	.. Standard, electric
Interior heater	.. Standard, fresh air
Safety belts	.. Extra, anchorages built-in
Interior trim	.. Leather seats, cloth headlining
Floor covering	.. Carpet
Starting handle	.. No provision
Jack	.. Scissor type
Jacking points	.. 2 each side under sills
Other bodies	.. None

MAINTENANCE
Fuel tank	.. 14 Imp. gallons (warning light for last 2 gal.) (63·6 litres)
Cooling system	.. 32 pints (including heater) (18 litres)
Engine sump	.. 15 pints (8·5 litres) SAE 10W/30 Change oil every 3,000 miles. Change filter element every 6,000 miles
Gearbox	.. 2·5 pints SAE90. Change oil every 12,000 miles.
Final drive	.. 2·75 pints SAE90. Change oil every 12,000 miles
Grease	.. 13 points every 6,000 miles and 4 points every 12,000 miles
Tyre pressures	.. F. 32; R. 32 p.s.i. (normal driving). F. 40; R. 40 p.s.i. (fast driving)

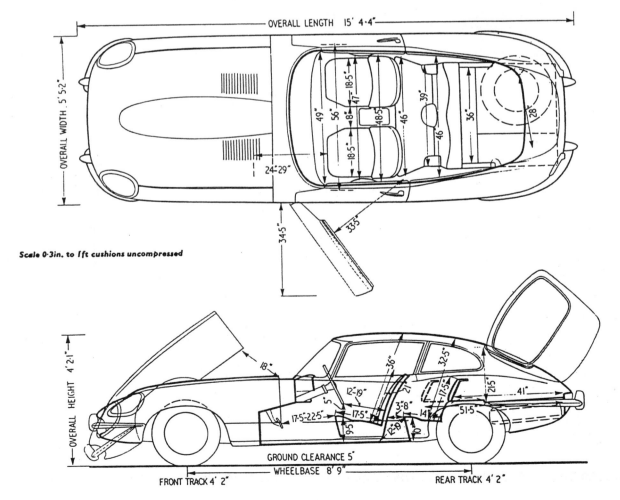

Scale 0·3in. to 1ft cushions uncompressed

The Jaguar E-type 2+2

AS regular readers know, I have already carried out a short road test of the new Jaguar 2 + 2, and now a full-length test has been made. The two cars differed, inasmuch as the previous machine had a manual gearbox and the subject of the present article was equipped with automatic transmission.

It might at first appear incongruous to fit a Borg Warner transmission to such a sporting machine, particularly now that the Jaguar manual box has become an excellent piece of equipment. Nevertheless, there is quite a considerable demand for automatic sports cars these days, particularly among the larger and more powerful models. Users who must drive a great deal in urban areas would certainly prefer this type of transmission, and there is a tendency nowadays for quite elderly men to buy sports cars, many of whom might choose the option demanding the least driving effort.

Obviously, it is good that these seasoned drivers are taking a new interest in the more civilized sports cars, for their freedom from accidents must improve the insurance situation for all of us. For my part, I would much prefer to have the do-it-yourself gearbox, but I admit that I greatly appreciated the easy driving that the automatic Jaguar gave me in London's heaviest traffic.

The design of the E-type Jaguar is well known, with its independent suspension on all four wheels and inboard disc brakes at the rear. Although fundamentally a high-performance sports car, it has all the elaborate sound insulation of the Jaguar saloons, and it is quite remarkably free from road noise over every sort of surface. The 2 + 2 model is 9 in longer in the wheelbase than the two-seater, allowing two occasional seats to be fitted behind the main buckets. Much better heat insulation is provided between the engine-transmission unit and the passengers—this was a weak point of the earlier E-types.

The famous Jaguar twin-overhead-camshaft six-cylinder engine now boasts a capacity of 4.2-litres. It has three SU carburetters and develops a gross output of 265 bhp with massive torque right through the range. At 27¾ cwt, the roomier 2 + 2 is still quite a light car and the efficient engine just plays with its load. Cars fitted with automatic transmission pull a higher gear (lower numerical ratio) than the hand-change cars at 2.88 to 1, which is used in conjunction with a limited-slip differential.

On the road, the car is marvellously effortless. There is something very special about a really good "six" and many people prefer them to eight-cylinder power units. The six is a long engine, and so a pretty impressive bonnet is needed to house it. Somehow this is all part of the character of the car and one soon becomes accustomed to the unusual length.

As a town car, the automatic E-type is excellent, though its considerable length and rather poor steering lock may cause parking to be a bit of a chore. The engine never gets bored with continuous traffic blocks and does not become hot or stall. The gear lever can be used in the D2 position—D1 allows bottom gear to be engaged and may cause some jerking in slow city driving.

Road test by JOHN BOLSTER

In general, the transmission behaves well, though it is not as utterly smooth as some of the more sophisticated American efforts. The pleasant centrally-mounted quadrant lever provides a lock-up position for holding a low gear, when the rev counter may be taken into the red sector if the ultimate performance is required. It also permits winding hills to be stormed without any unnecessary changing up and down.

Though some power is absorbed by the transmission, the instantaneous up-changes on full throttle certainly add to the acceleration. It is, indeed, seldom necessary to use more than half throttle when overtaking other cars. The cruising speed may be almost anything you fancy—110 mph is a nice, restful speed, for example. There is a praiseworthy absence of wind noise, and although this larger and heavier body must reduce the speed a little, the maximum of 137 mph is still more than satisfactory.

Dunlop SP41 HR tyres are now standard on these cars. In conjunction with the excellent suspension, they give high cornering power and a fine sense of control, with plenty of "feel" through the steering. On wet roads the rear end breakaway is fairly abrupt, but it can be stopped with a flick of the steering. The brakes are incomparably better than those of the earlier E-types, the car appearing to be arrested by a giant hand without a trace of a skid. The resistance to fading is impressive, but the hand brake is not notably effective.

Though the suspension does not feel soft, the ride is nevertheless most comfortable, with a total absence of pitching. There is only moderate roll during fast cornering, thanks to the low build and fairly wide track. Unfortunately, the headlamps are still pitifully feeble for so fast a car, being recessed behind plastic covers.

The interior furnishing and the instrument panel are pleasant, functional, and very much in the Jaguar tradition. The front seats are most comfortable and give good lateral location, the wood-rim steering wheel being instantly adjustable for position. The rear seats are really intended for children, but a very neat arrangement allows them to be folded away, when the luggage platform is usefully increased in size. My two large dogs found this space very much to their liking, and the surface does not scratch or collect dog hairs.

This compartment is accessible through a rear door which contains the large electrically demisted rear window. This door is heavy and has a rather crude prop which may fold up at the wrong moment. At the time of writing, I have some most spectacular and painful bruises to prove this, so I suggest that Mr Heath Robinson should be fired from the design staff! The door locks might be better, too—a common complaint with British cars nowadays, I am afraid.

A remarkable feature of this Jaguar is its fuel economy. The average owner will obtain a genuine 20 mpg, which is good going indeed for a 4.2-litre car of very high performance. Even quite a bit of 100 mph cruising seems to have remarkably little effect on this splendid economy.

Like all Jaguars, the 2 + 2 represents unbeatable value for money. Though many of us would prefer the manual gearbox option, myself included, the automatic version which I have been testing will certainly widen the appeal of the E-type. The longer body results in a more practical car, and the deeper windscreen, with slightly higher seating, gives an improved view and reduces the apparent length of the bonnet. Without doubt, Jaguars have done it again.

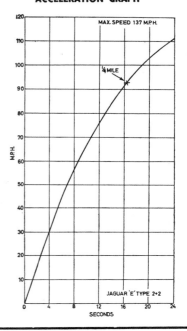

ACCELERATION GRAPH

SPECIFICATION AND PERFORMANCE DATA

Car Tested: Jaguar E-type 2 + 2 saloon, price, with automatic transmission, £2385 12s. 11d. including PT.

Engine: Six cylinders 92.07 mm x 106 mm (4235 cc). Twin chain-driven overhead camshafts. Compression ratio 9 to 1. 265 bhp (gross) at 5400 rpm. Three SU carburetters. Lucas coil and distributor.

Transmission: Borg Warner three-speed automatic gearbox with fluid torque converter. Hypoid bevel final drive, ratio 2.88 to 1, with limited slip differential.

Chassis: Central steel monocoque with multi-tubular extensions front and rear. Independent front suspension with wishbones, torsion bars, and anti-roll bar. Rack and pinion steering. Independent rear suspension with lower wishbones and fixed length driveshafts plus radius arms. Helical springs. Girling telescopic dampers all round. Dunlop servo-assisted disc brakes, inboard at rear. Centre-locking wire wheels fitted Dunlop SP41HR 185-15 tyres.

Equipment: Twelve-volt lighting and starting. Speedometer. Rev. counter. Oil pressure, water temperature, and fuel gauges. Ammeter. Clock. Heating, demisting, and ventilation system. Windscreen wipers and washers. Flashing direction indicators. Heated rear window (extra). Radio (extra).

Dimensions: Wheelbase, 8 ft 9 in; track, 4 ft 2 in; overall length, 15 ft 4½ in; width, 5 ft 5¼ in; weight: 1 ton 7 cwt 3 qrs.

Performance: Maximum speed: 137 mph. Standing quarter-mile: 16.4 secs. Acceleration: 0.30 mph, 4 secs; 0-50 mph, 6.7 secs; 0-60 mph, 8.8 secs; 0-80 mph, 12.9 secs; 0-100 mph, 19 secs.

Fuel consumption: 18 to 22 mpg.

JAGUAR 'E' TYPE 2+2

YOU COULD, ONE SUPPOSES, GET AN ADULT OF EVEN GENEROUS BUILD IN THE BACK IF HE OR SHE SAT SIDEWAYS, A COUPLE OF SPROGS, ON THE OTHER HAND, HAVE MORE THAN SUFFICIENT ROOM.

Immediately noticeable are the longer body and steep windscreen.

(Staff Photo)

IT'S two inches higher, nine inches longer and weighs an extra three hundredweight, all of which is the price you pay for being able to cart a pair of sprogs about in the 4.2-litre "E"-type 2+2. And, on top of all that, it doesn't accelerate quite so fast, nor has it such a high maximum speed. And frankly, none of it matters a damn—it is still a bloody good motor-car by any standards. It is superbly-equipped, comfortable, fast, safe, elegant still if a little less so than the lower shorter two-seater and altogether something of a Motoring Experience. Unfortunately, the car we had for test was fitted with the optional Borg-Warner Model 8 transmission, which goes with the very high rear axle ratio of 2.88 to 1 compared with the 3.07 job which goes with the standard four-speed box. Nothing against automatics, of course—it's just that we're old-fashioned enough to prefer the do-it-yourself version, and in spite of the fact that as fitted to the "E"-type you can play a lot of tunes on

it yourself, we prefer sporting carriages without the magic touch in the transmission. It transforms the character of the "E"-type: in its automatic form it's a pleasant, restful touring car; if it isn't as quick as the two-seater, or for that matter as the manual-change four-seater, it still doesn't hang about.

The mechanical specification doesn't change between the 2+2 and the two-seater except, as we said, that you get a higher cog if you specify the automatics, and of course the 2+2 is a bigger—an even bigger—motor-car. Apart from the increases in height and length, the wheelbase is greater, the doors are wider and the floor is lowered a bit. But apart from this everything remains as before. You still get the six-cylinder, twin-cam engine, developing 265 b.h.p. at five-four before you start having to subtract odd equines for accessories and so on—not to mention the magic gearbox —and measuring 92.07 mm x 106 mm bore and stroke to

112

give a capacity of 4,235 c.c. Compression ratio is 9 to 1, the go-juice gets fed into the works through three huge HD8 S.U.s and a cooling system which includes a thermostatically-controlled electric fan. You get at all this by undoing a couple of catches inside the car and swinging the whole front section forwards, where its long nose stops it going quite far enough for comfortable checking of the levels. An alternator copes with electrical supply and demand.

Inside the car you've got the traditional Jaguar instruments, all spread out in a business-like long line with the king-sized speedo (five inches in diameter and reading up to 160 m.p.h.) and matching tachometer slap in front of you. Underneath them are all those lovely switches, controling everything from the map-reading light to the electric screen-washers; this is also one of the few cars where you really have to press the tit to start the fire going—none of your turn-the-key tricks here. "E"-types have ignition switches AND starter buttons like we all had in the old days. The selector lever for the automatic transmission lives down on the floor where the gear-lever would be if it had a gear-lever, and there is a little quadrant for it to move in which tells you what you've got selected. There are the usual positions for parking lock, reverse and neutral, and for dashing about in a forwards direction you are given D1, D2 and a low-gear hold. What all this means is that D1 gives you bottom gear starts and uses all three ratios progressively until there is no further to go, while D2 avoids bottom gear, starts you off in second and makes life less brisk but, possibly, more economical. The low-gear selector means that you can hang on to bottom gear until the thing blows up if you forget to move it at the right time, while if you grab Low from top it will immediately make the thing change down from top to intermediate provided you aren't going too fast. Bottom is then selected automatically if the speed drops low enough.

In practice a D1 start, using a bit of power, will provide upward changes at 55 and 87 m.p.h., although if you're just trickling along in traffic you'll be in top gear by the time you're doing a shade over 30 m.p.h. Once you're in top, you can get hold of intermediate by using the kick-down, which will bang you into second cog and hang on to it until you're doing over ninety. Obviously, you can't use this technique if you happen to find a lower cog desirable as you rush into a corner, and this is where the low-gear hold comes in—you simply move the selector-lever one notch and intermediate gear arrives to report for duty. If, under these circumstances, your speed drops below 20 m.p.h. bottom gear will automatically be selected, and on "our" car this arrived with a helluva bang which we didn't like very much. At the other end of the scale, we didn't fancy hanging on to the low-gear hold until the rev-counter needle got to the red mark because of an appreciable lag between moving the lever back to one of the "D" positions and actually getting the upward change, which meant that for a measurable length of time you went on accelerating well into the red. Which is obviously a Bad Thing.

Obviously, you get maximum performance if you plant the thing in D1 and press hard. This, as we have explained, uses all three ratios in the box and, with the loud pedal well down towards the floor, the upward changes are carried out at a point well round the rev-counter. Driving it this way you'll get up to sixty in just over eight seconds, to the legal limit in ten-and-a-half and on up to, say, the ton in a bit over twenty, which is slower than the manual-change two-seater by about one second to sixty and by nearly three seconds to a hundred.

Top whack is quite well down by comparison with the manual-change two-seater, and well down too on the figure Jaguars quote as maximum speed for the manual-change 2+2. We got a shade under 140 m.p.h. compared with 149·8 for the two-seater, while Jaguars claim 145 for the manual four-seater. The difference, we suppose, is accounted for by the greater frontal area and, of course, in the case of 2+2 comparisons, by the extra power absorbed by the automatic box. But by any standards it is still a pretty swift old motor, and not one to be treated lightly.

We called it a four-seater just now: well, of course, it isn't, and Jaguars don't say that it is. We haven't the least idea what is actually meant by the words "two-plus-two" but what it invariably boils down to in practice is a two-seater with space behind the front seats which is upholstered and which will accommodate a couple of kids in reasonable comfort. Which is what this car achieves. You could, one supposes, get an adult of even generous build into the back if he or she sat sideways and wasn't going very far. A couple of sprogs, on the other hand, have more than sufficient room for the heads and legs as well as their behinds and ought to sit there happily lost in rapt admiration of Daddy's driving skill for mile after mile. If you happen to be running as a two-seater, well you simply fold the back seats away into the floor and you've got as much space for luggage as you get in the two-seater. There is some additional comfort to be found in the fact that the seats are great and caused us no fatigue of any sort even on long journeys; there is plenty of room in the well-furnished interior—even our six-footer had no complaints about the headroom in the front of the 2+2—with lots of space for odds and ends, and above all an unusually efficient sound insulation—even by Jaguar standards—which allows the car to waft along on almost total silence at three-figure speeds. The engine noise is almost completely damped out, only the things like the wireless aerial make windy noises and all you hear inside, apart from the wireless and the occasional soft click from the cigar lighter (real executive transport, this) is a low-pitched muffled boom from the exhausts.

What about comfort and handling? Well, on the first count there is practically nothing more to say. The 2+2 is comfortable, and the longer wheelbase probably allows it to ride more smoothly over bad surfaces. On the handling side, the increase in wheelbase and weight don't seem to have changed anything. The 2+2 handles with almost completely neutral characteristics until, eventually, it reaches a point at which gentle oversteer occurs, the tail sliding out ever-so-gradually and easily controlled. In fact, once you get used to the size of the thing you can chuck the "E"-type about a bit: a limited-slip diff. takes care of getting the power to the road and makes a powerful difference in the wet, and the steering, at 2½ turns from lock to lock, gives the right degree of control for somewhat vivid motoring which you can't really call "driving with elan" when you're in a Jag. Now can you?

Brakes? Certainly. Discs all round—inboard at the back—plus a powerful servo which combines with wheels which tend to stay firmly on the ground all the time to give extremely good braking—this is something you couldn't always say about the "E"-type. Nowadays that's all over, though, and the "E"-type's anchors bring it to a graceful halt with no fade that we discovered, and in exchange for a light pedal pressure. In fact, the pressure is so light that an owner hopping in after driving a car which needed a heavy old prod on the stoppers would be well advised to get used to 'em gradually, otherwise he could find himself shrieking to a halt in a cloud of rubber smoke while the 48-seater coach astern of him climbs up the back of the boot.

Petrol consumption isn't desperate when you compare it

with the sort of performance you're getting, plus the creature comforts that are thrown in. As an overall average you'd get about 18 to the gallon: if you do a long run in this country, now that we got this ruddy limit, you could get twenty, while shuffling about in and out of town seventeen would be nearer the mark. There's a fourteen gallon tank to give you a useful range, the gauge is pretty accurate and, like all Jaguars, they throw in a little light which flashes when more juice would be a Good Idea.

Are there flies in the "E"-type ointment? Yes. Quite honestly, the heating arrangements are really up to the standards of a £2,000 plus car, and the demisting bit definitely isn't, although this was greatly helped on the test wagon by an electrically-heated rear window. The other, greater snag is the lack of effective lighting for after-dark motoring. The headlamps probably lose a good deal by having to look through perspex windows, but whatever the reason they aren't up to the performance standards on either main or dipped beams. And with a sharp nose like that it isn't the easiest thing in the world to attach iodine-vapour spot-lamps to help out, either.

But nothing's perfect, and one way and another we reckon the 2+2 "E"-type is high on the list of cars most keen-driver family men would most like to own. If it ain't, it ought to be.

Above: even if she was wearing her mini skirt, the low door sill in the Jaguar would enable her to get out gracefully.

Below: the rear seating arrangement.

Below left: the usual superlative range of instruments.

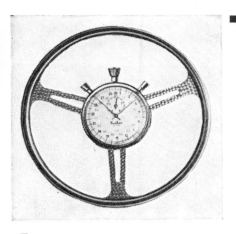

JAGUAR "E" TYPE 2 + 2

PERFORMANCE PANEL

Make: JAGUAR
Model: "E" TYPE 2 + 2

ENGINE

Starting:	Excellent
Idling:	Excellent
Flexibility:	Excellent
Vibration:	Excellent

TRANSMISSION

Clutch:	n/a
Gear Ratios:	n/a
Synchromesh	n/a
Gear Change	n/a
Gearbox Noise:	n/a
Final Drive Ratio	2·88 (see text)
Rear Axle Noise:	none

SUSPENSION

Roadholding:	Good
Roll Stiffness:	Average

Ride:	Good
Traction:	Good
Ground Clearance	Satisfactory

STEERING

Ratio:	2·5 turns lock to lock
Kick Back:	Good
Caster:	Good
Direction:	Good
Lock:	Poor

BRAKES

Fade:	Nil
Pedal Pressure:	Excellent
Response:	Excellent
Balance:	Excellent
Handbrake—position:	Good
—action:	Good

BODY

Finish exterior:	Good
—interior:	Excellent
Sound Level:	Excellent
Weatherproof:	Good
Entrance—front	Good
—rear:	Satisfactory

Front seat—comfort:	Good
—legroom:	Good
Rear seat—comfort:	Satisfactory
—legroom:	Poor
Driving position:	Excellent
Headroom—front:	Good
—rear:	Satisfactory
Boot:	Good
Other storage space:	Good
Ventilation:	Good
Visibility:	Good
Heating:	Poor
Instrument:	Excellent
Minor Controls:	Excellent

ELECTRICS

Headlights:	Poor
Other Lights:	Good
Windscreen Wiper:	Good

SERVICE

Frequency:	3000 miles
Accessibility—plugs:	Good
—spare wheel:	Good
—battery:	Good
—radiator:	Poor
—dipstick:	Satisfactory

Engine: Six cylinders, twin overhead camshafts; 92·07 mm. x 106 mm. bore and stroke; 4,235 c.c.; compression ratio 9 to 1; triple HD8 S.U. carburettors; seven main-bearing crankshaft; thermostatically-controlled electric cooling fan; 265 b.h.p. at 5,400 r.p.m.

Transmission (option on test car): Borg Warner Model 8 automatic transmission with gear selector quadrant on tunnel. Rear axle ratio 2·88 to 1; Hardy-Spicer limited-slip differential.

Suspension: Front, independent, with wishbones and torsion bars and an anti-roll bar; rear, independent, with tubular transverse links, radius arms and twin coil springs.

Brakes: Dunlop discs on all four wheels (inboard at rear) with vacuum servo assistance. Independent hydraulic circuits to front and rear.

Dimensions: Overall length, 15 ft. 4½ in.; overall width, 5 ft. 5¼ in.; overall height, 4 ft. 2 in.; ground clearance (laden) 5½ in.; turning circle, 41 ft.; dry weight, 22½ cwt.

PERFORMANCE

	m.p.h.
MAXIMUM SPEED	139·8
Mean of two ways	139·3

SPEEDS IN GEARS
(automatic transmission): Low—55

Intermediate—87

ACCELERATION	secs.
0–30 —	3·5
0–40 —	4·9
0–50 —	6·3
0–60 —	8·3
0–70 —	10·5
0–80 —	13·2
0–90 —	16·7
0–100—	20·5

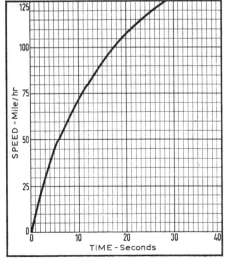

Manufacturers: Jaguar Cars Ltd., Coventry.
Price in U.K.: £2,245 including purchase tax.

GORDON CHITTENDEN PHOTOS

4.2 JAGUAR XKE 2·2

Grace, pace—and, now, more space

IT ISN'T DIFFICULT to get into an argument about a Jaguar. Everyone who has ever owned one, and many who never have, hold strong opinions about how good or how bad a Jaguar is. To the man who fancies the latest in modern, short-stroke, Vee-type engine with multi-throat carburetors, the long-stroke, 3-SU, inline six Jaguar is practically prehistoric. To the design nit-picker, the XKE was an unsatisfactory compromise taken off the racing D-type and the coupe body a mistake that never should have happened.

Yet the E-type is a car for the enthusiastic motorist. It is mechanically interesting, thoroughly pleasant to drive and is possessed of great character and charm. If the engine is basically old, it's still an overhead cam design and a better engine than most cars can boast, and if there were mistakes in the basic body design, it's still undoubtedly one of the sexiest shapes ever to catch a lady's eye.

When the E-type was introduced in 1961, it had the 3.8-liter version of the XK engine and a 4-speed manual transmission with non-synchronized first gear. Since that time there have been a number of changes and refinements made; the engine has been increased to 4.2 liters (by increasing the bore from 3.43 to 3.63 in.), the 4-speed gearbox is now fully synchronized and a 3-speed automatic transmission is offered as well.

The engine in the current 4.2 version is rated at 265 bhp at 5400 rpm. The 3.8 also offered 265 bhp but at 6000 rpm. The 4.2 offers more torque than the 3.8, however (283 vs. 260 lb-ft) at the same engine speed, 4000 rpm.

The most significant change in the latest model is the addition of sufficient length to make the coupe into a genuine 2+2. This was accomplished by stretching the vehicle by nine inches, the wheelbase being increased to 105 in. from 96. All the added length has been made in the passenger area; the doors are 8.5 in. wider, which has the side benefit of making it much easier for the driver and the first passenger to get in and out. The plus 2 seats are hardly full size and hardly suitable for long distance traveling but the whole idea of the extra seats is to make it a 2+2, not a family sedan. We made a perfect demonstration of the car's utility as a 2+2 after the Pebble Beach Concours when we transported a pair of stranded golf widows back to their motel in Monterey. They were admittedly a bit derisive about the lack of knee room but if we'd been driving one of the original XKE coupes, they'd still be stranded at Del Monte Lodge.

The roofline of the coupe has been raised by two inches to create more headroom and to increase the height of the windshield. This is a useful change, so far as the taller driver is concerned, and even the tallest member of our staff could find nothing to complain about on this score. The increased roof height has also required taller windows and this has resulted in a curious condition of rolled-down windows that don't completely disappear into the door.

The hinged back door offers easy access to a large flat luggage space. This area can be made even larger by switching the plus-2 seat back to its forward position. The spare tire is housed in a well under the luggage deck, a neat, out-of-the-way location, and there is a good assortment of practical tools in a roll-up kit furnished with the car.

Our test car was made available to us through the importer, Jaguar Cars Inc., and by arrangements kindly made by Johannes Eerdmans. It was shipped to the West Coast,

made ready at Charles Hornburg, Inc., service department and we picked it up from service manager Frank Bott. We must admit that we experienced a pleasantly anticipatory glow as it was turned over to us. It was a handsome pale green, had chrome wire wheels (as do all E-types brought in through regular channels) and the interior was finished in rough-grain tan leather.

When we drove it away, there were 138 miles on the odometer. We had the car for 10 days and during this time drove it more than 2500 miles. Time and tide being what they are, we don't often get to drive a road test car this much but we were especially glad to be able to put this many miles on the 2+2. Not only was it a pleasure to drive but it also gave us an opportunity to observe the car's behavior during a critical period of its existence. During this period the only defect we found was that the bulb behind the right hand turn signal indicator worked only intermittently. When it didn't blink, you had to tap it to get it going again. We also put in a fresh set of sparkplugs before doing our acceleration runs but outside of this, we did nothing more than change the oil at the 1000-mi mark as recommended by the owner's manual. There just wasn't anything else that needed doing or that we could find to complain about. Even the clock kept reasonably accurate time.

The larger doors make it easier to get in and out than it was in the earlier coupe and though the door sill is high (stepover height, 17.0 in.), ingress-egress techniques do not require contortions. Once seated, the driver feels that he is sitting high up. From this position he is looking out across an impressive length of hood and until he becomes used to it, there is a constant concern over the yard or so of vulnerable sheet metal that is beyond his range of vision.

The steering wheel has three inches of travel and this, combined with the good seat travel, makes it possible for almost anyone to be comfortable. The seats themselves, when we first tried them, seemed too small and we were prepared to find them tiring during a long drive. We couldn't have been more wrong and after several long stints at the wheel we decided they were among the most satisfactory seats we'd ever tried.

The dashboard is padded in the contemporary mode and the gauges and dials are set into a no-nonsense, non-reflective black panel. (No polished walnut to worry about, for which thanks are again given.) The instruments themselves are big, legible Smiths with white reading on black backgrounds. The instrumentation is suitably complete and the speedometer of our test car deserves special mention as it was dead accurate at 100 mph. A most unusual circumstance. The tachometer was wont to take an occasional leap, however.

The automatic transmission with which our test car was equipped is an option that adds $340 to the basic price. The gearbox is a Borg Warner Model 8, a 3-speed planetary gearbox with torque converter. It makes the car dead simple to drive and for anyone who is weary of shifting and clutching through heavy day-after-day traffic, we recommend the Jaguar 2+2 automatic without reservation.

That the automatic accounts for some loss in efficiency is undeniable but there is sufficient margin of performance with the 2+2 that we would not consider the loss worth thinking about in exchange for the convenience.

In all-out performance, the present 2+2 has a bit less

4.2 JAGUAR XKE 2+2

AT A GLANCE...

Price as tested	$6823
Engine	6 cyl dohc, 4235cc, 265 bhp
Curb weight, lb	3090
Top speed, mph	128
Acceleration, 0-60 mph, sec	8.3
50-70 mph (1-2 gear)	5.0
Average fuel consumption, mpg	17.3

4.2 JAGUAR XKE 2+2

zap than the original XKE. It's heavier, for one thing (curb weight of 3090 lb vs. 2720 for the E-type roadster), the frontal area is slightly greater (18.2 vs. 17.5 sq ft) and it has no more horsepower. In acceleration, our 2+2 with automatic got through the standing quarter-mile in 16.7 sec. This is hardly sensational, even for a car with a lb:hp ratio of 13.1:1 but it is certainly adequate. We might also note that the car had almost exactly 2000 miles on the odometer when we made our acceleration runs and that this is just barely getting into the broken-in stage with a Jaguar engine.

In top speed, our car showed a 2-way average of 128 mph. This was 5350 rpm and after the engine is thoroughly broken in there's no reason to suppose that a 2+2 wouldn't do the full 5500 rpm beyond which the engine should not

be taken "under ANY CIRCUMSTANCES," according to the factory manual. With the 3.31:1 final drive which comes as standard with the automatic, 5500 revs would be 132 mph and this sounds about right for maximum speed. In a recent test, the British magazine *Autocar* reported a top speed of 139 mph for a 2+2 equipped with the 4-speed gearbox and 3.09:1 rear end.

The handling of the Jaguar 2+2 is excellent. The suspension, independent at both ends, keeps everything where it should be and because it does everything so well, it is a car that inspires confidence. It isn't a slalom car, what with the long wheelbase and the sloping-away extremities out where you can't see them, but it is easy to drive quickly even on the twistiest normal roads.

Drivers who have owned Jaguars in the past will no doubt recall their concern for getting caught in traffic jams. We admit we were a bit wary with the 2+2 and thus kept one

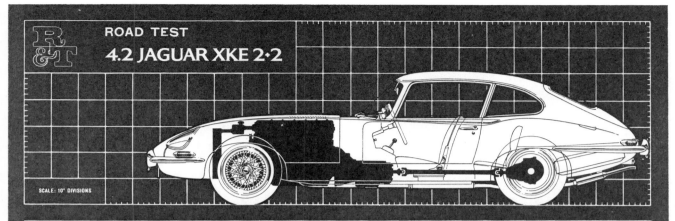

SCALE: 10" DIVISIONS

PRICE

Basic list.................$6070
As tested..................6823

ENGINE

No cyl & type...... inline 6 dohc
Bore x stroke, mm....92.1 x 106
In....................3.63 x 4.17
Displacement, cc/cu in.4235/258.4
Compression ratio..........9.0:1
Bhp @ rpm.........265 @ 5400
Equivalent mph...........129
Torque @ rpm, lb-ft. 283 @ 4000
Equivalent mph............97
Carburetors..........3 HD8 SU
Type fuel required.......premium

DRIVE TRAIN

Transmission: Borg Warner Model
8 automatic (torque converter
with 3-speed planetary gearbox).
Gear ratios: 3rd (1.00).....3.31:1
2nd (1.46)..............4.83:1
1st (2.40)..............7.94:1
1st (2.40 x 2.00).......15.88:1
Differential type......limited slip
Ratio................3.31:1
Optional ratios.....3.07, 3.54:1

CHASSIS & SUSPENSION

Frame type........unit with body
Brake type..................disc
Swept area, sq in.........461
Tire size 6.40–15
Make............Dunlop RS 5
Steering type.......rack & pinion
Turns, lock-to-lock.........2.5
Turning circle, ft..........41
Front suspension: independent
with unequal-length A-arms,
torsion bars, tube shocks, anti-
roll bar.
Rear suspension: independent with
lower A-arms, radius arms,
fixed-length halfshafts, coil
springs, tube shocks, anti-roll
bar.

ACCOMMODATION

Normal capacity, persons.......2
Occasional capacity..........4
Seat width, front, in.....2 x 18.0
Rear...................39.2
Head room, front/rear...40.0/37.0
Seat back adjustment, deg......5
Entrance height, in..........47.3
Step-over height..........17.0
Door width..............41.0
Driver comfort rating:
Driver 69 in. tall............95

Driver 72 in. tall............84
Driver 75 in. tall............84
(85–100, good; 70–85, fair;
under 70, poor)

GENERAL

Curb weight, lb.............3090
Test weight................3410
Weight distribution (with
driver), front/rear, %...49/51
Wheelbase, in..............105.0
Track, front/rear....... 50.0/50.0
Overall length............184.3
Width...............65.3
Height...............50.1
Frontal area, sq ft 18.2
Ground clearance, in.........5.5
Overhang, front/rear....36.2/43.1
Departure angle, deg.........20
Usable trunk space......see text
Fuel tank capacity, gal......16.8

INSTRUMENTATION

Instruments: 160-mph speedometer, 6000-rpm tachometer, trip
odometer, fuel level, water
temperature, oil pressure, ammeter, clock.
Warning lights: choke, brake fluid
level/parking brake, turn indicators, fuel level, high beam,
ignition.

CALCULATED DATA

Lb/hp (test wt).............12.8
Mph/1000 rpm (top gear)....23.0
Engine revs/mi (60 mph)....2500
Piston travel, ft/mi.........1820
Rpm @ 2500 ft/min 3600
Equivalent mph..........87
Cu ft/ton mi..............109
R&T wear index..........45.4

EXTRA COST OPTIONS

Included on test car: chrome wire
wheels, white sidewall tires,
tinted glass, overriders, automatic transmission.
Other options: radio.

MAINTENANCE

Crankcase capacity, qt........9.0
Change interval, mi.......3000
Oil filter type...........full flow
Change interval, mi.......6000
Chassis lube interval, mi.....6000

FUEL CONSUMPTION

Normal driving, mpg........14–19
Cruising range, mi........235–320

MISCELLANEOUS

Body styles available: 2+2 coupe
as tested.
Warranty period: 12 mos/12,500 mi.

ROAD TEST RESULTS

ACCELERATION

Time to speed, sec:
0–30 mph.................3.4
0–40 mph.................4.8
0–50 mph.................6.4
0–60 mph.................8.3
0–70 mph................10.5
0–80 mph................13.6
0–100 mph...............22.5
50–70 mph (1–2 gear)........5.0

Time to distance, sec:
0–100 ft.................3.6
0–500 ft.................9.3
¼-mile.................16.7
Speed at end, mph..........88
Passing exposure time, sec:
Car ahead going 50 mph.....5.6

SPEEDS IN GEARS

High gear (5350), mph........128
2nd (5500)................89
1st (5500)................54

BRAKES

Panic stop from 80 mph:
Deceleration, % G...........89
Control..................good
Parking: hold 30% grade.......no
Overall brake rating........good

SPEEDOMETER ERROR

30 mph indicated.....actual 29.0
40 mph...................39.3
60 mph...................60.2
80 mph...................80.0
100 mph...................100.0
Odometer correction factor...0.995

ACCELERATION & COASTING

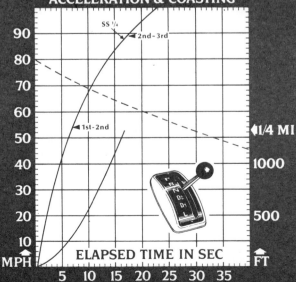

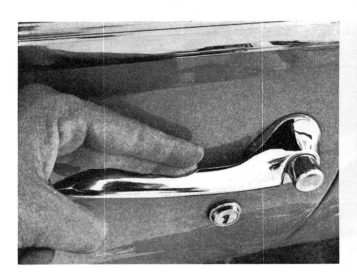

eye on the water temperature gauge almost constantly. We relaxed after being caught on a hot summer Sunday afternoon and spending over a half hour creeping a yard at a time over the last hills into Los Angeles from Santa Barbara. The needle went up to the 100°C section of the dial (which goes to 110°) but never went any higher. The same spot on the gauge was reached later when driving across the Mojave Desert at high ambient temperatures but neither then nor when making all-out runs did the needle go higher. However, the electric cooling fan comes on at 80°C and since the engine in our test car ran that hot nearly all the time, the fan stayed on most of the time. This is a curious way of doing things as the purpose of a supplemental electric fan is to have it come on under severe conditions when additional air circulation is needed, not to have it running (and using power) whether it is needed or not.

It is not easy for us to assign the Jaguar its proper place in the automotive scheme of things. We expect a lot from it and we get a lot. Yet there are curious little disappointments such as louvers that aren't quite perfect, crooked little ripples in the sheet metal that reveal an uneven surface, little bits of trim that didn't get glued properly. And over the most severe section of our ride evaluation road, the body of our test car was so full of rattles and squeaks that it almost made us laugh.

On the other hand, it's obvious that we expect too much. Because of its beautiful lines, its handsome engine, its luxurious interior, its good road manners, its excellent brakes and all its other virtues, we tend to class it with cars costing far more and thus demand the same sort of perfection we feel we have a right to expect from a $10,000 Iso, a $14,000 Ferrari, or a $15,000 Aston Martin. This may be unfortunate but it also demonstrates just how great a value the Jaguar really is.

". . . and thou beside me, sweltering in the wilderness."

'Cook—with an E'

A Buchan laddie goes home in style

by Rab Cook

AS I pulled up outside the Saltoun Arms Hotel in Fraserburgh, a saloon drew alongside. The passenger, a youth of about 18, called out: "Michty! Fit d'ye get oot o' that?"

"'s near's damn't a hunner an' forty," I said, dropping back into the Buchan Doric language without really realizing it. He thought for a bit, looked at the E-type from stem to stern and said with awe: "Losh—that's twice the speed limit". In Buchan, you see, they seize on the basic essentials. . . .

I suppose that, before going any further, I should explain about this Buchan and Doric business. The very north-east corner of Scotland is Buchan, an ancient Celtic territory which lies between the rivers Ythan and Deveron but which in spirit stretches from Stonehaven to Buckie. About 4,000 years ago the Beaker Men arrived there after a long walk from Central Europe via Holland —probably they left because they couldn't stand the cooking—and their skull structure is plainly evident in the North East even today, giving lie to the story that the Vikings completely wiped out the Picts. The Doric language is a sort of ancient Northumbrian (goodness only knows how it got there) which the people talk when they don't want visitors to know what is happening. Should you feel that it *isn't* a different language, but just a dialect, try working out: "Thon feel limmer's fair connach't th' neep hasher", which is quite a normal sentence up there. Non-Picts of any breed will find this somewhat tricky and would be floored even by a simple question such as: "Fa's 'at?"

Lest you doubt the relevance of any of

this to an E-type 2+2 automatic I must point out that Buchan has retained its unique character and people because it is in a corner which everyone who travels from Aberdeen to Elgin or Inverness cuts across. So my arrival there with this silver-grey bullet was somewhat akin to wearing a mini-skirt at Ascot. For example, the *Fraserburgh Herald* published an item in its "Round and About" column, telling its readers that one R. Cook, assistant editor of *Motor,* was on holiday in the Saltoun (pronounced "Salt'n") Arms: last year, when I turned up for the same length of time with a Rover 2000, they took not a bit of notice. Unfortunately they rather spoiled the whole thing by saying that I was a native of Macduff whereas I'm from Banff, the deadly rival town on the opposite bank of the Deveron.

The point is that having an E-type, even a borrowed one, makes quite a difference. The whisper goes around the hotel. People who wouldn't normally bother go out of their way to smile at you and engage you in conversation, usually starting: "I've just been having a look at your car. . . ." At one stage the grapevine got a bit tangled and one fellow guest was overheard remarking to another: "The manager of this place must be *coining* it—he's got an E-type".

Now why, you might ask, should a person who lives in London point the nose of an E-type to the north (no, the car wasn't magnetic) instead of south or east where there are no nasty 70 limits? Why spend a fortnight doing 2,477 miles on British roads when the Autostrada del Sol is calling? Well, for a start, 2½-thousand miles at 19.92 m.p.g.

comes to just over £35, which is a fair old hole in the travel allowance. Next point is that I like to get back home now and again to keep in touch with the basic thought processes and indulge in some of the local customs, like seeing how much malt-flavoured soda water you can drink in an evening. But the matter of real importance is this cut-off aspect of the North East—you can go for miles and never see another car yet the roads are well surfaced and, since it is a fairly flat part of the world (surprised?) the open bends are a sheer delight. In Buchan, you really *can* go pleasure motoring, even in 1966, and because it is an agricultural area with many small farms, the road network is an exceptionally comprehensive one—there are good roads absolutely everywhere. There are also miles and miles—quite literally—of completely uninhabited golden sands, sand dunes, little villages with tiny harbours cowering under cliffs and as much solitude or company as you may want.

One feature of the roads is their long-straight/tight-bend/long-straight layout, so a car with considerable acceleration is just what you want. Having an automatic gearbox makes it better still because once you are used to it you can get instant gear changing with a mere flick of the right foot. The local drivers are another feature. They are either very fast and very, very competent, or else very slow and so thoroughly hopeless that you will never credit it unless you go there. In fact, they are so bad that the fast ones *have* to be competent otherwise they don't survive. With such thin traffic the rearview mirror becomes a redundancy and look-

Family gathering. Brother Cook gets shirt sleeve dirty on cowling; Mother Cook says: "Is that all engine?"; Cook-type Cook watches to see that nothing gets pinched.

Above: The effect that the E-type had on members of the Aberdeen Ladies' Pipe Band was quite remarkable. They manifested one Sunday evening in the square in front of the Saltoun Arms in Fraserburgh. Or, womanifested . . .?

Right: Mother's country cottage. . . . Actually, it is Craigievar Castle, near Alford in Aberdeenshire, and belongs to the National Trust for Scotland. On certain days you can see inside it.

ing to right and left comes into much the same category. After all, if you have met nothing at a road junction for the past 40 years, why should there suddenly be an E-type driven by a mad journalist bearing down on you today? What's so special about today?

So, in your E-type, you regard every side road, farm road, field gateway and rustling in the grass with the gravest possible doubts. The engine makes a lovely moan as you raise and lower your foot and now and then Messrs. Borg and Warner change gear for you. Warner, by the way, made lovely, smooth changes but Borg was a bit jerky at times—he took over when the kick-down button was pressed. You dart along like a minnow or like Wordsworth's Reaper—stop here, or gently pass. On the rare occasions when you do come up behind another car you pull right in and study his behaviour for a while; usually, you have to give him a hoot and then wait until he makes that sudden dive for the nearside that means he's heard you. The very good drivers, on the other hand, give no trouble whatsoever and immediately you come into view they give a solitary wink with the nearside indicator to say: "OK, I've seen you." Very comforting, if unorthodox. You can pick out Scottish drivers on English roads by this trick.

With an E-type, you can tell when a driver ahead has seen you in his mirror if he is carrying passengers because they all suddenly turn their heads and look. Often, I just lurked behind to see how long this would take—the record was three miles.

But, usually, the roads are quite empty and with such a beautifully balanced car you go round corners by steering with your right foot as well as using it to change gear—just a flick does the trick—and you think deep thoughts about insurance companies who charge a small fortune for covering what must be one of the safest cars ever built. It's like changing direction while swimming—you don't do anything except decide that you want to do it. "Your wish," says the E-type, "is my command."

The trip north from London was through the worst driving conditions I've ever experienced, and that's saying something. Man, it *rained,* and at 45 m.p.h. you were being very brave and passing everything else on the roads. I'd always thought that small passenger compartments steamed up in such conditions, but this one blankly refused to do so. The outside of the screen got into a terrible state with oily smear and the remains of dead flies and even the three wipers couldn't cope. At the first opportunity I bought a supply of Trico SR-12 and motored happily onwards thereafter—just a squirt gets the dirt (variations on a theme). It is, I think, comforting to have at least *occasional* glimpses of the road.

Other drivers' reactions to an E-type seem to vary in different parts of the country. In Scotland, they were downright interested and kept asking to see the engine. In London, they just look, quite expressionless. In the Newcastle area they carve you up, shout at you when you overtake, and generally

Cook— with an E

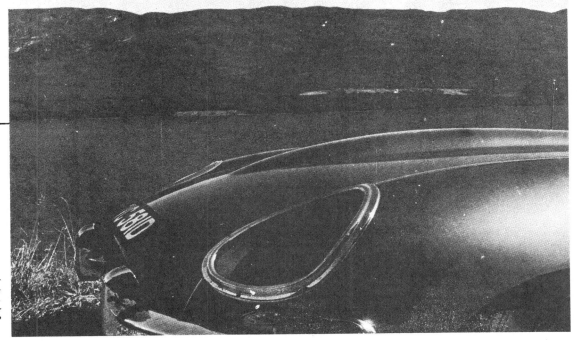

The stretch of water in the background is Loch Ness so whatever is that nearer to the camera?

behave in a most remarkable manner. I've never seen anything like it. Why? It happened on both the north and southbound trips. In general, though, the sight of an E-type doing a very steady and precise 70 m.p.h. seems to have a sobering effect on other drivers. You see them rushing up behind and then settling down to 70 astern of you. Same applies to lesser limits right down to 30. Again—why?

Passenger reactions vary, too. My mother, looking at the rev-counter instead of the speedo, remarked that it felt a lot faster than 40. It was, it was. My brother commented that it was "a bit bumpy" when we were doing 30 m.p.h. over a few manhole covers but shut up once the trigger had been pulled on the open road. Another chap settled in, took a firm grasp of the passenger grab handle and then let go and relaxed completely after we'd done about a mile. I think you'd have to be a really hairy driver to frighten a passenger with this car. No doubt you can frighten other drivers by just coming alongside at 30 or whatever they're doing, suddenly kicking down and vanishing over the horizon like a bit of wet soap. This must be especially impressive on long, steep hills; it certainly impressed me. I can't help thinking that this is the sort of car my mother brought me up to deserve. No native of Buchan should be without one.

Certainly, I had the best holiday ever. The sun shone for practically the whole fortnight and I came back to the office bronzed—but set about reverting to the pale shadow of my former self. The car was a sheer delight—to drive on the twists and turns and on the straights, or just to look at parked in some shady corner by a babbling Cook. Happiness is E-type shaped.

Then, oh, woe is me, they came and took it away. As I tell people on the phone: "It's Cook—without an E."

M

Picture of the village of Pennan taken from the middle of the harbour—while the tide was out.

A common enough scene when you go north with an E-type. The amount of interest in the car was quite phenomenal.

THE SYMBOL

"Those things are hell in the parking lot," muttered the simian boob to my right.

He smiled with sadistic resentment, relishing in perverted thrills at my meticulous ministrations over her voluptuous body.

Wise men said long ago that a Jaguar driver should have lots of rejoinders on hand for envious clods like this, so I replied quickly, accusingly, "*These* aren't the things that are hell in parking lots."

The scrutinizing ritual continued as I looked for body damage on the side of the XKE 2+2 facing his outrageous domestic with its deadly door swinging ominously.

You learn quickly, with a XKE 2+2, to develop an air of stoic superiority, even though your emotions rebel. If you find a nick in the paint, you only shake your head lightly in disgust, when all along you're struggling to quell an agonizing scream. If a car tries to park alongside, you want to leap sacrificially in front of the 2+2, but you've learned to merely stand imperiously alongside and stare in disdain at the driver.

The boob continues his taunt. "I wouldn't have one of them for all the money in the world."

I countered, "Obviously. First, you need good taste."

Suddenly I realized he had done it. I should have been aloof, but now he's hooked me. Those wise men warned against this. Everyone knows it's one of the world's greatest cars, but get involved, they said, and the real knowledgeable sort can make you feel pretty uncomfortable simply by picking on its past faults.

Already the boob has a point. It *is* hell in a parking lot. Okay, so the E-type body is still perhaps the most sensational design in existence . . . it's also one of the most vulnerable.

But somehow that doesn't seem to matter. It's a Circe, and few can ignore its seduction. Others gather quickly, as now. A funny thing about the 2+2 — few people fondle it, perhaps because it represents a certain dimension of excitement they know they will never, or wouldn't dare, attain.

There's an odd characteristic about the 2+2. Both its length and wheelbase have been extended a full nine inches, the roof is two inches higher, doors are 8½ inches wider, yet it is still identifiable as an XKE — to the extent that a degree of conscious effort is necessary for the layman to distinguish it from the coupe.

"Ain't much room in the back seat, is there?" rasped a different voice. The complacency bubble broke. Yet, all you do is open the door and let the heady aroma of natural leather waft through the air. While his objectivity is temporarily impaired, quickly explain that it has just as much room as any other 2+2, and that entry and exit is much easier, though still difficult, and the inside is much more comfortable, with seats now having 2-position rake adjustment. Then change the subject to something that emphasizes Jaguar's automotive authority.

Such as the dash. Packed with toggles and dials and levers, it has a complexity that appears to require either a degree or blood relationship for full rapport. Presumably, this also implies that ownership is bound to be select. Below the dash is a shelf, similar to that in the sedans, and the glove compartment now locks. Best of all, there are vent directional vanes, and when combined with the 2+2's slab-sided windows, air finds its way around much easier.

If the overt appearance of the 2+2 doesn't silence the critic's cry, there is an alternative. Since the advent of the XKE, a mere lifting of a hood has inspired awe in spectators and confidence in the driver. This is a property approached by no other car, regardless of price. Not that other engines aren't as impressive . . . only because others can't expose such a naked display of mechanical flamboyance.

And, let's face it. All those old wives' tales about this engine's temperament are now unfounded. In fact, envious chidings about oil consumption, overheating and the like can be used to stultify the critic, because these problems were eliminated when the 4.2 engine was created. In spite of its longevity, it is one of the most advanced of the day. After all, how many other production cars can boast dual overhead cams, hemispherical combustion chambers, chrome-plated top rings, seven main bearings and sufficient flexibility for an optional Borg-Warner Model 8 automatic — 3-speed, planetary, with torque converter that is confused with low-end performing but impressive at speed, shifting with a slam, consistently, at 5000 rpm.

Torque peaks at 283 lbs.-ft. at 4000 rpm and hp is 265 at 5400, but the weight of the 2+2 — 310 pounds more than the coupe — lowers performance noticeably, and the automatic's 3.31 final drive ratio does the same to top speed. But when you're doing 135 mph, this becomes purely academic.

I gave them one last chance to sweep their eyes over the chromed wire wheels, excellent 11-inch vacuum-assisted disc brakes and unequal length A-arms and tube shocks hanging outside that incredible engine, then lowered the front half of the car, lashed it securely from inside, and reached for the starter, casually — to make it appear accidental — hitting the windshield wiper switch and setting off a wall of flagellating arms that simultaneously clean nearly every square inch of the windshield and block your vision. But with *three* wiper blades, can you blame a guy for showing off?

That unmistakable Jaguar purr had them all contented now — all except the skeptic who intentionally kept firing questions with the hope of delaying me long enough for the engine to overheat. I accommodated him with repartees about the independent suspension all around that gives a ride so good it could even use stiffer front shocks. That cornering harder than the purpose of an XKE 2+2 presents induces initial understeer that quickly turns into something beautifully neutral and not at all that much different from the smaller XKE. That the car's stability remains constant to well above 110 mph.

The temperature continued to rise along with my anxiety. Then I remembered the thermostatically controlled fan that kicks on at 80°C. It did, and it was a classic put-down that closed the skeptic's mouth for good.

Suddenly it occurred to me that I learned something by exposing myself and the 2+2 to life. Those wise men are outdated. Evasion is no longer necessary. In fact, to the contrary, the opposition's envy can now be used as part of the strategy to prove the worth of this car. I had been taught that Jaguar is a symbol, that it has been one for a long, long time, and that this time it's better than ever. And I had been taught that this is a Jaguar that lets you behave as a proper Jaguar driver should: you stand silently, masterfully, proudly alongside and let the 2+2 speak for itself. /MT

SOME KIND OF CEREMONY ACCOMPANIES EACH MOMENT WITH AN XKE 2+2

Betraying its high-speed, grand-touring nature is a top two inches higher than the coupe, giving more comfort while subduing some of the sexiness of the E for the more modest enthusiast. All the bugs are gone from that beautiful engine, and a 9:1 compression ratio makes it tractable for at-speed touring or slugging around the city. Three SU carbs don't damage mileage as much as you might expect. You can expect as high as 16 mpg, as low as 10.6 if you're disrespectful. There are instruments for everything, plus lights for choke, brake fluid level, fuel level, emergency brake, ignition, high beam, turn signals and flasher system. Top of back seat slides forward for more room behind. And it's still an XKE.

PHOTOS BY BOB D'OLIVO

Acceptance tests of a modified E-type being carried out at Willow Run Airport Ypsilanti, near Detroit. Apart from new cars getting through the test, the emission control requirement demands a 50,000 mile continuous road test with standards checked every few thousand miles

E-TYPE
TO AMERICAN SPECIFICATION

EXHAUST emission control has been almost as thorny a problem as the new Federal safety regulations for the 1968 American selling season. The work load on both counts has been so intense that several British manufacturers have withdrawn many models from the North American scene in the hope of getting the others approved in the time.

Because Jaguar deliver 85 per cent of E-type production to the USA and Canada it was the obvious car to concentrate on. Even so, the pressures were unbearable at times; well over £250,000 was committed to the safety and emission control programmes, and at times over

one-third of the entire Jaguar engineering strength was involved in the programme.

Meeting the exhaust emission requirements has been solved, on the E-type, by fitting twin Zenith-Stromberg 175CD2 Duplex carburettors and special manifolding in place of the triple 2in. SU units still retained on other E-types. The Duplex Strombergs have a small-diameter choke tube effective at low engine speeds, in addition to a normal choke tube only coming into operation higher up the rev range. This means that gas velocity is kept up at all times, and to ensure more perfect mixture formation, gas is led across the top of the twin o.h.c. head, pre-heated

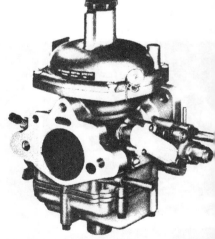

Most of the cockpit changes needed to meet Federal requirements centred on switchgear and door handles, with more padding to the centre console

''Air pollution'' E-Type engines have this intriguing twin-Stromberg set up and the Duplex manifold to replace the triple SU set-up more familiar to British eyes. The tube across the cam covers carries a fuel/air mixture across from the carburettors to the pre-heat chamber above the rear exhaust manifold, then back to the inlet port at low engine speeds only

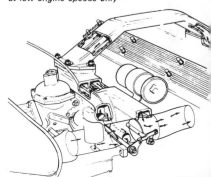

Two carburettors, instead of three, and a polished duct over the cam covers distinguish the American specification E-type engine

against the exhaust manifold, then fed back into the actual inlet manifolds. In addition, production tolerances are tightened up as much as possible, and a special Lucas distributor looks after more stringent ignition control requirements. To make sure the engines stay in tip-top condition, Jaguar have printed the list of parameters on the air-cleaner box, such as idling rpm and static ignition advance, which make the achievements possible.

The combination of inlet manifolding less suitable than before for maximum power production, tighter ignition and mixture controls, and modified carburation, has meant an unavoidable power loss of 20 bhp or 7.5 per cent; the new figure is 245 bhp at 5,500 rpm. Conversely, specific fuel consumptions have been much improved.

We borrowed a 2+2 E-type equipped with the 3.54-to-1 axle ratio normally installed for all North American territories; in Britain and Europe 3.07-to-1 is standard. Tyres, by the way, were the new Dunlop SP Sports (standard on the latest E-types) which include interesting moulded-in water passages.

The results were entirely predictable. Less power and rather low gearing nearly balanced each other out; in fact this test car was heavier than the car tested fully in June 1966 due to some experimental items under development and

rather more test gear, so it was not quite as lively. Fuel consumption would certainly have been appreciably better on the British axle ratio, but the 3.54 ratio dragged it down to a similar overall figure.

Some of the edge has been lost in out-and-out acceleration, particularly towards the top of the rev range. Gear changing points are at considerably lower speeds, and on this car we limited ourselves to the recommended 5,500 rpm. There was no opportunity to take absolute maximum speed figures, but since the car easily exceeds the 5,500 rpm in top gear, we were

happy to limit ourselves to the equivalent of 123 mph when testing at MIRA.

Nevertheless, to reach 100 mph in 22.6 sec is still excellent for a £2,250 occasional four-seater, and in many ways we preferred the lower overall gearing for Britain's crowded roads. Performance figures apart, the E-type remains a delightful car to drive, slow or fast; it is still astonishingly docile, and we were able to take acceleration figures from a mere 10 mph in top gear with the 4.2-litre engine turning over lazily and smoothly at only 460 rpm. With its modified carburation, pick-up is clean and forceful at any time once the engine is thoroughly warmed through. A lot of choke was needed for cold morning starts. There are *two* electric cooling fans side-by-side and a bigger radiator to look after the much increased heat rejection to cooling water that is characteristic of these modified engines.

Fuel consumption figures are intriguing. At steady speeds the emission-control car is markedly inferior to the British version, yet the overall figure was almost the same as before. Overall the gearing is 11.5 lower on this car, and our previous 2+2 spent much of its time being hammered round the passes and motorways of Europe, while the emission control car suffered several hundreds of miles of congested and restricted Britain. From this we might assume that part throttle and accelerating fuel consumption states have been improved, and that better use is being made of the fuel in all normal driving.

The new "safety interior" is certainly neater and more modern looking than that of the previous E-type. Most of us were glad to see the starter switch now combined with the ignition lock—this now lives down on the steering column, doubling with a steering lock. The hazard warning, when operated, sets all four flasher lamps working together, and makes the stationary car very obvious.

A battery-condition voltmeter has now replaced the ammeter in the facia design, and the clock is in the centre of the car instead of at the base of the rev-counter. Door handles and window winding levers are well out of the way of front seat passengers in any E-type, but these have been re-located and re-styled to give maximum safety. No changes have been made to the steering, and—surprisingly—padded leather has not yet replaced the wooden-rim on the wheel.

In all other respects, this is still a perfectly representative E-type. Handling, brakes, docility and general refinement are as enjoyable as ever; the 2+2 is still remarkable value for money.   □

Performance Data

Figures in brackets are for the 2+2 E-Type tested in AUTOCAR of 10 June '66.

Acceleration Times (mean): Speed range, gear ratios and time in seconds.

mph	Top (3.54)	(3.07)	3rd (4.50)	(3.90)	2nd (6.16)	(5.34)	1st (9.49)	(8.23)
10-30	6.5	(6.6)	4.8	(5.0)	3.4	(3.3)	2.4	(2.3)
20-40	5.5	(6.6)	4.1	(4.6)	3.0	(3.3)	2.4	(2.3)
30-50	5.6	(6.5)	3.8	(4.7)	3.0	(3.2)	—	
40-60	5.6	(6.1)	3.9	(4.5)	3.6	(3.0)	—	
50-70	5.6	(6.1)	4.2	(4.5)	—	(3.7)	—	
60-80	6.6	(6.5)	5.3	(4.7)	—	—	—	
70-90	7.7	(6.9)	—	(5.4)	—	—	—	
80-100	8.4	(7.4)	—	(7.1)	—	—	—	
90-110	10.9	(8.6)	—	—	—	—	—	

FROM REST THROUGH GEARS TO:

30 mph	3.0 sec	(2.7 sec)
40 mph	4.5 sec	(3.9 sec)
50 mph	6.3 sec	(5.7 sec)
60 mph	8.3 sec	(7.4 sec)
70 mph	11.0 sec	(9.8 sec)
80 mph	14.1 sec	(12.4 sec)
90 mph	18.2 sec	(15.4 sec)
100 mph	22.6 sec	(19.4 sec)
110 mph	29.9 sec	(24.2 sec)

Standing quarter-mile 16.3 sec (15.4 sec)
Standing kilometre 29.5 sec (28.1 sec)

MAXIMUM SPEEDS IN GEARS:

	mph	kph	rpm
Top (mean):	123 (139)	197 (224)	5,500
(best): (see text)	123 (141)	198 (227)	5,500
3rd:	95 (108)	153 (174)	5,500
2nd:	68 (73)	109 (118)	5,500
1st:	44 (48)	71 (77)	5,500

FUEL CONSUMPTION AT CONSTANT SPEEDS (mpg)

30 mph	29.2	(29.0)
40 mph	28.2	(29.0)
50 mph	26.7	(27.6)
60 mph	24.8	(26.2)
70 mph	22.2	(26.0)
80 mph	20.0	(24.2)
90 mph	18.6	(22.6)
100 mph	15.7	(20.4)

OVERALL FUEL CONSUMPTION:
18.7 mpg; 15.1 litres/100km (18.8 mpg; 15.0 litres/100km)

The new range grouped together, with the latest 2 + 2 coupé, complete with more screen rake, in the foreground. The seat headrests are fitted to US specification cars only

NEW FOR '69

Series 2 Jaguar E Types

USA ''federalized'' bodywork adopted, slight frontal style changes, and more raked screen on 2 + 2. No price increase

Headlamps have been moved forward yet again, 1.5in. beyond their 1967 ''exposed'' position, and 4.5in. ahead of their original sunken point. Headlamp cutouts are bigger, as is the radiator air intake

This group shows the still lovely lines of the E Type, not at all marred by compulsory USA-Federal changes

A mid-show surprise from Jaguar, who release revisions to the E-Type range, which become Series 2. Body style revised to meet latest USA Federal safety regulations, now standardized for rest of world. New bonnet nose with exposed headlamps further forward and full width bumper. New big tail lamps and exhaust system. More raked screen for 2 + 2. Adwest Pow-a-Rak power-assisted steering becomes optional, along with pressed-steel disc wheels. No major mechanical changes, but braking system is now Girling. No price increases.

JAGUAR originally intended to release the Series 2 E-Types later in the autumn, but advanced production schedules allowed a quick change of plan and a surprise release literally in mid-Show. The range still consists of the three models—2-seat Roadster, 2-seat Coupé, and 2 + 2 Coupé. All continue with the same body and mechanical changes where appropriate, only the 2 + 2 getting its own slight re-styling touches.

The new cars have been designed round the very latest USA Federal safety regulations, but (unlike previously) these safety features are to be built into every E-Type, no matter what part of the world it is to be sold. However, one item—the lower powered emission-controlled engine—remains special to the USA; all other markets keep the triple-SU, 265 bhp (gross) engine which the E-Type has always used.

Most obvious changes are the slight styling re-touches brought about by new USA lighting laws. The headlamps have been moved forwar yet again (the last time was in 1967)—and ar now exposed rather frog-like, 4.5in. ahead o their original design position in 1961. The aero dynamic lamp covers were discarded last yea also; on the Series 2 the bonnet cut-out ha been broadened a little so that lamp spread i better than before. Less obviously, the front a intake has been subtly enlarged, by no less tha an effective 68 per cent, this getting more ai into the radiator—doubly important when th high heat-rejection controlled-emission engin is fitted for the USA. The front bumper is now full width, including a bar across the previousl uncluttered air intake, side lamps and indicato mouldings are substantially bigger, and ther are side reflectors in the front wings ahead o the front wheel arch.

The new interior, showing off the rocker switches, and the steering column lock/starting switch. On the very latest cars the rear view mirror is mounted direct to the screen

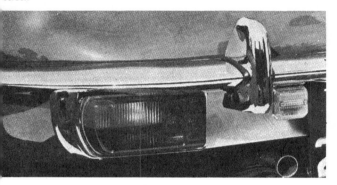

The new tail lamps have to be so large to satisfy USA regulations

New recessed door handles are well hidden in the door trims

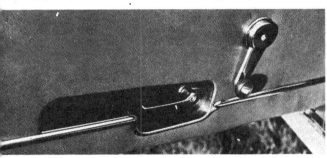

The new 2 + 2 screen is more raked though still the same depth; only two wipers are now fitted to this model

The 2 + 2 bodyshell receives its own individual styling change with the adoption of a much more stylishly raked windscreen, the rake angle having gone up from 46½deg. to 53½deg.; this has been achieved by moving the base of the screen forward while retaining the original crown line. An incidental change is that two large wipers have now been fitted to this body only, the other cars retaining their triple wipers.

At the rear, changes are confined to ultra-large tail lamp clusters, which don't suit the car at all but which are unavoidable due to latest regulations; and a full width panel between them designed to take all the world's licence plates. The exhaust system has been splayed out to clear the usual rectangular American variety.

Inside the car, the fully "federalized" facia panel is now standard on all models, with rocker switches in the central panel and, at last, a steering column-mounted combined ignition and starter key which also doubles as a column lock when removed. Door handles are recessed and big soft knobs are fitted to the winder handle.

Mechanically, the most important change is the addition of Adwest Pow-a-Rak power-assisted rack and pinion steering as an optional extra. This is basically identical with that adopted for the new Jaguar XJ6, fully described in our issue of 26 September. There is no change in steering ratio when this is specified.

Chrome-plated pressed-steel disc wheels are also offered as optional extras, though the wire-spoked variety, standard on the E-Type since 1961, are unchanged.

The steering column now incorporates a collapsible section of the expanded mesh Saginaw type, together with two universal joints, and is known to be ultra safe in a head-on collision.

As on the XJ6, the helix angle on gear teeth has been increased to provide even more silent running, but ratios are not altered. Borg Warner Model 8 automatic transmission is offered as an option only on the 2 + 2.

In spite of these changes, and the many other detail improvements phased into the car during its long and successful career, there has been no price increase, and the E-Type production lines—already flat out as always—will find it doubly difficult to keep pace with orders. □

Interior of this convertible looks something like a cockpit, which it is.

Rear suspension is mounted on a sub frame and insulated by rubber mounts.

AFTER A FEW MILES THE E SEEMS TO BECOME AN EXTENSION OF YOURSELF, A WILLING SLAVE THAT WILL OBEY EVERY WHIM. IT'S DESIGNED, BUILT, AND ENGINEERED TO CRUISE SAFELY PAST 100 MPH.

By ALEX WALORDY ■ The exterior of the XKE speaks for itself: the long sexy hood, the wire wheels, the streamlined shape. It has all the feel and trimmings of power, so naturally we had to try it out for size. Your feet are inside a cocoon, sandwiched between the body and transmission, the seat is form-fitting

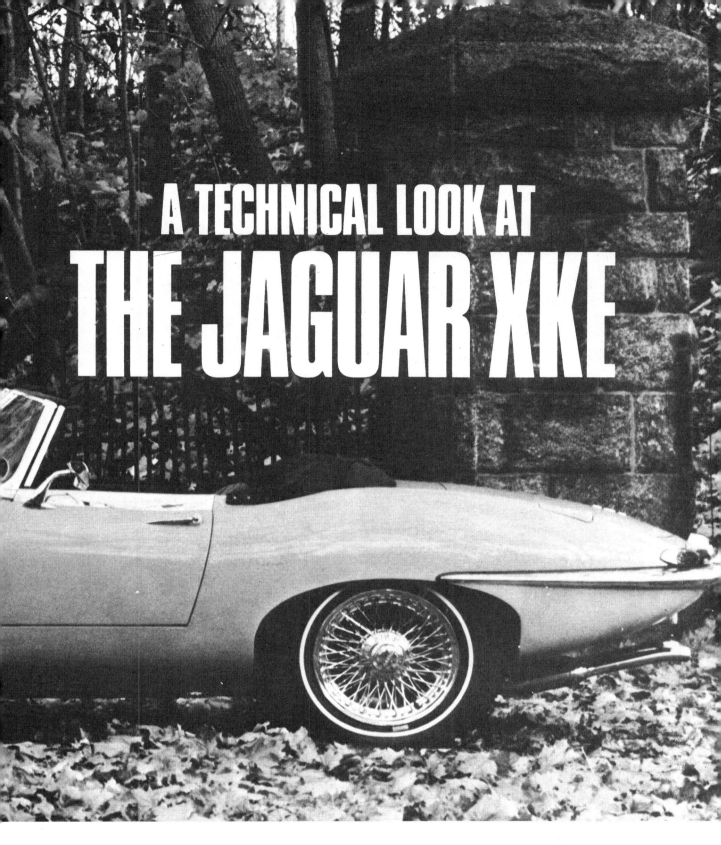

A TECHNICAL LOOK AT THE JAGUAR XKE

and the car fits snugly, like a well-cut English suit. We moved the seat all the way back, adjusted the telescopic steering column to its furthermost stop for that proper race-driver straight arm position. No dice! You need fingertip extensions to drive the car that way, so telescope was moved back out.

There is arm room to spare, but we wish we could say the same for headroom. Until you get used to it, which takes awhile, the roadster is likely to give you a case of claustraphobia, with its taut soft top, but then whoever heard of driving a convertible with the top up. Reclining the seats did help considerably.

THE JAGUAR XKE

Overhead cams actuate valves through cup type lifters. Engine is detailed down to a set of polished lift bars for service use.

In addition to the two stock thermostatically controlled electric fans, a third one is installed for air conditioned cars.

Pairs of throttles, one behind the other, reroute the mixture to the manifold at part throttle and idle, reducing emissions.

Long piston skirts and tall connecting rods minimize the side thrust against the cylinder walls, hence a longer engine life.

The hardtop two-plus-two coupe is far superior to the convertible or the roadster in terms of headroom and somehow seems more appropriate for the tall set. The two-plus-two has a nine inch longer wheel base than the roadster's 96 inches and all of the extra space has been alloted to a rear seat. That seat, incidentally, folds downand serves as additional luggage space which seems to be its most practical use.

No one will ever accuse the Jaguar of being short of instruments. As a matter of fact, they extend right across the dashboard, well into the co-pilot's area, and are underlined by a row of no less than ten flip-flop switches. They control everything from the lights to the three individual windshield wiper arms. The shift handle is right at hand, and the throws are short, sharp and well-defined.

After a few miles the XKE seems to become an extension of yourself, a willing slave that will obey your every whim. That rack and pinion steering takes just two and three quarter turns from lock to lock. It seems impossible to turn the steering wheel by the slightest amount without having the front wheels respond immediately and in just the right amount. The XKE is basically an understeerer, stable on the straights. Get it into a tight corner and all it asks for is that you push the accelerator down a bit further. At higher speeds the XKE comes into its own and by the time we had it wound up past the hundred mark, it seems to settle down into a comfortable cruising speed.

A gas-filled cell in these king-sized shock absorbers prevents aeration and foaming of the fluid, hence more accurate control.

Moving the disc brakes inboard reduces the unsprung weight. The suspension loads are handled by coil springs and shock absorbers.

A hydraulic slave cylinder operates a diaphragm type clutch and provides self-adjustment and no care during its natural life.

Dropping the engine reveals the square tubing front sub frame that bolts to the monocoque body shell which supports the engine.

That Jaguar front end is longer than a day without bread. Like Cyrano's nose, it represents an identity all of its own, and no one in his right mind would dare call it an idle piece of decorator's trim. Back in the glory days of Le Mans and D/Jaguars it benefited from extensive wind tunnel testing, which resulted, among other things, in a set of headlight fairings. California had never heard of such advanced technology, and the fairings had to go. We don't know just exactly what this did to the drag coefficient, but that Jag front end is still the sleekest nose cone around.

Stiffened by bulkheads and some very functional air ducts, the finger-shaped sheet metal also forms a long crushable structure that protects the main portion of the body shell and its occupants. Last, but not least, when you pop the two hood latches, the foot swings up slowly and majestically to reveal an amassment of impressive machinery.

The E's unit body forms a monocoque structure, a single rigid assembly with stressed sheet metal that envelops the occupants like a protective, snug fitting shell. From the firewall on forward, a sub-frame which bolts to the body shell supports the engine, ties in the front suspension and, in turn, provides a secondary crushable structure to protect the driver. The engine is pulled well back of the front end to provide more weight on the driving wheels and better traction. This also brings the engine into the widest portion of the car, and full *Continued on page* 142

JAGUAR XK E

$5584
West Coast P.O.E.

First significant changes since addition of 2+2 in 1966, bumpers front and rear are relocated, auxiliary lighting below rather than above bumpers. Twin exhaust pipes separated. Does not obsolete older models. Larger air intake for radiator. Performance and handling above average. Has high eye appeal. Manufactured by Jaguar Cars Ltd., Coventry, England.

Jaguar's 4.2 litre (258.4 cu. in.) twin overhead camshaft six cylinder engine has been with us now for many years. In its latest form, it puts out 246 bhp at 5500 rpm. Twin Zenith-Stromberg carburetors replace the three S.U.'s of the '67 model and are part of the smog device system. The effectiveness of this smog unit can be judged by the emission figures, hydrocarbons 135 ppm whereas the Federal requirements are for 220 ppm. The engine exceeds the intended requirements for California for 1970 by a large margin. The net loss to performance by the reduction in bhp from the three carburetor unit is some 20 horses. In general driving, they are not missed but if you want to show up at the drags, there will be a slight loss when run against the

clocks. As the car was never intended as a dragster, it is of academic interest. The other changes on the engine are more interesting. There are now two fan belts, one driving the alternator (from a larger pully thereby getting it cranked up a bit faster) and the other to the water pump. At the rear of the block, there is a better clearance for the water passage which allows the rear cylinder (No. 6) to run a mite cooler. This was the one that gave trouble if the engine ever ran overly hot.

Oil consumption, according to owners, is at last way down on this engine to a mere quart per thousand at the most. This same engine was also in the '68 model so a fair number of miles have been used to testify to this low figure.

The header tank has also been replaced by an expansion tank on the firewall and another bone of contention has been removed. Water hoses and the rubber trim will still require watching as the British still persist in using a high pure rubber content.

When the engine hood is closed down, it is supposed to form a seal around the wheel arches to prevent road muck from being thrown into the engine compartment. This it does not do and dirt and grit get in everywhere. It has been improved some over the older model but is not perfect yet.

The front suspension is independent by parallel wishbones, with torsion bars, telescopic shock absorbers and anti-sway bar. The rear suspen-

New type safety dash with recessed push-on switches but still the traditional Jaguar layout.

All this space and carpet too? The E-type trunk is surprisingly roomy and vinyl carpet-lined to avoid damage to luggage.

other trouble and the first item to go will be the wiper blades, followed a close second by the rubber trim between the bumpers and the body. Generous use of rubber lubricants is strongly recommended, and by this means, the owner can keep his car looking show-room fresh.

The addition of a 2 plus 2 filled the need for the market that liked the looks of the car and its status appeal yet had outgrown the four on the floor shifting. The automatic version obviously had to come and the extra two seats were a bonus. They are usable by adults in the 5'6" bracket but whether you can get four people in the car depends on the size of the driver. If he has his seat fully back, you have a three seater. Entry in and out of the four seater is easier due to the larger door (8½" over the two

sion unit is a complete assembly and is the most trouble free item on the car. It is fully independent comprising tranverse links, radius arms, quadruple coil springs with four concentric shock absorbers.

The ride is very good for a sports car with this potential and the car will smooth out the freeway joints but not

eliminate them completely. Coming out of a corner under power, the rear end sits down well and the car accelerates smoothly and maintains the chosen line without sliding around. On severe braking, the car will dive, naturally, but it is not really that noticeable to the driver.

The use of pure rubber will cause

the center of the instrument panel. This is the same size as the gauges and has even got a fast/slow adjustment screw. From all accounts, it performs well which is more than could be said for the older model, the owner had a 50/50 chance of it working at all.

An extra switch has been added to the panel for the rear window electric heater. This is now mandatory by law but the unit is one that Jaguars have used on their European models for years and is a reliable item. All safety laws have been met and the car now sports an adjustable headrest. The door latches have been recessed and are awkward to operate, there is certainly no possibility of opening one accidentally.

The front and rear of the car have had a face lift and the intake hole has been enlarged to allow better cooling. The turn signal lights at the front and the brake/turn combination at the rear are now below the bumper level. They have been enlarged considerably but as they are not now visible from the side, running lights have been added to meet safety requirements. These tend to detract from what would have been a clean side view of the car. The twin tail pipes have now been separated and the rear bumper position has been raised about 1 ½ ins.

The big change in the '69 car is that the brakes are now Girling discs all around. Previous owners will testify to the eternal squealing that haunted the car for the first 10,000 miles. This could be alleviated by rapid decelerations from speed but was not too practical a solution in many instances. The new discs appear to eliminate this problem but we will

Higher bumper, new rear light cluster and back-up lights, new exhaust pipe arrangement. All different for 1969.

seater) although the rear passenger requires a certain amount of agility to enter and exit, and it is something not easily done with grace.

The '69 model 2 plus 2 has had a subtle change in the front of the roof line and the windshield is much more raked giving it better aerodynamics and a bit more room inside. It has smoothed out the humped-back look

of the older model. Power assisted steering will be optional for this model in early '69, desirable for the little woman but not necessary for the average male.

The '69s have had a revamp of the instrument panel and the toggle switches have been replaced with the rocker type, all part of the safety requirements. The 'quarter' sized clock that used to be hidden in the tachometer dial has been dumped in favor of a good sized electric type in

wholesale. Parts are readily available although occasionally there will be shortages caused by the workers going on strike at the factories — an all too frequent occurrence.

All in all, the steady product improvement over the years is at last paying off and the '69 XKE is certainly one of the best to come down the pike in a long time. Its acceptance by the buying public is still high and it is one of the few cars that gets the sophisticated California Freeway drivers to turn their heads and take another look. If it's a toss up between a Jaguar and a Stingray to go on the front line at the restaurant parking lot, the Jaguar makes it a no contest ♠

have to wait a short while for owners' confirmation of this. The brakes are still hydraulically operated with a vacuum servo assist and are quite satisfactory for the little woman to operate without working out at the local 'Y.'

The interior seating is as before and the ventilation system has had minor improvements. They are still not the coolest cars to ride in but the factory is now installing air conditioning which eliminates this problem, albeit at a price tag of $485.00. This is almost $100 less than last year.

Knock off hubs (now require a separate attachment to remove them) are the standard wheel on the car. A mag type wheel will be available early in 1969.

The U.S. market is still the largest one for Jaguars and close to 80% of their entire production comes to these shores. Southern California is by far the largest buyer with upwards of 600 cars being sold in this area alone in a year. If the owner keeps his car for three or four years, he will invariably come out quite well. If he just prefers to add gas and forget it, then come trade in time, he will hurt badly.

In times of plenty Jaguars can be bought for $400 to $500 off on a clean deal. However, 1968 was a lean year for the dealers as regards availability and prices were much firmer. '69 looks like following the same pattern so the market for cream puff used ones should be extremely good. An edgy car will be at least two back of

Jaguar XKE
Data in Brief

DIMENSIONS

Overall length (in.)	207
Height (in.)	48
Turning diameter (ft.)	37

WEIGHT, TIRES, BRAKES

Weight (lbs.)	2466
Tires	6.40 x 15
Brakes, front & rear	disc

ENGINE

Type	6 cylinder DOHC
Displacement (cc)	4200
Horsepower	265

SUSPENSION

Front	wishbones & torsion bars
Rear	transverse tubular links and coil springs

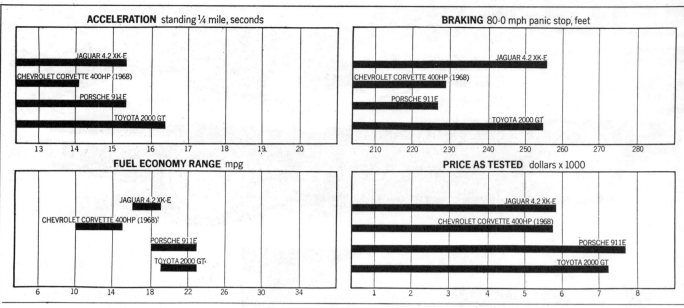

ACCELERATION standing ¼ mile, seconds

- JAGUAR 4.2 XK-E
- CHEVROLET CORVETTE 400HP (1968)
- PORSCHE 911E
- TOYOTA 2000 GT

(scale: 13, 14, 15, 16, 17, 18, 19, 20)

BRAKING 80-0 mph panic stop, feet

- JAGUAR 4.2 XK-E
- CHEVROLET CORVETTE 400HP (1968)
- PORSCHE 911E
- TOYOTA 2000 GT

(scale: 210, 220, 230, 240, 250, 260, 270, 280)

FUEL ECONOMY RANGE mpg

- JAGUAR 4.2 XK-E
- CHEVROLET CORVETTE 400HP (1968)
- PORSCHE 911E
- TOYOTA 2000 GT

(scale: 6, 10, 14, 18, 22, 26, 30, 34)

PRICE AS TESTED dollars x 1000

- JAGUAR 4.2 XK-E
- CHEVROLET CORVETTE 400HP (1968)
- PORSCHE 911E
- TOYOTA 2000 GT

(scale: 1, 2, 3, 4, 5, 6, 7, 8)

JAGUAR 4.2 XK-E

Importer: British Leyland Motors Inc.
600 Willow Tree Road
Leonia, N.J. 07605

Vehicle type: front engine, rear-wheel-drive, 2-passenger roadster

Price as tested: $5858.00
(Manufacturer's suggested retail price, including all options listed below, Federal excise tax, dealer preparation and delivery charges, does not include state and local taxes, license or freight charges)

Options on test car: Chrome wire wheels, $132.00; white wall tires, $27.00; AM/FM radio, $165.00

ENGINE
Type: 6-in-line, water-cooled, cast iron block, aluminum head, 7 main bearings
Bore x stroke.3.63 x 4.17 in, 92.1 x 105.8 mm
Displacement..................258 cu in, 4235 cc
Compression ratio..................9.0 to one
Carburetion..........2 x 1-bbl Zenith-Stromberg 175 CD2SE
Valve gear........Double overhead camshafts
Power (SAE)............246 bhp @ 5500 rpm
Torque (SAE)..........263 lbs/ft @ 3000 rpm
Specific power output........0.95 bhp/cu in, 58.2 bhp/liter
Max recommended engine speed...5,500 rpm

DRIVE TRAIN
Transmission............4-speed, all-synchro
Final drive ratio...................3.54 to one

Gear	Ratio	Mph/1000 rpm	Max. test speed
I	2.94	7.3	40 mph (5500 rpm)
II	1.90	11.3	62 mph (5500 rpm)
III	1.39	15.3	84 mph (5500 rpm)
IV	1.00	21.5	119 mph (5500 rpm)

DIMENSIONS AND CAPACITIES
Wheelbase...........................96.0 in
Track, F/R....................50.0/50.0 in
Length..............................175.5 in
Width................................65.2 in
Height...............................46.5 in
Ground clearance......................5.5 in
Curb weight........................2750 lbs
Weight distribution, F/R..........48.8/51.2%
Battery capacity..........12 volts, 55 amp/hr
Alternator capacity................720 watts
Fuel capacity.......................16.8 gal
Oil capacity.........................9.0 qts
Water capacity......................19.3 qts

SUSPENSION
F: Ind., unequal length control arms, torsion bars, anti-sway bar
R: Ind., lateral links and fixed length half-shafts, trailing arms, coil springs

STEERING
Type.......................rack and pinion
Turns lock-to-lock....................2.8
Turning circle curb-to-curb............39.8 ft

BRAKES
F:................11.0-in disc, power assisted
R:................10.0-in disc, power assisted

WHEELS AND TIRES
Wheel size.......................15 x 5.5-in
Wheel type........wire spoke, chrome plated
Tire make and size.....185 VR 15 Dunlop SP
Tire type...........Radial, tube type
Test inflation pressures, F/R.......32/32 psi
Tire load rating.....1480 lbs per tire @ 32 psi

PERFORMANCE
Zero to   Seconds
30 mph.........................2.0
40 mph.........................3.1
50 mph.........................4.8
60 mph.........................6.7
70 mph.........................9.2
80 mph........................11.9
90 mph........................15.3
100 mph.......................19.0
Standing ¼-mile........15.3 sec @ 90.0 mph
Top speed (estimated)...........119 mph
80-0 mph..................256 ft (0.83 G)
Fuel mileage.....16-19 mpg on premium fuel
Cruising range...................269-319 mi

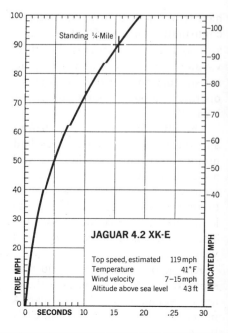

Standing ¼-Mile

JAGUAR 4.2 XK-E

Top speed, estimated   119 mph
Temperature   41°F
Wind velocity   7-15 mph
Altitude above sea level 43 ft

TRUE MPH / INDICATED MPH / SECONDS

CAR and DRIVER ROAD TEST

Jaguar 4.2 XK-E

Give it another year or two of loving attention
and it's bound to make the Queen's list of birthday honors

All you Faithful Readers still holding your breath for the V-12 Jaguar XK-F may exhale. It simply isn't time yet. But while we wait, here comes the XK-E for review again, still reeking with class. And since we haven't said a word about the car for a couple of years, we may as well examine the old lady and see how they've been amusing themselves over there at the factory for all this time.

If the apparent complacency in Coventry tends to infuriate you, look at it this way. Time flies for everyone except the Jaguar people. For them it passes in stately review. In this evolutionary context, the years have merely served to give them time to lovingly bring the XK-E to full bloom. A tasteful touch of refinement here, an unostentatious modification there. It's rather like breeding a Derby winner, or a Chelsea Flower Show champion rhododendron. As they undoubtedly say at Jaguar, "You simply can't rush these things, old boy. It takes time."

And then too, they probably talk about "not getting off a winning horse." Even if you're an automotive fire-in-the-guts, change for the sake of change, revolutionist you'll have to admit that that's what the Jaguar people have still got with the XK-E. They had one from the moment they unwrapped the first brakeless, over-heating,

Shelby Cobra-like, roughneck production model in 1962, and they've got one with the well-manicured, smooth operating, slicked down version we're talking about today.

On the other hand, look around in the market place to check on the XK-E's competition and you'll find yourself asking where it's all gone. Take $6000 and go looking for a well-mannered, luxurious 2-seater that doesn't label you *nouveau riche* or *boy racer*, and there's precious little left to choose from.

It comes down in the end to one of three cars; the Lotus Elan SE4, the Porsche and the XK-E's oldest rival on the American market, the Corvette.

For the conservative buyer, and you know in your heart that the XK-E buyer is a conservative, the Lotus Elan, at $4795, is something of a flier, even if Lotus has gone public. Porsche seems determined to price itself out of the market. And although the Corvette is backed by the General Motors Acceptance Corporation and is a fine and handsome machine, it's still the sort of car that one of these days Hugh Hefner is going to paint pink and give away to his Playmate of the Year. And if *that* doesn't affect your cultural taste, the Corvette, with the introduction of the aluminum 427 Chevy, has moved so far into the head-snapping, backside-booting performance world it has probably started to create yet another culture all of its own.

So, having selected and not settled for the E-type, in this case the 4.2 Roadster, let's see what you're getting for your money. Before launching into the list of "New Features of 1969" which, apart from a couple of major improvements, includes such innovating federal government inspired touches as a new license plate mounting assembly, new side marker reflectors and an unlegislated heavy duty alternator, it might be as well to review the basic and ancient formula for the XK-E.

Since the introduction of the 4.2 liter XK engine, which replaced the 3.8 in 1965, and the fully synchromesh 4-speed manual transmission (automatic is only available on the 2+2 model) introduced in the same year, the engine and drivetrain assembly

139

have gone basically unaltered.

The stressed steel monocoque body shell, with a tubular steel sub-frame assembly at the front and fabricated steel sub-frame assembly at the rear, also remains unaltered. It would be fairly tough to improve on this layout anyway. In the first place it provides extremely high torsional rigidity, responsible in large measure for the car's highly predictable and excellent handling characteristics. In the second place, it makes the car easy to mend, since both sub-frame assemblies are of the knock-off/bolt-on variety. Damage the monocoque tub and you're in a different kind of trouble.

Apart from the engine and transmission, the front sub-frame carries the suspension and the rack-and-pinion steering gear. The suspension, like a lot of other basic features, dates back to the Le Mans winning, super-heroic and faintly nostalgic D-Types. Two skinny wishbones are complemented by torsion bars mounted to extensions of the lower wishbones, with telescopic damper units and an anti-roll bar, also connecting the lower wishbones.

Dual coil springs are used at the rear with twin transverse links and trailing arms. The entire combination has that properly unruffled feeling, whether you're pounding through the potholes on New York's Lower East Side or skimming up Highway 1 in a big rush for a weekend at Point Concepcion.

So, on the surface, nothing seems to have changed much in the past two years. But beneath that Dietrich exterior the Jaguar refinement artists have been busily at work.

The big problem they've had with the straight-six XK engine since 1948 is keeping it cool. Imagine having a dohc, hemi-headed, 7-main bearing crank, 258 cu.in. kettle. Back in the days when consumers were called men and sports car buyers were known as enthusiasts, you just had to feed them a blast of cold air in the face, a sexy exhaust note and an open road and they'd sell as many cars for you as Coventry could make. When an XK120 owner saw his open road dissolve into a snarl of traffic he would light-heartedly whip off down a side road, or pull over and wait, rather than let his sleek-flanked thoroughbred boil itself dry surrounded by jeering 4-door conformists. Nowadays, with open roads as common as toad-in-the-hole, and enthusiasts only a wistful smile on Ken Purdy's lips, even sports cars must be silent and cool.

To this end Jaguar has gone overboard. The new cooling system is completely sealed with a catch tank to recirculate any water pressured out of the system. The air intake in the nose cowl has been enlarged by no less than 68%—which if anything enhances the E-type's looks—to get more cold air through the brass, crossflow radiator. A second thermostatically operated electric fan has been added. On air-conditioned models the fans work continuously; on standard models the fans come on as soon as the water temperature reaches 80° C. There is a new metered feed system to the aluminum head, with much larger apertures on the water channels leading from the block to the back of the head than to the front. This obviously forces more cold water to the rear three cylinders, which are without the benefit of the additional and incidental air cooling being supplied to the front three. The water pump has an increased capacity of 25% and the pump's gear ratio, relative to engine speed, has been increased from one-to-one to one-to-1.25. And in case all this extra whirring and shooshing and pumping still doesn't do the trick, the risk of the aluminum head warping has been cut to a minimum by lengthening the head studs from four inches to 12.

Ironically, the onslaught on the cooling system comes at a time when Jaguar has actually been forced to detune the XK engine to meet with U.S. air pollution control standards. The 258 cu. in. displacement remains unchanged, but the power output has been dropped from 265 hp at 5400 rpm to 246 at 5000 rpm. In the interests of cleaner air, the traditional triple HD-8 SU carburetor setup has given way to a pair of constant depression Zenith-Strombergs with a manual choke control, and an elaborate double manifold has been added between the inlet and exhaust manifold to to assure compliance with the Clean Air Act. More by accident than design, this has also resulted in a loss of torque (283 ft/lbs at 4000 rpm on the '67 models to 263 ft/lbs at 3000 rpm on the '69s) but, conversely, performance up to U.S. speed limits is actually improved over the 1968 triple carburetor setup (quarter-mile times have been reduced from 15.6 seconds to 15.3 at 90 mph). In addition, the engine revisions have lowered the torque curve into a far more useable area, which means you can prowl away in top gear from 1500 rpm on up, with no sign of strain. This is the kind of freeway flexibility that keeps your mind off driving when there's no real driving to be done anyway.

In the stick shift Jaguar of yesterday this would have been a blessed relief, but on the new cars changing gears is actually fun to do. The Laycock diaphragm clutch is light, without making you wonder if you've just put your foot into an empty hole, and it's smooth and progressive. There's a good stubby shift lever crouching right next to that great wood-rimmed, Duncan Hamilton, aluminum-spoked-drilled-for-lightness, flexy steering wheel with a picture of The Cat in black, white and gold mounted in clear plastic in the center. You don't exactly flick through the gears like you would on a ZF box, but the throws are short, and it's pretty tough to grab the wrong gear even in a panic.

The brakes are a sheer delight. They really are. Jaguar has replaced the old Lockheed discs with Girling variety—out-

CONTINUED ON PAGE 142

Time flies for everyone except Jaguar. For them it passes in stately review. In this evolutionary context, the years have merely served to give them time to lovingly bring the XK-E to full bloom with a tasteful refinement here and an unostentatious modification there

141

JAGUAR 4-2 XK-E
Continued from page 140

board on the front, inboard on the rear. The new discs are specially damped, with two operating cylinders on the outside face and one on the inside. They don't even squeal any more. Jaguar overcame this problem with great ingenuity, by machining a ⅜-in. groove out of the circumference of the disc and filling it with a soft iron core. It's getting better all the time.

The car is as well instrumented as a 707. Ten toggle switches controlling the lights, wipers and windshield washers, stretch across the center. And, right in front of the driver, there's a giant and highly legible tachometer and speedometer. But it's that huge wood-rimmed steering wheel that predominates the cool leather interior.

When you put this kind of a package together over eight years or more, you

should come up with a major and sophisticated automobile, and that's just what Jaguar has done.

Driving the XK-E grows on you in an impressive and unstoppable way. According to all the Jaguar ads you've ever read the car has a top speed of 150 mph, and with a 2.90-to-one rear axle ratio that may be perfectly true. But the standard final drive ratio on cars imported to the U.S. is 3.54-to-one which chops the top speed to near 110 mph at 5000 rpm.

To start with the car feels big and lazy. The long bulbous hood stretches away to infinity, and loafing along at the legal limit with the accelerator barely depressed is a sensuous experience in itself. The throttle feels as stiff as a dead pedal, but keep squeezing and the car responds with unnerving reserves of power. Bend it into a series of turns and the E-type suddenly

comes to life with a very satisfying, light but sure-footed feeling. The famous exhaust note crackles and rumbles, the servo-assisted brakes drag you down effortlessly and endlessly, and squatting on its haunches, the car tracks its way through corners with impeccable manners. The quicker you go the more the car seems to gather itself together. That long hood keeps pointing itself in precisely the direction you aim it.

There are drawbacks, but compared to the overall effect they become trifling. With all this going for you the wind noise at 80 is easily bearable. The angle of the leather seat backs is adjustable, but for tall people with big feet the pedals are too close together for almost anything except bare feet, and although even a mongoloid ape could straight-arm the steering wheel, his knees would be jammed up against the bottom of the wood rim. Adjust the rear view mirror once too often and it'll come off in your hand. The 2-speed triple wiper blades still manage to leave a large area of the curved windshield unswept, and the frame for the soft top is uncomfortably close to a tall driver's temple. But so what? The Jaguar XK-E is one hell of a lot of motorcar-cum-snob-appeal for under $6000. Give it another year or two and it'll even make the Queen's list of birthday honors, along with The Rolling Stones. ●

JAGUAR XKE

(Continued from page 133)

use is made of the extra packaging space to house a heater, battery and accessories.

At the right, space is throughly taken up by a pair of Stromberg carburetors and a king-sized air cleaner with twin snorkels that tune out some of the intake whoosh. There used to be three SU's on the side of the Jag engine but air emission controls killed that in a hurry. "The Stromberg's are as easy to work on as the SU's, but we liked the SU better", some of the mechanics confided to us. Up front, you'll find a pair of electric fans for the radiator and on air-conditioned cars there is an added fan mounted up front, plus a compressor and all trimmings, all neatly tucked away under that endless hood.

The 4.2 liters block is a tall affair with pressed in liners and seven rugged main bearing webs. Cast, solid skirt pistons, and hefty pop-ups provide a 9:1 compression. They, like the block, are unusually tall and therefore offer excellent control against rocking. Where today's engines tend to short, stubby slipper skirt pistons, and short rods that run at steep angles, the Jaguar rods are undoubtedly the longest in the industry, and just laze along with minimum side thrust on the pistons. They may look as old fashioned as an English colonial, but they do offer good engine life without inhibiting the rpm too much. The sides of these rods are well polished, to eliminate any potential imperfection or failure points. Completing the bottom end is a forged steel crank with cross drilled mains and jounals.

A cast aluminum oil pan with ample

cooling fins at the sides extends at full depth along the entire length of the engine. Since the Jaguars are essentially speed cornering and fast take off machines, an extensive amount of baffling is provided inside the pan to contain the oil during the more violent maneuvers.

The cylinder head is quite long and wide. In fact, it looks positively massive with its pair of integrally cast cam housings, but also turns out to be extremely light. Strategically located cam supports with bolt-on caps and bearing inserts are placed near the lobes to minimize deflections. The cams work against steel cups which slide in guides and operate the valves. Drillings in the cam lobes spray a substantial amount of oil and the cams run in what amounts to an oil trough so that lubrication is not wanting at any time.

Jag's long stroke engine fought off the emissions problem quite successfully and without need of an auxiliary air pump. Of course, it owes part of its success to the same old-fashioned long stroke to which most American car manufacturers are now beginning to turn. Point is that a long stroke engine results in a tight, compact, combustion chamber, hence lower emission. Also, the Jaguar has a hemispherical chamber and nothing could be much more compact than that (or better breathing).

One of the few concessions to emissions controls has been to add a pre-heating system that carries the intake mixture across the engine over to the exhaust side and back again at idle and low part throttle. An ingenious pair of throttles which work in series, one behind the other, help bypass the heating system offering a straight through path for the air-fuel mixture when full power is required.

The stick shift XKE has a straightforward diaphragm type clutch with a hydraulic slave cylinder to operate it. By balancing out the clutch return spring and the residual pressure in the hydraulic system, the system was made self-adjusting and requires no care during its natural life. For those who prefer an automatic, the Borg Warner three speed can be used without either D1 (first gear) or D2 starts. The detents in a shift lever are positive so that you will not completely lose touch with a stick shift unless you wish to just plunk it in "Drive" and leave it there.

Regardless of the transmission you pick, a short drive shaft takes the power from there to a differential that is bolted to a subframe. All rear suspension components also bolt to the sub-frame and the whole assembly is attached to the body shell by way of four "V" type rubber mounts. This insulates the body from vibrations and mechanical noises not already drowned out by the throaty twin exhausts.

When Jaguar first pioneered the use of disc brakes back in '54, it became their secret weapon for going deeper into turns at Le Mans and was credited with their win that year. The XKE, which in its own way is an updated, personalized D/Jag, continues the tradition with a set of four Girling discs that provide faultless stopping. Two-piston calipers are used front and rear and in addition there is also a pair of separate hand brake calipers acting on the rear brakes. For the benefit of the absent-minded professor, there is even a big red light that serves as a warning if the hand brake is on, or if the hydraulic system is low. ●

Road & Track Owner Survey
JAGUAR E-TYPE

JAGUAR WAS ONE of the two English marques—MG the other—that got the whole sports car thing going in the U.S. right after World War II, and the Jaguar E-type remains one of the most popular and coveted of the premium sports cars in today's highly competitive market. The E-type was introduced in early 1961 and was an astounding design then—its stressed-skin, partially monocoque structure, fully independent suspension, all-around disc brakes and way-out styling all seemed just too good to be true, and the dohc XK engine was just getting into its prime then. Since then the E has undergone gradual, minor refinement. In 1965 it got a larger 4.2-liter engine and a new all-synchro-mesh gearbox and it had to be modified to conform to U.S. safety and smog legislation in 1968 and 1969. Over the years it got many 'running changes" to improve its operation and reliability. Throughout its life, however, the E-type (like most other Jaguar models) has generated a word-of-mouth reputation of a definite lack of reliability—a reputation that has been impossible for us to confirm or deny until now.

We surveyed an even hundred owners of E-types. Eight had 1962 models, the first year designation of E-types sold in the U.S.; 7 were 1963s, 18 1964s, 12 1965s, 15 1966s, 24 1967s and 16 1968s. We thought it significant that just 27 of the Es were "only" cars, the rest coming from multi-car stables. Seventy percent of them were bought new, the rest used.

Because of the high proportion of multi-car ownership among our E owners, there was also a high proportion of owners who use their car less than 10,000 miles per year; the usual concentration of annual mileages in our surveys is between 10 and 15,000 miles per year. The highest odometer mileage reported was 82,000.

Reasons given by owners of E-types for purchasing them are pretty typical: 77% mentioned styling, 46% performance, 20% handling. The fact of multi-car status again crops up in how the owners use their Es—only 85% use them for daily transportation. And fully 31% use them in rallies,

which might give Jaguar's advertising people second thoughts as they aim their ads more and more at women and luxury-minded buyers. Asked how they treat their machines on the road, 51% said they drive "hard"—a high proportion—with 44% answering that they drive "moderately" and 5% "very hard." Among owners of other makes we've surveyed so far, the Jaguar owners are quite typical in that 63% of them follow the maker's maintenance schedule; the largest percentage of do-it-yourselfers we've encountered yet —24%—take care of their own E-types, a cultural oddity considering the price of the car!

Perhaps that 24% reflects the owners' dissatisfaction with their dealers. No dealer body has fared really well with our reporting owners; VW's dealers have done the best with 62% of the owners classifying VW service as "good." But a pattern is clearly emerging: the British cars seem to be the least well represented by their respective dealer organizations, and Jaguar is no exception, with only 31% of these owners feeling kindly enough to rate their dealers' service "good." The "poor" rating was given by 32%, fair by 20%, 9% said the service was very expensive (this is typical) and 7% said that their dealers were a great distance away. There are people out there who want Jaguars badly enough to drive a long distance to find service on them.

"Best" & "Worst" Features

THE E-TYPE, naturally, is another one of those cars whose handling is the most popular characteristic with its owners—fully 54% mentioned it. And the racy styling, long an outstanding part of the character of *any* Jaguar model, rated mention by 47% of the owners. Next came performance—acceleration, top speed, flexibility, good torque at low speeds, engine smoothness; all well known characteristics of the XK engine—which was mentioned by 43%. Comfort and luxury —particularly the expensive-looking and cockpit-like interior of the E—were noted by 16% as a favorite aspect. The 4-wheel disc brakes were particularly appreciated by 12%. Other items mentioned in smaller but significant numbers

New or Used?		How Many Current E-Type Owners Would Buy Another?	
Bought new	70%	Would	83%
Bought used	30%	Would Not	17%

How Owners Feel about Jaguar Dealers' Service	Problem Areas (Reported by more than 10% of owners)	(Reported by 5-10% of all owners)	Best Features
Rated "Good" 31%	Instruments	Carburetion	Handling
Rated "Fair" 20%	Cooling system	Electrical system	Styling
Rated "Poor" 32%	Oil Leaks	Tires	Performance
No opinion 17%	Generator	Differential	Comfort & Luxury
	Clutch	Upholstery & trim	Brakes
	Fuel pump		
Factory Maintenance Schedule Followed?	Starter		Worst Features
Completely 64%	Body Parts		Maintenance & Repairs
Mostly 12%	Rain Leaks		Ventilation
Not at all 24%			Overheating
	Owners Reporting No Troubles 7%		Lack of space
			Heater & Defroster

Road & Track Owner Survey
JAGUAR E-TYPE

were that the E is a great car for extended trips because of its relaxed gait and the fact that it rides very well.

For the first time in any of our surveys, the most frequently mentioned "worst" feature was maintenance and repairs. Sixteen percent of the E owners felt strongly enough about this aspect of life with an E to single it out. Next on the list came ventilation—the coupe owners were more sensitive to this—with 12% of the total mentioning the E's badly outdated ventilation system. Next came "overheating," a traditional Jaguar complaint and one which we will examine more closely a bit later; 8% of the owners mentioned it. Lack of space for people and luggage got 7% mention, and the heater-defroster was singled out by 6%. Eighteen percent of the pre-1965 models, which had the old Moss gearbox with crash first gear, rated that gearbox as a worst feature, but Jaguar finally laid this complaint to rest with the excellent all-synchro box. One Jaguar "problem" we expected to be high on the complaint list, oil consumption, was mentioned by only 2% of the owners. Apparently they accept this trait, which incidentally has been moderated somewhat in recent years with engine improvements.

Problem areas

THE XK ENGINE is a durable piece of machinery; in all 100 cars surveyed, only two had needed engine overhauls, each with an odometer reading of around 55,000 miles—and it may be significant that both had been purchased as used cars with the possibility of more miles on them than the odos indicated. One engine had seized because of coolant loss, but we can't blame engine mechanicals for that.

As indicated by the summary chart, the E-type has more than its share of problems as compared with the other makes we've surveyed:

	Number of Problem Areas Reported by more than 10% of the owners	Number of Problem Areas Reported by 5-10% of the owners
MGB	6	3
VW	2	3
Porsche	6	2
Volvo	4	6
Triumph	3	4
Jaguar	9	5

Specifically, the instruments were the E's greatest failing. Three times before (the MGB, Volvo, Porsche), instruments have been in the 10%-or-over bracket, but Jaguar's instrument troubles top them all. There were 49 mentions of instrument failures—not counting repeat failures. Sixteen were speedometers, 11 tachometers, 10 oil pressure gauges, 7 clocks, 2 temperature gauges and 7 unspecified.

The cooling system was the next big problem area; some trouble with it was reported by 43% of the owners. Twenty percent mentioned only "overheating" or coolant loss, and we can assume (as with the MGB) that many owners interpret a reading of (say) 200°F, as overheating when in reality it's not. This rather psychological area has been dealt with by Jaguar in the latest Es by a temperature gauge that isn't calibrated in degrees fahrenheit but rather in "cold, normal, hot" as on most American cars. But again missing the boat somewhat, Jaguar selected the "normal" range on the gauge so that the needle usually runs toward the top end of it! Coolant loss is another matter, of course, and so are the numerous failures of hoses and header tanks. Oil leaks, next

on the list, were reported by 19% of the owners and the 1967 model, for some unexplained reason, was the worst in this respect. Generators and alternators gave trouble to 17% of the owners, and there is some indication that the alternator, which replaced the DC generator when the 4.2-liter E was introduced in 1965, has given slightly more trouble than its DC counterpart. The fifth most frequently occurring problem was clutch trouble of a premature nature (that is, other than normal wear), reported by 13% of the owners.

Looking for an improvement trend in problems over the years, we analyzed these five problems in this way:

Problem Mentions per car

	1962	1963	1964	1965	1966	1967	1968
Instruments	1.1	0	0.5	1.0	0.2	0.4	0.3
Cooling	0.6	0.8	0.4	0.5	0.5	0.3	0.2
Oil leaks	0.1	0	0.1	0.1	0.1	0.3	0.2
Alt, gen	0.2	0	0.3	0.1	0.2	0.2	0.1
Clutch	0.1	0	0.1	0	0.3	0.3	0

The first conclusion from the above table might be that 1963 was a vintage year! It's also obvious that instrument failures have generally come down. So have cooling problems. There has been a succession of improvements: the hoses were improved gradually and were pretty well in line with domestic practice by 1966; in 1963 the header tank was revised for better flow; and in late 1967 a new cross-flow radiator and two (instead of one) electric cooling fans was standardized to cope with the demands of air conditioning. There have been two major changes in the clutch; it was first a Borg & Beck lever-operated clutch, then a Laycock diaphragm unit with the advent of the 4.2 engine and new gearbox, then in late 1967 a Borg & Beck diaphragm clutch. The two years of highest trouble frequency, 1966 and 1967, may reflect Jaguar's reasons for going back to Borg & Beck.

Component life

THERE WAS sufficient data to draw conclusions about the normal wear life of several areas of the E-type from this highly informative group of owners. Front brakes went an average of 33,000 miles between relines, rears 35,000—meaning that they would usually be relined at the same time. Clutch life, discounting the instances of premature trouble, averaged 38,000 miles. The Dunlop Road Speed (cross-bias) tires formerly used lasted an average of 17,500 miles and the radials now standard should go about 30,000. Spark plugs were generally changed at about 6500 miles, but Jaguar's current recommendation of 12,000-mile intervals probably more accurately reflects the life that can be expected of plugs in current Es.

Summary

IT SHOULD be obvious from the above that the E-type is indeed a comparatively troublesome car, as hearsay had led us to believe. But—and this isn't particularly surprising—its owners grin and bear it for the enjoyment of the car when it is working right. Why do we say that? Because 83% of them would buy another Jaguar, and that's about an average showing for all the makes we've surveyed so far. One owner, after describing his myriad troubles with brakes, clutch, cooling, pistons, oil leaks, and so forth, put it very well: "Believe it or not, I love my car. My next car will be another Jaguar." The remaining 17% won't buy another—nobody was "undecided" and half of them quote unreliability as their reason. Most of the remaining half are looking for a really new Jaguar, either because they feel the E is now outdated or because they disapprove of the recent styling revisions. We do expect a new model in a year or two, and hopefully the greater resources of Jaguar's new parent company BLMC will enable this respected innovator in sporting automobiles to achieve a higher level of reliability in the years to come.

JAGUAR E-TYPE COUPE

*U.S. safety and emission control regulations
result in some changes in a long-time favorite*

GORDON CHITTENDEN PHOTOS

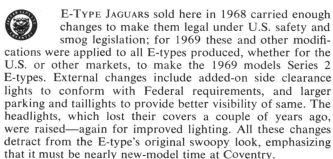

E-TYPE JAGUARS sold here in 1968 carried enough changes to make them legal under U.S. safety and smog legislation; for 1969 these and other modifications were applied to all E-types produced, whether for the U.S. or other markets, to make the 1969 models Series 2 E-types. External changes include added-on side clearance lights to conform with Federal requirements, and larger parking and taillights to provide better visibility of same. The headlights, which lost their covers a couple of years ago, were raised—again for improved lighting. All these changes detract from the E-type's original swoopy look, emphasizing that it must be nearly new-model time at Coventry.

Inside, the traditional toggle switches were replaced by rocking tablets, and crash padding was revised. The 3-carburetor, 265-bhp version of the venerable XK engine (introduced in 1949) couldn't meet the emission rules, so Jaguar opted for a 2-carburetor version with a dual induction system that developed 246 bhp. Latest models, the test car included, have a water-heated intake manifold rather than the dual induction system, dispensing with the crossover tract that took intake mixture across the cam covers to the exhaust manifold for heating.

Exciting though the E-type was when it was introduced in 1961, time has made it rather dated, inside and out. The interior, though retaining that wonderful smell of leather and the aura of a cockpit with a million controls and dials, lacks the spaciousness and ergonomics of more recently designed cars. Entry and exit are somewhat awkward and legroom is restricted. The rocker switches look nice and are labeled clearly, but one has to look at them to operate them because they're all alike. The heater controls, which have been revised, are recalcitrant and there's no modulation for temperature—just on or off. Wisely, we suppose (though we prefer numbers), Jaguar has omitted numbers on the temperature gauge so that the unknowing won't be alarmed at the sight of 210°F, and a battery voltmeter has replaced the ammeter of old; this latter seems a useful instrument, though one can't spot electrical trouble instantly with it. Our test car had factory-installed air conditioning, which was integrated nicely with the instrument panel and which worked quietly and effectively.

In performance, this latest E-type is still characteristically Jaguar but something has been lost in meeting the smog laws, not to mention the effect of increased weight due to air conditioning. The test car weighed 3020 lb, vs 2900 for our 1964 test car, and had a 3.54:1 final drive (vs 3.31:1). Quarter-mile times were within 0.1 sec for the two cars, but the 1964 car was doing 91 mph at the trap vs 86 for the 1969; 0-60 mph times were 7.4 for the 1964 and 8.0 for the 1969. For top speed in 1964 we took the maker's claim,

JAGUAR E-TYPE COUPE

which was 150 mph at 6300 rpm; the current 4.2-liter engine has a redline of only 5500 rpm, and this combined with the numerically higher final drive ratio leaves us with a top speed of 119 mph. This is pretty academic in America anyway; in acceleration, which should be about the same up to 70 mph (without A/C) as it was in 1964, the E-type is certainly no slouch.

By contemporary standards, however, the XK engine doesn't seem comfortable when it's driven hard. It likes to amble along at moderate speeds in 4th and has so much low-speed torque that gearshifting is rarely necessary; driven this way it is quiet and smooth. But when pressed it takes on a hard note, and cruising at anything above 3300 rpm (71 mph) seems a bit strained.

The all-synchro gearbox (new in 1965), though a bit noisy, shifts beautifully and has infallible synchromesh. The shift lever falls "readily to hand" and everything seems to fall into place to make the E-type one of those cars you can climb into and drive smoothly the first time.

The E doesn't have quite the absolute cornering power of a Corvette or Porsche these days, but it's still a car with a nice balance between handling and ride. Steering is accurate and light enough at speed, though it gets heavy in parking

and feeds back considerably on bumps. The car handles with neutrality and imparts confidence; there's little change of attitude if you lift your throttle foot in the middle of a hard corner. In all, it does better than we expected with such a narrow track (50.0 in.) by today's standards.

And it rides very softly most of the time; on big undulations it seems almost floaty but never gets out of hand. Rough roads bring out the worst in its body structure, which has little creaks going even on smooth surfaces and rattles quite a bit when it's jolted about. On the freeway the E is a restful car, with moderate wind, road and engine noise and excellent directional stability.

The 4-wheel disc brakes do a fine job, with moderate pedal effort and good feel for everyday driving plus good panic stopping and fade resistance for those times when brakes must be used to their limit. The old bugaboo of disc-brake squeal has been almost eliminated by steel wire set into grooves in the disc periphery.

We hear that a new engine is in the plans for the E-type this fall; probably the basic car will be with us for another year or two. As it stands, it's a pleasant car in normal everyday driving, and it has a style about it that still pleases a lot of people. It's still afflicted with a fair share of reliability problems, too (see the Owners Report in the July issue). In summary, we can't really say we didn't like it. But we do think Jaguar can do better—and will before long.

Jaguar's latest method of controlling emissions of the classic XK engine is this water-heated intake manifold.

SCALE: 10" DIVISIONS

PRICE

Basic list.................$5675
As tested...............$6495

ENGINE

Type...........6 cyl inline, dohc
Bore x stroke, mm...92.1 x 106.0
  Equivalent in.......3.62 x 4.17
Displacement, cc/cu in..4235/258
Compression ratio..........9.0:1
Bhp @ rpm.........246 @ 5500
  Equivalent mph.............119
Torque @ rpm, lb-ft.. 263 @ 3000
  Equivalent mph..............64
Carburetion.......two Stromberg
  175 CD 2SE
Type fuel required.......premium
Emission control....intake heating

DRIVE TRAIN

Clutch diameter, in..........10.0
Gear ratios: 4th (1.00).....3.54:1
  3rd (1.39).............4.92:1
  2nd (1.91).............6.74:1
  1st (2.94)............10.39:1
Final drive ratio..........3.54:1

CHASSIS & BODY

Body/frame: steel tubular frame
  with stressed steel panels
Brake type: disc, 11.0-in. front,
  10.0-in. rear; handbrake by
  mechanical caliper
  Swept area, sq in.........461
Wheels......chrome wire, 15 x 5
Tires.......Dunlop SP 185 VR-15
Steering type......rack & pinion
  Turns, lock-to-lock.........2.8
  Turning circle, ft.........37.0
Front suspension: unequal-length
  A-arms, torsion bars, tube
  shocks, anti-roll bar
Rear suspension: lower A-arms,
  fixed-length halfshafts, trailing
  arms, coil springs, tube shocks,
  anti-roll bar

EQUIPMENT

Options on test car: air conditioning ($482), AM radio ($110), white-
  wall tires ($27), chrome wire
  wheels ($132) tinted glass ($69)
Other: heated rear window ($41),
  AM/FM radio ($165), chrome
  disc wheels ($77)

ACCOMMODATION

Seating capacity, persons........2
Seat width................2 x 18.0
Head room................40.0
Seat back adjustment, deg.....65
Driver comfort rating (scale of 100):
  Driver 69 in. tall.............90
  Driver 72 in. tall.............70
  Driver 75 in. tall.............70

INSTRUMENTATION

Instruments: 160-mph speedo,
  6000-rpm tach, 99,999 odo,
  999.9 trip odo, oil press, water
  temp, battery voltage, fuel level,
  clock
Warning lights: generator/ignition,
  low fuel, high beam, directionals,
  hazard flasher

MAINTENANCE

Engine oil capacity, qt.........9.0
Every 3000 mi: minor op'l check,
  check fluids
Every 6000 mi: chg eng oil & filter,
  lube chassis
Every 12,000 mi: chg gearbox oil,
  tune engine & chg plugs, adj
  timing chain, chg air cleaner,
  major op'l check, oil can lube
Every 36,000 mi: chg brake fluid
Warranty, mo/mi......12/12,000

GENERAL

Curb weight, lb...........3018
Test weight................3360
Weight distribution (with
  driver), front/rear, %....49/51
Wheelbase, in............96.0
Track, front/rear.....50.0/50.0
Overall length.........175.3
  Width.................65.2
  Height.................48.1
Ground clearance, in.........5.5
Overhang, front/rear..........
Usable trunk space, cu ft.....6.5
Fuel tank capacity, gal.......16.8

CALCULATED DATA

Lb/hp (test wt).............13.7
Mph/1000 rpm (4th gear)....21.2
Engine revs/mi (60 mph)....2820
Engine speed @ 70 mph....3280
Piston travel, ft/mi.........1965
Cu ft/ton mi.................125
R&T wear index.............55
R&T steering index.........1.04
Brake swept area sq in/ton...274

ROAD TEST RESULTS

ACCELERATION

Time to distance, sec:
0–100 ft...................3.3
0–250 ft...................5.6
0–500 ft...................8.5
0–750 ft..................10.9
0–1000 ft..................13.1
0–1320 ft (¼ mi)..........15.7
Speed at end of ¼ mi, mph...86
Time to speed, sec:
0–30 mph...................3.3
0–40 mph...................4.5
0–50 mph...................6.1
0–60 mph...................8.0
0–70 mph..................10.9
0–80 mph..................13.7
0–100 mph.................21.7
Passing exposure time, sec:
  To pass car going 50 mph....6.0

FUEL CONSUMPTION

Normal driving, mpg.......15.9
Cruising range, mi..........267

SPEEDS IN GEARS

4th gear (5500 rpm), mph.....119
3rd (5500)..................86
2nd (5500)..................64
1st (5500)..................41

BRAKES

Panic stop from 80 mph:
  Deceleration, % g.........84
  Control................good
Fade test: percent of increase in
  pedal effort required to main-
  tain 50%-g deceleration rate in
  six stops from 60 mph......nil
Parking: hold 30% grade.....yes
Overall brake rating.....very good

SPEEDOMETER ERROR

30 mph indicated.....actual 29.2
40 mph....................39.4
60 mph....................59.8
80 mph....................80.2
100 mph..................100.5
Odometer, 10.0 mi....actual 9.95

ACCELERATION & COASTING

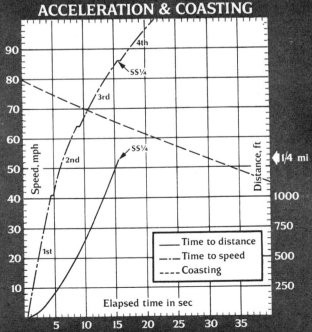

Time to distance
Time to speed
Coasting

Elapsed time in sec

Front air intake has been enlarged to help alleviate traffic delay heating problems.

THE 'E' TYPE — MAXIMUM STATUS MEDIU

Jaguar continues to win influential friends

Since its introduction in late 1961, the Jaguar XKE has had many imitators but so far, no one has quite come up with a styling shape that has been so durable or has captured the public eye in such a marked manner as the 'E' type. After eight years on the nation's highways, the 'E' will still cause the blasé Los Angeles freeway driver to turn and take another look, such is the lasting impression that the car instills in all who enjoy fine looking automobiles.

Naturally, there have been many refinements, some badly needed, over the years; but it takes the trained eye to tell exactly which model year he is looking at.

Jaguar philosophy in building the car is typical of the craftmanship heritage of the European coachbuilder. As they conceived the car, it is to them, perfect. Unfortunately, between the drawing board and the customer, many hands are involved and the end result is not always exactly as was hoped for. For some

reason or another, this is difficult for the designer to comprehend and it usually takes several years of retroactive modifications to ultimately come up with a well honed machine, in every respect, which approximates the original concept.

Such has been the case with the XKE. The body shell is basically the same as the original, which was derived from the highly successful 'C' and 'D' type racing cars. The changes under the hood and in the interior have improved the car in many respects but there are those who will say that there is yet room for much improvement in the present model. More on this later.

The racing heritage of the Jaguar is studded with many magnificent wins on the circuits of the world, with their more notable successes in the 24 hours of Le Mans. All this has been passed down into the 'E' type which has been raced with moderate success, mainly in Europe where lightweight versions were pro-

duced for racing purposes. But the overall design of the car was for high speed touring in the grand manner and not for the week-end racer. The Jaguar XKE is a fine example of British automotive thinking of using racing to improve the breed.

Reams of paper and gallons of ink have been used by automotive writers over the years extolling the virtues and vices of the Jaguar XKE's and at this point, ROAD TEST felt that a resume of what has gone before in this car might be of some assistance to someone contemplating buying a used car.

The 1962 introduction of the car had a steady procession of diehard enthusiasts trooping in to the showrooms to lay down their hard earned cash for the latest car from Coventry. For their money, they got the same basic six cylinder in-line twin overhead camshaft engine that had been around for some twelve years. The shape was exotic to say the least, with a good five year lead on anything that Detroit even had on the drawing boards at that time. The interior of the car was more suited to the smaller European build and the very early cars all had flat floor panels. This was changed in the middle of the model year when the present dished out floor was introduced. The early hoods were five piece units, the three main sections and the two louvers. This, too, changed early in production when the panels were punched out with

the American market yardstick rather than the top-end high speed touring as used in Europe.

The gearbox was changed in 1965 to a fully synchromeshed unit which was a sadly overdue requirement. The old box had stood the test of time but in this modern age, was certainly archaic.

The 3.8 engine was replaced with the new 4.2 unit with some subtle engineering changes, plus changing the electrics

Early XKEs had only fair braking at moderate speeds. New system gives excellent stopping power throughout speed range. There is no fade after repeated 60 mph stops, all in a straight line.

ONEY

the louvers included in the main center section. The outside key opening unit for raising the hood was changed to the present interior locking system and if anyone now owns one of these older models, it is indeed a rarity.

The main technical change affecting the performance of the car was in the braking system. There was excessive play in the pedal linkage and the master cylinder came in for replacement with a much more satisfactory system.

This eliminated the ghastly feeling of the car not stopping swiftly from moderate speeds although the high speed braking was never a problem.

The next important change came in late 1963 when the scraper rings on the pistons were altered. This all but eliminated the thirst for oil that was a talking point with early Jaguar owners. The rear axle ratio was changed from the 3.31:1 to 3.54:1 in 1965. This gave the car a better acceleration more in keeping with

to a negative ground and switching to an alternator. The torque curve was more suited to the rear end gearing with the result that better acceleration was forthcoming. This put it in a better light with the Corvettes at the traffic light Grand Prix but not to the point where it could stay with them. There is still no substitute for cubic inches.

Minor trim interior changes followed over the next two years and by mid

First major styling changes in years are most evident at the rear. Huge tail lights, new bumper line upset some purists.

1967, the first of the safety requirements began to appear. The headlight covers were the first to go in preparation for the 68 standards.

The knock-off hubs came in for their whacks under the safety campaign and

line engine has been with us now for almost twenty years. In this latest form, it puts out 246 bhp at 5500 rpm. Twin Zenith-Stromberg carburetors form part of the smog device which shows up in two variants. The original unit has a stainless twin tube enclosed in a single polished bracket that runs across the engine at the rear between the two carburetors and the exhaust manifold. This ducts the fuel/air mixture over to the hot exhaust side for pre-heating en route to the cylinders. With increased throttle opening, the butterfly valve in this manifold gradually closes until at full throttle, the mixture is going directly into the cylinders. The latest version of this item uses the hot water system in the engine to achieve the same result. It makes for a neater engine bay.

At the front of the engine, there are two fan belts, one driving the alternator and the other to the water pump. The pulley size is increased thereby getting the pump cranked up that little bit faster.

Over the shoulder viewing is fair, head restraints not too obtrusive. Other 'safety' features do little for safety, actually reduce convenience.

First time viewers are awed by the 'E' type's cockpit. Instrument and control array resembles an aircraft. Switches are clearly labeled, easy to use.

they were replaced with a tripodal type locking nut that required the old style knock-off to be fitted over it, then the owner could whale away in the old manner. This is one of those needless so called safety items that are quite useless. To our knowledge, no one has been seriously injured, if at all, by a knock-off hub since the Ben Hur movie and before that, when Queen Boadicea was 'having at' the Romans back in early British history.

1968 saw the end of the door arm rest and the tumbler switches on the instrument panel. Shoulder harnesses became standard and non glare wiper blades were there for all to see. Jaguar had always used the black matte finish on its dashboards so no changes were needed there. The engine came in for major revision due to the smog laws. The three 2 in. S.U. carburetors gave way to two 1 ¾ in. Strombergs and the power dropped from 265 BHP to 245 BHP. The *bete-noir* of Jaguar owners, the $40 header tank on the engine, was replaced with a small expansion tank on the firewall. With the high attrition rate of the old tank, due to the rusting effect caused by the high mineral content of the California water, this expensive unit has at

last removed a possible source of expensive engine overhaul if the driver didn't spot the temperature rise when the tank blew.

The old two blade electric fan was replaced by two four bladed electric fans and this went a long way in combatting the traffic heating problems with the older cars.

These changes briefly cover the background of the Jaguar XKE to the present time. It amplifies our original opening statement; the current car is an evolution of an original theme and not merely change for the sake of change.

Drive train

The Jaguar 4.2 litre (258.4 cu. in.) twin overhead camshaft six cylinder in-

At the rear of the block, there are two water passages providing better circulation for cooling around the number six cylinder. Crackle finish on the cam covers completes the new look on the old block.

The fuel pump is a Lucas electric and is located in the right rear wheel well. In recent years, this has proved to be relatively trouble free but should it act up, it can easily be reached for a couple of whacks, the standard emergency drill for this item.

The power is taken from the engine through a 9 ½ in. diaphragm single dry plate clutch. The fully synchronized box is really a very sturdy unit and little troubles have been experienced with it. The synchromesh is very good and cannot be beaten by speed shifting. The ratios are

XKE Coupe offers enormous cargo space virtually all open to view of passersby. There is a small, concealed cubby directly behind the seats.

Relation of throttle and brake is excellent. Competition heritage is evident in many subtle touches.

2.93:1 in first, 1.90:1 in second, 1.38:1 in third and fourth being 1:1. The spacing of the gears is satisfactory and combined with the good torque, gives the driver great flexibility in the acceleration range.

Power and performance

No matter how one looks at it, the Jaguar is really a car for touring in the true GT manner. Around town is not its natural habitat; you don't see race horses dragging milk carts. In Europe, such cars maintain high cruising speeds in the three figure bracket and with this type of driving, engine performance is at its optimum. However, in the 70 mph U.S.A., the Jaguar will turn in very creditable performance by most standards. In the standing quarter at Orange County International Raceway, it showed up a clean 15.70 sec with a trap speed of 88.4 mph.

Passing with this car is quite effortless. Merely by prodding the loud pedal, an extra 20 mph comes up in less than 5 secs. If the gear is dropped down one, the effect is even more swift. This makes overtaking on two lane highways a relatively safe operation.

The ride is extremely smooth and quiet, particularly in the air conditioned coupe and 2+2. The fully independent suspension contributes to this coupled with the Dunlop Super Sport radial tires.

Roadability and handling

The difficulty with the Jaguar on the open highway is in keeping the speed

down to the legal limit. The car moves effortlessly up through the gears and if the driver tends to become a little exuberant, the needle will soon be hovering over the 'ton' figure. At the high speed end, the car is probably one of the safest machines that a novice can drive without getting into trouble. The secure feeling while the car is at high speed allows a driver, who knows little about high speed driving techniques to do things with the car and get away with it. Plenty of warning is there before the car begins to breakaway on a corner and the swift steering response, allows it to be brought back into line. Naturally, anyone who tries high speed motoring without first going through a performance driving school, is asking for it but at least with the 'E' type, he does have a good chance of learning without it being fatal.

Cornering in the car is a satisfying experience and the 'E' performs best under power. Once the car is close to the apex of the turn, power should be smoothly applied and the rear end will squat down and the car will come through the bend in a smooth controlled manner. Mere wrist movements will relay the driver's slightest whim and the

Spare wheel, jack and tools live under trunk floor. Jaguar, like most imports, includes fairly complete tool sets with each car.

satisfaction of a turn well executed will result.

Rack and pinion steering gives precise control at all times. The 2+2 will have power steering later, presumably the same unit that was used in the 420 models which give road feel to the driver.

Although the 'E' type is a pleasure to drive on a long trip, the real fun with the car comes from a winding road in hilly country. There is ample power to throw the car around and the enthusiast can get all his thrills and satisfaction without going over the legal speed limits.

Brakes and safety

That Jaguar owners have survived some pretty hefty pile-ups is testimony to the strength of the monocoque type of construction of the car.

The braking system follows the required split system, which has always been standard on Jaguars. In facts, discs all 'round were introduced on all their cars from *1957* onwards. The latest

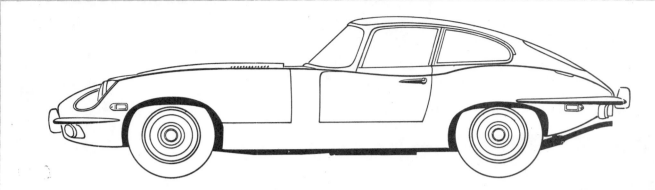

brakes are now Girling discs. These are much better ventilated and have at last eliminated the problem of squealing brakes on all previous models. Rapid decelerations from speed would alleviate this old problem but was not always a practical proposition in many instances. Now, they are quite superb and recorded 28 ft. per sec² plus. This being equivalent to a 138 ft. or better from 60 mph.

The hydraulic braking system is assisted by a vacuum booster making pedal effort quite low for the little woman.

The wide radial tires have excellent drainage characteristics and provide good traction in wet conditions. These tires were introduced on the '68 models, and owners report wear factors in excess of 30,000 miles.

All switches are now of the rocker variety and the dashboard retains its heavy padding from the earliest models. The interior conforms to all regulations. One annoying item is the glue used to secure the rear view mirror to the windshield. It does not stand up to the baking in the California sunshine and requires to be reglued using some of the local stickum, this cures it once and for all.

Comfort and convenience

Getting comfortable in a Jaguar is not an acquired skill, it is a function of size. From 5 ft. 6 ins. on up, the ease of entry depends entirely on the model. A tall person wears a convertible very snugly whereas a 2+2 by comparison, feels like a Lawrence Welk ballroom. The backs of the seats are adjustable for rake but the fore and aft travel is still on the short side for most tall people. The seat padding is much improved over the older models but does not give quite the lateral support of an Alfa GTV. They are not too satisfactory for long distance work due to lack of thigh support. It is felt that they could easily be improved, even within the confining size limitations of the cabin area. Throttle angle is rather too vertical.

Heating and ventilation are still not the greatest after eight years. The control knobs for defrosting require some experimentation before getting the maximum benefit from them. The amount of cool air that can be directed on the driver's feet is below what would be rated as satisfactory. Air conditioning is now available (factory installed) on all models and this goes a long way toward easing the problem. It is still not the answer for the driver's feet. The problem is due to the close proximity of the fresh air ducts to the hot exhaust side of the engine.

The arm rest on the door was removed in the '68 model to comply with the safety standards. This makes it uncomfortable for the driver who likes to rest his elbow at that position. Tall people can use the top of the door with the window lowered but again, this is not exactly comfortable and depends on weather conditions. Wind noise is unbearable with coupe or 2+2 windows open.

The long low hood tends to overwhelm new owners but requires little adjustment on the driver's part to get used to estimating the overhang at the front when parking the car. It is a wise driver who parks with the nose in a red zone.

Instrumentation has always been a strong point with Jaguar and the basic layout has been standard from its introduction. The main change has been in providing a battery operated clock in the center of the console. This replaces the quarter sized' one that used to be located in the tach. The instruments are Smiths and their reliability has improved greatly in recent years. All are easy to read and the driver is informed as to the engine's state of health. The main gauge is for temperature, especially after a few years of ownership; as this will soon let you know if you've had a hose failure. If the hoses are checked regularly, any leakage can be corrected without expensive servicing being required.

Economy

When the buyer has had to shell out some six thousand dollars on an 'E' coupe, economy of operation can not be expected to be the same as for a small import. However, the running costs for a Jaguar are not unreasonable for this price range automobile.

Gas economy, which is naturally not a consideration with this type of machine, is a useful 15-18 mpg. Oil consumption

With fully independent suspension, E Jag handling cannot be faulted. A novice can enjoy hard cornering.

is down to less than one quart per thousand miles, again, a far cry from the fifties when the engine seemed to take as much oil as the tank held gas.

Tune-ups are recommended every six thousand miles and depending on driving conditions, this seems to be fairly average. The cost will be around $32.00, including the lube and oil. The twelve thousand mile check-up will run close to $60.00 to $70.00, depending on just how much is done, such as whether the owner wants the tires rotated etc. Again, if this price is compared to a similar priced domestic, the Jaguar is a relatively inexpensive car to operate.

Availability of parts, at least in the Los Angeles area, is extremely good, There can be the usual shortages periodically if the factories go on strike back in England. This is completely beyond the control of the distributor.

The Jaguar price starts at $5873.00

or the convertible, equipped with chrome wire wheels, tinted glass and white side walls. All other items, disc brakes, limited slip, heater, harnesses etc., are all standard. The coupe, similarly equipped, costs $6105.00. Air conditioning is available for another $465.00 and is now installed at the factory making for a much neater arrangement. The +2 runs into more money and one fully equipped, with air and automatic will just tip over the $7000.00 figure.

Summary

When a Jaguar is ushered into the family, it is necessary to be aware of the fact that it is not something that can be ignored and left to the tender, or otherwise, machinations of the friendly neighborhood gas jockey. Dealership mechanics vary quite largely in degrees of skill and if you find a good one, stick with him

Meeting smog requirements has meant reduction from three 2 in. SU carbs to two 1¾ in. Strombergs. Horsepower, while down by 20, is still impressive.

Highly efficient double overhead cam engine continues to attract viewers at service station stops after 20 years. New models have twin electric fans.

and let him do the worrying over the engine tune-ups.

The latest carburetors are simplicity itself as regards setting up, BUT, there is more to tuning an engine than fiddling with the idle screw. They are also sealed, by law, and should not be tampered with.

The prestige of Jaguar ownership sets the buyer up as one with discriminating tastes, just to be seen with it is enough to set him apart. Next time you visit your favorite restaurant, just look at the front row in the parking lot and see how the 'E' types are parked, domestic iron takes a back seat every time.

Jaguar ownership is like marriage, you don't expect it to be all roses, but at least you won't want to be separated from it either.

Owners of the older models always swore they would never buy another, yet,

when the 'E' type came out, they were in line waiting to get their hands on one. When the 'E' type successor comes along, the enthusiasts will walk barefoot on broken glass to get another one. The loyalty to the breed would keep a psychology major working nights for a lifetime.

It all boils down to value. It's not that the Jaguar XKE costs $6000.00; it is more 'how can so much car be sold for *only* $6000.00?' To get way ahead of it, you've got to spend almost double the money. ♠

Jaguar XKE Coupe

Data in Brief

DIMENSIONS

Overall length (in.)	175.0
Wheelbase (in.)	96.0
Height (in.)	48.0
Width (in.)	65.2
Tread, front (in.)	50.0
Tread, rear (in.)	50.0
Fuel tank capacity (gal.)	16.7
Luggage capacity (cu. ft.)	n.a.
Turning diameter (ft.)	37.0

ENGINE

Type	DOHC in-line 6
Displacement (cu. in.)	258.4
Horsepower (at 5500 rpm)	246.0
Torque (lb/ft at 3000 rpm)	263.0

WEIGHT, TIRES, BRAKES

Weight (as tested)	3261
Tires	Dunlop radial 185 x 15
Brakes, front	disc
Brakes, rear	disc

SUSPENSION

Front	independent with parallel wishbones, torsion bars, anti-sway bar, telescopic shocks
Rear	independent, transverse links, radius arms, quad coil springs, quad concentric shocks

PERFORMANCE

Standing ¼ mile (sec.)	15.70
Speed at end of ¼ mile (mph)	88.40
Braking (from 60 mph, ft.)	138

SPOT CHECK: Jaguar E-type

Development details, dates, diagnosis: the second in our new
spot check series for owners and used-car buyers

Now in its 10th year the Jaguar E-type is selling at a higher rate than ever before, 270 per week being produced, of which 95 per cent are exported. This leaves a balance of some 14 cars, all of nearly 150 mph potential, still eagerly sought despite the 70 mph limit. Britain's return to the red-flag days is not crippling her ability to make successful, very-high-performance sports cars—and export them.

The car's evolution can be summed up as a blend of two parallel streams of development. On the one hand there was the Heynes-Baily-Hassan string of engines—produced to a clean-sheet-of-paper design—which went through an alphabetical series of development before reaching production. Mr W. M. Heynes lists the 1996 cc four cylinder (known as the XJ) as the true precursor of the subsequent XK units. It was one of these experimental 6000 rpm, 146 bhp fours that took Major Gardner to his world records in the 2-litre class.

From these beginnings sprang first an XJ 3.2-litre six and then the XK 3.4 production engine and its sisters. The

E-type used variants of first the 3781 and then 4235 cc engines. Running parallel were the chassis/body developments —where true chassis were used.

The proper ancestor of the E-type is the XK 120, which was introduced at the 1948 Earls Court Show and intended to be produced in very limited quantity—200 to be precise.

From race successes of XK sportsters stemmed the C-type (C standing for competition). The 3.4 of the two Peters, Walker and Whitehead, won the 1951 24-hour Le Mans classic.

Aside from the briefly seen "Jabbeke" prototype of 1953, the C-type evolved into the D-type. This was a monocoque-based design against the tubular frame of the C-type. Some of the D-types were characterized by tail fins stretching back from the driver's headrest.

With roadster development meanwhile going apace via the XK 120 to 150 series, and engine advancement proceeding with those and the sister 2.4 and 3.4 saloons (Mark I) etc., the competition side went on to the "Cunningham Car", a logical

successor to the D-type, evolved by the factory and borrowed by the American Briggs Cunningham for the 1960 Le Mans. It had a 2997 cc fuel-injected engine producing 295 bhp; it aborted in the actual race. The Cunningham car with its independent rear suspension and inboard disc brakes forms the direct link between the D- and E-types.

Less direct is the evolution of the D-type into a roadster, known as the XK SS, a rare model of 1957 made even rarer by a fire that finished XK SS production. Out of these antecedents came the E-type, unveiled in March 1961 at the Geneva Motor Show.

These antecedents are important because the E-type didn't follow the usual path of drawing-board conception and development-shop gestation. Instead it was a natural emergence placing Sir William Lyons in the enviable position of having a *new* model with *already proven* engine and mechanicals. This is the explanation why this 3.8-litre, triple-SU, 150mph sportster has been so remarkably free from a history of detail alterations.

A few minor points were quickly tidied in the introductory year. Water deflector shields were added to the rear hubs, a self-adjusting handbrake was devised, new bonnet catches (situated inside the car) installed and a heated backlight made an option on the fixed head coupe.

In 1962 footwells were introduced and the seats moved back (both were designed to increase legroom); the brake pedal angle being altered in consequence. The Dunlop disc brakes were given Mintex M33 pads.

The next season was more a year for technical changes. Universal joint shields were added to the rear driveshafts and thicker ($\frac{1}{2}$in.) discs brought in for the rear brakes. Pad material was changed to M59 (which is the recommendation to this day).

Dunlop SP41 radials became standard and the exhaust system, which was extensively modified, became much more efficient. The axle ratio started out at 3.31, went up to 3.07 and then was changed back to 3.31.

It returned to 3.07 in 1964 with the introduction of the all-synchromesh gearbox and the 4.2-litre E-type of October. A diaphragm-type clutch was next, plus an alternator, improved radiator, one-piece inlet manifold with a water rail, divided-circuit, tandem-servo braking and dirt shields on the front discs, new seats and revised interior trim, and pre-engaged starter. Better headlamps were also provided.

Detail improvements (the 3781 cc version was discontinued) included aluminized silencers, boot-hinge covers on the fixed head coupe, a lockable boot on the open car and improved fuel pump.

The development department had no

Mr Champness, workshop manager of Coombes of Guildford, being advised about work done on a car before delivery

major work to do for the 1965 season other than an improved screenwasher, getting some better waterproofing on the distributor and giving factory blessing to Dunlop's SP41.HR radials.

Frantic action behind the scenes in 1966 led to the introduction of the stretched-door 2 + 2 for that March, with its 9in. longer wheelbase (a new option was a Borg-Warner automatic gearbox).

In company with the new variant the fixed head coupe took on a wide ratio gearbox. All cars got a re-angled clutch pedal.

The next season, wide ratios appeared on the open two seater, the headlamp covers were removed and a much better plastic-type material replaced the canvas hood on the drophead.

Having got their wind, the development staff really had a show for 1968. Wheel spoke breakage meant revised hubs and spokes, the screen rake was revised to 2 + 2 styling, air intake was upped by 68 per cent, the headlamps brought forward, bigger indicator repeaters and brake lights fitted, twin reversing lights mounted just inside the overriders, wrap-round bumpers devised, and the facia given a set of rocker switches and improved heater and choke controls. Wiper-motor power was also increased.

From October 1968 twin reversing lights, inboard of the overriders, were featured. Note new exhaust system

Triple SUs and the new modified manifold with water heating: the three carburetters are the HD8-type SU with an enormous air cleaner mounted immediately behind the offside front wheel

Overhaul costs

Spares	New Price, Outright			Reconditioned Price		
	£	s	d	£	s	d
Complete engine	475	0	0	—		
(Manual)	—			198	0	0
(Automatic)	—			188	0	0
Manual gearbox	105	0	0	62	0	0
Automatic gearbox	155	4	7	51	0	0
Torque converter	31	2	6	n/a		
Crankshaft	n/a			17	0	0
Pistons (each)	5	10	8	n/a		
Water pump	10	0	0	n/a		
Timing chain, upper	2	16	9	n/a		
lower	2	7	3	n/a		
Valve, inlet		11	10	n/a		
exhaust		19	6	n/a		
Decoke gasket set	4	6	4	n/a		
Fan belt		16	8	n/a		
Alternator	18	11	6	14	4	6
Distributor	12	10	0	8	15	0
Starter motor	37	15	0	26	8	6
Clutch cover assembly	7	8	3	6	8	11
drive plate	5	10	9	n/a		
release bearing	1	4	7	n/a		
master cylinder	2	11	6	n/a		
slave cylinder	3	1	1	n/a		
Differential	91	0	0	30	0	0
Half shaft (each)	12	6	0	n/a		
Brake master cylinder	11	17	11	n/a		
pads, front (set)	4	5	0	n/a		
rear (set)	3	12	6	n/a		
Dampers (each)	4	14	0	n/a		
Coil springs (rear, each)	1	17	10	n/a		
Manual (incl. 4.2 supplement)	4	6	7	—		

This little lot was dubbed the Series 2 and arrived in October 1968.

The tempo was kept up for the 1969 season. New camshafts gave quieter running and allowed still longer service intervals.

Cold-start, ballast-resistor ignition systems reached Coventry as did the steering lock, a gas-filled bonnet stay, arm rests on the doors, a clock powered by the car battery, and revamped backs to the seats with apertures for fitting headrests, and the optional extra of powered, Adwest, steering.

The 1969/70 period saw the introduction of the non-eared hub cap for all wire wheel cars and the arrival of the disc wheel as an option (these wheels were dearer, which is a reversal of practice with more mundane cars).

For the benefit of *Motor*'s many overseas readers, the home-market models—comprising about 5 per cent of current E-type production—differ in minor details from export models, which themselves are not identical for all markets abroad.

In 1968 Jaguar spent over £250,000 complying with the United States' Federal safety regulations, and more money since on meeting exhaust emission standards. The main feature here has been, for 1970, elaborating the 1968-introduced duplex manifold system to reduce the carbon monoxide content of the exhaust gases from 1.5 to 1 per cent, achieved by warming the air supply to the carburetters to 120 deg. F.

An incidental by-product of all this work has been a betterment in fuel consumption of about 5 per cent coupled with a 5 per cent power loss above 4000 rpm. **B.M-S.**

Headlamps and flashers are a good guide to quick dating of the car (see text). This is the latest version

Pocket diagnosis

Oil consumption of 150 miles per pint, and better, is acceptable. Worse than this denotes need for attention

A dry rack in the steering may be nothing worse than the previous owner forgetting to give the rack-and-pinion a squirt of grease, as the book stipulates. The nipple is rather liable to be overlooked

A front-end knock over bumps, and/or uneven front tyre wear, may be nothing worse than a worn bottom ball joint, which should be de-shimmed or renewed according to its condition

Brake squeal can occur if the wrong pads are used. M59 is the right stuff

Braking troubles may be less serious than you suppose. It's vital that the callipers are kept clean; there's a groove between cylinder and piston that fills with debris and prevents full retraction of the piston when clogged

Slop in the steering column may be nothing more than a worn top bush. The latest type is plastic and takes only half an hour to slap in

Ideally oil should be checked after an overnight stand. At the very least, with a hot engine, allow 5 min. for levelling or you'll waste your money and risk over-oiling trouble. Same applies to the water; let the car stand. Jaguar, in fact, like both to be checked cold

Brakes need checking every 3000 miles—yes, even the handbrake pads—as wear may not be even. Rears have twice the life of fronts with many drivers

A cold-condition buzz on 95 per cent of automatics is due to oil being circulated between gearbox and converter. Don't worry about it. Both Jaguar and Borg-Warner are trying to cure this feature

Don't forget to clean out the plug recesses before unscrewing the candles. They can accumulate small stones—which then promptly drop down inside . . .

Timing chain noise may (or may not) be less serious than you fear, having heard diabolical rumours about the cost of renewing the bottom chain. Try the tensioner on the top one first. If the noise quietens, well and good. If it doesn't (and there's no tensioner on the bottom one up to 1964), confirm rumours

When overhauling, don't classify worn cam-followers (tappet buckets) as serviceable. Any chatter marks suggest need for renewal.

If you want a quick demonstration of instant valve damage put the head down on a flat surface or turn the camshafts independently. In case one, some valves protrude below the joint face; in case two, the valves will tangle. Result in both cases: bent valves

Oil round the differential—and it's not unknown—must be attended to (first check the diff breather) Penalty is lubricant-soaked brake gear and perhaps a big bill for a new Powr-Lok.

Twin cooling fans were introduced in 1968. Here is the right side fan of a pair

Side-flow radiator and single fan feature on this 1967 car. The alternator was fitted during 1964

Dirt shields were added to the front discs in 1964 as worn here by a 1967 (F) model

LIFETIME'S AMBITION

Tester meets E-type at last

By J. R. Daniels, BSc

It isn't possible for anyone to drive everything. But it was clearly wrong that the E-type had eluded one of our test drivers for so long

FOR SEVERAL years, I had been uncomfortably aware that there was a gap in my motoring education. Horror of horrors, I had never driven a Jaguar E-type. Events had conspired against me; I left one magazine just before it got its road test E-type, and arrived at *Autocar* too late to try the last example to pass through their hands. The strain of keeping my guilty secret was beginning to tell. I could not join in arguments with people like my wife, who *says* she wouldn't be seen dead in an E-type; or with some highly respectable drivers (like Dave Thomas) who still rate it among the best driver's cars on the road.

My scepticism towards Dave's point of view was, perhaps, understandable. Too many of the E-types one sees on the roads are driven badly, or slowly, or both. The visual appeal of the car is so obvious that some people are bound to buy it for this alone.

The only way I was ever going to sort it out was to make a pilgrimage to Coventry and spend a day driving an E-type. Jaguar found they could produce a 2 + 2 Coupé on the day suggested, and so the meeting was arranged.

The car has lost something as history has progressed. At one time it was good for 150 mph on the right day and the right tyres, but that was before the Americans started their drive on pollution. Not only was "my" car up to the latest anti-emission standard; being a 2 + 2, it also has extra weight and extra frontal area to contend with. Still, an assessment of maximum speed—or even a string of stop-watch figures—was not part of the programme. The object was simply to live with the car for a day and see how many of my prejudices could be swept away.

The E-type seems smaller once you are in it than it appears from outside. There is still the long bonnet in front of you, and it should be part of every new driver's briefing that there is another 18in. of it you can't see. Visibility generally is not a strong point, since the rear quarters leave a blind spot as well. The driver's sitting position is rather low, and somebody as big as me finds the width adequate but no more. There is rearward seat room to spare, however, and space has been found to provide a good pedal layout. The steering wheel position and rake are well nigh perfect. In Jaguar tradition, instruments are comprehensive and legible, but their exemplary layout is not echoed in the minor control layout.

I was spared the indignity of automatic transmission, and noted with interest that the middleweight clutch was nicely progressive in its action. The gearbox in this car, with over 20,000 Jaguar-owned and maintained miles behind it, was as smooth and sweet as you could wish, betraying its age and its torque capacity only by unfashionably long movements.

"Unfortunately" used to be a stock prefix of mine when reporting that any test car had power steering. This is one prejudice which started to take a real beating about three years ago, when all at once several British and German systems convinced me that power assistance didn't *have* to leave you in total ignorance of what was going on under the front wheels. Thus it is with the E-type. Its system never takes all the effort out of steering, it just keeps it light enough never to be tiring. There is always plenty of feel, and a pleasant self-centring effect which never becomes vicious and permits tidy exits from all sorts of corner.

One must, I suppose, always set off for the first time in a car like this wondering what will happen when the accelerator is pushed to the floor. Will the rev counter flip into the red before you can reach out for the gear lever? Will instability set in? Will it become so noisy that you can no longer hear yourself think?

To its immense credit, the E-type does none of these things. There is never any real kick-in-the-back sensation, even in first gear. Instead, there is a steady pressure from behind and a rising but muted thunder from the front. Lesson one: the E-type makes smooth driving easy. Provided you have your wits about you, the red line is easily respected. With standard gearing, first gear goes to over 40 mph at 5,000 rpm. Second takes you beyond 70 mph, and third would be good for almost 100 mph. Maybe the fine edge of responsiveness has been sacrificed to flexibility. Despite a forewarning, the ability to trickle along in top at 10 mph—clutch fully engaged, no cheating—took me by pleasant surprise.

It was a long time before I remembered to think about the brakes, which is some measure of their unobtrusive efficiency. Any car in the E-type's class is ruined unless the brakes are smooth, progressive and very strong when needed; there is no suggestion that Jaguar have fallen down on the job. In view of their pioneering work with disc brakes, of which the E-type has four, it would be surprising if they had.

The handling was on a par with everything else, with a proviso or two. It is no use asking any car to do the impossible, and it is easy enough to bring the E-type into a corner 20 mph faster than you think. Even when you are established on your line, the presence of that much power makes it possible to overdo things. Yet there is no longer any doubt in my mind that the E-type can still out-corner most things on the road. It appreciates a smooth, racing sort of approach—none of your rally-type antics—and getting towards the limit it develops a tendency to "nibble", twitching gently towards oversteer. This effect is felt earlier with the power off, and I don't think I would have the courage to brake in mid-corner. Overall, however, it's very impressive.

This much you can learn when driving is the sole objective of the day. There are other things . . . the ride, which is good; the ventilation, which is poor. When it came to giving the car back, I did so grudgingly. It's not a perfect car, and I could write a list of more or less important things which would improve it. But I can see what the enthusiasts like about it; over and above its roadgoing virtues, it has real character which I hadn't expected to find. □

The roadholding and low roll angle of the E-type conspire to make this 50mph shot look as innocuous as it felt. The direction of the front wheels shows that the car was in virtually neutral steer, exactly holding the intended line

E-TYPE REVISITED

After nearly 10 years, we find we can still get excited about driving an E-type Jaguar.

LIKE the MGB, the E-type Jaguar has been around for nearly a decade and in that time has lost none of its magic appeal. It phased out the XK 150 S in 1960 with a 3.8-litre version and in 1965 the updated 4.2-litre was released. SCW tested a 4.2-litre version in '65 and it wasn't until recently we were able to sit our eager backsides in a soft top version.

While other top priced sports cars have changed over the years, the E-type still remains the same — a long, low, lithe, begging-to-go piece of machinery. Not many cars can hold the same appeal and attraction for nearly 10 years and still blow the minds of enthusiast and the mini-skirt brigade. Heads still turn to gaze in awe as an E-type slides past on the highway and all the gold rules like "thou shalt not covet" are instantly forgotten as you envy the guy who who has the money to buy.

Only minor changes have been made to the E-type over the years and then only to comply with the American safety anti-emission laws. The E-type is a big seller in the States. One noticeable change, although not immediate, is the missing perspex covers over the headlights. They were the first things to go in the American safety laws. Instead of being set back in the guard, the headlight now protrudes slightly and has a small fin running back along the top of the guard to streamline the look — quite effective and not at all unpleasant. The knock-offs are also missing from the wire-spoked wheels (another US safety rule).

Entry to the E-type is quite different from other sports cars because you've got that big sill — part of the monocoque construction — to step over. The action is more of a step over and down than just in to. Quite advantageous if you admire female legs. Once inside, the car seems to wrap itself around you and even in the passenger seat you feel very secure, although leg room is still sadly lacking. With the driver's or passenger's seat right back, it's impossible to sit with legs outstretched.

The view of the three-spoked woodrim wheel

Only real noticeable change for 1970 for the E-type is the new headlight treatment. Gone is the familiar perspex cover and the headlight is now set slightly forward.

Another modification is the knock-ons. Because of American safety rules, these have also been replaced. However, the rest of the exterior remains the same on the sleek beast.

and down the long bonnet with the power hump in the middle is magnificent. It makes you want to fire-up the engine and head for the open road. An E-type is not for posing. It has to be driven and no excuses are needed to head for the open road or take the weekend trip Interstate.

But for all its get up and go, the E-type is still content to cruise the streets of Sydney's Double Bay or Melbourne's South Yarra in top gear at 35 mph. But this is not the way to enjoy the smooth power of the big twin-cam engine. Feed the high-octane to it through the triple SU carburettors and it will leap away in absolute obedience.

As in all high-performance cars, a tight rein has to be kept on your boy-Fangio leanings. At 6000 rpm, first gear will run out at 54 mph; second, 86 mph; third, 117 mph and top around 150 mph. But the real magic comes in its cornering ability. You'll find you can sit and throttle-steer it all day. It becomes very pleasant to set up a corner with the right amount of lock, and then guide the car through with just that extra bit of throttle. You can have an enormous amount of fun at any level of its gargantuan performance scale, and if used sensibly, in complete safety.

For all this, the car still has its minor faults, such as the ridiculously small and shallow boot of the pyjamas-and-toothbrush type. And the lock release is still mounted behind the driver's seat. With the hood folded down, it's almost a knuckle-barking effort to get to it, let alone pull it to open the rear lid.

But little sins like this can be forgiven because the sheer pleasure of driving the car and enjoying its appetite for road miles is compensation enough . . . The seven and a half grand price tag is another thing.   #

Comparing the coupé and 2+2

The E-type Jaguar has figured fairly regularly in AUTOSPORT road tests since its original appearance in the issue of March 17, 1961. That issue was a sell-out, so great was the interest in the new Jaguar, and since then the machine has undergone many changes. It might be said that it is less a hairy sports car more a practical GT these days, with the net result that it is probably capable of putting up higher average speeds on long continental journeys, while certainly its occupants feel much more fresh and relaxed at the day's end.

Perhaps the greatest improvement was in the brakes, which were barely adequate at first for the tremendous speed potential of the car, and the new gearbox added greatly to the pleasure of driving. The earliest models lacked space for a large driver and changes were soon made to the seat, pedals and floor. There was also a heat problem, caused by hot air passing down the transmission tunnel and warming the interior of the car in summer; successive improvements have been made in this direction. The Series 2 E-types, announced in 1968, had a new radiator, twin electric cooling fans, and a redesigned water pump pulley to increase the rate of flow. All these things, and a much larger air intake, lowered under-bonnet temperature to the benefit both of the engine and the occupants.

The original 3.8-litre engine was replaced by the 4.2-litre, which gave a lot more torque for acceleration but cut 500 rpm off the top end. Lately · this unit has been redesigned with long studs going right through the cylinder block, to remove the loads from the block face, and new camshafts give longer and more silent service.

The first 3.8-litre E-types were capable of nudging 150 mph. However, as 80 per cent of the cars are sold in the States, it was necessary to remove the headlight fairings to comply with federal regulations, and this, coupled with the larger air intake, reduced the maximum speed. In any case, the bigger engine reaches its normal maximum revs at 137 mph or so, though one can have a short burst up to 140 mph without much risk. Very few owners ever used the 150 mph maximum and the latest car, with its improved acceleration and brakes, could run rings round its predecessor. The lights, though less artistic in appearance, also work better without their coverings, and those stray beams have been eliminated, which caused angry flashing from approaching motorists even though one had dutifully dipped.

In addition to the strictly 2-seater version of the E-type, a 2 Plus 2 model was introduced to widen the appeal of the Jaguar. At first this was a less attractive car because of its more restricted windscreen, but when the Series 2 E-types were introduced the rake of the screen was increased from 46½ deg to 53½ deg from the vertical. This made a phenomenal difference to the appearance, and now there are those who prefer the looks of the 2 Plus 2 to the two-seater, because the longer body brings the immense bonnet into better proportion.

This is a composite road test because I took the performance figures a little while ago with a 2-seater. However, I was then able to borrow a 2 Plus 2 to the latest specification, and it was most interesting to compare the two cars. The 2 Plus 2 has an increase of 9-ins in the wheelbase and a slightly higher roof line, the front seats being similarly raised. The rear seats are ideal for children, or two adults could use them for short distances, which a man sitting crosswise could be quite comfortable for a longer journey. The seat back folds down to give a very large luggage platform when only one passenger is to be carried.

Though there is an increase in weight and frontal area, the difference in performance is very small and can scarcely be felt. The stopwatch reveals that it is only at the top end of the performance scale that the two-seater would draw away noticeably. If one permitted the engine to over-rev, the more compact car would perhaps have an extra 2 or 3 mph, but both models are similarly geared and can exceed 5500 rpm in top gear, which is supposed to be the limit.

In spite of a longer wheelbase, the 2 Plus 2 feels just as compact as the 2-seater to drive. Both cars corner equally well, a moderate degree of understeer being convertible to neutral handling or a gentle oversteer by the suitable application of power. With a 110 mph third gear and an 80 mph maximum in second, it is always possible to call the immense torque of the engine to one's aid.

As in all Jaguars, road and wind noises are very well subdued. The twin-cam engine has had so many years of development that it remains just as far ahead of the opposition as it used to be when it won repeatedly at Le Mans. It has that glorious exhaust note which only a "six" or a "twelve" can produce, but it is virtually silent when ticking over at 70 mph or cruising at 110 mph on a whiff of throttle. The brakes stand up well

After nine years' production, with only detail changes, the E-type coupé is still striking in appearance.

to hard driving, remaining just as potent even when they smell hot. The handbrake, once a weakness, is now very effective.

Though the seating position of the 2 Plus 2 is a little higher, this is not perceptible unless one steps straight into it from the two-seater. The 2 Plus 2 which I drove was fitted with power-assisted steering, an extra which some might call gilding the lily, since the standard steering is quite light even at low speeds. Once the driver is used to it, the ease of handling is very pleasant and will no doubt be appreciated on the American market, especially as the price is reasonable.

The E-type Jaguar is a wonderfully easy car to drive, with vast reserves of power for safe overtaking and remarkable top-gear flexibility. Indeed, very little gearchanging is called for unless the driver wants to use the full performance potential. It is this flexibility, allied with high gearing and a low-drag body shape, that makes the car so astonishingly economical on petrol.

It is difficult to be critical, for so many of the early shortcomings have been removed. The headlights, though improved, do not allow the full performance to be used after dark, and the effective ventilation would be better still with adjustable " eyeball " outlets for the fresh air. The E-type still compares amazingly well with GT cars of more than twice its price and, though the 2 Plus 2 is longer, the temptation to increase the width has been resisted. The car is narrow enough to be nippy in traffic and on winding lanes, while the long bonnet does not worry the driver except when emerging from a driveway onto a busy road.

When I have not driven an E-type for some time, it is always a pleasure to try the latest version. The sheer performance and the modest price are still almost beyond belief, and the ride is as outstanding as the roadholding. This spectacular sports car is now highly civilised but even more fun to drive.

Car tested: Jaguar E-type 2 seater coupé, price £2465, and E-type 2 Plus 2, price £2709 14s 2d. Extra: Power-assisted steering, £74. All including tax.
Engine : Six cylinders, 92.1 mm x 106 mm, 4235 cc. Twin chain-driven overhead camshafts. Compression ratio 9 to 1. 265 bhp (gross) at 5400 rpm. Three SU carburetters. Lucas coil and distributor.
Transmission: Single dry-plate diaphragm spring clutch. 4-speed all-synchromesh gearbox with central remote control, ratios 1.0, 1.328, 1.973, and 3.04 to 1. Hypoid final drive, ratio 3.07 to 1.
Chassis: Combined steel chassis and body with separate sub-frames. Independent front suspension by wishbones, torsion bars and anti-roll bar. Rack and pinion steering. Independent rear suspension with wishbones, fixed-length driveshafts, radius arms and two pairs of coil springs. Telescopic dampers all round. Servo-assisted disc brakes all round. Centre-locking wire wheels fitted Dunlops 185-15 ins radial ply tyres.
Equipment: 12-volt lighting and starting with alternator. Speedometer. Rev counter. Water temperature, oil pressure and fuel gauges. Voltmeter. Clock. Heating, demisting, and ventilation system. Windscreen wipers and washers. Flashing direction indicators with hazard warning. Reversing lights. Cigar lighter. Radio (extra).
Dimensions: Wheelbase, 8 ft (2 Plus 2, 8 ft 9 ins). Track, 4 ft 2 ins. Overall length, 14 ft 7.3 ins (2 Plus 2, 15 ft 4.4 ins). Width, 5 ft 5.2 ins. Weight, 1 ton 5.4 cwt (2 Plus 2, 1 ton 7.4 cwt).
Performance: 2-seater coupé: Maximum speed, 142 mph. Speeds in gear: Third, 110 mph; second, 80 mph; first, 51 mph. Standing quarter-mile, 14.9 s. Acceleration: 0-30 mph, 2.8 s; 0-50 mph, 5.5 s; 0-60 mph, 7.2 s; 0-80 mph, 12.2 s; 0-100 mph, 17 s; 0-120 mph, 30 s.
Fuel consumption: 20 to 25 mpg.

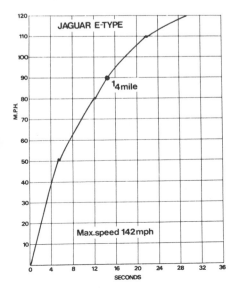

There is no difference between the coupé and 2 + 2 at the rear.

The twin cam engine has had so many years of development that it is still immeasurably superior to its competitors (above). The interior is well appointed in true Jaguar style.

Jaguar

Ever since British Leyland Motor Corporation took over Jaguar, the firm has fallen woefully behind in both the production of existing models and the fielding of officially "leaked" new ones. Cases in point are the continued scarcity of the XJ sedan in the U.S. and these obviously carryover XKE's which are only intended to keep the name alive until the long awaited V-8's and V-12's arrive. And when they do, Americans probably won't see them for another couple of years. The situation has reached the point where Sir William Lyons, supposedly retired with all of his BLMC stock derived from the merger in the safe, is reported as restive and scheming to pull Jaguar along with Rover and Triumph out of the doddering combine.

All of this is not to imply that we're plugging for more styling changes in the XKE's. They are a timeless design, and we can't help but remember when Sir William improved his 120 with the 140 and then spoiled the lot with the bulbous 150. What BLMC's committees would do to an XKE is best not thought about. The sole styling change for '71 is a chrome strip around the grille aperture to give it a little protection from parking lot cowboys. It would still be advisable, however, to buy yourself an accessory guard and leave it in place at all times except when showing off the car at a charity concours. The chrome strip will dent too, and so will the metal under it, putting you into double jeopardy.

If the time has come to trade your elderly XKE (the E-type first appeared in 1961, back in the heyday of fender

fins) on a new one, you'll get a dual overhead cam six of 4.2 liters displacement and 245 horsepower. This is 0.4 liters more displacement and 20 less horsepower than the original which hardly seems like a step forward. This engine apparently is intended to soldier on as standard fare even after the advent of the multi-cylinder units which will go into the sports cars first.

Although BLMC don't say so directly, the 2+2 appears to be a casualty at least for the American market. References in releases issued with the new models cover only the coupe and roadster. Present styling of the latter two got a fair working over in 1969, mostly a widening of the grille aperture for much-needed additional cooling and a controversial heightening of the bumper at the rear. The loss in horsepower can be blamed on emission controls as a switch was made from three S.U. carburetors to twin Zenith-Strombergs.

Until this year, power steering as an option was reserved for the 2+2 but it is now available for the two-passenger models. It assists the same delightful rack and pinion system that unaided, was one of the main reasons

Sleek and pretty as ever, the '71 Jags in two-passenger coupe and convertible form must be considered interim models until the V-8 and V-12 appear.

that people bought Jaguars. The boost is $160 extra and air conditioning costs $482, these being the only factory options you can add to the $5,734 tag for the roadster and the $5,934 for the coupe.

Data in Brief
Jaguar XKE
ENGINE: 6-cylinder dohc, 258.4 cu. ins., 4200cc, 245 hp at 5500 rpm, 263 lb.-ft. of torque at 3000 rpm, dual Zenith-Stromberg carburetion.

DRIVELINE: 4-speed manual transmission, rear drive.

SUSPENSION: Independent torsion bar front, stabilizer, independent quadruple coil rear, carried in subframe.

BRAKES: Girling discs front and rear, power assisted.

STEERING: Rack and pinion, power optional.

DIMENSIONS: Wheelbase 96.0 ins., length 175.4 ins., width 65.3 ins., height 48.0 ins., weight 2464 lbs.

JAGUAR E-TYPE COUPE

Towering performance, superb braking and sexy good looks make the ageing E-type an unforgettable motor car

—types are old hat. Anyone with even a sketchy interest in motor cars knows that Jaguar's voluptuous speedster has been around nigh on 10 years.

Despite that, the E—Type is still the head—turningest, crowd—stoppingest glamour car around.

It may not have the exotic, way—out specifications of a Lamborghini Miura, or Ferrari GTB4 or Maserati Ghibli. But for sheer "presence" it is unbeatable.

We were fortunate to be able to put close on a thousand miles on a new E—type coupe recently, and it impressed us from the moment we climbed aboard until the moment we regretfully handed it back to British Leyland.

It impressed us with its comfort (we have reservations there, but more about that later), it's effortless performance, great handling and roadholding, and enormously powerful brakes.

We drove it from Melbourne to Sydney on an extremely hot day, and even "loafing" we covered the distance in about nine hours. Of course loafing in an E—type is anything up to 100 mph, and in fact we had the speedo hovering around the 90-100 mark for much of the way.

The most impressive facet of the E is the absolute ease of its performance. The Falcon GT — which performs about equally — makes by comparison a great song—and—dance when it is driven fast. The Jaguar's towering performance is achieved with consummate ease, and considerably more silence than the GT.

Considering its performance, fabulous looks, comfort and

appointments, we think that it is a car in the best Jaguar traditions. When you also consider that it costs $8389 it begins to look an even better buy — and this after almost 10 years in existence.

The E—type was, when it went on sale almost a decade ago, a car that confronted the Ferrari/Maserati clan head on but at a fraction of the price.

Today, there are many other cars that do this, but all of them are more expensive that the E. Which means of course that it is in many respects, a bargain.

The current E differs from the original car in that it's engine is 4.2 litres, against 3.8.

The engine is of course, the legendary XK double ohc that powered C and D—types to victory at Le Mans. In the E it produces 265 bhp at 5400 and 283 lb. ft. of torque at 4000 rpm.

The engine is a long—stroke design — it was conceived and put into production long before the current fad for short stroke grew popular — so that it has enormous flexibility and enough low—speed torque despite "tall" gearing, to make around—city

trickling and freeway loafing an absolute breeze.

The test car was fitted with the standard four—speed manual transmission that proved to be excellent in use. The weak link in Jaguar's drive train has traditionally been the manual transmission, but this latest 'box is beyond reproach. The radios are "right", the movement smooth and precise, and the synchromesh very strong. It is not a weak link any more.

For those driver's who prefer shiftless motoring, the E—type is available with Borg Warner dual range "8" automatic transmission. This is similar to the unit we experienced in the XJ6 and it is good.

Suspension is all independent — a refined system of wishbones and transverse torsion bars at the front with hydraulic dampers and anti—roll bar.

The rear suspension is more complex — lower wishbones, a half—axle as the upper arm, with trailing lower radius arms, four coil springs and four telescopic dampers to provide the suspension medium.

The system works well. The E—type rides smoothly for a sporty car, and

handles all but the choppiest of surfaces with aplomb. Radial ply tyres are standard — the test car was fitted with Dunlop Aquajets — and there is a moderate amount of "thump" over irregularities.

Steering is rack and pinion with 2.5 turns of lock and a 41ft. turning circle. It is wholly in keeping with the car's character — quick, precise, and responsive, but with sufficient well damped "feedback" to keep the driver well informed of changes in the road surface.

The steering wheel itself is big in diameter and thin—rimmed. Alloy spokes and a wooden rim date it somewhat. A smaller, thicker, leather—covered wheel would be more in keeping with the car in this day and age.

Fabulous performance is matched by equally fabulous brakes. Four wheels discs are fitted, and these are carried on the wheel hubs at the front, and inboard, adjacent to the differential at the rear.

The fronts are just under 11in. diameter, the rears are 10in. The circuitry is duplicated, as it necessary by law these days, and a moderate servo—assistance makes heavy application easy.

The sleek body, developed after extensive wind—tunnel tests more than 10 years ago, but strangely still as chic a shape as ever, is made of stressed steel, of a patented monocoque construction with a front sub—frame in tubular high—tensile steel (carrying the engine, front suspension, and forward hinged bonnet and front wings.)

We felt at home with the car the moment we slipped aboard. The cab is a very snug fit, but despite this has sufficient leg and head room to accommodate drivers well over six ft. in height. The seats are adjustable for length and height, and the steering wheel is also adjustable, thereby ensuring a sufficiently wide range of ergonomic variation to ensure comfort for most people.

There is unfortunately, no "dead pedal" for the left foot, so that it is forced to rest, somewhat uncomfortably, on the floor, next to the big transmission tunnel. Other minuses in terms of comfort are the too—thin steering wheel rim (you get used to that) and the fresh air ventilation which is practically non—existent, and as a consequence totally inadequate for Australian summer conditions. Try as we might, with all manner of combinations for the semi—flow—through ventilation, and the wind—down windows, we weren't able to get a satisfactory arrangement.

The ambient temperature for most of the time we had the car was about 80, but our Melbourne—Sydney run was done in 100 deg. heat, which made the Jaguar's cab pretty unbearable.

CONTINUED ON PAGE 166

DATA SHEET- JAGUAR E-TYPE

Manufacturer: Jaguar Cars Ltd, UK.
Test car supplied by: British Leyland, Sydney.
Price as tested: $8,389

ENGINE

Water cooled, 6 cylinders in line. Cast iron block, seven main bearings.
Bore x stroke: .... 92.1 x 106 mm
Capacity .... 4235 cc.
Compression .... 9 to 1.
Carburettor 3 50 HD8
Fuel pump .... electrical
Fuel tank .... 14 gallons
Fuel recommended .... super
Valve gear .... dohc
Max. power (gross) .. 265 bhp at 5400 rpm
Max. torque .... 283 lb.ft.
Specific power output ..... 62.6 bhp/litre
Electrical system .. 12v, 60 amp hr battery, 45A alternator.

TRANSMISSION

Four speed manual all synchro gearbox; single dry plate clutch.

Gear	Ratio	Mph/1000 Rpm	Max. mph
Rev......	3.085	—	
1st.	2.681	—	50
2nd.	1.739	—	73
3rd......	1.270	—	101
4th.......	1.000	23.2	137
5th			

Final drive ratio .... 3.07 to 1

CHASSIS

Wheelbase .... 8ft. 0in.
Track front .... 4ft. 2in.
Track rear .... 4ft. 2 in.
Length .... 14ft. 7 in.
Width .... 5ft. 5¼in.
Height .... 4ft. 0in.
Clearance .... 5½in.
Kerb weight .... 26cwt.
Weight dist. front/rear 49.6/50.4 percent
lb/bhp .... 10.6lb.

SUSPENSION

Front: Independent, wishbones, torsion bars, anti-roll bar, telescopic shock absorbers.
Rear: Independent, wishbones with semi-axle as upper arm, trailing lower radius arms, 4 coil springs, 4 telescopic shock absorbers.
Brakes: Front: 10.98 india disc, rear: 10in dia inboard disc, dual circuit, servo-assisted.
Steering .... rack and pinion
Turns lock to lock 2.50
Turning circle .... 41ft.
Wheels: Knock-off wire with centre lock hubs and 185 by 15 tubed radial ply, Dunlop Aquajet/tyres.

PERFORMANCE

Top speed .... 137 mph
Average (both ways) .... 137 mph
Standing quarter mile .... 15.5 sec.

Acceleration

Zero to	Seconds
30 mph	2.7
40 mph	3.9
50 mph	5.6
60 mph	7.6
70 mph	9.7
80 mph	12.5
90 mph	16.0
100 mph	20.5

	3rd	top
20-40 mph	4.4	6.4
30-50	4.2	6.3
40-60	4.1	6.4
50-70	4.5	6.7

BRAKING: Five crash stops from 60 mph

Stop	percent G	pedal
1	.98	53 lb
2	.98	53 lb
3	.95	50 lb
4	.95	50 lb
5	.98	50 lb

Consumption; 21.2 mpg over 950 miles including all tests; 23-25 mpg in normal country and suburban use.

Speedo Error;

Indicated mph	30	40	50	60	70	80
Actual mph	32	42	52	62	73	83

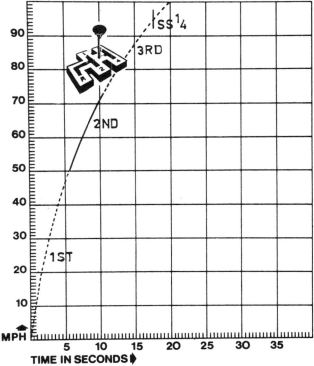

ACCELERATION CHART

tss ¼
3RD
2ND
1ST

MPH — TIME IN SECONDS ▶ (5 10 15 20 25 30 35)

HOW JAGUAR COMPARES

MAXIMUM SPEED (mean) M.P.H.

(70 80 90 100 110 120 130)

Jaguar E-type ($8389)
Falcon GT ($4725)
Porsche 911T ($9953)

0-60 M.P.H. SECONDS

(25 20 15 10 5)

Jaguar E-type
Falcon GT
Porsche 911T

M.P.G. Overall

(10 20 30 40)

Jaguar E-type
Falcon GT
Porsche 9IIT

STANDING START ¼ MILE (secs)

(20 10)

Jaguar E-type
Falcon GT
Porsche 911T

E-TYPE JAG.

CONTINUED FROM PAGE 164

The fact that the car doesn't have those much—maligned swivelling quarter vents added to our discomfort, and we finally resolved that any Australian who bought an E—type coupe or 2—plus—2 without specifying air—conditioning was making a grave mistake.

Occupants are located in such close proximity to the big engine and transmission that the cabin would be hot even in wintery conditions, with the result that air conditioning would be a year round "must".

Dunlopillo padding — is excellent. The seats look nothing special, but they serve their occupants very well over both short and long distances.

Naturally, the car doesn't roll much anyway, and the big sills and close—fitting doors keep people in place. But stiff backs and tender backsides just aren't a part of the E—type picture.

Instrumentation is very comprehensive and traditionally arranged on the black vinyl—covered dash.

Directly in front of the driver and visible through the top half of the wood—rim wheel are matching tachometer and speedo, the former reading to 6000 rpm, and the latter to 160 mph.

Ranged across the dash centre are gauges for fuel, water, amps and oil pressure, together with a small, but painfully—accurate clock.

Beneath that clutch of instruments is arranged a line of tumbler switches for hazard warning four-way flashers, map, interior side, and headlights, two—speed wipers, washer, and fan.

The controls for fresh—air inlet are located on either side of the dash centre, and they're unlike anything we've ever seen before. What's more they don't work particularly well, as we've already explained.

Before the passenger is located the world's smallest glove—compartment (lockable) with just enough room for — you guessed it — a pair of gloves.

Fortunately, there's additional stowage space in a cubby between the seats, beneath a padded centre flap.

Behind the seats is a large luggage area, which can be further enlarged by lowering the forwardmost panel, which when upright, forms a bulkhead to stop luggage catapulting under heavy braking.

The luggage area is protected by rubber and chrome rubbing strips, which tended to turn up and catch in our luggage.

The load area is sufficiently large to take the luggage of two people. week.

Access to the luggage area is gained through a side—hinged back door, the release catch for which is located by the driver's seat. The door swings left and is locked in place by an articulated bow.

From a practicality viewpoint, the E—type stands up very well. It is further enhanced by the forward—hinged bonnet which tilts to reveal not only the engine but the entire front suspension, thus making routine service extremely easy.

It's an easy car to drive. The position behind the wheel is "right", although forward visibility is hampered by the attenuated bonnet line and the enormous power bulge right down the centre of the bonnet.

A couple of times we misjudged the length of the car's bonnet and fetched it up (gently) against obstacles.

We learnt our lesson early and allowed ourselves a very wide safety margin thereafter.

The car starts easily without choke and drives very sweetly, slipping through the gears without effort (although the clutch is on the heavy side) and generally responding like a true thoroughbred.

The car is absolutely no effort to drive and visibility to the rear is (surprisingly) not as restricted as the rakish fastback and smallish rear window suggests.

On the open road the coupe is in its true element, eating the miles with an insatiable 100 mph appetite. We could cruise at 100 mph continuously and the oil and temperature gauges would never budge from their proper marks, despite the high ambient temperatures.

In short bursts we ran it higher, reaching 125 on one appropriately straight stretch. Even at 125, the E—type still had tons in reserve, and should run close to 140 mph.

The car is an almost neutral steerer, seemingly unaffected by closure of the throttle in corners, and quite content to whistle around corners at any speed the driver chooses. It gives a feeling of enormous security, and we never once succeeded in wrong—footing the car.

The suspension works well; soaking up bumps smoothly and generally, with great silence. Unfortunately, the test car developed an undiagnosed rattle that spoiled the limber, cat—like effect otherwise created.

The brakes worked fabulously well. Closing speeds in a car capable of ton—up cruising have to be judged very carefully, and once or twice we found ourselves narrowing the gap much too rapidly. It was then that we appreciated the enormous power of those four—wheel discs which washed off speed with ridiculous ease.

Cruising in this manner the car returned about 20 mpg — which gives, on its 14—gallon tank a modest range of 280 miles. Driven more sedately, the car will return 23 or more mpg, which is a tacit compliment to the slippery tunnel—tested shape.

The E—type is a perfect "poser's" car. It turned more heads than any car we've driven, despite the familiarity of its shape. But it is no cream—puff. Point it up a fast winding road and it will lay down a time for which no apology is needed. It is a sleek, fat cat, with muscles where they are needed. We enjoyed driving it, despite the 10 year wait. Let's hope we don't have to wait so long for the much—rumoured, long—awaited V12 F—type, XL12, or whatever it might be called. ∎

Buying An E-Type

The impossible dream? Former E-type owner Paul Skilleter, and former E-type restorer Michael Brisby, say that a six-cylinder E-type for restoration could be a good bet — if you know what you are in for . . . .

The E-type Jaguar was a legend in its own time — between 1961 and 1975 when E-types offered a combination of refined but potent performance, looks, quality and value for money that was unrivalled. Even today it is still *the* dream car for many people.

It is over twenty years since the announcement of the E-type, but it is unlikely that anyone driving one for the first time will be disappointed — provided that the car is in good condition it is remarkably easy to drive

(Above) Assistant Editor John Williams owned this 3.8 E-type — spotlights should not obstruct the air intake, these were fitted for an advertising picture.

The 3.8-litre E-type is still beautiful and potent by modern standards. Slim bumpers, small bonnet air intake and glass fairings over the headlamps make this the "purest" E-type for many people. External bonnet lock, flat floors and restricted seat travel were all developed out of the car shortly after production commenced. The seating and brake servo were not thought quite up to the rest of the car.

For Restoration

The Fixed Head Coupe was equally as handsome as the Open Two Seater but had more luggage capacity and was very slightly faster. Most cars sold in Britain had a stick-on front number plate on the bonnet above the intake and at the time the police took a dim view. The owner of this 4.2 Series One car has repositioned it for aesthetic reasons.

on the open road or in city traffic. By sportscar standards it is quiet, comfortable and practical, and yet if you want it, there is still more real performance than most people will ever want to use. In short the E-type is one of the most practical supercars ever made, and also one of the cheapest to run.

Unlike many other great cars the Jaguar E-type has never been reduced to the level of being something you could not give away with a year's tax and a full tank of petrol! While prices definitely did suffer a serious set-back about two years ago, they have steadied and it would not be surprising if they now began to climb again a little each year, because demand exceeds supply. Good unrestored cars have become few and far between, and as the cost of a full professional restoration is frightening, the price trend for a good or restored example can only be upwards.

Unfortunately the E-type has not been granted immunity from rust, or deterioration of its suspension, braking and mechanical components, and all too often buyers under-estimate what they are taking on when they land themselves with a superficially reasonable E-type.

An E-type which is not right in all the important departments can be described as a dangerous animal waiting to kill, and there are

The 4.2 litre E-type superseded the 3.8 and brought with it an all-synchromesh gearbox, improved brake servo and better seating; this is a Series One roadster. Outwardly there were very few changes until the introduction of what is known as the Series 1½.

no shortcuts to getting a good E-type — you either search very carefully and pay a lot for a genuinely good one which must then be carefully preserved, or you spend a lot of time, money and effort putting a bad one to rights step by step, from end to end. Experience shows that a mediocre E-type which "needs tidying" almost always needs a total rebuild just as much as a rough one "suitable for restoration" — which costs much less to buy in the first place.

If you are buying an E-type the condition of the bodyshell is more important than any other aspect of the car. Unfortunately, other

6-cylinder E-Type Specifications

	3.8	4.2	2-plus-2	4.2 S2*
Capacity	3781cc	4235cc	4235cc	4235cc
Wheelbase	8'0''	8'0''	8'9''	8'/8'9''
Length	14'7½''	14'7½''	15'4½''	14'7½'/15'4½''
Max. speed	146 mph	147 mph	140 mph	137/143 mph
0 - 60 mph	7.5 secs	7.3 secs	7.8 secs	7.5/8 secs
Av. consumption	18.5 mpg	18.5 mpg	17 mpg	18/16.5 mpg

* 2nd figure 2-plus-2

Production figures

Model	RHD	LHD	Total
3.8 Open two-seater	942	6885	7827
3.8 Fixed-head coupe	1798	5871	7669
4.2 Open two-seater	1182	8366	9548
4.2 Fixed-head coupe	1957	5813	7770
4.2 2-plus-2	1378	4220	5598
4.2 S2 Open two-seater	775	7852	8627
4.2 S2 Fixed-head coupe	1070	3785	4855
4.2 S2 2-plus-2	1040	4286	5326
Total 3.8 Cars:	15,496		
Total 4.2 Cars:	22,916		
Total 4.2 S2 Cars:	18,808		

The 'Series 1½', of which there seem to be [a] surprising number about, lost the headlam[p] covers (improving night driving considerabl[y] but retained the small side and rear ligh[ts] above the bumpers of the earlier cars. The plus-2 and roadster are pictured here with t[he] Anglo-French 'Jaguar' fighter plane.

For Restoration Six Cylinder Variations Bu

than in exceptional cases, the only way to be absolutely sure that the precious shell is sound is to see it stripped bare of paint and trim — a fresh coat of paint and a partial re-trim can be a cover-up of all sorts of major faults. Fortunately, however, there are other checks you can make inside half an hour that will tell you what sort of car you are faced with, without the need for such drastic measures.

But before you get too depressed about the whole idea of owning an E-type, the following points should cheer you up — few E-types have been bad enough to have been scrapped over the past five years or so, and a determined person with skill and sufficient funds can rebuild a car from little more than fragments. The scarcity of parts that arose as factory spares ran out has been very largely met by the specialist firms who are generally more interested in acting as suppliers to home restorers than in doing full restorations on their premises.

Not that rebuilding an E-type is something we would recommend as a first restoration project, although several people have done it. It is a major undertaking, but the trade and knowledge-able Jaguar enthusiasts know that it is possible,

The Series 2 cars had much more exposed headlamps and bigger side and tail lamps below bumpers. The rear number plate went below the bumper, and the bonnet air intake was enlarged.

behind the wheel, always assuming that the car you are contemplating buying can actually

The 2 + 2 Fixed Head Coupe was a long wheelbase version of the E-type with heavier gauge sills and sundry other revisions to the floor pan. Introduced with the 4.2 engine in Series One form, their evolution followed that of the two seaters. The cars last better (structurally), but have always been considered a "poor relation" because of their slightly less well balanced proportions.

which is one of the factors that have kept the price of complete wrecks stable — not cheap but not increasing dramatically.

Driving The Car

With a car which can deteriorate so badly if neglected, it pays to look over the danger points of an E-type carefully before getting

be driven! *Then* you can see what you can learn from a drive.

Jaguar engines should start promptly and within two or three minutes it should run evenly and without very much clatter — though some detectable tappet noise is a good thing. Oil pressure should be 40 lbs per square inch hot, and if it is less than thirty pounds per

square inch something is wrong — either minor like the sender unit, or oil pressure relief valve, or major like bearing trouble.

The gearbox should not be too noisy and the clutch should begin to taken up quite early in a long travel. First gear is high and some care with the clutch is required to get away smoothly. Both the early gearbox and the later all-synchromesh unit are strong but the early cars have usually very little synchromesh left and welcome a fairly slow, gently, change. First gear especially on the 3.8 cars is far from quiet, but beware of grinding or grating noises from this ratio or reverse — parts to repair are both expensive and scarce.

Insurance

You would be foolish to try and insure your E-type with a High Street broker — join the JDC's E-type Register, or go to a specialist classic car insurance broker, who know that E-types are now treasured 'week-end' transport and have a far better claims record than, say, new Cortinas do. If you are over 25 and have a good record, then an E-type will actually be cheaper to insure than the said Cortina, through one of these special schemes. But watch out if you are under 25 and/or have a bad record.

g An E-Type For Restoration Buyir

The engine, radiator, front suspension and steering rack are mounted on a removable sub-frame. Many sub-frames have been damaged by drilling, incorrect jacking, accident or internal rusting. The tubing must be examined inch-by-inch — repair is for experts only and replacements are costly if available.

Continued

There is more to removing, fitting or even lifting an E-type bonnet than one might expect. Accident damage (particular ly around the intake) and rust when the wings meet the centre section, ahead of the front wheels and below the headlamps can all make it worth obtaining a new bonnet. These cost around £500 in primer from BL, but even with the fitting and painting charges to add on, it will often be better than attempting to repair a bonnet which is past its best.

▼

You have to work with E-types to appreciate how many are run with faulty steering, braking and suspension despite the car's performance potential. Be prepared to overhaul all the running gear.

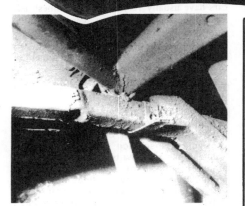

Bent and cracked sub-frame tubes like this are potentially lethal. Damaged tubes must be completely replaced — not a job for the home-restorer.

What to pay

A non-runner in almost any condition from a pile of bits to a recent MoT failure can be described as 'for restoration', so the price band for an off-the-road E-type is wide. However, the price should hinge on monocoque (centre section) condition, and completeness (many of the smaller chrome fittings are hard to find now). Dismantled cars with possibly the wrong engine, 'scrap' monocoque and front sub-frame, and perhaps incomplete can be bought from £500-£1,200. Complete cars, with correct engine, reasonable front sub-frame, the right engine (albeit needing an overhaul) and a restorable monocoque go from between £1,500-£3,000 depending on condition and whether open or closed (the former fetching approx. 20-40% more than a fixed-head).

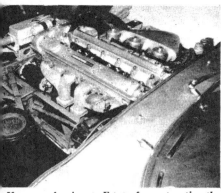

If you are buying an E-type for restoration the engine and transmission could be the least of your worries; Jaguars are mechanically tough and will do a lot of hard work, and spares are generally not a severe problem. However, all sorts of minor items can be difficult to find so make sure nothing is missing.

The engine has to come out for clutch and gearbox work — some people cut the shell to avoid this and such damage must be repaired. Damage to the lips of the bulkhead and the engine steady bracket as shown here, can tell you quite a lot about the previous usage and maintenance — a high mileage in town or a driver that slips the clutch because first gear is a bit high can wear a clutch out in 12,000 miles, which otherwise can last for more than 100,000 miles. Steel heater pipes running through the bulkhead cavity rot, and are very difficult to replace.

Typical parts/services costs

Front floor section	£15.00
Inner sill	£13.00
Boot floor	£40.00
Door skin	£22.00
Complete door	£125.00
Rear wings (FHC)	£80.00
Bonnet complete	£530.00
Monocoque rebuild based on existing front bulkhead and tunnel	£2,200
Engine rebuild	£950.00

Note: all prices approximate and not inclusive of VAT.

Removal of the air cleaner drum and the battery carrier on either side of the car will reveal the lower sub-frame mounting points — if there are signs of trouble here the car almost certainly needs a major rebuild. Here the sub-frame has been removed — note hole in bulkhead panel next to the mounting point!

The sills of an E-type are very, very important. If you are buying a car for restoration, new sills will have to go on.

Unfortunately, rusty outer sills are only the tip of the iceberg — in many cases the car will require new inner sills and floors, and you should look inside the car for evidence of patching and false panels as have been fitted to this shell. An untouched but rotten car might be the best bet as a total restoration project, as you avoid having to deal with (and possibly pay for) other people's bodges.

If the lower outer front sub-frame mounting or outer sill are a bit suspect, this is what you are likely to find when the sill is removed — a new inner sill is definitely required here.

Roadsters are particularly prone to almost breaking their back just below the rear door post and adjacent to the rear bulkhead. That hole in the floor should be the mounting point for the radius arm which helps locate the rear axle and suspension assembly!

If you can get new doors they will be expensive, and rusty ones can be very difficult to reconstruct. The doors are hung on a single hinge which wears particularly badly on 2 + 2 — hinges are over £20 if you can get them.

An E-Type For Restoration Buying

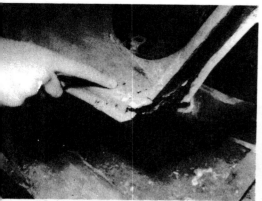

Quite a few E-types are now rotting at the base of the screen pillar and at the top of the door aperture — not an easy area to repair.

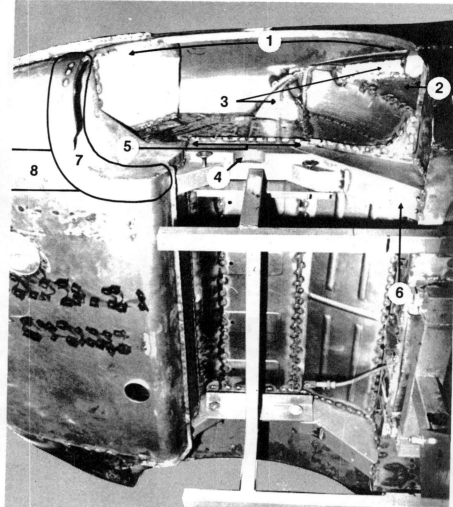

This extensively rebuilt shell on a stand allows us to pinpoint several rear-underside rust trouble spots: 1. Edge of wing above wheel (coupes); 2. Rear sill end and lower part of door post (roadsters) or wheel arch (coupes); 3. Hood frame recess (roadsters); 4. Bump stop mountings — sound outer surface can disguise internal rot; 5. Bottom edge of wheel arch above chassis box section; 6. Anti-roll bar mounting points; 7. Forward outer corners of boot floors and lower rear corners of wheel arches; 8. Joint between outer and centre sections of boot floor.

Continued

Specialists

These are almost too numerous to name individually but include:

Martin E. Robey, Whiteacre Road, Industrial Estate, Nuneaton, Warks. (0203 386903). *Extensive range body parts, monocoque rebuilds.*

Forward Engineering Co., Barston Lane, Barston, Solihull, W. Midlands. (06755 2163). *Engine rebuilds, & rebuild kits.*

British Sports Car Centre, 303 Goldhawk Road, London W12. (01-741 7823/4). *Wide range of parts inc. chrome etc.*

FB Components, 35-41 Edgeway Road, Marston, Oxford. (0865 724646/7). *Steering, suspension, brake components, chrome parts etc.*

G.H. Nolan, 1 St. Georges Way, London SE15 (01-701 2785). *Wide range of parts esp. mechanical.*

Phillips Garage, New Canal St., Digbeth, Birmingham (021-643 0912). *Reconditioned engines, spares and repairs.*

Norman Motors, 100 Mill Lane, London NW6 (01-431 0940). *Wide range of mechanical/body parts, some s/hand.*

Suffolk & Turley, Unit 7, Attleborough Fields Ind. Estate, Garrat St., Warks. (0682 381429). *Trim and interior restoration.*

Jag Unlimited Ltd., 1 Ness St., London SE16. (01237-5529). *New and s/hand parts.*

G.W. Bartlett Co Ltd., Unit 29, Llantarnam Park Ind. Estate, Cwmbran, Gwent. (06333 73664). *Trim kits, materials.*

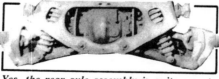

Yes, the rear axle assembly is quite easy to remove, but with its four springs and dampers, four universal joints, numerous bushes, inboard rear discs, calipers and handbrake assembly, is expensive to overhaul. If you put the work in the hands of specialists, be prepared for a £650-£800 bill. Check the condition of the wheels, hub splines and bonded rubber sub-frame mountings.

The top forward corner of the rear wings on a roadster rust, and the edges of the recess for the hood frame inside the car also suffers. On the fixed head, similar trouble is avoided because there is an inner wheel arch, but that is accompanied by a rot problem above the wheel arch where the body is double skinned.

Clonks as the drive is taken up can come from any number of sources including worn hub splines, universal joints and differential and sub-frame mounting bushes which have deteriorated.

Before the car has built up any appreciable speed try the brakes gently. The early 'bellows' servo has been known, on isolated occasions, to go off duty just when it is needed and is therefore viewed with suspicion, but most owners have driven thousands of miles and never been given cause for panic or complaint.

The steering of an E-type should be reasonably light, and being rack and pinion you can expect accurate response accompanied by some kick back at the wheel rim over broken surfaces.

Those of us who have served our apprenticeship with ageing E-types would urge newcomers not to try using a fraction of the car's potential performance until the car has

e For Restoration Under The Skin **Buyi**

Boot lids and tail gates are hard to come by. Panel above the number plate and the number plate panel itself rot quite badly. Most E-types are ready for a new boot floor if they have not had one already, unless they have been very well looked after. Fitting new panels requires skill and patience, but good reproduction parts are now available if you shop carefully.

been given a very thorough going over, and we would not place any particular reliance on an MoT — so please take it very gently at first!

The E-type's excellent ride and effortless performance can land a newcomer in trouble — it is easy to arrive in situations going a great deal faster than you expected. However, while the E-type's grip is easily bettered by many modern family saloons, its safe handling qualities make it fair to say that the car is both easier to drive — and to drive briskly without much effort — than most people would expect. Just watch that long and partly invisible snout when manoeuvering in tight corners, though!

Restoration — How Difficult

Finding an E-type for sale at a price which takes into account that the need for a rebuild is not all that easy; today you stand very little chance of finding anything below £1,000, and may well have to find nearer twice that for an open car, but scouring classified advertisements in magazines and even newspapers and being prepared for a long search would be a wise approach. A very worthwhile move

would be to join the Jaguar Drivers Club and studying the pages of their magazine, the *Jaguar Driver*.

Before even considering buying a Jaguar E-type for restoration, it is a very good idea to think for a long time about what you are letting yourself in for. Some novice restorers have tackled an E-type and carried out a very good job, but many others have found that they got into trouble and either had to sell the car for what they could get or call in professional assistance.

Rebuilding the bodyshell is indeed a major undertaking requiring considerable skill (your welding will have to be particularly good), and constant reference to how the car was made and to the correct shapes and profiles is necessary. The trim, although comparatively straightforward, is still a major hurdle for amateurs and no matter how well you carry out the metalwork, the trim and especially the final paintwork will make or break the end result.

The mechanical side of the car cannot be ignored simply because of the cost (you could easily spend £1,500 on the engine and gearbox), but it is still structural condition of the shell and front sub-frame, and the need to get the brakes and steering working properly, which *must* be the principal concerns. Remember — even an E-type with a badly running, worn-out engine can go quite fast enough to be lethal if the other basic essentials of the car are not up to the mark.

To sum up, the rules of the game are: make sure you know exactly what you are buying by examining every part of the car's structure carefully and persuading the vendor to adjust the price according to what's rotten and what is missing. Then cost out the work needed by

Condition of the interior of both the 4.2 (shown here) and 3.8 litre cars is important because of the cost of re-trimming — which can be into four figures. Kits are available for the competent do-it-yourselfer though. Some of the vinyls for the earlier cars can no longer be found.

obtaining quotes for parts and (if you cannot do it yourself) the all-important monocoque rebuild (allow an amount for 'extras' for hidden defects discovered during this work). If you can still afford it, then go ahead!

A rebuild or good original E-type is (and I speak here as a past-owner of a 1962 3.8 litre fixed-head which I used every day) an extremely reliable and practical sports car even in the eighties — though remember that in today's terms (if the original purchase price of around £2,000 is adjusted for inflation) it is a £15,000 motor car and has maintenance and parts prices in line with such. So while an E-type *is* cheap to run compared with an Aston Martin, Ferrari or Maserati, do not expect to be able to rebuild or maintain it on an MGB-type budget.

It is hardly possible to restore an E-Type Jaguar to "new" standards and hope to get your money back in the short term, so if you are determined to tackle the job. It makes much more sense to think about what you *really* get for your money and effort — and that is, one of the great high performance cars of all time. □

A nostalgic sight — a compound full of newly completed Series 2 4.2 E-Type Jaguars. Wouldn't you like to take your pick? Incidentally these cars were for export markets and the car sold well in America.

Clubs

There is only one club in Great Britain which caters for E-types, and that is the highly active E-type Register section of the Jaguar Driver's Club. Besides all the events organised, technical features appear in the A4 monthly magazine, and the club has a Parts Department with full-time professional parts manager who knows E-types inside out. For an application form (if you have not got a Jaguar or SS you can join as an Associate Member) write to: Tony Rea, JDC, Jaguar House, 18 Stuart Street, Luton, Beds.

An E-Type For Restoration Buying

Rob Giordanelli on running an E-type without breaking the bank

Rob stands by his E-type road-racer. "I intended to keep it only six months, but I've owned it now for nearly 12 years"

There's a school of thought to the effect that E-type ownership is now all about five-figure, professional rebuilds, heated garages and hard-fought concours awards. And if the car isn't totally original, right the way down the line, then it's hardly fit to be seen on the road. Needless to say, Rob Giordanelli doesn't go along with these contentious guidelines …

By his own admission, Rob bought his E-type – an early one, chassis no. 192 – when the car was in average condition, needing work. The engine was misfiring and the brakes virtually non-existent, he recalls. That was in December 1971, nearly 12 years ago. Since then, Rob's kept the Jag on the road, maintaining it himself all along the way; his car may, today, have some E-type purists tut-tutting but he's proved, if you like, that it isn't always necessary to spend a fortune keeping an E-type in shape.

The Giordanelli 3.8 E-type, built on October 20 1961, has been systematically restored and modified over the years to the point where it may look standard (wheels apart) yet, below the skin, it's been updated to make it faster and handle better.

Modified cylinder head

Currently, the car is running with a modified cylinder head – the ports and manifolds have been enlarged and polished – with carburettor needles matched to suit. The clonky Moss 'box has been replaced with the later, stronger 4.2 unit and the back axle ratio lowered from 3.3:1 to 3.07:1. Brake discs and pistons have been renewed and competition pads fitted, together with an additional servo.

On the suspension front, Spax adjustables replaced the standard shockers and stiffer rear radius arm bushes also toughened up the running gear. The back wheels feature a degree or two of negative camber, plus increased offset to increase the track. The car is thus set-up to do well as a road car-cum-racer, and Rob's custom-made straight-through exhaust system not only helps engine breathing, it has the effect of making the E-type sound glorious …

Rob remembers he bought the car for just £400, a typical figure then for an early E-type in good to average condition. "In those days, people were buying old E-types and crashing them right, left and centre" he said. "I bought mine because it represented cheap speed but honestly, the number of E-types that used to be written off at around that time was just ridiculous!

Over the years, Rob has restored his own car 'rather like the Forth Bridge', to use his own words, and also repaired E-types belonging to other people. An XK 150 was another of his restoration projects.

He's rebuilt 828 WFM, which until recently was used everyday (at one point he was even using it as a tow truck!) for a fraction of the cost of a professional rebuild but for all that has few regrets.

While in his tenure, the E-type has had a bare-metal respray and pair of new rear wings (in 1982), plus new floor sections, door skins and inner sills. The inner sills have been renewed and reinforced with thick plating to increase the monocoque's rigidity. Battery carriers? The car's had two or three of them.

As for the E-type's colour, that's been changed three times ("the originality boys wouldn't like that!" quipped Rob). From 1971 until 1976, the car

In action at a very wet JDC Silverstone meeting

His hairy turbo Modsports racer wasn't a success

was red; from then up to 1982, it was British Racing Green but now it's silver. So why the changes?

"When the car was red, it used to stand out like a sore thumb and people couldn't help but notice it. Eventually I found myself being embarassed at being seen in such a flashy car so I sprayed it green. That was great – no one saw it – but after a while it became boring. The trouble was, when I changed it to silver, everyone began to see it again and one night the car was vandalised. Still, that's E-types for you.

"The car certainly hasn't had a £10,000 rebuild but I reckon that, in many ways, it's just as good. This talk of not being able to repair an E-type for less than ten grand or whatever is just a lot of baloney as far as I'm concerned. My E-type may not be pristine or original through and through yet it goes, stops and certainly isn't dangerous.

"Nowadays you see E-types advertised at crazy prices and I even heard of one put up recently for around £25,000. I don't honestly believe anyone ever sells an E-type for that kind of money. Surely, most people go out with maybe £5000 or £6000, to buy the best car they can find? Looking at it that way, I can't really see that these ground-up, better-than-new E-types are really worth the money."

Competitive on tracks

Rob's E-type has figured competitively on the tracks on three occasions. His racing career started though, in the early seventies with a Special Saloon Lotus Twin Cam-engined Anglia. After that he became deeply involved in his own turbocharged E-type project …

"I built that car from scratch, doing everything myself. It was going to be raced as a Modsports car; I did millions of laps on test days but never managed to race it. In the end I ran out of money and had to sell it for tuppence. It cost me a fortune.

"When it was going properly (it was giving over 400bhp) it *really* went but it had this terrible misfire which I couldn't cure. Now I know the fuel lines were too small. In hindsight, it's probably just as well I didn't race it because it was diabolically unstable on the straights.

"With the 3.8 turbo out of my system, I raced 828 WFM, twice at Silverstone in '79 and once at Brands. In one race, the JDC's Production Jaguar event, I came first overall while in the Inter Marque, Aston, Ferrari, Porsche and Jag club race I finished fourteenth, third Jaguar home. Just for the record, in that second event, I beat Nick Mason's 250 GTO, John Atkins' Dino 246 GT and François Duret's DB4 – not bad for home-brewed, road racer.

"I bought this E-type, intending to keep it for six months. I've now had it for close on 12 years and maybe the time has come to part company with it. Why? Well, I now have a family to consider so an extra pair of seats wouldn't go amiss. With that in mind I might go for a manual XJS because I think one of those might be a good bet in years to come.

"Quite frankly, I also fancy a change. I find I don't drive it nearly as fast as I used to on the road – and as I'm not interested in posing in the E-type at the pub, I'm somewhat stuck to know what to do with it. Of course, it still looks great and has the performance but so do quite a few modern cars.

"To make it respectable, there are a few things that do need doing, I'll admit that. The head's a little clattery, the front wings needs touching up and some of the interior could be more original. The front subframe could also do with some work. But overall, it's a good solid car; it's served me well enough and it could, if need be, do well in a race tomorrow. If anyone, incidentally, would like to make me an offer I can't refuse, they can reach me on Sunbury-on-Thames 86819."

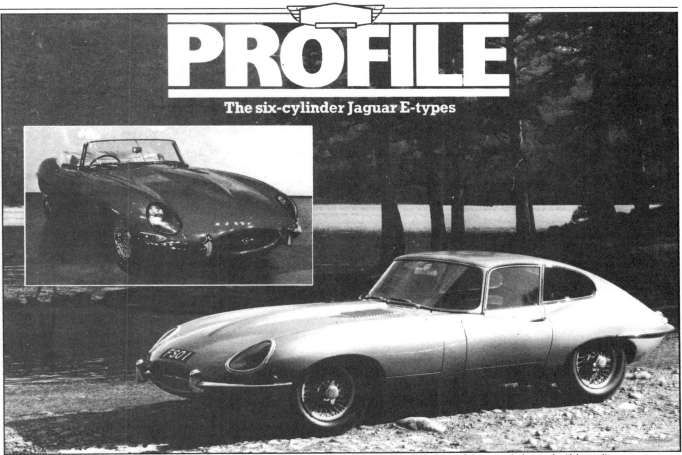

The Series One E-type in open and closed forms – 'it has a sheer beauty of line which easily beats the Italians at their own particular game' said the pundits

Eternal E

When launched in 1961 the E-type Jaguar was an immediate hit. One of the true instant classics, it remains a practical and desirable buy today. Peter Nunn is your guide

Enough superlatives have been lavished on Jaguar's E-type over the years to warrant a charge of 'overkill' being brought forward, some might say. But while there may be a grain or two of truth in that statement, it has to be said that the E-type is one of those rare cars that does, in fact, deserve the full eulogy treatment. Some versions are certainly better than others, but pristine or tatty, the car is, for sure, a bona fide 'classic' and always will be.

For many enthusiasts, the six-cylinder E-types, built between 1961 and 1971, are the purest of the breed, with the original Series 1s the finest of all. Because these XK-powered cars are more plentiful, cheaper to buy, easier to maintain and better suited to the average enthusiast than the later 5.3-litre V12 E-types, we've decided to concentrate here on the E-types 'sixes'. Stay tuned, though, for a follow-up V12 piece at a later date.

The origins of the E-type story can be traced back to the immortal XK 120, and the Le Mans-winning D-types of the fifties. The XK 120, Jaguar's beautiful 1948 creation was easily the best car of its day but inevitably it had to make way for progress sooner or later, and the XK 140 and 150 variants, which were more refined, though heavier developments on the theme, stayed in production until the early sixties. The E-type, then, was to be the replacement for Jaguar's acclaimed XK line, which was getting rather long in the tooth by this time.

At Le Mans, Jaguar scored a hat trick of D-type victories during the mid-fifties, following Duncan Hamilton and Tony Rolt's stirring second place in a works D-type in 1954. But after the '56 race Jaguar officially withdrew from racing – ostensibly to draw up a successor for the D-type; yet it was not to be. The fire in February 1957 and the urgent need to develop a 'new' XK meant that any competition plans had to be abandoned. Behind the scenes, however, work was progressing on a car that would ultimately run at Le Mans but not in Jaguar's own colours . . .

Three prototypes built

It's now a well-known fact that Jaguar built three prototypes of the car that would be known eventually as the 'E-type'. The first, christened E1A ('A' for aluminium), was constructed along D-type lines during 1957/58; running with a 2.4 XK engine, it was designed by William Heynes and styled by Malcolm Sayer in conjunction with Sir William Lyons. The car, which had what we now know as an unmistakable E-type outline, served as a mobile test-bed for Heynes' new form of independent rear suspension, utilising fixed length drive-shafts as upper links, the complete assembly being attached to the monocoque. This car had an active and varied life and was later joined by a second, steel-bodied prototype.

But it was the third car, known internally as E2A, that really showed how things were developing at Jaguar. Intended purely as a sports racer for the works' planned re-entry to racing in 1958/59, the car was, in effect, a second-generation D-type. It had the older car's style of central monocoque and tubular front chassis section – but at the back a hypoid differential, matched to inboard disc brakes, linked up to fabricated lower wishbones and fixed drive-shafts acting as the top half of a twin wishbone system (*à la* E1A), an anti-roll bar, four coil spring/damper units plus light alloy wheel hubs on either side.

Apart from the engine – a 3-litre, dry-sump XK unit with aluminium block – the rest of the car was substantially D-type. The styling, too, owed more than a little to that of the Le Mans winner and, in hindsight, showed how the E-type (then not far off) would look.

The works lent the car to Briggs Cunningham for the 1960 Le Mans 24 Hours yet despite being quick in practice, the car dropped out with a blown cylinder head gasket, brought on by fuel injection problems, having at one point climbed as high as third place. After Le Mans, the car (now 3.8-powered) went to America where it enjoyed some success before returning to England and honourable retirement.

The scene was now set for the dramatic unveiling

of the production E-type at the 1961 Geneva Show, where the car understandably created a major sensation. On looks alone, the car was fabulous, from front to back, and from top to bottom. And 265bhp of 3.8-litre XK engine under the bonnet ensured the car was no café racer. But the pricing was yet another blow to the senses; once again, how on earth could Jaguar produce such an aesthetically-clean, race-bred piece of excitement for such a comparatively low price?

From the E2A came the monocoque shell, clothed voluptuously with metalwork supplied by Abbey Panels while the 3.8 engine/transmission unit came from the old XK 150S. At the front, a complex tubular cradle supported the engine, wishbone and torsion bar front suspension (an anti-roll bar was also fitted), rack and pinion steering and massive front-tipping bonnet. But the big news was at the back; the ingenious irs of the E2A was enclosed in a compact, rubber-mounted subframe to keep road noise and mechanical vibrations at bay, the diff also being insulated from the cradle for quietness. Fore and aft location was achieved by twin radius arms, mounted either side of the subframe.

Dimensionally, the E-type was shorter, wider and significantly lighter than the bulbous XK 150S. Aerodynamics also favoured the new cat in a big way, and the sleek interior with its neat and tidy dashboard and facia complemented the car's outstandingly smooth exterior profile to a tee.

The motoring press naturally went overboard over the E-type. At the epic Geneva Show JVB was one of those allowed to drive 9600 HP, the second fhc built, and his comments still make illuminating reading today.

Quiet and flexible

'Here we have one of the quietest and most flexible cars on the market, capable of whispering along in top gear at 10mph or leaping into its 150mph stride on the brief depression of a pedal. A practical touring car, this, with its wide doors and capacious luggage space, yet it has a sheer beauty of line which easily beats the Italians at their own particular game.'

In his test JVB was evidently greatly impressed by the car's silence and noise suppression. The gearbox received the thumbs down for its un-synchro'd first but as John so rightly pointed out, first need hardly ever be used. Due to a strong side wind the famed 150mph fell short at 148.1mph but 0-60mph took 6.8sec and the standing ¼ mile dash just 14.8sec. In other words, the E-type was electrifyingly fast – so much so, in fact, that John was moved to comment nonchalantly '145mph came up from time to time during ordinary road motoring . . .' But few private owners seemed to be able to manage the 150mph achieved at great expense and trouble by the weeklies.

Nevertheless, the E-type was now a production reality and an instant hit wherever it went. In the all-important US market, where the car was known as the XK-E, it received an ecstatic reception from press and public alike. When manufacture started in earnest, lhd export market cars, and particularly those destined for America would outnumber right hook E-types by as much as six to one, which meant that the E-type was a rare sight on British roads during its early life.

Right from the word go, E-types began to be used in competition. In April 1961, Graham Hill gave the car its maiden victory at an Oulton Park BARC race, Roy Salvadori's sister car finished third behind Innes Ireland's DB4 GT. But from then on, the E-types had to battle hard against Ferrari's 250GTs and from '62 onwards, the glorious 250 GTOs, yet at international level major race victories were few and far between.

Despite the efforts of such drivers as Graham Hill (with the very hot ECD 400/4WPD), Dick Protheroe (with CUT 7), John Coombs (with BUY 1) plus Roy Salvadori, Jack Sears, Peter Lumsden and Peter Sargent, the E-type failed to shine in important races principally because it was too heavy, and the opposition was too tough! That the works couldn't really spare the time to develop it to its full potential didn't help either. Out of two Le Mans entries (1962 and

This Theo Page cutaway drawing from Autosport *is of the original Series I coupé, and shows clearly the neatly designed independent rear suspension and inboard rear disc brakes*

1963), one privately-entered Cunningham E-type finished fourth, although a number of GT category wins were achieved during the latter year and, in America, the E-type was campaigned enthusiastically at Sebring and other tracks. But again, major wins eluded them.

The exciting 'lightweight' E-types, made available during 1963, nearly put all this to rights. Made extensively from aluminium and powered by alloy block, fuel injected 3.8 engines, developing in one particular case 344bhp, these five-speed works cars certainly looked good. In early 1963, Hill's competition E-type scored three GT wins at Snetterton, Goodwood and Silverstone and at the Nürburgring 1000kms, German Peter Lindner astounded everyone by initially leading a class field headed by some very potent Ferraris, in his competition E-type, shared with fellow countryman Peter Nocker.

The lightweights (in all, 12 'genuine' cars are thought to have been built), were now coming on and other bright spots during 1963 included a second at Rheims for Protheroe, an Avus win for Nocker and a Snetterton GT first for Peter Sutcliffe. But at the prestigious Le Mans and TT events, the Ferraris were still dominant.

Into 1964 the picture was little brighter in spite of some very competitive drives put in by someone called Jackie Stewart. Protheroe's special-bodied competition E-type (Jaguar's Malcolm Sayer had devised its low drag shape in 1962, in an effort to counter the GTO offensive), won its class at Rheims though the Sarthe 24 Hour marathon and TT brought more disappointments. Thus it may only be co-incidence that Jaguar's decision to give up their interest in the competition programme more or less co-incided with the death of the unfortunate Lindner, killed in his aerodynamic lightweight E-type at Monthléry at the end of '64. Certainly, from '65 onwards, the E-type never figured in top class results, though in less exalted categories, it was – and still is – very much a force to be reckoned with, witness Roger Mac's well-deserved successes in present-day historics, for example.

In October 1964 Jaguar introduced the 4.2 E-type, which circumvented most of the earlier 3.8's shortcomings. The bigger engine meant even better flexibility and low-range pulling power and the all-synchro 'box that went with it was judged to be a vast improvement over the 'agricultural' Moss four speeder, fitted previously. The brakes were improved too as were the seats, and overall, the 4.2 was regarded as a definite step in the right direction, especially as performance remained the same and the car was now easier to drive.

The 2+2 was the next E-type variant to be introduced, this slightly controversial addition to the range arriving in the spring of 1966. A 9ins longer wheelbase and 2ins increase in height enabled the car to carry two adults and two small children in tolerable comfort though, as a penalty, some of the graciousness of the Series 1 fhc had to be sacrificed. Automatic transmission became available on the 2+2 (an E-type first), mainly to help the car sell well in America.

SPECIFICATION	Jaguar 4.2 coupé (S1)
Engine	In-line 'six'
Capacity	4235cc
Bore/stroke	92.07×106mm
Valves	Twin ohc
Compression	9:1 (8:1 optional)
Power	265bhp (SAE) at 5400rpm
Torque	283lb.ft (SAE) at 4000rpm
Transmission	Four-speed manual (auto, later option)
Final drive	3.07:1 ratio
Brakes	Discs/discs with servo
Suspension F.	Ind. by torsion bars, wishbones, anti-roll bar, telescopic dampers
Suspension R.	Ind. by wishbones, fixed drive-shafts, coils, telescopic dampers
Steering	Rack and pinion
Body	Monocoque, all-steel
Tyres	6.40 - 15

DIMENSIONS	
Length	14ft 7¼in
Width	5ft 5¼in
Height	4ft 0in
Wheelbase	8ft 0in
Dry weight	25⅔cwt

PERFORMANCE	
Max speed	152mph
0-60mph	7.5sec
Standing ¼ mile	15sec
Fuel con.	17/19mpg

PRODUCTION	
Years built	Oct 1964 – Oct 1968
Nos built	7772
Price when new (inc tax)	£2032 (1965)

Traditional English sportscar cockpit, with man sized steering wheel, a full array of instruments and leather trim galore

In much the same way that the original XK 120 progressed to the heavier and comparatively ponderous XK 140 and even more-so XK 150, so the E-type gradually began to put on middle-age spread as it grew older. The first danger signs became apparent in late 1967 when the car started to succumb to US federalisation in various forms – detuned engine and so on – yet Motor Show 1968 brought even more changes, necessitated by the stringent demands of the North American market.

A list of the alterations imposed (few could actually be classed as improvements) can be found under the 'Production history' column. Suffice it to say, the Series 2 E-type lost much of the original's matchless elegance, but the really bad news concerned the new-found performance – or lack of it.

To compensate for the energy-sapped XK engine's reduced power output and the car's slower acceleration, Jaguar lowered the axle ratio on US-bound cars which dropped the top speed to around 130mph. And with full emission gear in situ (principally twin Strombergs and Duplex manifold) the XK could only manage a lacklustre 177bhp – kid's stuff compared to the original's 265bhp. Furthermore, the gradual call for rationalisation decreed that, eventually, the federalised US-spec 4.2 became standard issue, at home and abroad. Luckily for enthusiastic drivers, this dire state of affairs was not allowed to remain unattended for too long, for in March 1971, Jaguar gave the car a new (and final) lease of life by introducing the 5.3-litre V12 Series 3 E-type. But that is another story . . .

So much for history, yet what of the E-type today? Its protagonists, it seems, are clearly divided. 3.8 enthusiasts covet the 1961-64 cars because they were the first to be introduced and, in fhc guise, were the fastest of all standard E-types, according to the tests. 4.2 drivers, on the other hand, tend to regard the 3.8 as a little unrefined, particularly in the braking department! 4.2s were more civilised, in comparison.

Production history

First shown at the '61 Geneva Show, the E-type was introduced officially to the home market in July that year. Prices for these first 3.8-litre cars ranged from £2097 for the beautiful open roadster to £2196 for the fixed head coupé – sensational prices that even undercut the XK 150 'S', then just withdrawn from production.

During the winter of 1961/2, several minor refinements were made to the seating, footwells and brakes and '62 cars also featured re-aligned pedals and changes to the bonnet locks. Between '62 and winter '64, further detail improvements were phased in, mainly with respect to the running gear, but October '64 marked the arrival of the 4.2 E-type, a more refined breed of cat.

From the Mk X came the 4235cc straight 'six', developing 265bhp and greater torque. An all-synchro 'box, coupled to a new diaphragm clutch, was the other important talking point, the car at last being relieved of the cumbersome Moss 'box with unsynchronised first. Additional improvements included an engine alternator (in place of a dynamo), pre-engaged starter, higher final drive ratio, copper flow radiator and a new Lockheed brake servo. The exhaust came in for attention, too.

A leather-faced dash and pair of seats offering more generous lumbar support were the principal interior changes, though a between-the-seats oddments box was a useful addition. But externally, the Series 1 4.2 was virtually indistinguishable from the 3.8 it supplanted (for the record, the 3.8 ran alongside the 4.2 for a brief period – officially until October '65 – and, so the story goes, some late versions had the all-synchro 'box fitted).

In March 1966, Jaguar introduced the stretched 2+2 E-type, the original two-seater coupé continu-

Type	Engine	Dates	Total
Series 1	3.8	Mar 1961-Oct 1965	15,500
Series 1	4.2	Oct 1964-Oct 1968	22,922
Series 2	4.2	Oct 1968-Mar 1971	18,794

E-type prototype, E2A, at the 1960 Le Mans test day

First race at Oulton: Salvadori leads eventual winner Hill

Others tried to improve on the original – this is Frua's offering

ing alongside unchanged. Popular opinion has it that the 2+2, with its more deeply-raked windscreen and larger side windows, wasn't quite as striking as the fhc but two rear-seat passengers, travelling in some degree of comfort, could now be accommodated.

To go with various minor improvements (facia parcel tray, larger glove box and so on), Jaguar offered the 2+2 in automatic guise, with the US market in mind. The results were mixed – performance and handling suffered slightly and the 'box itself could have been smoother, but the E-type magic was still there, if slightly diluted, some felt.

The so-called 'Series 1½' E-types were produced during late 1967. These cars, which paved the way for the forthcoming Series 2s, pioneered several of the later cars' features. Thus, in the interests of US federal regulations, the headlamps were exposed, the 'ears' on the wire wheel spinners deleted, and dashboard rocker switches appeared. Twin Strombergs, in place of triple SUs, were also fitted, for tighter emission control but alas, the engine's power output took a sharp nose dive, though fuel economy improved slightly.

Earls Court 1968 saw the introduction of the Federal-conscious Series 2 E-types. Externally, the differences amounted to an enlarged bonnet 'mouth', the fitment of one-piece bumpers front and rear with bigger flashers and sidelights underneath, and repositioned headlamps. Ad West power steering was now optional, along with chrome bolt-on wires. Twin engine fans became standard, as part of the (optional) air conditioning system.

Other changes included square number plates, reversing lights and, for the 2+2, a shallower-raked windscreen. The exhaust tailpipes had to be re-routed. Inside, some detail alterations were introduced for safety's sake.

From then on, until the end of 4.2 production in March 1971, few significant changes took place but increasing modernisation meant that home-market and US-bound cars had begun to look more like each other by the turn of the decade. The E-type was now slower than ever before and significantly down on power so Jaguar, to their credit, decided to do something about it, and the Series 3 V12 was the result.

Officially, there was talk of a six-cylinder, emission-spec Series 3 at the time of the V12 E-type launch, and the car was actually catalogued in some quarters, but were any built or offered for sale? Nobody seems to know for certain.

Buyers spot check

There are essentially three ways to buy an E-type. First, one can go the long way round by picking up a near-derelict car with a view to a complete, ground up restoration. Opting for a mid-range example in 'average' condition is the second choice, with splashing out on an A1 original or completely-restored concours candidate the third and most expensive route to adopt.

Obvious? Perhaps, but the trap that many people fall into is to pay out for what appears to be a sound mid-range car, only to find out later to their cost that it needs as much rectification work as a tatty banger costing maybe half the price. For that reason, some sources suggest either going cheap or expensive as an 'average' E-type can be a risky proposition for the unwary. Also it's very easy for a skilled (but unscrupulous) panel beater/sprayer to make a sow's ear pass superficially for a silk purse. The motto, then, is to take your time and check over the car you are thinking of buying very, very carefully. If you can arrange for thorough, expert assessment from a Jaguar specialist, so much the better – it could save you a fortune in the long run.

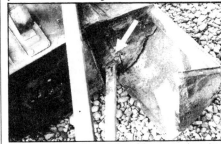
All important area, front tubular subframe mounting point

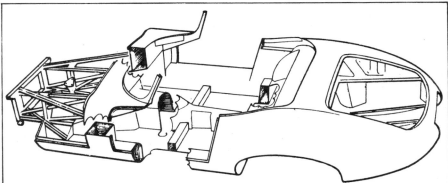
One of the features of the E-type was that a conventional chassis was replaced by a monocoque developed from the D-type

In general terms, any E-type can now be restored, whatever its condition, but it's important that, as far as possible, all the parts are intact. On early cars, for example, hood frames, chrome parts and interior mirrors are now almost impossible to find.

It's the condition of the monocoque and front tubular framework that's all important but trouble around the rear axle subframe is another make-or-break factor. In particular, if the monocoque rails locating the rear subframe are found to be wanting, or if the rear floor sections supporting the radius arm cups are on the way out, then that's very bad news. Corroded sills are not such a serious matter – they're relatively cheap to have replaced, but rust in the two regions already mentioned or in the rear anti-roll bar area could well write off the car.

If battery acid has been allowed to drip onto the front tubing for any length of time, then there's a good chance the tubes in question will need replacing. If matters have deteriorated to that point, then the whole frame will need to be removed (an engine-out and suspension-off job), checked and rebuilt, or renewed, as necessary.

Other body checkpoints include the wheelarch lips – run your fingers around the edges, feeling for any ominous changes in thickness – the boot floor and interior floorpan. Check the doors for security and alignment (E-type doors are sometimes difficult to close) and the extremities of the front scuttle, at the foot of the 'A' posts. The rear wings should also be inspected, along with the bonnet, which can rust around its lower edges. If you've managed to get this far and all seems OK, then make sure all the opening panels are correctly aligned without any nasty gaps.

On the mechanical front, the main problem area is, once again, that independent rear end. If the rear discs need attention or the calipers need replacing – and there are four of those at £96 each – then steel yourself for a hefty repair bill as the subframe will have to come down. And that's a job for a garage, not the d-i-y man.

XK engines can cover 100,000 miles or so without trouble if properly maintained, but watch out for any signs of burnt oil, significant water loss or cracking around the head or block. Having the engine compression tested is a good idea yet don't be surprised by a low oil pressure reading – quite a few XK gauges are like that. Noisy timing chains are another clue to old age but, like worn valve gear, need not necessarily be viewed with alarm.

Transmission checks are usually straightforward. With manual 'boxes, a noisy first gear sometimes occurs but the condition isn't too serious. Synchro rings can also have a fairly short life if abused. With a 2+2 auto, however, check the changes up and down the range carefully; rectification of worn internals could be costly. The rest of the drive-line, propshaft, diff and so on, has a good record for reliability.

Remember that E-types have the traditional Jaguar ability to continue driving hard and fast even though down-at-the-heels and perhaps rotten throughout! A neglected car can be trouble, for sure, but parts and the expertise to make the car well again are not too hard to find.

Rivals when new

By necessity, this has to be a short listing, for in terms of outright performance, gracious styling and, above all, sensational value for money, no car has ever been able to match the E-type.

In America, the Corvette and Mustang squared up to the Jaguar on both road and track (and on record as well, as in the sixties Californian pop duo Jan & Dean came up with an unlikely tale of how an XK-E and a Stingray duelled all the way to 'Dead Man's Curve', only for the Jag to career off the road while the Corvette continued in triumph. Really!).

The Mustang line chopped and changed so often that it's difficult to regard it as a serious rival to the E-type (or XK-E). Finesse, which the Jag possessed in abundance, was not its strong suit. On the home market, Aston's DB4 and DB5 stood close comparison with the E-type in several respects bar production totals and pricing, while Daimler's quaint SP 250 could be termed a rival of sorts due to its lovely V8 engine.

A brand new E-type monocoque at Martin Robey's premises

Lovely line up – a row of clean E-types at a club meeting

Where marque image was concerned, the Mercedes 230-250-280SLs were seen by some as competitors to the E-type, which again undercut all three on pricing by a healthy margin. Perhaps Porsche with the evergreen 911 series provided the closest competition of all?

Clubs, specialists and books

With a membership total currently standing at around the 8000 mark, the Jaguar Drivers Club is one of the country's principal enthusiast car groups. The club's base, Jaguar House, is situated at 18 Stuart Street, Luton, Beds LU1 2SL (tel: Luton 419332) and at the time of writing, a year's subscription is set at £15, with a £5 joining fee.

Within the club, there's a flourishing E-type Register, run by George Gibbs of Burghclere Grange School, Burghclere, Newbury, Berks. The Register looks after the interests of its members via a lively column within the pages of the JDC's monthly magazine *Jaguar Driver*, and International E-type Day, held this year at Peterborough in August.

When the talk turns to Jaguar specialists, the E-type driver is really spoilt for choice. To try to sort the wheat from the chaff, as it were, an independent organisation – the Jaguar Specialists Association – was set up not so long ago and the latest list of members appears below in no particular pecking order. But it should be stressed that there are some first-rate concerns specialising in the Jaguar marque that don't appear on the list for one reason or another and that election to the JSA list doesn't necessarily imply a recommendation. Nevertheless, here are the names and addresses:

British Sports Car Centre Ltd, 299-309 Goldhawk Road, London W12; Roger Bywater Engineering Ltd, Unit 4, Hillgate Ind. Estate, Carrington Field Street, Stockport, Cheshire, SK1 3JN; Classic Autos, 10 High Street, Kings Langley, Herts; Classic Power Units, Tile Hill, 18 Trevor Close, Coventry; D.K. Engineering, 10/16 Hallwell Road, Northwood, Middlesex; Coventry Auto Components, Gillingwood, Waste Lane, Berkswell, near Coventry, Warwicks and Deetype Replicas Ltd, South Gibcracks Farm, Bicknacre Road, East Hanningfield, Chelmsford, Essex.

Forward Engineering Ltd, Barston Lane, Bartson, Solihull, West Midlands, B92 0JP; Alan George, Plot 11, Small Firms Compound, Dodwells Bridge Ind. Estate, Hinckley, Leicester; A.W. Hannah, Central Garage, Snaith, near Goole, Humberside; Bill Lawrence Esq, 9 Badgers Walk, Dibden Purlieu, Hampshire and Lynx Engineering, Castleham Ind. Estate, St. Leonards-on-Sea, East Sussex, TN38 9NR.

Phillips Garage, 103/7 New Canal Street, Digbeth, Birmingham, B5 5RA; R.S. Panels, Kelsey Close, Attleborough Fields Ind. Estate, Nuneaton, CV11 6RS; S.S. & Classic Restoration, Cemere Green Farm, Cemere Green, Pulham Markets, Diss, Norfolk; S.S. & L. Automobile Engineers, Homefarm, Holmlea Road, Datchet, Berkshire; Suffolk & Turley, Unit 7, Attleborough Fields Ind. Estate, Garrett Street, Nuneaton, Warwicks and Swallow Engineering, 6 Gibcracks, Basildon, Essex.

Other firms to note include Oldham & Crowther (Engineering) Ltd, 30/31 Ivatt Way, Westwood, Peterborough, PE3 7PG; Warren Pearce Motors, 59 South Street, Epsom, Surrey, KT18 7PX, and Olaf P. Lund & Son Ltd, 40 Upper Dean Street, Birmingham, B4 4SG.

One firm in particular, Martin E. Robey Ltd of Poole Road, Camp Hill Industrial Estate, Nuneaton is well worth contacting if brand new Jaguar panels or advice on restoration matters are needed.

And in London, George Nolan's legendary shop full of new and used Jaguar parts is worth keeping tabs on. Based at 1 St. George's Way, London SE15, Nolan's is a veritable treasure trove of elderly Jag bits and George's knowledge of which-part-went-where-and-when is equally well founded. Your own local JDC rep should also be able to supply the low-down on other specialists who are doing a good job in your area.

Heading the Jaguar sports car book list must be Paul Skilleter's epic *Jaguar Sports Cars* (Haynes). Running at 360 pages, it's a superb book that's highly recommended. Paul also penned the useful *The Jaguar E-types* in MRP's popular 'Collector's Guide' series. Long-time Jaguar devotee Denis Jenkinson recently had his E-type memoirs published by Osprey under the heading *Jaguar E-type Autohistory* – and very good they are too.

E-type bibliomaniacs will want to have Chris Harvey's *E-type – The End of an Era* (Oxford Illustrated Press), Andrew Whyte's *Jaguar The History of a great British car* (Patrick Stephens), the same author' *Jaguar E-type* 'Superprofile' (Haynes), and the various Brooklands Books reprints of original road test material.

Prices

Pinpointing precise guidelines for the prices of individual E-type models isn't always possible, we understand. According to Martin Robey, there's no marked differential in 3.8 and 4.2 prices, it being very much down to personal taste and preference and the condition of the car. There is, though, something of a premium on roadsters and, by and large, Series 2 cars seem to attract slightly higher prices than the original Series 1s.

Using Martin's 1-2-3 thinking (see 'Buyers spot check'), a car bought ripe for restoration, probably as a non-runner, might command anything from £2500 upwards. Moving up, the sometimes tricky mid-range cars, that are generally neither good nor bad, tend to fall in the £4500 to £7000 bracket, the upper limit obviously representing an E-type in excellent order.

The tricky one is the third category; just how much is a fully-restored, immaculate throughout E-type worth? The short answer is, of course, precisely what someone is prepared to pay for it. But a complete, ground-up restoration might end up at around £15,000, Martin Robey reckons, though he has heard of ones that have gone even higher. Whether you consider an E-type to be worth that kind of money is, again, a matter of personal opinion – but look at it this way, what is available new today at the price that can match the E-type's charisma and formidable power? The answer is – not a lot.